920
R456

Rilke at the age of twenty   *Drawing by* KOLO MOSEN

RAINER MARIA RILKE

BY

E. M. BUTLER

*Henry Simon Professor of German Language and Literature in
the University of Manchester; Fellow and Associate of
Newnham College*

CAMBRIDGE

AT THE UNIVERSITY PRESS

1941

By the same author

THE SAINT-SIMONIAN RELIGION IN GERMANY
THE TYRANNY OF GREECE OVER GERMANY

CAMBRIDGE
UNIVERSITY PRESS
LONDON: BENTLEY HOUSE
NEW YORK, TORONTO, BOMBAY
CALCUTTA, MADRAS: MACMILLAN
TOKYO: MARUZEN COMPANY LTD

To

I. B. H.

CONTENTS

Author's Note   *page* ix

INTRODUCTION   1

CHAPTER I

JANGLED BELLS, 1875–1899
    1. Growing pains   13
    2. Juvenilia.   30

CHAPTER II

SPIRITUAL HOMES, 1899–1902
    1. Russia, 1899–1900   49
    2. Worpswede, 1900–1901   86
    3. Westerwede, 1901–1902   116

CHAPTER III

LATIN LESSONS, 1902–1914
    1. Rodin, 1902–1906   139
    2. Paris, 1906–1910   171
    3. Playing truant, 1910–1914   212

CHAPTER IV

WARS AND RUMOURS OF WAR, 1914–1921
    1. The Non-combatant, 1914–1919   249
    2. The Refugee, 1919–1921   283

CHAPTER V

THE CRISIS, 1921–1922
    1. Muzot   307
    2. Angels   316
    3. Orpheus   340

CHAPTER VI

THE END, 1922–1926

1. Personal death   *page* 361
2. Last words   375
3. Transformation   398

CONCLUSION   415

Bibliographical Note   426

Index of Names   429

Index of Works   434

AUTHOR'S NOTE

A list of the abbreviations used in the foot-notes will be found
at the end of the Bibliographical Note. Unless otherwise
stated, I must be held responsible for the translations in this
book; but Mr J. B. Leishman, the well-known Rilke translator, who has rectified some errors of fact in the biography,
has most generously allowed me to use his fascinating verse-
translations of Rilke's poems either *verbatim* or making any
alterations I liked, a courtesy which I trust that I have not
abused. The extent to which I am indebted to this author will
be apparent in the foot-notes.

Amongst those who knew Rilke personally, my greatest
debt of gratitude is to Baron Eduard von der Heydt, the
nephew of one of Rilke's closest friends and kindest benefactors. During an unforgettable summer at Monte Verità
near Ascona, I had the great pleasure and privilege of listening
to Heydt's memories of Rilke, whilst being treated to the same
munificent hospitality which his uncle Karl so often showed
to the poet. I should like to thank this princely patron of art
and letters once more, this time in print, for his friendship
and help. Many other friends and acquaintances of Rilke's
have been outstandingly kind in answering my letters and
questions. I treasure (as who would not?) some pithy postcards written by Bernard Shaw. The Russian artist Leonid
Pasternak made me a present of his published memoir of
Rilke in proof, including his portrait of the poet. Stefan
Zweig, Gertrud Ouckama Knoop and Nanny Wunderly-
Volkart have all written me long and revealing letters about
him; and Judith Cladel gave me some important first-hand
information about Rodin.

As regards unpublished sources, both the *Inselverlag* and
the *Rilke-Archiv* kept me severely at a distance; but, owing to
the kind offices of a friend who wishes to remain anonymous,
I was nevertheless able to see transcripts of important
manuscript material; and Professor Fiedler magnanimously

permitted me to use some unpublished autograph letters in his possession. Professor Ernst Zinn was indefatigable in answering questions about the dates of various poems; and Sophie Brutzer sent me transcripts of Rilke's Russian verse.

Mrs Chadwick, to whose work all students of Russian oral literature owe so much, took endless pains in helping me to trace the sources of Rilke's versions of some *byliny* and *skazki*; and Mr G. C. Grant of the International Book Club has zealously collaborated throughout by hunting down and procuring many journals and books essential to this study and often out of print. I should have been in a poor way without his assistance.

My thanks are due on another score to Miss Janet Bacon who read the book in typescript and saved me from many a stylistic calamity by doing so, an act of mercy continued during the proof-stage by Miss I. B. Horner, who has in addition shouldered the burden of the Index. In considering this debt, together with the long list of I.O.U.'s which precedes it, I feel, to quote Rilke, that I have had "an *ee-normous* mass of help." But since authors desire publication first, last and all the time, my deepest gratitude should perhaps go to the Syndics of the Cambridge University Press for accepting this particular book at this particular time.

E. M. B.

September 1940

Introduction

INTRODUCTION

The disruptive forces let loose in this age (and they do not date from yesterday) are responsible amongst other things for rending poetry and life apart. This is a tragic situation which may end by brutalising humanity irretrievably, and has already seriously inhibited the civilising function of poetry. It is true that great artists and writers (at the height of this as of every other situation) continue to master life and to interpret its mystery. But the widening gulf between the war-haunted, machine-driven multitude and the heart-stricken modern poets is such that words cannot carry over it. Mankind as a whole is unaware of the visions life is engendering; whilst creative poets and artists, cut off from the common roots of humanity, are becoming markedly eccentric, disdainful, ambiguous and remote. Yet they are conditioned by the times they live in like everyone else. Vitally affected by the march of science, they have for many generations now been striving for new forms and a different language in order to express the altered aspect presented by life owing to such revolutionary thinkers as Darwin, Einstein and Freud.

For the spirit of life, rushing through and overflowing the deep but eroded channel of Christianity, seems to be on its way to rejoin some unknown sea as yet uncharted by humanity. Many individual poets have had strange visions of life throughout the ages, and isolated modern writers are prophetically inclined; but the earlier poets are forgotten, and the present divorce between popular and poetical modes of thought deprives the latter of universality, so that the fear expressed by Santayana in 1916 is still not dissipated:

The greatest calamity, however, would be that which seems, alas! not unlikely to befall our immediate posterity, namely, that while Christianity should be discredited no other religion, more disillusioned and not less inspired, should come to take its place.[1]

---

[1] G. Santayana, *Interpretations of Poetry and Religion*, New York, 1916, p. 116.

The new religion which seems to be gathering impetus is certainly one of disillusion, but it is nebulous and does not come from the mythological subsoil which nourishes great religions. Schopenhauer's ruthless and tragic Will, Nietzsche's merciless Superman, Proust's hoary enemy Time have certainly moulded and modified the thoughts of men; but they are intellectual conceptions rather than spiritual revelations. Still less inspirational energy and power inform the synthetic paganism established in Germany for political ends, which is a caricatured version of Schopenhauer and Nietzsche, and with which the dreams and the visions, the faiths and the fears of the people have nothing to do.

A more hopeful sign is the well-named renascence of wonder which has been rapidly deepening among poets since the end of the eighteenth century, producing such visionaries as Hölderlin and Blake, and perhaps Rainer Maria Rilke in our times. I say perhaps, for the subject of this study is still a mystery to me, and one which I shall never fathom. Amongst all great modern poets his mythological aim is the most indubitable; since the whole of his work is one long unremitting effort to represent life and the universe in the terms of his own strange philosophy. But his vision is so kaleidoscopic and shifting, so deeply impregnated with ambiguities and fundamentally irreconcilable notions that the threads which should lead one to the heart of the maze too often snap in one's hand. The uncommon penetration of an English critic has recently shed much light on this darkness, a light to which I am deeply indebted;[1] but the question underlying the present study still awaits a decisive answer. Has the work of the greatest German poet since Hölderlin real religious validity; or is it merely the mysterious expression of a one-man dream? Rilke remains baffling, partly because he belongs to an age which does not think poetically, but partly because he willed it so. If many modern poets have little or no desire to be generally understood, Rilke often aimed at misleading his readers, using in a private sense words which seemed to bear their

---

[1] E. C. Mason, *Lebenshaltung und Symbolik bei Rainer Maria Rilke*, Weimar, 1939.

traditional meaning, and wrapping himself in a cloak of darkness woven from esoteric symbols. He will not abide our question, and we should let him go free had he not spoken so often and so urgently of his message and mission to humanity.

The matter is still further complicated by the legend of Rilke the seer-saint, so industriously circulated by adoring friends and contemporaries. I could instance dozens of passages from dozens of books (many, though not all, written by women) so hagiographical in tendency and sentimental in style that it would be unfair to the poet to quote them. But the following extract from a letter to me by one of Rilke's most intimate friends will give some idea of the prevailing attitude. It was written in answer to an enquiry about the length of her acquaintanceship with Rilke and the number of his letters in her possession. The information was withheld, and it was considered, as will be seen, highly irreverent to ask for it:

R. M. Rilke was unique, one of those who come to this world perhaps once in every hundred years. He came to fulfil a mission, he was sent. Everyone who studies his works must feel that. Therefore there is no human standard by which he can be measured on this side. And if he himself was so touchingly human among us and for us, this was a part of his great loving-kindness and desire to help, which never failed. For *he* knew how hard the life of man is. But his greatest self, his real self, is very high and far above us; and that is his singing, his nearness to God. . . . Of what importance can it possibly be to know how long I knew him, or how many of his letters I possess? That one was permitted to know him and to help him, that is the miracle. . . . He never belonged to this world, and his life was dedicated to *his mission*, of which he was most deeply conscious.

Rilke himself was partly responsible for this most prejudicial legend, although he was probably aiming less at creating a saint-like impression than at appearing as a high priest of poetry. But even those latter-day critics who have understood this and realised his formidable genius, have continued the sensational tradition of the hagiographers by luridly illuminating his spiritual dangers and difficulties, so that they

appear as some sinister and tragic sin against the very spirit
of life. In this they are following in the footsteps of Kierkegaard, who certainly influenced Rilke and made the excruciating choice between life and art seem doubly and trebly fateful.
For Kierkegaard himself was vividly aware of the perils
inherent in genius:

That such an existence as genius, in spite of its brilliance,
magnificence and importance, should be sin, it certainly requires
courage to understand; and one can hardly understand it at all until
one has learnt to moderate the hungry longings of the soul.[1]

It is a courage however which many of Rilke's more able
critics have possessed in abundance; and Kierkegaard's
conceptions, elaborated and systematised by Jaspers and
Heidegger into the well-known Existence Philosophy, have
become the plank from which they lecture one and all about
Rilke's life and art. These ready-made interpretations with
their inevitable catchwords and parrot-cries and their
Teutonic overemphasis tend to simplify overmuch Rilke's
human situation, but they have clarified some obscurities in
his work, which undoubtedly reflects the dual aspect under
which he regarded his own existence: as that of a man charged
with a great and glorious mission, and of one labouring under
the doom or curse of genius.

On the whole, however, he was on the side of poetry, and
aimed at showing in his person, conduct and works that poets
and poetry are divine in their own right, above and beyond
religions and gods. But he did this so ambiguously, that both
his behaviour and his poems appear superficially saint-like, an
impression fortunately belied by a careful scrutiny of his life,
his actions and his utterances. This reveals, on the contrary,
genius and self-assertion to a marked degree, a gallant
struggle for poetical existence and the grim determination to
survive. Yet Rilke also possessed an intense desire for self-
surrender. The story of his life consists in his increasingly
successful efforts to harness the latter emotion exclusively to
the service of his art. It led to self-dedication, and also to the

---

[1] S. Kierkegaard, *The Concept of Dread*, 1844, chap. III, § 2.

immolation of others, to whom he was fully as ruthless as he was to himself; but almost imperceptibly, for his unyielding obduracy was masked by wistful evasiveness and elusiveness. It was a protective colouring. His gentle manners, his sensitive mind, the skill and fluency with which he used religious terms seemed to prove that he loved humanity and worshipped God. Whereas in reality he recognised only the god of art and Rainer Maria Rilke his prophet, and was stirred to deepest and purest enthusiasm for those kindred spirits who felt and did the same.

So much at least seems to emerge from his voluminous correspondence. Nearly all Rilke's letters are permeated by that intangible element which differentiates poetry from the prose of life. Few indeed came straight from his heart, or even from his mind; none came straight from the shoulder. Even when he wished to be most simple and direct, his sense of style intervened, his sense of what a poet should be. It was by no means an impeccable style, being too mellifluous, and at times distressingly precious. The impression he wished to create is so clear-cut that his real personality suffers. Like an actor who has completely sunk himself in his part, he becomes what he represents, his own idea of a poet. But he was in fact so nearly his own ideal, that the real poet Rainer Maria Rilke often breaks through the mask of his aesthetic double. It is a mysterious business altogether; and the problem has been greatly complicated by the manner in which his correspondence has been given to the world.

The editors, Rilke's daughter and son-in-law, have done what in them lay to deprive the published letters of biographical value, not to speak of the confused, inconsistent and double-crossing manner in which the fifteen volumes, by no means uniform in shape, size or method have gradually seen the light of their financial day. The editorship leaves much to be desired, and the method of selection is at least as unsatisfactory as the system of publication. All 'unsuitable' references to living persons have necessarily been omitted; but discretion goes so far as to delete in some volumes the beginnings and endings of all the letters, as well as all references to Rilke's private life, personal relationships and material circumstances.[1] In so-called augmented second editions some of these gaps have been filled at the expense of passages in the first editions which under the Nazi *régime* might seem politically unsound. Yet, even in its present slovenly and mangled condition, Rilke's published correspondence is a most arresting phenomenon, and of incalculable critical and biographical value if it is read with a mind open and aware of the attempts at mystification. For it is not only full of disconcerting gaps, it is also misleadingly presented. The suppression of many facts, events and circumstances in the poet's life is less serious than the deliberate omission of those passages from his letters which might have revealed the real and natural man. One deduces at least that such passages have been expunged, for one can hardly believe that they do not exist, although Rilke himself tended to dwell almost exclusively on the spiritual side of his nature and existence. The editors have probably thrown overboard what ballast this strange vessel carried, since they admit to banishing the personal element from the early correspondence, in which nature had probably not yet been altogether suffocated by art. One is therefore continually in the region of surmises, and there is hardly a sentence in the biographical sections of this book which should not be accompanied by the saving clause 'to judge by the published letters'. Let it stand here and now at the outset, if not once and for all. Many of the conclusions I have been tempted to draw on this challenging but insufficient data may prove to be wide of the mark; but at least they have not been biased by the discernible tendency towards mystery-making and hagiography behind the drastic omissions and skilful selections in the letters, which weight the balance on the seraphic side, and which devitalise Rilke's personality, a result to which his own rather monotonously beautiful prose has also largely contributed.

These letters therefore are not ordinary letters. They were written for the most part as works of art and wisdom; and we have no means of knowing whether or not this was Rilke's

[1] Cf. *B. 1902–1906*, pp. 8 ff.; *B. 1906–1907*, pp. 7 f.; *V.B.* p. 11.

constant practice, and how much vitality he has lost. To judge by the extracts of his diary-letters to Nanny Wunderly-Volkart given by Salis in his book on Rilke in Switzerland, a good deal has been pruned away. The published correspondence, emerging from the editorial beauty-parlour, has sacrificed those distinguishing marks and blemishes which give character to the noblest features. Lines have been erased, angles have been smoothed out. If a certain artificiality is the final impression one derives from Rilke's letters, it should be remembered that they have been through a strenuous treatment before being presented to the world; on the other hand, it must not be forgotten that they lent themselves admirably to such a course. The correspondence, the monographs and the biographies of Rilke's contemporaries must all be scrutinised with the care and scepticism with which medieval scholars interpret the lives of saints, or with which members of the distinguished Society for Psychical Research investigate the claims of mediums. Yet the mistake would be gross indeed if, in exploding a mere legend, one should overlook a miracle. For the presence of a great poet is a miracle in any age; and that Rilke should have lived his life, had his thoughts and written his works in the present era is fully as miraculous as if the flame of the forest should suddenly bloom and blossom in some ear-splitting factory of deadly explosives.

It is tragically relevant to-day to see how Rilke came to terms with life in the twentieth century, how he suffered under it, and what effect war produced upon his life and art. The fact too that he was a German born in Prague, almost certainly with Czech blood in his veins, that he was an idealist and an extremist and cannot be weighed in the balance of common sense; all this has made the study of his personality and works absorbingly and painfully interesting to the writer.

Chapter I

JANGLED BELLS, 1875–1899

1. *Growing Pains*
2. *Juvenilia*

CHAPTER I

JANGLED BELLS, 1875–1899

1. *Growing Pains*

Heinrich Heine once asked the pertinent question, whether poetry might not be considered a symptom of sickness, resembling the pearl which is produced by the stimulus of disease. Certainly the story of Rilke's childhood and youth reveals such suffering as a sensitive mind could hardly have endured without the relief of the poetical discharge which accompanied it.

René Maria Rilke (as he was baptised) was born in Prague on December 4, 1875, the seven months' child of Joseph and Phia (Sophia) Rilke, neither of whom seems to have been fit to have children at all, far less so sensitive and defenceless a one as Rilke. He was called René as a sign that he was sent to them in the place of the first child of the marriage, Sophia, who was born in 1874 and died in the same year. René was brought up as a little girl until he was five, dressed in girls' clothes, with long curls, and given dolls to play with. A most remarkable essay he wrote on dolls in later life shows with what loathing he remembered those toys, so closely associated with his early years.[1] On the other hand, his intimate sympathy with young girls, and his intuitive understanding of them probably date back to the time when he half believed that he was a little girl himself. The coddling and dressing-up were probably the work of his mother; but his father showed the same kind of attitude in fussing about his son's health, changing his nurse twenty-four times in the infant's first year, and later laying down hygienic regulations for the purpose of hardening the little boy. That he should ever have permitted René to be treated like a girl is all the stranger since he destined him from birth for a military career. An officer himself, he had been obliged by lack of means to quit the army and

[1] *G.W.* IV, pp. 265 ff., written early in 1914.

accept a small post as a railway official in Prague. His son was to compensate him for this sacrifice, a natural if egotistical desire which took little account of the child's predispositions. The mother, much more temperamental and endowed with a much stronger personality, was the type whose self-dramatisations would earn for her to-day the epithet exhibitionist. She wrote verse, played at being a great lady, and was a fervent Roman Catholic. She was probably as unreal as Rilke declared her to be in later life. Although she encouraged her little son in his artistic and poetical leanings, she played on his emotions, and he spoke of her with bitter resentment as soon as he was of an age to judge, whereas he mentioned his father gently and with respect. He complained that his mother had cruelly neglected him, leaving him entirely to the tender mercies of a vicious servant, and only paying any attention to him when she wished to parade him in his new clothes before her friends. Alternately spoiled and ignored, coddled and hardened, he was a permanent bone of contention between his mutually incompatible parents. His was the story with which Byron's life has made us all so familiar; it belongs to the dark ages of child-psychology when parents ruled the roost. Phia at last, unable to stand Joseph any longer, retired to Vienna with a more sympathetic companion, and René was packed off at the age of ten to the military academy of Saint Pölten; he was later transferred to the senior branch at Weisskirchen, making five years' incarceration (it is hardly too strong a word) in all.

These institutions, probably neither better nor worse than the average of their kind, provided for boys of tender years and adolescent lads that more than Spartan training beloved of military martinets. René was by temperament and upbringing peculiarly unequal to the insensate demands made on his physical endurance and mental resilience. He was soon recognised by his hardier comrades to be the German equivalent for a milksop and was bullied accordingly. None of the masters, officers or petty officers was enlightened or humane enough to protect or spare him; the rigid efficiency of the system allowed no special treatment and recognised no special cases.

It seems almost a miracle in the circumstances that Rilke survived at all. As it was, the harshness of the discipline and the brutality of his comrades affected his health and caused him such agony of mind as hardly bears thinking of:

In this new phase of my young life I was all too familiar with that dastardly and manifest heartlessness which, impelled by pure bestial lust for murder (the expression is not too strong) does not even stop at torture.... Consider... how terribly the assault of such savage and unmerited brutalities must have echoed in the still undefiled sanctuary of a childish heart. What I suffered then can be compared with the greatest woe of the world, even though I was a child, or rather because I was one... I suffered blows without ever returning them, or even repaying them with angry words. In my childish mind I believed that my endurance brought me near to the merits of Jesus Christ; and when I once received a violent blow on my face, so that my knees trembled beneath me, I said quietly to my unjust aggressor—I can still hear it to-day: 'I suffer this, because Christ suffered it, quietly and without complaint, and whilst you were hitting me I was praying to my God to forgive you.' The miserable coward stood stiff and silent for a moment, then he burst into mocking laughter, in which all the others to whom he communicated the outcry of despair joined with yells of derision.... And it was on that very night on which my birthday came round... that I sat up in my bed, folded my hands and prayed for death. An illness would have been a sure sign that my prayer was answered, but no illness came. Instead the instinct for writing poetry developed at that time, which comforted me....[1]

I do not believe that I would have been able to live my life... if I had not for decades on end denied and suppressed all memories of the five years of my military education.... And even later... that long affliction of my childhood, great out of all proportion to my years, seemed incomprehensible to me. I could understand that impenetrable fate as little as the miracle which released me from the abyss of the unmerited misery at the very eleventh hour.... I left the

---

[1] P. Leppin, *Der neunzehnjährige Rilke; Die Literatur*, August 1927, pp. 631 f.; letter from Rilke to Valéry David-Rhonfeld, dated December 4, 1894. Cf. *B. 1892–1904*, pp. 37 f. for a similar but more restrained version of his sufferings given to Ludwig Ganghofer in a letter dated from Munich, April 16, 1897.

military academy at the age of sixteen, exhausted in body and damaged in mind, retarded...cheated of the most innocent part of my strength.... When Dostoyevski's *Memoirs of the House of the Dead* first fell into my hands, it appeared to me that I had been initiated since my tenth year into all the horrors and despairs of convict-prisons.... Dostoyevski was a young man, an adult, when he suffered a completely intolerable fate; in the mind of a child the prison walls of St Pölten, measured by the standard of its helpless and forsaken heart, could take on similar dimensions.[1]

This second passage, separated in time by more than a quarter of a century from the first, shows an increase if anything in the bitter resentment with which Rilke regarded his school-days thirty years later. It was written in answer to a letter from a former master of the academy, General Sedlakowitz, who had taught Rilke German grammar, and had in all innocence recalled himself to the memory of his distinguished pupil, speaking with quite unconscious irony of the golden age of youth. After months of silence he received such an indictment of the whole institution and such an analysis of the tragic effects it had produced on the poet's mind, that he must have realised vividly if belatedly how blind he had been to the torments undergone before his eyes.

The harrowing tale is not quite done. During the later period of his school-days Rilke made friends with a boy called Oscar, whom he spoke of to Valéry David-Rhonfeld as Fried. This lad was probaby older than René, about whom he wrote a compassionate letter to Joseph Rilke:

Filled with the warmest sympathy for René, I venture to put in a kind word for the poor boy. I also thought at first that his condition was purely imaginary, but I now realise after a fortnight's continuous observation that unhappily it is real, as far as I can judge. I have just been for almost a fortnight in the hospital with him, and I noticed that his headaches got much better. He was merry and talkative, in a word he was not seriously ill. The regimental surgeon discharged him yesterday, and when he came up for a moment this

[1] Cf. *B. 1914–1921*, pp. 350–357, for the letter from which these extracts are taken; written to General Sedlakowitz from Schloss Berg am Irchel, Zürich, December 9, 1920.

morning he looked ill, complained of terrible headaches, and was trembling in every limb. In short he had obviously great difficulty in keeping on his feet.[1]

The relief and happiness which this friendship brought to René was of short duration. After an absence from the school on his grandmother's death, Fried returned completely altered to the boy who had been living for that moment. Their fellow-pupils, disliking and almost certainly misinterpreting the nature of the bond between them, had reported them to the authorities, who had warned Fried to leave 'the fool' alone. The latter was left to the consolations of his own mind, to poetry and religion, until at last his health became feeble enough to procure him a tardy release from the inferno of his boyhood. It is just as conventional and as well-worn a story as his early life at home, and recalls public-school novels of the more lurid and distressing type; but the turn of the screw was given by the rigid military training, enforcing a day which began at four in the morning, and included marches, exhausting drill and bathing out of doors in all seasons and weathers as well as the educational routine. Like all young boys Rilke longed to excel at these physical exercises, but did so only in day-dreams, from which he would be rudely awakened by taking a toss from his horse at the most glorious moments of his imaginary feats of courage, daring and endurance. Riding at least, although he was never anything of a horseman, gave him some moments of mental exhilaration and revealed its poetical side. Then too the feeling that he was better than his schoolfellows undoubtedly procured him some alleviation, though it will have done little to endear him to them, and was in danger of turning him into a prig, as the letter to Valéry shows. But the knowledge that he was different was not only the fundamental experience of these years, but actually, besides making him a pariah, on one dramatic occasion inspired terror and respect. One Christmas Eve, when they were all packing for the holidays which René was to spend with his father, a brutal senior, seeing the little boy lost in happy dreams beside his brimming valise, tossed it

[1] C. Sieber, *René Rilke*, Leipzig, 1932, pp. 93 f.; n.d.

up to the ceiling and broke into coarse laughter as the contents
scattered over the room. Suddenly, to his own surprise and
even horror, René heard his voice saying loudly and emphatically: 'I know that you won't get home for the holidays.' His
tormentor began to laugh, slipped, fell and broke his leg.[1] He
did *not* get home for the holidays, and this evidence of
prophetic or psychic gifts earned for their owner a not un-
enviable reputation in that barbarous community.

Rilke felt, as many a poet has felt in similar circumstances,
that until and unless he could transform his tormenting
memories into art he would not be cured of the after-effects of
his disintegrating experience. But another instinct, and it
proved the stronger, urged him to suppress the past altogether.
The 'military novel', which he looked upon as a duty, was
never written, but two short sketches were achieved: *Pierre
Dumont*, not dated but early, in which he described the excruciating 'last day' before the entrance to the academy; and
The Drill-Class, 1899, in which he portrayed the terrors
attending physical instruction. He got no further with the
attempted representation of his past torments, and fell back
on the other way of dealing with them. He banished them as
far as possible from his consciousness, and rarely referred to
them even in private letters.

Apparently stoical, such an attitude is not truly courageous,
and the letters to Valéry and Sedlakowitz are fraught not only
with resentment against the military academy, but also with
extreme self-pity. In the lad of nineteen this seems natural
if unattractive; in the distinguished and successful poet of
forty-five it is pathological. Rilke's incurable grief for his mis-
handled youth inclined him to an almost maudlin tenderness
towards himself which was one of his outstanding weaknesses.
It often disfigures his private letters and was noticeable too
in his bearing. A personal acquaintance described him to
me as a shivering, pathetic person, who always looked as
if he were about to complain, although he practically never
did so. This emasculate self-pity was, if not created, then

---

[1] M. Saint-Hélier, *A Rilke pour Noël*, Bern, 1927, pp. 14 ff.; cf. also E. v.
Schmidt-Pauli, *Rainer Maria Rilke, Ein Gedenkbuch*, Basel, 1940, p. 34.

certainly increased by the prolonged strain he had undergone
in his boyhood, unprotected and alone. It was thanks to the
resilience of youth that he nevertheless managed to survive
mentally as well as physically. Fast, frivolous and gay at the
school of commerce in Linz where his father sent him after
Weisskirchen, he was probably trying to get the better of
harrowing memories; but it would not do; he absconded
before the dreary course was completed with an instructress
several years older than himself. His father was in despair
until René's uncle Jaroslav Rilke offered to pay for his further
education, which included cramming for the entrance examination to the university of Prague and his studies there from
1893 onwards. During this period he lived with a paternal
aunt in wretched health and spirits according to his *fiancée*
Valéry David-Rhonfeld. Nevertheless, poetical schemes and
poetical dreams were keeping his mind alert; and the few
letters available show him immersed in various literary
ventures, appealing for advice and help to several so-called
'masters'; establishing contact with the poetical stars of his
day, seeking and finding publishers for his poems, and
determined to dedicate his life to art and not to law. On the
death of Jaroslav in December 1892, his daughters seem to
have grudgingly continued their father's financial support.
Certainly Rilke's studies were not cut short. He was at the
university of Prague until 1896, at Munich until 1897 and at
Berlin from then onwards. He also managed to undertake a
certain amount of travelling, including a trip to Venice and
Arco in 1897 and to Arco, Florence and Viareggio in 1898.
The most dismal of these university years were those which
he spent in his native town. The long autobiographical story
Ewald Tragy, probably written in the winter 1899–1900,
shows how solitary and how scornful he felt in the society of
his relations, none of whom even began to understand the
aspiring young poet. His misery was lightened, however, and
his life was sweetened by his engagement to Valéry David-
Rhonfeld, or Vally as she was generally called. She was a year
older than René, in happier and more affluent circumstances,
the first of those many women to whose sympathy, affection

...ke owed so much. And she was the only
...ublicly turned against him. She helped him
...es, encouraged him in his poetical efforts and
...pient of his confidences. She also pampered and
...e outer man, providing him with more delicate fare
...s placed before him at home. Rapturously grateful at
...me, Rilke nevertheless broke off his engagement when
...eft Prague for Munich, wishing to be unhampered by any
ties in the pursuit of his poetry. Vally, who remained single,
never forgave him. In 1928 she sold his letters to Hirschfeld
and allowed him to publish her memories of the young poet.[1]
She made him out to have been a pretty poor specimen of
humanity: neurotic, dyspeptic and suffering from boils.
Repulsively plain except for his eyes, he horrified her at first,
until pity melted into love. His family have retaliated by protesting that Rilke's relationship with Vally was the most
trivial of *amourettes*. The impassioned tone of the one letter
available belies this interpretation; but both that and the
scanty references in a Prague diary show that some cupboard-
love was present in his feelings for Vally, also his lifelong
predilection for elegance and comfort. Her real function,
however, was to provide him with an emotional outlet during
this depressed and depressing period. It may have been
because she was an artificial social butterfly that Vally seems
to have left so little impression on his mind; more probably
still, she was almost entirely obliterated from it by a much
more important relationship formed when Rilke removed to
Munich in September 1896, if not already during his visit to
that city the preceding March.

Ewald Tragy portrays a timid, aspiring and modest young
man dazzled at first by the big words and resounding phrases
of a would-be brother poet, a certain von Kranz, who has been
identified as Wilhelm von Scholz.[2] The trenchant criticism

[1] C. Hirschfeld, *Die Rilke-Erinnerungen Valéry von David-Rhonfelds: Die
Horen*, Berlin, 1928–1929, VIII, pp. 714 ff. Spite apart, her account tallies
closely with Rilke's own published letter to her in *Die Literatur*, and with the
references to her in a fragmentary diary of 1893 which is still unpublished, as are
also the 130 letters he wrote to her.

[2] By E. C. Mason. He also identifies Thalmann as Wassermann.

levelled at this author betrays the underlying arrogance of the
observer, also apparent in a letter from Prague full of spiteful
wit about the self-advertising antics of a writer called Zlatnik.[1]
As for Ewald Tragy, that rather half-baked young man (as
Rilke purposely represented him to be) was, for all his
apparent diffidence, the very reverse of humble, sneering at
his philistine family and inexpressibly shocking one of his
aunts by declaring: 'I am a law unto myself, and the monarch
of my own soul; there is no one above me, not even God.'[2]
He had, however, the saving grace of being able to recognise
his superiors, and indeed was in danger of becoming almost
too subservient to them; as witness the passionate outburst of
weeping which overtook Tragy in Thalmann's room, when
that blunt and laconic genius persisted in ignoring him.
Thalmann (probably a pseudonym for Wassermann) opened
Tragy's eyes on the subject of phrase-making and bombast
and gave him a glimmering of a notion of what reality might
mean. This was quite enough to throw the hero into a violent
fever filled with the strangest dreams. Small wonder that, on
his recovery, he uttered a poignant 'cry for motherliness' in
a long letter to his absent mother which was never sent off,
since that slender, nervous lady who was proud if strangers
called her 'Miss' would not have understood it.

The 'cry for motherliness' was not however unheard in
Munich, where Rilke became acquainted with Lou Andreas-
Salomé, a Russian by birth, one of those interesting and
problematical women who so often beset the paths of poets.
Fourteen years earlier, being then only twenty, she had
stirred Nietzsche to his very depths, maintaining her own
poise under the impact of his powerful personality to the
extent not only of refusing his offers of marriage, but also
(less comprehensibly) of withstanding the fiery pathos of
Zarathustra. Owing to the mischief-making propensities of
Nietzsche's sister, great, indeed irredeemable, damage was
wrought in the philosopher's mind by his encounter with Lou,
whose book on Nietzsche is still valuable to-day. She was

[1] Cf. *B. 1892–1904*, pp. 15 f.
[2] Rainer Maria Rilke, *Ewald Tragy*, Munich, 1929–1930, p. 38.

almost certainly innocent of the more unsavoury charges brought against her by Lisbeth Nietzsche; but her intellect seems to have been too dominant and critical, one might almost say too masterful, to make her anything but a danger to that abnormally sensitive and distrustful genius. She was of the type more prone to captivate than to be subdued; and one feels that so young a girl who could combine admiration for Nietzsche with cool judgment must have been formidably unyielding. She was now married to a scholar of oriental languages who was shortly to profess them at Göttingen; and her relationship with him, which seems to have been a happy one, was probably accurately indicated by the nickname of Loumann given to him by their friends. Unscathed by her encounter with Nietzsche, she had no cause to dread the fire of genius; and indeed Rilke, thirteen years her junior and apparently ten times more sensitive, shrinking and vulnerable than the man with the now darkened mind, would seem to be the one whom the relationship might imperil. But it is ill prophesying about unknown quantities. He came to her, as he put it, still almost a child to a rich woman and she 'took him into her arms and gently rocked his soul'.[1] So far so good, as he naïvely said himself; but there was this susceptible young man, already all but broken by his boyhood's experiences, in the power of a fascinating and dominant woman. Strangely enough Lou, who had withstood Nietzsche emotionally, seems to have succumbed to Rilke whilst preserving her intellectual empire. As far as can be gathered from the tone of the poet's diary written in the spring of 1898 and addressed to her, they were lovers before Rilke left for Italy that April. He may even have been the father of the child she was then carrying and which he was expecting with tense and tremulous excitement. Certainly there was a passionate sympathy between them, whatever the actual facts of the friendship. On receipt of some unspecified news from

---

[1] This quotation and the following analysis of the relationship between Lou and Rilke are based on the journal he wrote in Florence, Viareggio and Zoppot between April 15 and July 16, 1898, generally called the Tuscan diary. It is still unpublished.

her (probably about the birth of the child) Rilke left Italy to rejoin Lou and to learn a rather bitter lesson. He was filled with the glories of art and nature which had been revealed to him in Italy; and his head was almost bursting with magnificent theories about art. In spite of an encounter with Stefan George in Florence which had temporarily shaken his self-esteem and was probably accountable for his abrupt flight to Viareggio, Rilke felt, and with justice, that the sojourn in Italy had added many cubits to his stature. He was now, he believed, Lou's equal and even more than that, since he would be able to enrich her with his experiences, the priceless gift of his journal. He was cruelly undeceived. Far from being overwhelmed by the greatness of what he had written, Lou seems to have accepted it very coolly (as was natural from one who had withstood *Zarathustra*) and to have stolen his thunder in their conversations. Rilke's revulsion from her was in proportion to his frustrated desire to dazzle. For a moment he actually hated her because she was too great, oppressing him by her superiority, towering above him and making him appear like the meanest beggar. There was probably some quarrel, but it did not last long. Rilke brought himself to accept the situation, and finally did so with almost rapturous humility. Lou was his beloved and holy one, unique amongst women, the goal, nay the thousand goals of all his striving.

This conclusion to his analysis of the course of their friendship and the emotions it had aroused in him was cancelled out however by the last pages of the diary, which deal with the nature and function of art. And indeed, except in the passages addressed to Lou, the journal as a whole is the very reverse of humble. Not for nothing had Rilke been in close personal and intellectual contact with Nietzsche's sometime disciple; and the sketch entitled *The Apostle* written early in 1896 shows that he was predisposed to this influence.[1] In the journal a more individual and interesting use was made of Nietzsche's

---

[1] Rilke wrote *The Apostle* early in 1896 before his removal to Munich, which he had visited in March of that year. He said at the time that this story was a half satirical, half deeply serious confession of faith; cf. *B. 1892–1904*, p. 22. A Nietzschean outburst in *Ewald Tragy* also suggests that he harboured such feelings in 1896.

theories than the mere dramatic summary given in the sketch. Applying the doctrine of the superman to the tribe of artists, Rilke asserted with great vigour and gusto that they, already sealed and set apart, would in the future survive and bring forth a greater race, whilst ordinary human beings would gradually die out and perish. The hard, arrogant, imperious tone he adopted about the people, the *bourgeois*, the philistines, the tourists and the critics in this journal; the dogmatic manner in which he proclaimed the complete and utter isolation of artists from their fellow-men, and the absolute incomprehensibility of art to the lay mind are only less striking than the ecstasy he reserved for the works of nature and art in Italy, and for women and young girls. His prophecy, too, that the spring of the Italian Renaissance was at last about to produce a summer in modern times; his expressed conviction that he had a message and a mission to humanity further go to prove that Rilke was experiencing those heady sensations which attack young artists with such mysterious force. He was uplifted and inspired by the certainty that he belonged to the chosen people and he probably found in that knowledge the necessary self-defence against the threatening domination by Lou. For his preoccupation with the Italian Madonnas and his hushed reverence towards the phenomenon of motherhood cannot disguise the fact that in a poetical and adoring way he was relegating women to the sphere which popular prejudice has always assigned to them. There is more eloquence than originality in his ukase that, since children are their works of art, they have no need (and indeed no right) to produce others. They reach fulfilment in child-birth and can then become beautiful prophetesses to the artists about the glory of the goal. It sounds very well, especially in Rilke's language; but it would be unlikely to appeal to that expectant mother, Lou Andreas-Salomé, already the author of poems and books of a quality not yet displayed by Rilke. It will have been all the less acceptable to her since, however great the importance of motherhood, Rilke so clearly gave the palm to art, maintaining that the bulk of humanity is creative in religion, women in child-birth, and artists in their art, which is nothing

more nor less than the creation of God. One can well understand Lou's lack of any real enthusiasm for Rilke's journal, a
coolness which was probably responsible for the final remarkable pages written in Zoppot.

Rilke's Catholicism had not long survived his release from
the military academy. At the age of eighteen he wrote a poem
reproaching Christ for laying claims to divinity. There is a
savage Nietzschean attack on Christ in *The Apostle*; and the
Christ Visions of 1897 deal with various aspects of the tragedy
of a man who was believed to be a God.[1] In the journal Rilke
denied the existence of God except as the creation of artists.
The God of his own day was merely the oldest work of art, he
declared, in a very bad state of preservation and patchily restored. In a word he was dead, and none but the artists could
create his successor:

And now the final value of this book is the recognition of an
artist's call, which is only a path and will finally fulfil itself in a
mature existence. With every work of art which you lift out of
yourself you create space for some kind of power. And the last, who
will come after many generations, will carry everything within him
which is powerful and real around us, for he will be the greatest
space, filled with all power. Only one will attain to that; but all
creators are the ancestors of this solitary man. There will be nothing
outside him; for trees and hills, clouds and waves are only symbols of
those realities which He finds within himself.[2] Everything has
flowed together within him, and all the powers which, hitherto
separated, have been in conflict, tremble beneath his will. Even the
ground beneath his feet is too much. He rolls it up like a praying-
mat. He no longer prays. He is. And when he makes a gesture he
will create, hurling into infinity many millions of worlds. Maturer
beings will first multiply and then segregate themselves and after
a long struggle at length achieve One who holds everything within
him, a creator of this eternal kind, a Colossus in space, one with
plastic gestures. Thus every generation winds like a chain from God
to God. And every God is the complete past of a world, its utter-

[1] Cf. M. Sievers, *Die biblischen Motive in der Dichtung Rainer Maria Rilkes*,
Berlin, 1938, pp. 78 ff. for details and quotations from these poems which are
still unpublished.

[2] I retain Rilke's solitary capital for He.

most meaning, its harmonious expression and at the same time the
possibility of a new life. How other far distant worlds will ripen to
Gods I do not know. But for us art is the way.... I feel therefore
that we are the ancestors of a God and that with our deepest lone-
linesses we are reaching out through the centuries towards a
beginning. That is what I feel.

However much this fantastic vision of the future may owe to
Nietzsche, the self-assertion of genius apparent throughout
the diary, to the point of extravagance in the Zoppot post-
script, is a reassuring sign that Rilke had overcome the more
fatal consequences of the military academy; and far from being
lamed for life as he was apt to declare later, was filled to overflowing with the feeling of creative strength. The part played
by Lou in this liberation was probably quite as vital as the
revelation of Italian art; in all likelihood it was she herself
who gave him the weapon with which he resisted the dangerous
side of her influence; but what it was that wrested it from his
grasp is not so easy to see.

The Tuscan diary is unique among Rilke's early writings as
far as these are known. With the exception of *The Apostle* and
some passages in *Ewald Tragy*, the youthful poems, stories,
letters and published diaries are chiefly remarkable on the
subjective side for their wistful, humble and gentle tone. The
virility, the vainglory, the fervent acceptance of life as a
whole, the dislike and contempt of pessimism and morbidity
differentiate this journal sharply from the themes and the
attitudes elsewhere adopted. It is also noticeable for an
almost Stopesian worship of 'radiant motherhood', partly
inspired by his great affection for his friend Francesca Countess
of Reventlow who had given birth to a son in January 1898,
partly by Lou. This adoration was shortly to yield (and indeed
was already yielding) to a more pathological cult of untouched virgins. It is certainly possible to admire both
aspects of the 'eternal feminine'; and Rilke reserved an
honourable position for mothers in his later works. But his
deepest feelings were from now onwards consecrated to
young girls, and he came to harbour an uneasy dislike of
motherhood which destroyed the state he adored. I believe

myself that, probably in Viareggio and certainly before he had
completed the first version of *The White Princess* in July 1899,
he lived through some emotional crisis or underwent some
spiritual shock which left an indelible impression on his mind.
Either his natural anxiety about Lou's confinement which may
have ended badly, since he was dismayed by the news she
sent him and planned to rejoin her at once; or some other and
perhaps stranger revelation of the kinship between love and
death aroused in him something like hatred for the male, fear
and distrust of sexual love and a morbid horror of child-birth.
Whatever the shock or the crisis may have been, it was to
reverberate through his poetry until the end of his life, inspiring him with a poetical passion for young girls linked with
great sympathy and expressed predilection for all who die
young. This latter emotion dictated some moving pages in the
Tuscan journal in connection with the fate of Giuliano dei
Medici, slain by the knife which was aimed at his elder
brother Lorenzo, cut off in the spring-time of his life, leaving
his poems to perish unsung in the heart of his young peasant
lover, who died shortly afterwards in giving birth to his child.

The theme of girlhood, love and death was certainly already
latent in his mind when the incident occurred which inspired
The White Princess. Indeed, his elaborate description of it in
the journal contains the embryo of the dramatic sketch. It
impressed him profoundly, and he still remembered the
episode vividly in 1924.[1] It took place in Viareggio, where he
inhabited a large villa with marble balconies and pillars and a
garden running down to the sea. One morning when he was
working on his balcony he heard the gravel crunch below,
and looked down to see a black brother of mercy standing
motionless on the garden-path, obviously there to beg for his
order, not venturing to approach, but hoping to be noticed.
He was wearing a black mask, and appeared among the
auriculas, poppies and red roses like a shadow cast by some
towering giant, and indeed like death itself. Not as the fell

[1] Cf. Hermann Pongs, *Drei unveröffentlichte Briefe Rilkes: Dichtung und
Volkstum*, Stuttgart, 1936, xxxvii, 1, p. 113; letter to Pongs from Muzot,
October 21, 1924, for this later account of the incident; there is also a shorter
one in *B. 1892–1904*, p. 437, to Ellen Key in 1904.

sergeant, however, but rather in the guise of a servant who had been summoned, and was now awaiting further orders. Rilke watched breathlessly, half expecting some fair-haired girl, or some strong silent man to appear on the terrace and, immersed in deep thoughts, to follow the friar out of the garden for ever. Meanwhile, the latter, having gently rattled his alms-box without effect, was slowly and with many hesitations preparing to retreat, when he was arrested by the appearance of a young lad who had been sent out to give him a coin. This led the friar to resume his station on the garden-path, motionless as before. Rilke, as immobile as he, imagined the blond young girl, whom he had visualised earlier, sending out the lad to give the black brother her heart, saying: 'Take that, and precede me. I was mistaken. It is true that I am tired and that I cannot love; but let me still gaze at the beauty all round me.' Unwillingly and incredulously the figure of death retreated with many hesitations and backward looks to the garden-gate where he stopped beneath the plane-tree; whilst the girl, leaning against the marble pillar, the weeping lad cowering beside her, gazed out at the distant sea.

In spite of this poetical transference, the recurrence of the real friar after he had seemed to be off, unnerved Rilke, who began to think that if he made some involuntary gesture, the sinister apparition with the masked face would approach him to solicit alms, and having received them, begin to wait again until someone else would also appear to be beckoning to him. In 1924 he declared that he had been paralysed with terror lest this should happen. In the journal he disclaimed all fear; declaring that, on the contrary, the whole incident had aroused in him an indescribable sensation of reconciliation, peace and blessedness. But something else was to happen which retrospectively made the visit of the friar seem really uncanny. A favourite dachshund belonging to the house was accidentally killed that evening, an event which Rilke might not have associated with the occurrence of the morning, if he had not happened to come across the dog behaving very strangely in the afternoon. Generally more than willing to respond to Rilke's advances, it remained mournfully inert now, and seemed to be sunk in melancholy brooding. Deep, mysterious, dumb, it resembled a sphinx more than a dachshund. So Rilke thought at the time, and was puzzled but not alarmed. When he heard of its death, however, he remembered the black brother of mercy whom he never afterwards forgot. Though he was emphatic in the journal about his lack of fear, the panic he remembered in 1924 underlay the works this incident inspired; and in the journal, too, uneasiness is apparent. He may well have experienced both the utter peace and the acute dread, even if not simultaneously; for his lifelong ambiguous attitude to death seems to have germinated in Viareggio; and it is probably significant that, shortly after the incident of the friar and the dog, came the disturbing letter from Lou.

Three great experiences moulded the childhood and adolescence of René Rilke: the military academy, the encounter with Lou Andreas-Salomé, and whatever the unknown factor was which created the symbolism of *The White Princess*. All three left deep marks on his life and works; although the first, which has been so much stressed by Rilke and his critics, was aesthetically the least important, great though its influence was. The horrors undergone at school were to haunt him through life, but their inhibitive effect upon his genius was not nearly so great as he imagined; and their positive aesthetic effect produced the great symphony of fear played out in *Malte Laurids Brigge*, the supreme manifestation of an important aspect of his work. Lou Andreas-Salomé liberated and inspired him, as the Tuscan journal proves, and was to be a lifelong spiritual influence. It was under her aegis and Nietzsche's that he conceived at the age of twenty-one those great leading ideas which were the condition of existence of *Duino Elegies*. As for the complex of emotions and thoughts in which a black brother of mercy and a dead dachshund fortuitously became involved, whoever or whatever was the origin opened up a trail in the poet's mind which blazed its way through the whole of his subsequent work, achieving its final goal in the *Sonnets to Orpheus*. The years 1896–1898 were perhaps the most crucial years in Rilke's life, since they

determined his poetical course and implanted in his spirit the
conception of a mission which was nothing less exacting than
to found the religion of art.

2. *Juvenilia*

Yet there is little enough in Rilke's early published works,
few of which antedate the year 1896, to show the transformation which was taking place in his mind or what strange
visions and notions inhabited it. This was partly because he
was rushing too early into print, as the publisher Adolf Bonz
insinuated in 1897, only to be hotly contradicted.[1] Stefan
George gave utterance to the same opinion during their
meeting in the Boboli Gardens in Florence; and Rilke,
probably very much piqued at the time, was later entirely of
George's opinion. The poems, the stories and the plays which
he wrote before 1899 were all abhorrent to him afterwards.
He considered them negligible and insincere, devoid of skill,
obviously the products of a damaged mind; not even representative of the period, since he had withheld from publication
his less contemptible efforts.[2] The abnormal discrepancy
between his ideals and achievements, between the Tuscan
journal and his *juvenilia* written at the universities of Prague,
Munich and Berlin, is certainly remarkable, and must, I think,
be attributed to the shades of the military academy. The cruel
element of life and reality, thrust violently into his consciousness before he was old enough to assimilate it, produced
highly unreal escapist poetry on the one hand, on the other
distressingly morbid prose-fantasies varied by crude efforts at
grim realism. From 1898 onwards his poetical genius began
to shine through his verse, but his prose showed little sign of
it until several years later; and his literary adolescence extended well into his twenty-fifth year, no unusual phenomenon
with great poets, especially when, like Rilke, their develop-

---

[1] Cf. *B. 1892–1904*, pp. 48 ff.
[2] Ellen Key, *Seelen und Werke*, Berlin, 1911, p. 167.

ment has been stunted in youth, and when into the bargain they belong to those highly civilised members of society who come slowly to maturity.

The quantity if not the quality of the verse produced between 1894 and 1899 is proof of the determination of the author to succeed. He kept on shaking verses out of his sleeve like a poetical conjurer, more and more of it and better in kind: *Life and Songs*, 1894; *Wild Chicory, Songs given to the People*, 1896; *An Offering to the Lares*, 1896; *Crowned with Dreams*, 1897; *Advent*, 1898; *In my Honour*, 1899. All this verse, slowly rising from mediocrity to mystery, has one common quality. It is pure poetry uncontaminated by reality. Limpid, lucid, often trivial but never unmelodious, it cannot hold the attention for very long; the mind slides away from its facile charm, soothed nevertheless by music and grace.

Life and Songs, dedicated to Vally but written at Linz, is now long since out of print and very rare; I have not been able to procure it. The second collection is available in a volume containing early verse, prose and dramas, published during the author's lifetime with his grudging permission in an edition limited to one hundred copies.[1] *Wild Chicory* comprises seventeen poems in which the ideal is clearly folk-like simplicity, and which are colourless in the extreme; but some of the poems from contemporary journals printed in the same collection have more individuality; and one rather ugly diatribe against the philistines reminds one of the Tuscan journal.

An Offering to the Lares has Prague for its theme; it shows but the faintest traces of inspiration. The influence of Heine (of a trivialised not to say a vulgarised Heine) pervades the metre, the technique and the very moods. The descriptions of the monuments, the evocation of the atmosphere, and the chronicling of moments in the history of one of the most fascinating cities in Europe by one of the greatest poets it has produced resulted in something so uninspired and derivative, that youth and inexperience cannot be the only cause.

[1] *Aus der Frühzeit Rainer Maria Rilkes*, Leipzig, 1921.

Determined as he was to write poetry, Rilke chose his native town as the subject nearest to hand. It was a natural choice; but it was symptomatic of that poetical insincerity which he took so many years to overcome. Rilke disliked Prague, and never thought of it as his home.[1] Not really because he was a German born in a Czech town, as nordic patriots would like to believe; but because it had been a wicked stepmother to him. His childhood was like a confused bad dream; and now living none too comfortably with an aunt, forsaken by his mother, in bad odour with his father for breaking down at Weisskirchen and playing the fool at Linz; uncertain about his future and out of tune with his surroundings, he had little enthusiasm to spare for the scene of so dismal an adolescence. He was later to speak of Prague with extreme dislike and to shun it almost morbidly. The poems he forced to flower on such unnatural soil are as artificial and as devoid of vitality as one would expect them to be. There is one noticeable exception. The music of the songs and of the language he heard all round him every day must already at this period have been part of his own interior rhythm. This did not break through into his poetry until later, since Heine's rhythms were different; but it can be heard in *Folk Tune* like bells sounding softly rather far away.[2]

Crowned with Dreams belongs to that region of languid, impotent and die-away visions which melancholy young poets affect. It is sincerer than the preceding collection, for it gives impressions of landscapes seen through certain moods which the writer had experienced. The emotions are rather titivated up, and are made to perform Heinesque gyrations, but the superficial vapourings are genuine, and some of the poems effective if facile:

> This yellow rose on Monday
> The lad did give to me.
> I carry it on Tuesday
> To his fresh grave—and see!

[1] Cf. C. Du Bos, *Extraits d'un Journal 1908–1928*, Paris, 1931, p. 285; B. 1906–1907, p. 253; B. 1907–1914, pp. 9 ff.
[2] *G.W.* I, p. 61.

> How on its petals leaning
> You may clear droplets view.
> But tears to-day their meaning,
> And yesterday 'twas dew.

There, but for the grace of workmanship, goes *The Shropshire Lad*, whose author would never have passed 'leaning' for drops of water; and would have disdained to fall back on 'see' for the sake of a rhyme.[1]

The preponderance of death in *Crowned with Dreams* is too typical of adolescent poetry to call for comment. But Rilke's choice of epithets: 'languid—faded—dark—dying away—repressed—sad—pale—still', with their appropriate nouns and verbs, indicates a preference for decadent values which often exercise over vital and vigorous young men the attraction of opposites. But there was real languor behind Rilke's youthful pose which affected those dragging rhythms where Heine's thraldom had been overcome. And the Rilkean rhyme-scheme, which begins to appear in this collection (*abbba* with amplifications and variations), almost suggests that the writer was too tired to stop, or to resist the compulsion of the rhyme. It is inspiration by default, as it were, but inspiration none the less:

> Along the silent house the windows flare;
> The garden's heavy with the scent of roses,
> Above the white massed clouds the sky reposes,
> And twilight in the moveless air uncloses
> Its pinions bare.[2]

Advent shows little promise except in the almost complete emancipation from the manners and methods of Heine. Jens Peter Jacobsen was now Rilke's poetical star; but Dehmel, Liliencron, Hofmannsthal and others, to whom he dedicated a poem apiece in the section called *Gifts*, undoubtedly contributed to stir the waters of his mind; and produced the state-

---

[1] *G.W.* I, p. 113, Rilke used the words *lehnen* and *schau*.
[2] *G.W.* I, p. 128.

ment of his poetical aim inspired by those ideals which gave
significance to the Tuscan journal:

> This is my fate:
> By desire consecrate
> To go thro' all days wending.
> Then, strong and great,
> Deep into life go sending
> Roots that appear unending—
> And through pain's gate
> Far out of life be tending,
> Out of time's gate.[1]

It is as if with a strong effort of will Rilke were shouting
out a message he had received, lest he should forget it. The
emphatic, almost violent metre, the short hard words, the
virile bracing tone, suggest a very different conception of the
sorrow that was to mature him from the pale poetical melancholy he indulged in during the greater part of this collection.
The prophetic vision of his future career, during which he was
indeed to penetrate deep into life and grow far out of life and
time, is in the strongest possible contrast to the poetical ideal
represented in another poem in the same book portraying a
dim and desolate maiden who was much more truly Rilke's
early muse than the virile prophet of the other poem.[2] Weeping
for purple tents, dustless roads and strange melodies, winding
roses in her hair and despairing of love, she strayed hither and
thither rather ineffectively in a vague, musical land, returning
(to quote from another poem):

> Without a crown and empty-handed—
> but so young.[3]

In my Honour (now entitled *Early Poems* and considerably
altered in 1907) was the first collection to receive the author's
later approval. It was signed Rainer Maria Rilke, a symbol of
his determination to break with his youth and to undergo a
radical change. The power of transformation is indeed the
outstanding feature of this collection, and was henceforward to
be for Rilke the poetical process *par excellence*. He had in

[1] *G.W.* I, p. 167.   [2] *G.W.* I, p. 234.   [3] *G.W.* I, p. 223.

superabundance the more feminine than masculine qualities of receptivity, subtle comprehension, penetration and sympathy, characteristics, by the way, which he shared with his Slavonic compatriots and not with his nordic ancestors. Sympathy, whether emotional or spiritual, carried to the lengths to which Rilke could carry it results in the lowering of the barriers between the self and the non-self. The two become indistinguishable, the self merging into the non-self, the non-self flowing inwards into the self, like the river and the sea. The emotional compulsion to achieve such commingling is mystical by nature; its clearest poetical expression is in the lyric.[1] *In my Honour* abounds in poems in which the desire to become as the wind or the trees, or twilight, or the roses trembles on the verge of the actual transformation.[2] The roots which Rilke had invoked in *Advent* were in fact now beginning gently, gingerly to put out slender filaments into life, or the non-self, though not always with marked success. Sometimes the process was arrested on the way and doubled back into similes, personifications and symbols, occasionally feeble or even grotesque, as in the fantasy about roses, where he visualised them as women walking two by two, arms round each others' hips, the red roses singing and the white ones gently falling.[3] On the whole Rilke was naturally more successful when he expressed his sense of oneness with the phenomena around him than when he tried to represent their inner reality; there is more than one poem in which his experience of being part of all existence found mysterious and arresting words:

> Alone I can never be.
> Many before me going
> And away from me flowing,
> Were weaving,
> Weaving
> At the I that is me.

---

[1] As the term 'mystical' is used with widely different connotations, I ought perhaps to say here that I use it to designate the quality or the gift of being able to establish contact with a spirit or spirits other than oneself or outside oneself.

[2] *G.W.* I, p. 356.   [3] *G.W.* I, p. 285.

> And should I sit down beside you,
> Saying gently: mind you,
> I've suffered.
> Who knows who
> Murmurs it too.[1]

Besides these isolated efforts to achieve or express inter-penetration, there are two cycles of poems in this collection which deal in a sustained fashion with two special themes. Both of these were to be permanent subjects of inspiration and of paramount importance in Rilke's later poetry. The first cycle is called *Angels' Songs* and contains seven poems about angels; none of them is outstanding, nor is the symbolism underlying the conception clear; but they are interesting experiments in the art of evoking what might be called angel-psychology from within and not from without. The relationship between the poet and the guardian angel, for instance, is described by the poet, but from the angel's point of view. It stunted and impoverished him, until at last he was set free to cleave the silence of the stars once more with mighty wings. These poems seem to have been inspired by visual memories of those Italian pictures which had made such a strong impression on him in Florence. They were now intensified into vision:

> In my most secret dreams I'm holding,
> And will forever, that strange wing-folding
> That stood behind him like a cypress white.[2]

The *Maidens' Songs* (as the trilogy *Maidens, Songs of the Maidens* and *Prayers of the Maidens to Mary* is generally called) were conceived and partly executed in Viareggio and represent the apotheosis of maidenhood. The songs these young girls sing and the prayers they utter come drifting up from their subconscious minds and are cloudy with mystery. They themselves are compared with myths, with May, with the sea; they are spring and longing incarnate, blooming without aim, yearning for they know not what. They are melody in

---

[1] *G.W.* I, p. 361; cf. also p. 362 for the same theme; and pp. 354 and 355 for a similar contact with the spirit of twilight and evening.

[2] *G.W.* I, p. 278.

perpetual motion like the waves, and their songs will slowly
fade when the bridegroom comes. Baffling to themselves,
they know that when their fate is revealed to them they will
vanish away, none knows whither.[1] Their mothers have grown
grey with grief, they remember their former smiles like forgotten songs; they too bloomed once, but then they were
broken in a great storm-year. The girls long for such a storm
to come to them, but no wind stirs. They wait tremulously;
always together like sisters, they laugh, play and sing in the
golden light of day; but when night falls a distance seems
to separate them, and the bridegroom seems near. Their
thoughts then turn to Mary, and flicker round her, fitfully
illuminating themselves and her, ardent but impotent flames:

> O, let me be pain of the pain you're bearing;
> O, together let us be sharing
> The hurt by the self-same miracle.[2]

The trilogy closes with a piercingly sad small voice rising up
to God from a choir of invisible nuns.

The embryonic state of girlhood is well brought out by the
fragmentary and nebulous nature of the songs the young
things sing and the prayers they utter; more telling still, they
are indistinguishable from each other, a drifting plurality of
girls singing and speaking together or one of them speaking
for all. The total effect is of a haunting, far-off melody, of an
elusive scent vanishing on the air, of intangible presences
floating gently away, of transience and fragility. Yet the
sentimentality inherent in the subject has not altogether
dissolved by the awe-stricken treatment. Nor has one the
impression of being in the heart of a mystery, but on the
contrary of groping round the periphery, in danger at any
moment of seeing *The Soul's Awakening*, or hearing *The
Maiden's Prayer*. The essential unreality of Rilke's young girls
was divided perhaps only by a hair's breadth from the inner
reality he was aiming at expressing. The insubstantiality of
his vision is not to blame for the fact that his maidens appear
like poetical shams beside the figure of a Gretchen. Rilke was

[1] *G.W.* I, p. 304.   [2] *G.W.* I, p. 342.

unable in these poems to evoke the dark background on which his vision of maidenhood flowered. He had also gone inward rather than outward to discover girlhood's soul; the self-love and yearning with which he regarded these creatures of his fancy tainted them with a certain sickliness and improbability which blighted their youthful grace.

The plays of the early period, which Rilke later dismissed as beneath contempt, are, with the exception of *The White Princess*, extremely dreary. *Equal and Free*, a proletarian drama, is now lost, and nothing is known of it but Vally's amusing description. *Vigils* and *Mountain Air*, still in manuscript, have been analysed.[1] *Now and at the Hour of Death*, *Hoar Frost*, *Little Mother* and *Without being Present* have been published.[2] Represented against a background of grinding poverty or middle-class squalor naturalistically depicted, pure but mistaken young girls surrender their virtue to gross old men or coarse commercial travellers from motives of filial piety, fortunate indeed if nothing worse than incest results from their selfless actions. A disreputable night-scene infected by the presence of a corpse; a philistine young couple haunted by a dead girl's ghost; a younger sister innocently arousing her brother-in-law's repressed sensuality; such were the unattractive persons and such the unprepossessing themes handled by the self-same René Rilke who wrote such ethereal and 'beautiful' verse.

The early stories reveal similar preoccupations and dependence on models. Gerhard Hauptmann had dominated Rilke's dramas. *The Christ Child*, dated 1893, the same year as Hauptmann's *Hannele's Ascension*, is so extremely like it in treatment and theme, that its main aesthetic difference lies in its being a story and not a play. *The Apostle*, 1896, is a Nietzschean outburst; *United*, 1897, a pallid reflection of Ibsen's *Ghosts*, 1887; and *The Flight*, 1898, irresistibly recalls Wedekind's *Spring-Awakening*, 1891. More independent and more interesting are the *Two Prague Tales*, 1899, dealing

---

[1] Cf. J.-F. Angelloz, *Rainer Maria Rilke, l'évolution spirituelle du poète*, Paris, 1936, pp. 93 ff.

[2] In *Aus der Frühzeit Rainer Maria Rilkes*.

with the Young Czech movement and its victims, a pathetic dwarf in the first story, an unhappy young student in the second. Rilke obviously laboured hard at the atmosphere, which has a certain antiquarian fascination to-day; but the lack of real sympathy with his native town and its inhabitants resulted in local colour of the painstaking kind. Death, which plays a tragic part in these two tales, is the central theme of *Sacred Spring*, 1897, *Aunt Babette's Death* and *The Anniversary*, 1898. Thwarted spinsterhood is luridly depicted in *The Secret*, 1898; the unsavoury physical peculiarities of old age in *Old People*, 1898; blindness is sentimentally delineated in *The Voice*, 1898; consumption, love and religion unite in *All in One*, 1898, to produce a gruesome finale; the phthisical hero, whose carven Madonnas, to his great distress, grow under his hands into effigies of the woman he loves and who is another's, begins to hack away at his hands instead of carving the wood. There is a blood-curdling note in *The Laughter of Pán Mráz*, 1899; and queer, nightmarish sensuality in *The House*, 1900. In short, to read Rilke's early stories and sketches is to sup on horrors, actual and aesthetic, all of them in the worst of bad taste. The discomfort they produce is all the greater because of the highly wrought poetical prose. The supreme literary inspiration in Rilke's life, Jens Peter Jacobsen, affected the themes with their orientation towards death, the technique with its subtle soul-analysis, and above all the suggestiveness of the style. Rilke, who first read Jacobsen in 1896, regarded him throughout his life as a supreme master, paid tribute to him again and again, and acknowledged a debt great beyond calculation. He learnt Danish later in order to read Jacobsen in the original; but at this period he used German translations, a course I have faithfully followed.

Jacobsen died of consumption in 1885 at the age of thirty-eight, having produced two novels, *Marie Grubbe*, 1876 and *Niels Lyhne*, 1880; also a volume of short stories, *Mogens*, 1882. They are fascinating books, containing passages that positively take one's breath away: Marie Grubbe among the roses, and the terrible death-bed scene of Ulrik Christian Gyldenlöve in the same novel; Edele in her gypsy dress in

Niels Lyhne; the rain-storm in *Mogens*, and many more remain vitally fresh in one's mind, after the desultory plots and
even the subtle characterisations have ceased to affect one.
They are not purple passages, for Jacobsen was too delicate a
worker to indulge in those; but, as far as one can judge from
mere translations, they have an intoxicating quality. Strikingly great proportions these novels have not; and although
the characters are real, they have been analysed and syn-
thesised almost out of existence. But the strange iridescent
light playing over the whole gives it a value hard to define; it
is as if seemingly solid objects and homogeneous personalities
were being insidiously resolved into their component parts,
exhaling in the process a fragrance intimately disturbing, the
aroma of poetical dissolution, the poetry of decadence itself.
This heady influence, exerted over Rilke when he was barely
out of his teens, can be felt fermenting in his early stories—
not altogether to their advantage. Jacobsen's aesthetic preoccupation with death and decadence took on a personal and
emotional colouring in the young man's morbid fantasies
on macabre, gruesome, hysterical or sickly themes. The
artistry of Jacobsen's prose degenerated into preciosity
and the analytical technique was drenched in sentimentality;
nevertheless the discovery of this model did much to
give homogeneity to Rilke's prose, and to set his feet upon
a path which was to lead him finally to *Malte Laurids
Brigge*.

The tyrannical influence of Heine over Rilke's early poetry,
of Hauptmann over his dramatic sketches and of Jacobsen over
his prose shows the extremely suggestive nature of his
genius. The first, the least important, was the most quickly
thrown off, and in 1899 Rilke's personal lyrical note was
already to be heard. Hauptmann and naturalism were not
so easy to escape from; and Jacobsen, to whom Rilke was
drawn by a strong affinity, inaugurated a new era in his
work.

During the early period it was his curious and distressing
practice to use prose for fantasies so ugly and at the same
time so sodden with sentiment, aesthetically speaking so

perverse, that if one knew only these writings one could argue
with some show of reason that his mind was like a sink. In a
particular sense this is true. If most minds and memories
strongly resemble sieves, letting a great deal slip through
into unexplored mental regions where it generally does more
good than harm, subsiding, cohering, mouldering like a heap
of dead leaves to form fertile soil for the spring, Rilke's
memory was abnormally retentive, and allowed very little to
escape. In fact it resembled the impermeable surface of a sink
whose one inconsiderable outlet is all too easily choked. Most
of us know by experience what happens when an attempt is
made to get rid of accumulated refuse by clearing out the
passage. It was the same situation in Rilke's tales: his effort
to rid himself of horrible memories stirred up malodorous
dregs. What was unique in him was the hard and fast line he
drew between poetry and prose. In these early years his
verse was so carefully filtered, distilled and even disinfected,
that no trace of reality, its salt, its savour, its indefinable tang,
remained to give it ponderance. His prose, heavy with
poetical jargon, was thick with realities of the glutinous sort,
not transformed aesthetically, but in a process of decay. In
neither vehicle was reality assimilated. It was separated out
from the one, it polluted the other. Yet an exception must be
made for that haunting drama which he called *The White
Princess*, and whose acknowledged genesis was the incident of
the friar and the dachshund in Viareggio. What other experience was welded into this he never openly acknowledged.
But in the play in question, finished early in July 1899, remodelled and expanded in November 1904, girlhood met the
poetical destiny of Rilke's dreams. This lyrical drama sur-
passes in interest, beauty and mysteriousness anything that
had hitherto come from Rilke's pen. It was generated by
terror certainly, and by love almost indubitably; by an
imaginative terror, and by a metaphysical love. The influence
of Maeterlinck, with whose works Rilke was much occupied
at the time, pervaded the dream-reality of the atmosphere, in
which life-sized puppets are manipulated by an eerie fate; but
the influence of Jacobsen's *Plague in Bergamo* was even more

inspirational.[1] The scene is laid in sixteenth-century Italy, in
the garden of a princely villa by the sea. The White Princess
and her young sister Monna Lara wait through a long afternoon until sunset for the lover of the princess, for whose sake
she has kept herself untouched throughout the eleven years of
her marriage to a violent and passionate husband. To-day for
the first time since their wedding the prince has ridden away
with his retinue into the woods, leaving her mistress of the
castle and grounds. Her lover sends her a message to
announce his arrival from the sea at nightfall; he will land
when she waves her scarf as a signal that it is safe. The
messenger interrupts a conversation between the two sisters,
a queer entranced duologue about dreams and death, love and
life which has hardly its equal, outside Rilke's poetry, for sheer
mystery combined with stark sensuality. Equally strange,
and very gruesome, are the speeches made by the messenger
describing the ravages of the plague in the towns and villages
he had passed through that day. Monna Lara is petrified with
horror; her sister, lost in dreams, hardly hears what he says,
until the word 'death' penetrates her consciousness; and even
then she remains immune from the terror behind his words and
unmoved by his warning against the ambiguous brothers of
mercy who are prowling about everywhere, gaining access to
all the houses, performing last offices to the dying, carrying
out the dead, but bringing in who knows what? A feeling is
abroad that these birds of ill-omen accept ransom from the
living, who fear to withhold it. Monna Lara, shattered by her
first revelation of death in its most horrible form, implores her
sister to render aid to the stricken; and the latter, still half in a
dream, dedicates herself to their service from to-morrow onwards; to-night she belongs to her lover. This speech, the
only one in prose, is significantly enough the only occasion
when the plague comes uncomfortably, almost palpably, close.
Monna Lara retires into the villa as the sun goes down to
prepare her sister's bridal bed; and in a long, detailed and

[1] There are several articles by Rilke about Maeterlinck in periodicals during
the years 1898 and 1899. The intense interest persisted until 1901. Jacobsen's
Plague in Bergamo is a magnificent and terrible tale which clearly impressed
Rilke profoundly.

beautiful rubric Rilke describes the approaching sound of oars and the appearance of the black-masked brothers of mercy whispering in the background. The White Princess catches sight of them just as she is about to wave, and stands rooted to the spot in terror. In vain does she struggle to pull out her scarf as the sound of the boat comes slowly nearer, hesitates, goes past and gradually dies away. The sunset, a moment before flaming in the castle windows, dies down and is extinguished. The princess has ceased to fight against her paralysis; she is absolutely still, and the figures in black are creeping closer. Then from an upper window a curtain is drawn back, and something light and slender, like the figure of a child, is seen waving and beckoning; there is a moment's pause, and then the figure waves again, heavily and slowly as if in farewell.[1]

The silence in which the tragic catastrophe is accomplished is like the noiseless panorama of a dream, dissolving into itself on the brink of some unutterable horror. Although it is nowhere explicitly stated, the idea that the loss of maidenhood spells terror and a gruesome death is suggested, almost represented, in this strange and poetical play.

The uncanny sensations Rilke had experienced in the villa at Viareggio were not eliminated from his nervous system by their sublimation in *The White Princess*. They continued to work in his mind and began to poison it. On November 7, 1899, about four months after the publication of the play, he translated his broodings into prose. This sketch, which he called *The Grave-Gardener*, was amplified and printed in 1903 under the title *The Grave-Digger*. Sickly with sentiment and grisly in the extreme, it is on quite as low a level as the worst of the preceding tales, and the eeriness of the original experience has gone. The story runs as follows. There came to San Rocco one day a new grave-digger of a poetical turn of mind. He told the burgomaster's sixteen-year-old daughter Gita that he was a gardener; and indeed he turned all the

---

[1] This is an analysis of the longer (1904) version; there is only one speech about the plague in the 1899 version, and it is much less luridly described; cf. *Pan*, Berlin, 1899, 5th year, 4th number, p. 281; this bears out my contention of the longevity of horror in Rilke's mind.

graves into flower-beds, and made other beds to correspond with them on the opposite side of the churchyard. For a time all went well, and the few funerals which took place that spring were like flower-feasts; but then the plague broke out; and the people, believing that the grave-digger had brought it about by preparing flower-bed graves, came out to stone him. Gita, who had preceded them to warn him, was killed; but the plague, attacking some of the assailants, scattered their ranks. That night, after the 'gardener' had buried Gita, the people returned drunk and dangerous with cart-loads of corpses and dying men. They started hurling them over the wall, until the grave-digger bashed in the ringleader's head with his spade, and made off into the night 'like a conquered man'.

The jarring combination of sentimentality about death with revolting physical details of its manifestations shows what macabre thought-associations had been engendered by the experience in Viareggio. That one and the same mind could elaborate one and the same experience in two such diametrically opposite ways illuminates the cleavage between the poetical and non-poetical strata of Rilke's consciousness. If his early poetry as a result sounds rather like a eunuch's song, his prose-fantasies on the other hand sometimes resemble visions generated in an absinthe den. The one lacks the reality, the other the sanity of life. The glamour of gallantry is absent from both. Yet gallantry was not absent from Rilke's make-up. His youthful dreams of excelling at sports; his passion for riding; the way he clung to his uniform after he had left the military academy; his schoolboy war-poems; his ardent response to Detlev von Liliencron's masculine, vigorous and dashing ballads; and last but not least the Tuscan diary—all this shows that there was a streak of something heroic and virile in his nature which did not belie his stouter-hearted forebears.

The Lay of the Love and Death of Cornet Christopher Rilke, written down in a white heat of inspiration one stormy autumn night in the year 1899, combines dream-wishes of youthful comradeship with reminiscences from Liliencron, memories of Giuliano dei Medici and the psychic impression made upon him by the features and fate of a young namesake in the past. His lay is a heady mixture of prose and verse, and the hero as young, chivalrous and gallant as any knight of romance. Riding with his comrades against the Turk in 1662, fresh, bewildered, clean as a whistle, he seems in the literal sense to have been an inspired creation. The pageantry of his death, brandishing his burning flag surrounded by enemy troops, has a stinging freshness about it different indeed from the sick-room atmosphere of the stories and the hot-house air of the poems. This venture into the world of chivalry and romance comes considerably nearer to reality than Rilke's ultra-modern stories or his super-ethereal verse. It was his first hymn of praise to those who die in the flower of their youth; and here again love and death were in close proximity.

The rather sickly-sweet bells of Rilke's early verse were jangled, out of tune and harsh in his prose; whilst the works produced in both media lacked the saving grace of reality. The aversion from real life engendered in the military academy dictated neurotic or morbid representations of its horrible side, grotesquely distorted. The escapist illusions in verse were insignificant on the whole because of their feeble vitality and were illusory in the derogatory sense, as the following directions for staging *The White Princess* indicate:

The sea extends into the audience; the breakers are visible in the proscenium. The actors therefore look straight at the audience and at the same time their eyes reflect the wide sea. *The sea can only be brought on to the stage in the eyes of the actors.* The attempt to represent the infinite by a blue cloth would be too disturbing to the atmosphere of the play.[1]

Staged out of doors with the sea in sight, *The White Princess* would be in its ideal setting. Failing that (and Rilke was thinking of an ordinary theatre), the despised blue cloth could create the illusion of its presence, that or some better stage-device. These are the only two possibilities. Rilke demanded instead of reality or illusion based on reality the suspension of

---

[1] *B.u.T.* p. 18; to Cäsar Flaischlen from Schmargendorf, July 13, 1899. The italics are Rilke's; and need I say that atmosphere stands for *Stimmung*?

a natural law: the actors, gazing out over (say) a Berlin audience, were to reflect a non-existent sea in the sacred name of 'atmosphere'. No such miracle would be likely to occur and no such illusion be created. Rilke's early poems have the ghostly blankness of beautifully framed mirrors reflecting mere shadows; his early prose works were distorting mirrors. In both cases he represented through the medium of his art much that he refused to contemplate directly, preferring to see it as in a glass, darkly.

Otherwise, once his school-days were over, nothing in the scanty evidence available suggests that he himself was as ethereal or as morbid as his works. In particular what the Americans would call his love-life seems to have been much more normal than one would expect from the author of *Maidens' Songs* and *The White Princess*. His departure from Linz in the company of some woman of easy virtue; his engagement to Vally; his relationship with Francesca Reventlow and with Lou; his friendship in Italy with Lou's compatriot, Helene Woronin—all this indicates that, until the year 1898, women played their traditional parts in his emotional, intellectual and spiritual development. In that year, however, a change came over the spirit of his dream. René merged into Rainer Maria Rilke, a very much deeper and subtler personality, and one who seems to have been through some distressing crisis which had left deep marks on his mind.

Chapter II

SPIRITUAL HOMES, 1899–1902

1. *Russia*, 1899–1900
2. *Worpswede*, 1900–1901
3. *Westerwede*, 1901–1902

CHAPTER II

SPIRITUAL HOMES, 1899–1902

1. *Russia*, 1899–1900

Although Rilke returned to Italy early in March 1899, it was probably with a divided mind, for his whole being was now straining towards Russia, the native land of Lou Andreas-Salomé, of Helen Woronin and of Tolstoy, whom he had begun to read at Linz, and whose challenging pamphlet *What is Art?* had moved him to reply that it was nothing more nor less than the creator of future gods.[1] The relationship in which he stood to Lou (a mutual friend[2] called him her disciple) was enough in itself to fire him with a tremulous enthusiasm for that unseen land which acquaintance with it was to confirm.

From the day Rilke first set foot in Russia until the day he died he regarded this country as his spiritual home, an attitude often adopted by persons who know little enough about the countries of their choice. There are, of course, some striking examples of strange geographical or racial affinities: Lawrence and Arabia, Lady Hester Stanhope and the Near East are cases in point. But Goethe's feelings for Italy and Rilke's for Russia illustrate the truth of the disillusioned Russian proverb applicable to so many nostalgic persons, that happiness is there where we are not. The one pined for Italy, the other for Russia all their lives; but neither of them settled in the country of his dreams and both of them lived as best they might on the memory of two visits. Goethe's first journey was at least of a respectable length; and he more than once tried to win his way back to Italy. But Rilke, who spent less than six months all told in Russia, never seriously attempted to return, a fact which arouses some scepticism about the reality of his feelings.

[1] *Über Kunst* in *V.u.P.* p. 42; written in 1898.
[2] Frieda von Bülow; see *B.u.T.* p. 420.

He set out for his first visit accompanied by Lou and her husband, so highly charged with her emotional preposessions, that Russia had few surprises to offer:

When I first came to Moscow (he later told Ellen Key), everything seemed familiar and known from of old. It was at Eastertime, and it moved me as if it were my Easter, my spring, my bells. It was the city of my oldest and deepest memories; it was a continual recognition and greeting: it was home.[1]

Whether this feeling of familiarity was due to racial sympathy as Rilke seemed to think,[2] or to what Goethe would have called anticipatory or intuitive knowledge of it, or to personal emotions and preconceived ideas, it was sufficiently strong to make him feel certain that Russian things would help him to name those 'shrinking and reverent emotions' of his soul which had been yearning for aesthetic expression ever since his childhood.[3]

Having spent a week in Moscow, where he saw Tolstoy, and six weeks in St Petersburg, Rilke returned to Germany determined to go back and to profit more intensely. He kept in touch by correspondence with his Russian friends, and he tried to keep his memory green with Tolstoy by sending him one of his books. He also worked like a beaver at his Russian studies. He and Lou stayed for six weeks at Meiningen with Frieda von Bülow that summer and exasperated their hostess by their feverish industry. She hardly saw anything of them, for they were immersed in the study of the language, history, literature, art, civilisation and politics of Russia, and labouring with as much phenomenal industry as if they were preparing for the most appalling examination. When they all met at meals Lou and Rilke were far too exhausted for intelligent conversation. His reading knowledge of Russian grew apace; before the middle of March 1900 he had already translated

[1] Ellen Key, *op. cit.* p. 159; n.d.

[2] Rilke's purely Germanic orgins have been much stressed; his features would suggest that he had Slav blood in his veins; and the residence of his family in Czechoslovakia for many generations before his birth certainly affected his temperament and outlook. He himself liked to believe that the Slav element was there; cf. *B. 1892–1904*, p. 438 and *B. 1921–1926*, p. 236.

[3] *B.u.T.* p. 17; to Frieda von Bülow from St Petersburg, June 7, 1899.

Chehov's *Seagull* into German, and was reading the great
Russian writers in the original without much trouble. Although he never spoke the language well, his Russian letters,
written during the second visit, astounded his correspondents;
his verse renderings of Lermontov and Drojin are poetical if
not skilful; and his original Russian verse shows facility. He
made several translations from the Russian both before and
after his second visit, some of which are now lost; but his most
ambitious undertaking, a rendering of the twelfth-century
epic poem, *The Lay of the Band of Igor*, finished in 1904, which
marks the end of his Russian studies, is not very successful,
being rather turgid and Ossianic in style, to judge by the two
printed fragments.[1]

During his second visit Rilke, much better prepared for
seeing Russia and understanding it, also saw considerably
more of it. He was in Moscow for three weeks in May; he
then travelled through Tula (from where he visited Tolstoy in
Yasnaya Polyana) down to Kiev and Poltava in the Ukraine.
In the company of Lou, whose husband was not with them on
this occasion, he went by boat up the Volga from Saratov
through Kazan and Nijni Novgorod to Yaroslavl. Here they
stayed for three days with some peasants before returning to
Moscow on July 5. From July 18 to July 25 they were near
Zavidovo in the province of Tver as the guests, first of the
peasant-poet Drojin and then of his overlord Nikolai Tolstoy.
The final month was spent in St Petersburg. Here and in
Moscow Rilke frequented artists, writers, university pro-
fessors and journalists; he visited picture galleries, museums,
libraries and theatres, and generally behaved like an intelligent tourist with literary and artistic leanings, who intends to
write up the country he is studying. The journey to the south
was in the nature of a pilgrimage through Holy Russia.
Tolstoy, 'the eternal Russian' (as Rilke had labelled him
when he called on him in 1899), the sacred city of Kiev, the
illimitable steppe, the hallowed waters of the Volga, the god-
fearing *moujiks*, Drojin the peasant-poet, were all stages of a
voyage of discovery into that promised land; though whether

[1] *Prager Presse*, February 16, 1930; *Inselalmanach*, Leipzig, 1931.

or not he penetrated to its ultimate reality remains a very moot point. I think myself that in spite of his gallant efforts his equipment was too slight.

I have been living for three days in a little hut, as a peasant among peasants (he wrote triumphantly to his mother from Yaroslavl); sleeping without a bed and sharing the frugal meals inserted now and again into their heavy working-day. As the weather was fine, this primitive mode of existence had much to recommend it, and the frugality of the meals corresponded to my simple needs.[1]

'A peasant among peasants.' Lou said that she would never forget the expression that irradiated his countenance when one of the women kissed him on parting[2] with the words: 'You too belong to the people.' It was a charming thing to say, and showed that almost clairvoyant sympathy of the Russians as a race; but it was the exact opposite of the truth. A more highly civilised and complex person than Rilke it would be hard to find; the very strength of his desire for simplicity and primitive conditions was one of the symptoms of decadence seeking its cure, as witness the visit he and Lou paid to the peasant-poet Drojin in 1900. Rilke told Du Bos in 1925 that one day whilst he was in Russia, he received a letter from this unknown brother-poet, begging him to come and stay with him; adding that he had just built himself a little *izba* to write in, and wanted Rilke to baptise it first.[3] Actually the initiative came from the German side, and the Russian had to be coaxed and flattered into giving the invitation.[4] Sofia Nikolayevna Schill, a Russian writer who had made Rilke's acquaintance in the winter of 1899–1900 in Berlin, was the go-between, and a very anxious one too. She considered Rilke's enthusiasm for Russia excessive, and his admiration for Drojin's poems (which she had lent him) perplexing. But willy-nilly she had to open negotiations

---

[1] Quoted by Sophie Brutzer in *Rilkes russische Reisen*, Stallupönen, 1934, p. 6.

[2] This is a Russian custom which still survived among the humbler classes in 1917; cf. L. Andreas-Salomé, *Rainer Maria Rilke*, Leipzig, 1929, p. 25.

[3] Du Bos, *op. cit.* p. 285.

[4] S. D. Drojin, *Der Deutsche Dichter Rainer Maria Rilke*, tr. by A. Luther, *Das Inselschiff*, Leipzig, 1929, p. 225; the following account is based on this article, which prints letters from Schill and Rilke.

which, begun in March 1900, finally deposited Lou and Rilke
at Drojin's humble door towards the end of July. It was not as
humble as it had been in March. Drojin, bowing to his fate,
had thrown himself on the mercy of Nikolai Tolstoy, who had
reconditioned the whole house to make it fit for the distinguished foreigners.[1] Well might Sofia Schill express her fears
that the guests would put Drojin to a great deal of inconvenience; whilst the fear she did not utter, that Lou and Rilke,
'who love Russia and everything Russian passionately',
would almost certainly be disillusioned with Drojin, his *izba*,
and his village, flickers between the lines of her letters. She
ought to have known them better; they were determined to
be pleased. One likes to think of them sitting round the
samovar that evening, while Drojin, at their request, read
some of his poems out loud. But one shares in his perturba-
tion next morning when he found that they had arisen at dawn,
whilst he was still asleep, and were wandering barefoot in the
dewy meadow by the river, on nothing more solid than a glass
of fresh milk. He determined to be up before them next
morning and to go gathering flowers and mushrooms with
them; but he put on his big top boots, for he could not quite
swallow their story of the health-giving properties of barefoot
rambles in the dew. Rilke wrote a glowing account of the visit
to his mother, from which however it emerged that they were
only three days in the 'little newly-built hut', and then
accepted Nikolai Tolstoy's invitation to migrate to the castle
where 'I gratefully enjoyed all the comforts of the fine house,
and all the beauties of the fertile park'.[2] It was probably a
relief to Drojin as well, who was also a guest at the castle.
Meanwhile Sofia Schill in the Crimea was much relieved to
receive enraptured accounts of the visit from the wanderers, and
wrote expansively to Drojin, thanking him warmly for all he
had done, once more apologising to him for the inconvenience
he had suffered and repeating that both Lou and Rilke were a

[1] Both Schill and Drojin took Lou Andreas-Salomé (the daughter of a Russian
general) to be German; Schill believed her to be Rilke's cousin; this relationship
was probably assumed for convenience in travelling together.

[2] Brutzer, *op. cit.* pp. 9, 67 f.

little inclined to 'idealise our Russian reality'. No harm had evidently been done by allowing them to see a carefully staged portion of it; but nothing real or lasting came from this idyllic visit. Rilke's letter of thanks, written in Russian, contrasts oddly with Sofia Schill's fervent gratitude; it is stilted, conventional and almost cold:

I would just like to thank you again for the days spent with you, which were so rich in every kindness and friendliness.... In the evenings... I read your poems far into the night out loud to myself; and I hear in my imagination your voice which is so full of happiness and love of your native land.... With all best wishes to yourself and your family, Yours warmly and sincerely, R. M. Rilke.

These were the only personal remarks in the letter, which gave an account of his studies and visits to the Alexander Museum, and ended with an apology for grammatical errors. Much the same tone prevailed in the few subsequent notes and postcards. A long letter Drojin wrote to Rilke in the beginning of 1913 was returned through the dead letter office; and another effort to communicate with him in September of the same year, care of his publishers, received no answer. The gulf between the peasant-poet and the intellectual aristocrat was never effectively bridged.

If Rilke never really knew what Russian peasant life was like, he refused for many years to acknowledge that he had been granted a remarkable revelation of the Russian temperament by Tolstoy at Yasnaya Polyana. There are three different extant accounts of the visit made in May 1900. The first, the authorised version, was concocted in a letter to Sofia Schill the day after the event. The second is apocryphal, an incomplete poetical reminiscence, the rough draft of a letter to his fellow-pilgrim Lou, dated September 15, 1900, and written in Worpswede on hearing that Tolstoy was very ill. The revised version is an oral description given to the author Maurice Betz twenty-five years later.[1]

---

[1] Cf. *B.u.T.* pp. 37 ff., 308 ff.; and M. Betz, *Rilke Vivant*, Paris, 1937, pp. 153 ff. There is also the less detailed account reproduced from Rilke's conversation by Charles Du Bos in his *Extraits d'un Journal*, pp. 246 ff. The impression made by Tolstoy on Rilke tallies with the one given to Betz. There are some variations in detail and a good deal of retrospective characterisation.

One would naturally expect the last account to have gained
in glamour and romance what it had lost in accuracy. The
reverse is the case. The deep impression the whole affair had
made on Rilke's mind was not obliterated by the passage of
time, which had on the contrary dissolved the mists of
romance. The devotion to truth learned from Rodin, and
perhaps too the well-informed interest and psychological
shrewdness of his French audience, made of the latest version
by far the most realistic account of the three, and one moreover
which tallies with what is known about Tolstoy in the last
years of his life.

When Rilke and Lou had called on him in Moscow in 1899,
they had stayed with him for several hours and had been most
kindly treated. He had accepted a copy of *Two Prague Tales*
and had tried to persuade his visitors not to encourage
popular folly and superstition by attending the Easter celebra-
tions. It need hardly be said that he did not succeed; but
they were too tactful to advertise their contrary intention, and
the meeting seems to have been an unqualified success. Not
so the visit to Yasnaya Polyana. Even the highly idealised
account Rilke gave of it at the time showed that. The story he
told Betz twenty-five years later revealed it as a terrifying
affair. Lou and Rilke, uninvited and unwanted guests, went
through a good deal of discomfort to get to Yasnaya Polyana,
but it was nothing to what they suffered once they had arrived.
They had some difficulty in obtaining an entrance, which
indeed they almost forced. The great man, confronted with
them in the hall, barely greeted them and then made off.
Chiefly in the company of his eldest son, they hung about for
the better part of the day, more or less ignored by the rest of
the household, snubbed by the countess; immured for some
time in a little waiting-room from which they listened trembling to a succession of violent scenes between Tolstoy and his
wife; and were finally swept off for a walk in the park with
their unorthodox host instead of having lunch. Tolstoy quite
clearly failed to recognise them at first, never fully placed
Rilke, and even during the walk seemed hardly aware of his
companions. At the time Rilke gave a vague but grandilo-

quent account of the conversation which he later owned he
had only very imperfectly understood; and a touching description of Tolstoy as a stooping, gentle, fragile, fatherly,
benevolent old man. Actually he was terrified, as he also
acknowledged later, by the fierce, wild, majestic, almost
demoniacal personality of the formidable Russian. The latter
was in one of his towering rages that day, a fact which Rilke
hushed up in the first account, whilst graphically describing
the ill-humour of the countess. He himself made such a slight
impression on Tolstoy that the latter subsequently denied
that he had ever met the young man who went through so
much to achieve the encounter. But Tolstoy remained an unforgettable figure in Rilke's eyes. What is more, he grew in
stature as the years went by, and Rilke came to understand
him retrospectively. This was true of Russia altogether; it
was only gradually assimilated by its spiritual inhabitant, who
said of it later to Ellen Key:

> Russia became reality for me, but at the same time the profound
> and daily realisation that reality is something distant which comes
> infinitely slowly to those who have the power to wait.[1]

He had not that power in 1900, nor any marked desire for
reality, let alone for facing personally painful truths. He
much preferred the soothing form of make-believe in which he
had enveloped the disturbing day at Yasnaya Polyana. When
he returned to Germany, far from acknowledging the negligent fashion in which he and Lou had been treated by the sublime old man, he regaled his friends with glowing accounts of
the visit. He mentioned such descriptions several times in his
diary, but did not reproduce them, and it is a noteworthy
fact that the allusions to Tolstoy are infrequent in the published correspondence, and rarely refer to his books. Nevertheless such allusions as do occur are in an ascending scale of
admiration and comprehension, and contain tributes to the
genius and the tormented saintliness of the Russian.[2] But the
final word remained to be spoken. In October 1924, two years

---

[1] Ellen Key, *op. cit.* p. 159; n.d.
[2] Cf. *B. 1902-1906,* p. 203; *B. 1907-1914,* pp. 115, 299, 326; *B. 1914-1921,*
pp. 65, 92 f.

before his death, in answering a *questionnaire* by Hermann
Pongs, Rilke denied categorically that Tolstoy had influenced
him in any way, beyond confirming his 'discovery' of Russia.
This was no more and no less than the truth; but when he
went on to say that Tolstoy's figure embodied for him in 1900
the tragic destiny of one who had totally misunderstood his
task in life, this must be taken as a retrospective idea of the
man whose gigantic stature and problematical nature were
revealed to him gradually with the passing of the years. Yet
there was a sting in the tail of one of those tremendously long
sentences which wind their serpentine course through so many
of his letters:

The meeting with Tolstoy (whose ethical and religious *naïvetés*
had no kind of attraction for me, especially as shortly before my
second journey I had read the scurrilous and ludicrous pamphlet
What is Art?) had therefore an effect exactly opposite to the one
which he probably aimed at producing in his visitors; infinitely
removed from agreeing with his voluntary resignation from art, I
noticed how the artist had secretly kept the upperhand even in his
most involuntary actions; so that, confronted with his life, so full
of refusals, the opinion that aesthetic inspiration and achievement
were in the right, the conception of the might and the right of art,
and the certainty that I was called to that glorious struggle were
intensified in my mind.[1]

Here again Rilke was telling the truth up to a point. He
certainly never agreed with Tolstoy's rejection of art; but the
awe-stricken tone of his descriptions in 1900 contradicts the
latter-day denial of his earlier enthusiasm. This bears the
stamp of resentment, a resentment particularly curious since it
appeared for the first time so many years after the cause for
anger (whether personal or aesthetic) had been given. This
lingering malice may have been melted away by the sun of
comedy which warmed his descriptions of the famous meeting
to Betz and Du Bos the following year; but it was there, and
rather startlingly there, in 1924. This is the second trace in
Rilke's life of his grudge-bearing capacity. The letter to
Sedlakowitz about his school-days and this letter to Pongs

[1] H. Pongs, *op. cit.* pp. 108 f.; dated from Muzot, October 21, 1924.

both suggest that he was slow to forget an injury done to his genius. In the case of the military academy, he believed it to have been stunted and maimed; in Tolstoy's case he knew it to have been ignored by the disconcerting deity he had come to worship. He had been rejected, he and his offerings of first-fruits. At the time he was too far gone in self-deception to acknowledge even to himself that it had occurred. Completer comprehension came to him later, fascinating but also fretting his mind by emphasising the tragic antithesis between saintli-ness and art. And so it came about that the revelation of the tormented soul of Tolstoy bore no literary fruit.

It would be untrue to say the same thing of the Russian experiences as a whole. But Russia did not affect Rilke's art to nearly so great an extent as one would have expected from the profound impression it made on him, and which, recurring again and again in his letters, was more or less as follows:

It was a vast, holy, far-distant land, ancient and eternal, many, many rivers away. On the Volga, that quietly rolling sea in the midst of immeasurable plains, suddenly giant forests would rise up like night. And beside that mighty river stood the towns he still inhabited, whose gardens rustled over his head, and whose churches (reflected in the water in softened white and dimmer gold) rang out their great bells morning and evening in his ears. For it was a land prone beneath great bells which culminated in Moscow. That city had overwhelmed him by the first sight of its sublime glory: citadel after citadel; rampart after rampart, resplendent in gold, radiant colours and shimmering white; and over all this profusion a spring day or a moonlight night, so that fairy-stories grew dim beside this reality: the melodies of the East played on the organ of humble thoughts; as on that unique Easter night, long, strange, disturbed, when the people crowded together, and the great Ivan Veliki clanged out and struck Rilke's heart, with the never-to-be-for-gotten message: Христосъ воскресъ! Russia was and remained his spiritual home, this was one of the great mysterious certainties by which he lived; should he ever be granted a real home, it would be there in that vast suffering country of his imperishable love.[1] And if

---

[1] The word suffering (or sorrowing) was used with reference to the Russian-Japanese war in 1904.

his heart had room in it for anything but landscape, if there were a place in it for a town, that city, he had never doubted it, would resemble Moscow.

Russian songs, sung by blind men and children, wandered like lost souls round him, touching his cheek and his hair, musical emanations from a people whose essential brotherhood, nearness, neighbourhood were amongst the great experiences of his life. These simple, serious human beings were deeply aware of the fundamental things of life; divinely patient, they lived fragments of infinitely long and mighty lives, over whose shortest moments brooded the dimensions of gigantic aims and unhurried developments. They were surrounded by eternity; they belonged to the future, becoming not being, those deeply humble, very lonely people, each one carrying a world within himself, full of darkness like a mountain, full of distance, uncertainty and hope. And over them all was a God, a God with nothing final about him, always growing and being transformed. This Russian God broke into Rilke's consciousness, so that the poet lived for many years kneeling in the antechamber of his name.

Like God, and like Rodin, the Russians were creators, slowly and passively developing under the hands of life; thus showing their kinship with inanimate things and proving their ancestry. They were made perhaps to let the history of the world pass them by, so that they might join later with their singing hearts in the universal harmony of all things. Meanwhile, until the sign should be given, they waited, like a violinist, who sits in an orchestra, holding his fiddle carefully, so that nothing shall injure it. This natural patience, this slow evolution, which they shared with the tribe of artists, made of a Russian revolutionary, like Maxim Gorki, a contradiction in terms. Russians as a race were about as fit to make revolutions, as a cambric handkerchief to mop up ink; that is to say, they could do it excellently by the most ruthless misuse of their qualities, and the most total misapprehension of their predestined functions.

Could it really be possible, he wondered in 1921, that there was still any life in that distant country, and that it could still find its way over to us? Yes, it was possible, he affirmed in the year of his death. Russia, that unforgettable, mysterious fairy-tale, was still as near and dear to him as it had been in 1900, a sacred memory, forever part of the foundations of his being. The real Russia, the deep immortal Russia, had only withdrawn into the secret underground region whence sprang its roots, as it had done once before during the Tartar invasion. We ourselves might not witness its resurrection, but who could doubt that it was still there in its dark retreat, invisible to its children, but preparing with its divine slowness for a future which might be thousands of years hence?[1]

Meditating over Rilke's vision of Russia, one can well understand why it was that he assured himself so emphatically in his journal, on his return from his second visit, that he had in truth experienced all this and had not merely dreamt it. To which one might reply that, though he had seen Russia, he had seen it in a dream; and that, as Lamb said, 'There is no canon by which a dream may be criticised', for 'we do not know the laws of that country'. No, we do not know the laws of Rilke's Russia, we have never met its mythical inhabitants, the dreaming, inarticulate peasant-poets, fit temples for the Russian soul, humble incarnations of God. We do not know it, but we have heard a great deal about it; perhaps we have heard too much. In my young days (which coincided with the outbreak of the last war) the Russian peasant, the Russian soul and the Russian God were apt to flow into a trinity in the mouths of those who reproduced current Western ideas about Russia. They were vague, yearning, adolescent ideas, whose partial truth was much obscured by their total unreality, creating a nebulous region, generated by facts but floating away from them. Rilke's dream-country was based on real experience. But to read about it in 1940 is like being young again in 1914, and to be steeped once more in the unconvincing glamour of some Never-Never land. For he approached the peasants, as he had approached Tolstoy, blinded by preconceived notions, unable to observe. The vices, suspiciousness, idleness and obstinacy of the *moujiks*, which caused Tolstoy who loved them so deeply such agony of mind, never entered into his consciousness; and the savagery of the Slavonic temperament was as much outside his experience in 1900 as the cruelty of a

[1] Cf. *B.u.T.* pp. 53, 147, 268, 419; *B. 1902–1906*, pp. 125 f., 142 f., 213, 222; *B. 1906–1907*, pp. 116, 251 f., 253 f.; *B. 1907–1914*, p. 335; B *1921–1926*, pp. 76, 184 f., 363 f.

Russian winter. He was in truth merely a summer tourist in a rosy dream. Add to all this the fact that Rilke's Russia was pre-war, and one can only repeat Lamb's cry: 'We do not know the laws of that country.'

And yet no one who knew it when he did, or even (as I did) during the last war, will deny that he interpreted one side of it as only a poet could. Quite apart from his descriptions of the country which often evoke a whole landscape in a single line, he penetrated, partly by intuition, to something very deep-seated in the inhabitants of that land. Well can I believe that a simple peasant-woman told Rilke the story of her life with such simplicity and greatness, that he found himself treating her as an equal, and returning the compliment in kind;[1] that Nikolai Tolstoy's wife did exactly the same thing, but took four days over it;[2] and that a young man with a rose between his teeth, and most handsome to behold, poured out to Rilke the tale of his emotional perplexities on the subject of two sisters for three hours on end in a hotel bedroom one night.[3] Class distinctions and race distinctions were no barrier in Russia to confidences of this nature; nor were introductions necessary for the communion of souls. It is a truism that the Russians as a race are experts in the soul. Quite as great experts as Rilke thought. I have seen those self-same peasants, with whom he had such idyllic summer-time relations, verminous, mangled and mutilated carried into field-hospitals to die. Their patience, their resignation, their heroic fatalism were all that he said, and more. I have heard illiterate, almost subhuman *moujiks* say very strange things on their death-beds, showing that instinctive grasp of spiritual essentials, which he also noted. But I have seen the other side. Literate and illiterate, the Russians are deeply preoccupied with the soul, but not necessarily with virtue. It is not only in the pages of Dostoyevski that those strange conversations occur, which reveal so much of the baseness as well as the nobility of human nature. This psychological profundity is far

---

[1] M. von Thurn und Taxis-Hohenlohe, *Erinnerungen an Rainer Maria Rilke*, Munich, 1933, p. 12.

[2] Brutzer, *op. cit.* p. 9.   [3] Du Bos, *op. cit.* pp. 289 f.

removed from Western 'soulfulness', it can be fiendish, and that is what Rilke did not see. The Russians are a very strange people, as their history shows; dangerous, because they are extremists; incalculable because they are always in a state of flux. Their spiritual range is incredibly wide; they can swing down to the depths of depravity, up to the heights of holiness and down again without disintegration of personality. Hence their almost disconcerting lack of the power of moral condemnation; they know too much to judge. Kindness is not the right word for the Russian attitude towards sinners, since it savours of condescension; it is such complete understanding, that it almost seems divine. Yet their cruelty and treachery are in the strongest contrast to this virtue, as are also their terrifying passions to their winning gentleness, their ruthlessness to their self-abnegation and their arrogance to their humility. Rilke did not acknowledge, or did not realise, their satanic aspect, which, no less than the mystical and inextricably intertwined with it, makes of the Russians what they are: a race which towers as high above Western European standards as it falls far beneath them; whose terrific spiritual possibilities are fraught with terrible dangers. Only superlatives can really describe them; even Chehov's men and women are superlatively dim and desolate; and how superlative is their скука compared with boredom, *Langeweile* or *ennui*. The безгранигная грусть степей, the limitless sorrow of the plains, has no counterpart outside Russia, the vast land of tragic extremes. There is, however, a lighter side to all this. The Russians have a delightful and all-embracing sense of humour, reflected in their literature. They can be extremely good company; for they do not always talk of God and death when sitting round the *samovar*. They have endearing and startling habits. If the impression that predominates is one of dreaming immemorial forests, of wide roads, infinite space and a fierce, sad people; one also remembers the engaging custom by which banks closed down at 3 p.m. in the orthodox way, but left just enough room between the shutter and the ground to crawl through on hands and knees and transact one's business after hours. And if a rapacious *izvozchik* could solemnly curse one down to the third and fourth generation because one had only doubled his fare, the coaxing voices of the soldiers playing variations on all the diminutives for the word 'sister' would have melted the heart of a stone, though it was cupboard-love that inspired them.

Rilke's Russia seems ill-nourished to one who has known the reality; lacking in that arresting mixture of evil and good which is such a revelation to the Westerner. It is perhaps the fate of spiritual homes to be devitalised by their inhabitants; and it has certainly been the fate of Russia in the past to attract the type of mind which poetised reality unduly. Rilke's unique spirited description of a savage Russian was made in 1913, when he had outgrown his love of make-believe:

She is living with the Russian like a sister, immensely relieved, she says, not to love him, because 'he would drag any woman who loved him about by the hair'. He is a savage, a Mordvinian, a Siberian, good-natured but terrible, who makes the persons he loves definitely unhappy....His vast studio, part of which serves as a dormitory, is in such disorder that one would certainly call it a landscape if it were out of doors. They sleep on mattresses among piles of things scattered about and forgotten....At the moment the Russian has some amateurs who are interested in his work. (I remember having seen a gigantic Christ on the Cross, expressing with that musical disorder which the Slavs introduce into sculpture the final agony.) He has therefore some money, but his good-nature and carelessness cause the pennies to vanish as rapidly as running water; the days and nights are spent without any attempt at organisation; they sleep now and then, they rarely eat; but he smokes perpetually since living as an exile in a strange land, because he is home-sick....I think that she is very unhappy, and is burning herself away....[1]

The lapse of time brought to Rilke a truer notion of Tolstoy, of his visit to Yasnaya Polyana, and of the savage aspect of the Russian character; so that the book he was preparing to write about Russia the year before he died would have probably been illuminating in the extreme.

[1] *B. 1907–1914*, pp. 280 ff.; to the Princess Thurn und Taxis from Paris, March 21, 1913; the girl is Rilke's little *protégée* Marthe.

In 1899 and 1900, however, his literary attitude towards Russia was that of a gentleman-journalist. To begin with the language; he took it by assault, but he never really mastered it, nor loved it truly enough to wrestle with the grammar till it blessed him. He allowed it to slip from him later, and was unable to talk in Russian with Gorki in 1907. It was much the same with Russian art. He flung himself into the study of Kramskoy, Ivanov, Levitan and Vasilyev, intending to make literary capital out of them in a series of essays, or a monograph on Russian painting. This scheme dwindled down to two articles,[1] and his interest in Russian art was eclipsed by his interest in Worpswede, about which he produced a study instead. His translations from the Russian failed to catch on, never amounted to much, and were abandoned in 1904. Nor was his enthusiasm for Russian literature of that solid kind which results in the acquirement of real knowledge. His reading was planned on an astonishingly wide scale, ranging from the ancient *byliny* down to contemporary writers, and including the study of history, art and civilisation. But like the young man's time-table in *Love and Mr Lewisham*, Rilke's scheme proved too comprehensive and exacting to be carried out. To judge by his references to Russian authors and their works, and by the books in his possession when he died, which have been listed by Brutzer, he was on far from intimate terms with the great novelists and poets. An exception should possibly be made for Dostoyevski. Rilke read and re-read *Poor Folk*, and translated an episode from it which is now lost; he always spoke of it with the greatest enthusiasm. *White Nights* he also read in Russian; the *Letters from the House of the Dead*, *Crime and Punishment*, *The Idiot* and *The Brothers Karamazov* probably in German; and he possessed a Russian copy of *The Diary of an Author*. There is no evidence that Rilke finished *War and Peace*, which he began to read in Russian in 1900; he read *Resurrection* in German, *The Cossacks* in Russian, and some of the pamphlets and stories. Of Turgenev he only knew *The Diary of a Sportsman*; some stories by Gogol, but not *Dead Souls*; Chehov's

[1] Printed in *Die Zeit*, Vienna, October 19, 1901 and November 15, 1902.

Seagull, which he translated into German (this rendering also is lost); he may have read *Uncle Vanya,* which he wanted to translate after hearing an account of it; but he mentioned no other plays by this author, and never referred to his tales. He knew Pushkin's *Tsar-Sultan,* probably *Poltava* and *Boris Godunov* and some of the poems. He possessed copies of Goncharov's *Oblomov* and of Krylov's *Fables*; he knew Drojin's poetry well, and translated several of the poems, also trying his hand at Lermontov and Fofanov; he seems to have had a bowing acquaintance with Nekrasov, Garshin, Lomonosov, Fyet and Tyutchev; he saw Griboyedov's *Too Clever by Half* in Moscow, and A. K. Tolstoy's *Tsar Fedor* in Berlin; he also knew and translated *The Lay of the Band of Igor,* and he had clearly read some of the ancient *byliny* and *skazki.* There is a good deal of guess-work in this tentative list, which may do Rilke more or less than justice. All one can say for certain is that his references to Tolstoy's novels are astonishingly meagre; and that for many years Dostoyevski was quoted solely as the author of *Poor Folk.* Rilke first alluded to Raskolnikov in 1910; in 1912 he enumerated *White Nights,* *The Idiot* and *The Brothers Karamazov* as books which might fittingly be read after being initiated by *Poor Folk*; in 1914 he referred with high praise to *The Diary of an Author,* and to *The Idiot,* as probably Dostoyevski's finest book; and in 1920 he mentioned *The Dead House.* Except for *White Nights* and *Poor Folk,* Rilke seems to have read Dostoyevski relatively late and in German translation; until 1912 his highest praise was reserved for *Poor Folk,* Dostoyevski's first novel, which gives only a faint foretaste of his psychological powers and has none of the greatness and depth of his maturer work. Here again, comprehension and insight came to Rilke very slowly.[1]

Rilke's early enthusiasm for Russian literature was imaginative and inspirational; but little true assimilation took place, again with the possible exception of Dostoyevski, whose effect on *Malte Laurids Brigge* will be considered later. His strictures on Chehov's *Seagull,* after he had finished translating

[1] Cf. especially *B. 1907–1914,* p. 327 for a fine page on Dostoyevski in 1914.

it in March 1900, differ not at all from the conventional
Western attitude towards an art which, to quote Virginia
Woolf, demands a 'very daring and alert sense of literature'
to be grasped.[1] Rilke complained of the lack of dramatic
development, of the strongly retarded action, of the long-
winded conversations and of the resultant boredom; in a
word he reproduced the *clichés* of the unenlightened;[2] and
seems, after an unsuccessful attempt to get hold of *Uncle
Vanya*, to have lost interest in Chehov; generalising again,
but this time to the author's detriment, on one of the minor
works.

He had a 'Russian corner' in his rooms in Schmargendorf
and wore the Russian peasant blouse as late as 1904. There is
even a tradition to the effect that he behaved like a Russian,
and spoke broken German interspersed with Russian phrases.[3]
He told Hulewicz in later life that during this period he had
written only Russian, and had decided to settle in the country
for good; but that he had later realised that this would mean a
complete surrender.[4] Both the tradition and the reported
conversation underline something a trifle histrionic in Rilke's
attitude towards Russia and its language; he had wondered at
one time, he told Du Bos in 1925, if he ought not to write in
Russian rather than in German because he was so deeply
convinced that Russia was his real home.[5] Some letters, and
eight poems, all of them disfigured by grammatical mistakes;
an insuperable difficulty with the oral language which less
gifted linguists have mastered; and finally his failure to return
to the country of his spiritual adoption even for a brief visit
after 1900—all this seems to show that Rilke was inclined to
romanticise his connection with the country; dispassionately
contemplated, it was neither so close nor so deep as he liked to
believe, nor so real. Had it truly meant as much to him as he

[1] V. Woolf, *The Common Reader*, London, 1925, p. 223.
[2] Cf. *B.u.T.* pp. 28 f., 32 ff.
[3] See Brutzer, *op. cit.* p. 2; a communication made to Brutzer by Korfiz Holm.
[4] Communicated by 'Mgr.' in the *Prager Presse*, February 16, 1930.
[5] Du Bos, *op. cit.* pp. 284 f. The letter Rilke wrote to Lou Andreas-Salomé
on his death-bed began and ended in Russian; for he clung to the last to his
spiritual affinity with Russia.

thought, he could not have kept away from it. It might not have been practicable to settle there; but, considering his travels across and beyond Europe before the war, the pull towards Russia, the real Russia, cannot have been strong. The fear of a 'complete surrender' sounds like a retrospective excuse. Possibly he felt, on the other hand, that the Russia of his dreams would not have survived a third inspection of the reality.

Hence perhaps his deep and genuine dissatisfaction with the poetical effects of his second journey. On September 1, 1900 he wrote in his diary that either he had observed nothing with his whole being, or else his powers of observation were less closely connected with his creative gifts than he had thought. Either of these two alternatives, he added, was a wretched one.[1] On September 27 he said that the daily losses of the Russian journey were a terribly unnerving proof of immature eyes, which had been unable to receive, to hold or to let go, 'laden with tormenting pictures, passing beauties by on the way to disillusions'.[2] He was evidently not so blind to the harrowing side of Russia on the second journey as he appeared. Perhaps that was why he never returned, and why the book about Russia, like the book about the military academy, was never written.

The first visit, too short and bewildering to allow painful impressions to intrude, brought forth an immediate poetical harvest: *The Book of Monkish Life* in verse and *Tales about God* in prose, written in the autumn and winter of 1899.[3] Partly inspired by Russia, both works originated in Italy, and derive from the Tuscan diary, the cyclic poem in particular being a beautifully ambiguous and highly mysterious expression of Rilke's overweening ideas about art. Russia provided

---

[1] *B.u.T.* pp. 266 ff. Again the rough draft of a letter to Lou Andreas-Salomé.

[2] *B.u.T.* p. 342.

[3] *Das Buch vom mönchischen Leben,* the first part of *Das Stundenbuch,* published in 1905, was composed from September 20 to October 14, 1899. *Die Geschichten vom lieben Gott,* first published under the title *Vom lieben Gott und Anderes,* 1900, were written from November 10 to 21, 1899.

his vision of a nameless future God with a country to inhabit, full of spiritual promise and suggestive local colouring, and also helped to clarify his thoughts about the Renaissance. From the outset his enthusiasm for Italian art was crossed by his hostility to Christianity which had inspired its greatest paintings. He had contrasted art and religion as two irreconcilable opposites in the persons of Botticelli and Savonarola, and had symbolised his mixed emotions about the Renaissance by describing it as a glorious spring whose summer was yet to come. In *The Book of Monkish Life*, this simile was made still more pointed:

> The branch which the tree of God out over Italy throws
> Already has bloomed.
> It might, who knows?
> Have wished to bear premature fruit; but doomed,
> In the midst of blooming it flagged and swooned,
> And it will no fruits be bearing.
>
> Only the spring of God was there,
> Only his son, the word.
>
> .　　.　　.　　.　　.
>
> Alas, not yet has she brought forth the highest,
> And the angels who to her are nighest
> Comfortless and strange around her stand.
>
> .　　.　　.　　.　　.
>
> But with a branch which ne'er was like the first
> Will God the tree out into summer burst,
> Ripened and rustling, and will be fulfilled.
> It will be in a land where men are stilled
> With listening, lonely everyone like me.[1]

In a Russian poem written in the winter of 1900 Rilke explicitly compared Italy in May, serene and empty, with the wind-filled spaces of the steppe, where 'God darkens'; for he was firmly convinced that the future revelation would come from Russia, and eclipse the revelation of Christianity which he represented as having occurred in Italy some thirteen hundred years after the life of Christ. This is a striking in-

[1] *G.W.* II, pp. 194–197.

stance of his uncompromising belief that nothing has any real
existence except in art, a much stranger and more challenging
point of view than his denial of the divinity of Christ; it
enabled him to reject the Italian Renaissance on apparently
religious grounds. In a long poem excluded from the cycle
when it came to publication and now printed by Mövius,[1] the
Russian monk (the fictitious author of the book) was represented as writing a letter to his Metropolitan on this subject.
It seemed to the monk that Michelangelo and others like him
had been almost guilty of blasphemy in their attempts to
represent God; this was false worship, limiting the limitless,
imprisoning him in time, betraying him and stealing him
from humanity. The inner meaning of a reproach which seems
strangely inconsistent at first sight as coming from Rilke with
his notions of creative art, sprang from his dislike of the
Christian God, whom he had declared in the Tuscan journal to
be dead, the oldest work of art and very badly preserved. He
naturally therefore looked askance at the men of genius who
had restored him, preferring those Russian *ikons*, humbly and
devoutly painted by his monk. For these, being conventional
representations prescribed by tradition, concealed rather than
revealed the nature of God's mystery. And indeed, according
to the monk, God should be sought in things, which the artists
should represent, thus gradually, patiently and infinitely
slowly approaching to the creation of God:

> Work-people are we: prentice, pupil, master,
> Building, oh lofty middle nave, at thee;
> And sometimes comes to us a stranger, faster
> Than light, our hundred minds to master,
> And trembling shows us a new craft for thee.
>
> Upon the swaying scaffolding we're mounted,
> And in our hands the heavy hammer swings,
> Until we're kissed by some hour yet uncounted,
> Radiant with all the knowledge it's surmounted,
> Coming from thee, like to the sea-wind's wings.

---

[1] R. Mövius, *Rainer Maria Rilkes Stundenbuch*, Leipzig, 1937, pp. 209–215.

> Then, while the nearby mountain hearkens,
> Blow upon blow our hammers fulminate,
> Thy coming contours dawn and radiate,
> We shall not let thee go until it darkens,
>
> God, thou art great.[1]

The metaphor of humanity (that is to say the artists) building at the great cathedral God (or art) runs throughout the cycle, and is in fact its central idea. But Rilke's future God, the spiritual heir of all the artists who have preceded and helped to form him, a divine aesthetic creator on a colossal scale, was sufficiently like the Jehovah of Genesis (for whom Rilke always had a sneaking sympathy) to allow him to make a highly ambiguous and misleading use of the word God, embracing times past, present and yet to be in a manner at times surprisingly orthodox, but only apparently so. Rilke's seemingly religious monk was worshipping at the shrine of art, and seeking a God that never was on sea or land. This deity was endowed with some peculiarly Russian characteristics and a mystic affinity with the peasants. He was described as a *moujik* with a beard, as a blind old *kobzar* (minstrel), wandering over the vast plains of the Ukraine, which were likened to the soul of the poet who was awaiting him. These notions derive from Russian fairy-tales; whilst the conception of the essential futurity of God (which no orthodox believer would acknowledge) has the sanction of the Slavonic mentality. Deeply imbedded in Russian minds is a feeling for imperfectiveness or becoming, which might have affected their notions of God, although it does not seem to have done so. Their natural liking for and affinity with what is not finished, final, static and complete is manifest in their retention and development of the imperfective verbal aspect. The Slav

does not care to stand outside an action to register, to analyse, to judge, he wants to live into it, he craves 'knowledge by experience'....The imperfective...dominates Russian language and Russian literature; shall we be far wrong if we conclude

---

[1] *G.W.* II, pp. 191 f.

that the imperfective is the leading note in general Russian psychology...?[1]

Persons, actions and conditions still in the process of becoming and therefore impossible to judge are phenomena which strongly attract the Russian temperament; and Rilke's God, though he is not the God of 'orthodox' Russia, is imperfectiveness incarnate. Nothing fixed or final can be said about him; and since Rilke was experiencing him from within, he changed his aspect with every mood of the poet, appearing like a terrified little bird at one moment, infinitely remote and awe-inspiring at another, dependent for his meaning (as the monk acknowledged) on the existence of his votary, on the poet's creative mind. The startling divergences and antitheses of Rilke's God, creature and creator in one, are resolved by his one constant quality, darkness or obscurity, emphasised throughout the poem. For indeed this grandiose symbol of Rilke's allegiance to art is neither a subjective nor an objective deity. It was not a God but a passion which inspired the gravitating, rushing and soaring rhythms, the genuine ecstasy, the profundities and altitudes of this poem which described a dream the like of which no poet had dreamt before. The inexhaustible flow of images to evoke a being whom such similes obscure, as the poet maintained, resembles a fountain of light, shooting up, wavering and falling in showers of iridescent drops; mounting again like a pillar of liquid fire to splash down in radiant cascades; playing in absolute solitude against impenetrable darkness; and playing on until the unreal nature of divinity merges into the divine nature of unreality; then the fountain dies down whispering:

> And these his songs go flowing
> Murmuring back to him,[2]

and darkness wins the day.

Rilke's genius was for poetry and not for prose, a fact indicated by his early stories. But even allowing for this, the

[1] J. E. Harrison, *Aspects, Aorists and the Classical Tripos*, Cambridge, 1919, pp. 23, 33.

[2] *G.W.* II, p. 225.

discrepancy of talent between *The Book of Monkish Life* and *Tales about God* is remarkable, and all the more so since both derive from the same religious ideas. The first is impressive and significant; the second pretentious and puerile. The cyclic poem is the work of a great imaginative mind; the stories would seem to emanate from a greenery-yallery *littérateur*. By introducing the God of *The Book of Hours* into the school-room, Rilke inevitably mutilated the greatness of his conception and shattered the fragile world of fairy-tales as well.

God is the hero of nearly all these thirteen stories 'told to grown-ups for children', in an affectedly simple style. The style is indeed the worst feature of the book, since it remains constant; whereas some of the tales are on a much higher level than previous and even subsequent stories; although this is not saying very much. But Rilke's belief in the creative power of art brought about an extraordinarily impressive moment in the tale in which Michelangelo recognised God in the stone he was forming, and by doing so transformed God into the stone from which he was to liberate him. This and two other tales which have Italy for a background are interesting, and the same may be said with more reservation of the three stories about Russia. But the whimsical humour with which each new tale is introduced in turn, the gentle wistfulness, the fanciful notions, the patronising airs make of the whole something perilously close to puppydom. They are told to a neighbour with children of her own, to a 'stranger' (Christ), to a lame friend, an unenlightened schoolmaster, an amiable but fussy young man, a grave-digger, to the clouds and the dark; and someone always repeats them to the children. God is represented anthropomorphically, chiefly as a creator, a divine sculptor, whose tragedy lies in the fact that he has never seen his supreme creature man as he really is; for he has not yet beheld him naked. Owing to the clumsiness of his hands when he was moulding him and keeping his eye on the earth so that nothing untoward should happen there, man dropped down before God had seen him; by the time he had finished scolding the culprits one of those minutes had passed

which are a thousand ages on earth, and behold there were
millions of men on the face of the globe, all of them dressed in
hideous clothes, and therefore unrecognisable. The mischief
was done, and the divine hands were in deep disgrace. Ages
passed again. Unable to bear the situation any longer God
determined to send down his right hand to take on the shape
of a man and stand naked on a hill-top, so that God should see
him. Meanwhile the left hand covered the wound on God's
right arm, so that his blood should not bespatter the earth.
(The story, awkward enough in all conscience, is rendered
still more clumsy by the fact that Christ and the Holy Ghost
have to be referred to throughout as 'she' owing to the
gender of hand.) When the left hand saw a figure in a red
cloak stumbling up a hill under a heavy burden, and recognised
her sister, she left the wound to look after itself in her efforts
to get free and help her. Blood rained down from heaven,
and everything was obscured. God nearly died, the right
hand has not recovered yet, and no one knows what really
happened on earth, for nothing will induce her to tell. This
story, told to the 'stranger', God's right hand, once more a
pilgrim, is (I make haste to say) by far the worst in the
collection, and it may have been affected by an incident witnessed by Rilke, which would partially account for the
peculiarly distressing details.[1] God is now forced to seek for
man amongst those too poor to wear many clothes, and has
determined to bring them to such a pass that they shall become
stark naked. Those therefore who, like the unenlightened
schoolmaster, foolishly endeavour to clothe the poor are doing
God a disservice. Meanwhile he will reside in a thimble if
children imagine him to be there; or in stones for Michelangelo to shape; and is so benevolent as to step out into the
middle of the sky and stay there for days on end, to give three
cantankerous painters something better to do than fall off the
rim of the earth in their efforts to avoid each other. An old
Venetian Jew sees him from a housetop in the ghetto when he
catches sight of the sea; and a modern woman knows that he
was once and will be again, for he has left his unmistakable

[1] See below, p. 99.

traces in all beautiful things. The children who are represented as listening to these stories and asking for more, were fore-runners of Peter Pan and Blue-Birdish into the bargain. Rilke's fairy-tale of death, in which death blooms as a pale-blue flower, is indeed so extremely like the scene in *The Blue Bird* when the flowers shoot up from the graves, and someone exclaims: 'There *are* no dead', that it looks as if for once Rilke had influenced Maeterlinck, instead of, as heretofore, the other way round.[1]

The stories considered so far are more Rilkean than Russian; but the three tales in the collection based on Russian sources show whence the orientation godwards came and also what was wrong with the style, which was influenced by Slavonic folk-language. Rilke had in fact discovered the *skazki* and *byliny*, the one to his doom, the second to his glory. Both are oral types of literature, the first recited in prose, the second sung or spoken to music. The *skazki*, of whose origin little is known for certain, are generally popular in tone and primitive in their notions. Many of them are fairy-tales; others, deriving from *byliny*, are legendary and historical. The *byliny* have a tradition of at least a thousand years behind them, and probably originated in court poetry. They are heroic narratives, historical tales from the days of Vladimir I (988) if not before, down to 1831, or thereabouts. This very rich literature, which has been steadily added to throughout the ages, is now on the wane as far as the creation of new poems is concerned, but far from extinct as a living form of entertain-ment in the remoter and less civilised parts of Russia. Rilke never heard the *skaziteli* (*byliny*-singers) himself. His know-ledge was based on the Russian, French and English collections which had been made from 1850 onwards when general interest in this oral literature was first aroused.[2]

---

[1] *L'Oiseau bleu* was written in 1908.

[2] Rilke possessed a small volume of *byliny* in the Русская классная Библіотека; A. N. Afanasev, Русскія народныя Сказки, 3rd ed. Moscow, 1893, in 2 vols.; W. R. S. Ralston, *Songs of the Russian People*, London, 1872, from which he took copious notes. He also clearly knew A. Rambaud, *La Russie Epique*, Paris, 1876; and may have known R. N. Rybnikov, Пѣсни собранныя, in the first edition, now unprocurable.

It was, or so I believe, the study of the *skazki* which had such an adverse effect on Rilke's prose style. If the attempt of a Westerner to write like a literary Russian results in 'an affectation of goodness and simplicity which is nauseating in the extreme',[1] the effort to reproduce the tone of primitive Slavonic fairy-tales grafted on to the manner of Jacobsen was foredoomed to the unmitigated preciosity pervading Rilke's stories about God. Actually the three which were based on the Russian *skazki* sin less gravely in this respect than some of the other tales in the collection; but the narrator's introductions and comments are peculiarly affected. The best of the three is the tale entitled *How Treachery came to Russia*; and this is probably because, though not a literal translation of the original *skazka* which Rilke possessed, it keeps fairly close to it, omitting some concrete details and adding some imaginative touches.[2] The story relates how the subject kings refuse to pay tribute to Ivan the Terrible and even threaten to dethrone him, unless he succeeds in solving three riddles. Rilke gives neither the riddles nor their solutions, which figure largely in the Russian versions. An old peasant, whom the tsar meets building a church, supplies him with the answers to all three, and accepts as a reward one of the twelve casks of gold which the thwarted kings are now forced to give to Ivan. The latter cannot bring himself to part with a whole cask; and fills the one destined for the peasant three-quarters full of sand, laying some gold on the top. But the peasant, none other than God himself, knows what Ivan has done, and tells him that he has introduced treachery into Russia for all time.

The difference between the primitive Russian's child-like belief in God and the civilised German poet's efforts to adopt it, is illustrated by a comparison of this story with the non-Russian tale invented by Rilke and called *How it befel that the Thimble became God*. It is told to the clouds, and the narrator

---

[1] V. Woolf, *op. cit.* p. 221.
[2] Cf. Rybnikov, *op. cit.* Moscow, 1909–1910, II, pp. 715 ff.; Afanasev, *op. cit.* Moscow, 1914, IV, pp. 258 f.; Rambaud, *op. cit.* pp. 269 f. Rilke used details given by Rambaud and Rybnikov but not by Afanasev.

pretends to be a cloud himself for the sake of his audience, a cloud hovering over a country described as 'twilight with things'.[1] He recounts how a group of seven children decide to pretend that a thimble is God, so that they can carry him about with them, turn by turn, in their pockets, and thus save him from getting lost by their negligent and peevish parents. 'For', says the eldest, a boy called Hans, 'any object can be God, one has only got to tell him so.' Marie, the youngest of the seven, loses the thimble at the end of the week, and a stranger (God) finds it for her. The appearance of God at the end of these two tales has a diametrically opposite effect on the reader. In the first case, it induces suspension of disbelief, but not in the second. The one has the matter-of-fact attitude towards the supernatural of all genuine folk-tales; the other is a wistful parable on the text 'Unless ye be as little children....'.

The 'treachery' *skazka* came from Olonets in the North. *The Song of Justice* takes place in the Ukraine. Rilke probably invented the story after reading Rambaud's description of the blind old *kobzar* Ostap Vyeryesai singing the Song of Justice at the archaeological congress in Kiev in 1874.[2] Rambaud, who heard him sing this and many other songs, gave an abridged version of this particular one in French; Rilke's German version approximates very closely to Rambaud's, being a slightly shorter rhymed reproduction, in parts a literal translation. The hero of his story is also a blind old *kobzar* called Ostap, who stirs up his hearers to revolt against their oppressors, the Polish *Pans*, by singing this famous song. The tale is full of local terms and local colour, partly borrowed from Rambaud, partly from Rilke's own memories. By a very Rilkean twist at the end of the tale, the listener proclaims what the narrator did not know: that the blind old minstrel was God, whom Rilke had also described as a *kobzar* at the end of *The Book of Monkish Life*.

---

[1] *Wladimir der Wolkenmaler*, written during the same period, makes great play with clouds of tobacco-smoke, and also deals with God.

[2] Rambaud, *op. cit.* pp. 434 ff. *Kobzar* is the Ukrainian term for minstrel; derived from the *kobza* (or *bandura*), a stringed instrument rather like a large mandoline. Rilke appended a prose note about *kobzars* to the original manuscript of *Das Buch vom mönchischen Leben*.

How old Timofei sang on his Death-Bed reads more like Rilke than Russia, though it may derive from a *skazka* I do not happen to know. It is chiefly used as a vehicle for Rilke's notions of *byliny* and *skaziteli*, and is disfigured by sentimentality. It is the tale of an old *skazitel*, Timofei Ivanitch, who knew all the songs of all Russia, amongst them such with words like *ikons*, and melodies, which no one, peasant or Cossack, could hear without weeping. But he gave up singing when his son and poetical heir Yegor married in spite of his disapproval and went to Kiev. In vain did the villagers, left desolate without his songs, implore him to sing to them as before, Timofei turned his head to the wall and remained obstinately mute. Yegor, hearing that Timofei's days were numbered, abandoned his wife and child and returned to his father to learn his songs and enter into his inheritance. For days and nights he listened; then the old man died. Yegor stepped out of the hut after Timofei was buried, and began to sing as his father had sung before him; but there was a new mournful melody in all the refrains; this was probably because of his grief for wife and child whom he never saw again.

Rilke's *skazki* were all told to the brave but pathetic cripple Ewald, who passed them on to the children. He was therefore playing the traditional part of the Russian *kalyeki* (cripples), itinerant singers who purvey chiefly narrative religious poetry; these minstrels are traditionally supposed to be lame, and often blind as well. The stories communicated to the children by the German *kalyeka* are sufficiently like their Russian models to be fairly acceptable. The God who appears in two of them has nothing whimsical about him, and suffers under no visual or mental deficiency of the kind which made Rilke's God incapable of discovering a naked man. One is perfectly willing to believe in him on Rilke's word alone; whereas if a voice from heaven vouched for the truth of that dreadful fantasy of God the creator and his mutilated right hand, one would still instinctively hope to discredit it. But if the Russian stories themselves are free from the faults which disfigure so many others in this collection, the passages which introduce them, describing Russia, the *byliny* and the *skaziteli*,

are steeped in sentimentality of a thoroughly Western brand.
Amongst other things Russia is hailed as a land in which
the inhabitants address, indiscriminately and touchingly, both
God and the tsar as 'little father'. This is a misrendering
which, since the appearance of Jarintzov's book *The Russians
and their Language*, will, I trust, never be made, at least in
English, again.

Rilke was fated to make it, not only by temperament, but
also because he belonged to a generation which, as Beerbohm
says, thought it essential to 'be able to converse with
moujiks about *ikons* and the Little Father and anything else—
if there were anything else—that *moujiks* cared about'.[1] In
1916 Jarintzov made it abundantly clear that the maligned
moujiks never had talked and never would or could talk about
the 'Little Father':

It is high time to explain that the famous 'Little father' does not
mean 'little' father at all! The Old Russian word for father,
*batushka, does not suggest an atom of the tone in which 'little father'
or the German Väterchen is pronounced.* This way of translating it is
sickly-sentimental! No, *batushka* is used either in a grave, defer-
ential way...or else it is used in a very argumentative tone....One
cannot even imagine the two Russian words for 'little father' ever
pronounced in our land at all!...The combining of this particular
noun with this particular adjective is absolutely unthinkable; it
could not be borne by a Russian mind.[2]

Rilke translated *batushka* by *Väterchen*, although he should
have known better. For in one of Afanasev's tales, which he
used for his prose story *The Dragon-Slayer*, a father and
mother address their son as *batushka*, which ought to have
made him pause.

After hearing the 'treachery' story Ewald asked the
narrator if he had got it out of some book, and was sorrow-
fully told that such was indeed the case, because all the *skazki*
and *byliny* were now dead and had been buried by the scholars
in their books. This funeral dirge was very premature. As

[1] Max Beerbohm, *And Even Now*, London, 1924, p. 291. Italics mine.
[2] N. Jarintzov, *The Russians and their Language*, Oxford, 1916, pp. 50, 198.
The italics are hers.

late as 1928 the brothers Sokolov heard nineteen *byliny* sung
by one *skazitel* near Lake Onega, and thirty-seven by the star
performer. In 1932 *byliny* were being sung by peasants who
had never heard of Lenin or Stalin, and there is some hope that
they are still being sung to-day.

Rilke's patronising sneer at the scholars who buried the
skazki and *byliny* in books provokes the question: Who really
loved them best? Men like Rybnikov, who spent years of
their lives tracking the *skaziteli* down, stoically and cheerfully
undergoing hardships, privations and even perils in the
process; who associated with illiterate and suspicious peasants
for months on end in order to gain their confidence and hear
their songs; who interested themselves in their affairs and
had the police ban on the *kalyeki* removed, so that they were
once more allowed to sing in public at fairs and ceremonies;
who faithfully and accurately edited their finds, thus saving a
unique oral literature for posterity just in the nick of time; or
Rilke, who never penetrated into districts remote and un-
civilised enough to hear *byliny* sung; who exposed himself to
no hazards, underwent no discomforts, undertook no grinding
labour to become acquainted with them; but who, using without due acknowledgment the scholars' 'funeral' books, senti-
mentalised and sophisticated the literature they contained,
striking poetical attitudes as he did so? This purely rhetorical
question emphasises the unreality of Rilke's enthusiasm, and
the second-hand knowledge which inspired it.

If the *byliny* are not dead yet, it is perhaps because they are
full of a vitality, vigour and liveliness which Rilke missed, for
he represented them as being unrelievedly mournful, blurred
with melancholy and dim with time. Actually many of them
are humorous, and all of them have the freshness which is the
hall-mark of oral literature. His own poetical *byliny*, a cycle
rather oddly entitled *The Tsars*, written in 1899, remodelled
and published in the second edition of *The Picture-Book* in
1906, the last concrete evidence of the inspiration of Russia,
are in a very different category from his imitations of the
skazki, being original, strange and fascinating in the extreme.
This cycle contains six poems, two of them taken from the

Kiev *byliny* cycle, another dealing with Ivan the Terrible, and
three with his son Fedor. They are highly imaginative and
very finished poems. Rilke gave a striking picture of Ivan IV
towards the end of his reign, creeping about the Kremlin in
terror and madness; even more subtle is his evocation of
Fedor, the last of the Ruriks, 'the pale tsar', dreaming uneasily on his throne, surrounded by fierce and threatening
boyars; listening to the great bells of Moscow, the voices of
his mighty forebears, who used him up for their heroic deeds,
sapping his strength long before he was born; standing in the
twilight before a richly bejewelled *ikon* of the Madonna, like
an *ikon* himself in his stiff encrusted robes; whilst his face,
like the Madonna's in her oval frame, fades away to meet hers,
and two golden garments shimmer in the hall. In these poems
Rilke seized and exhibited the inner reality of spiritual states
of mind in that penetrating manner of which he was past
master. He not only comprehended Fedor, he *was* Fedor, the
last exhausted scion of a long and renowned line.[1]

The two legendary poems are in another category: more
narrative than descriptive and more symbolical than evocative.
They are interpretations, rather than versions, of the two
famous *byliny*, *The Healing of Ilya of Murom*, and *Ilya and
Nightingale the Robber*.

> Who is there who could tell us about the old days,
> About the old days, and what happened long ago,
> About Ilya, Ilya of Murom?
> Ilya of Murom, the son of Ivanov,
> He sat among the stay-at-homes for thirty-three years;
>
> There came to him poor brethren,
> Jesus Christ Himself, and two apostles:
> 'Go, Ilya, and bring us a drink!'
> 'Poor brethren, I have no use in my arms or legs!'
> 'Stand up, Ilya, do not deceive us!'
> Ilya stood up, exactly as if nothing were the matter. . . .[2]

---

[1] These four poems are not, as far as I can discover, based on any of the
historical *byliny*.

[2] Translated by N. K. Chadwick, *Russian Heroic Poetry*, Cambridge, 1932,
p. 59. Kiryevski's version of the *bylina*.

The pilgrims then prophesy that Ilya will become a mighty hero, and that he will not die in battle; but they warn him to avoid the heroes Svyatogor (literally holy mountain), Samson, Mikula and Volga Vseslavitch (all heroes belonging to an earlier cycle). Ilya then goes to help his parents in the fields, performs prodigies of labour and great feats of strength; and finally sets off on his adventures riding a foal which he had trained according to the pilgrims' instructions. Rilke kept to the outline of *The Healing*, though he condensed it greatly, and introduced it mysteriously, giving it a prehistoric setting:

> 'Twas in the days in which the great hills came,
> The trees were rearing up, still far from tame,
> And into armour climbed the mighty river.
> Two unknown pilgrims shouted out a name,
> And roused at length from years of being lame
> The giant of Murom, the mighty Ilya.[1]

This strange beginning makes one rather wonder if the 'hills which were on the way' and the 'river which was getting into armour' stand for Svyatogor and Volga Vseslavitch, either improperly understood or twisted into prehistoric mythological figures rather than legendary heroes. Certainly the poem as a whole dissolves the legend into a nebulous mist clouded by symbolism. Ilya is represented as riding on and on, perhaps for thousands of years, for who can reckon time when a hero wills? He may have been lamed for a thousand years too. Those who sit for many years in their deep twilight will travel far. Rilke identified the 'Old Cossack' with Holy Russia, awakening from an immemorial trance to perform great deeds, and step out into a future heavy with promise. Reality (which in the poem is compared to the miraculous, measuring the world with arbitrary measures and thinking nothing of thousands of years) is that slow-moving reality, coming to those who have patience to wait, which was one of Rilke's definitions of Russia.

[1] *G.W.* II, p. 97. Rilke's metre forces one to accentuate Muróm; it should be Múrom; and Ílya, when it should be Ilyá.

Even stranger is his version of *Ilya and Nightingale the Robber*. This outstandingly popular *bylina* is puzzling in itself. Nightingale may have been 'a robber chief, perhaps also a merchant, who had his "nest", or home, beside the high road from Chernigov to Kiev, whence he swooped down on passing caravans';[1] but the name remains strange, especially in conjunction with the fact that he was represented as sitting in an oak-tree, or in a nest spread above seven, or nine, or twelve oaks; and that he assaulted the passers-by 'not with a weapon, but only with his robbers' whistle';[2] or, as another account has it:

> Nightingale whistles like a nightingale,
> He shrieks, the wretch, like a wild beast:
> The dark forests bow to the earth,
> All the herbage and grass withers up,
> The azure flowers wilt,
> Every mortal creature falls dead.[3]

Or again, according to another: 'First nightingale whistles like a nightingale, then the robber hisses like a snake, and the third time he howls like a wild beast.'[4] Ilya wounded Nightingale by shooting out his right eye with an arrow from his bow, and then led him to Prince Vladimir at Kiev. At the Prince's express command Nightingale uttered his extraordinary war-cry, and paid for it with his life:

> At that nightingale whistle,
> At that wild beast roar,
> A tremendous pother arose.
> The dark forests bowed to the earth,
> And the pinnacles of the houses were bent awry,
> The glass windows were shattered,
> And every mortal creature lay lifeless....

---

[1] Chadwick, *op. cit.* p. 66.
[2] Afanasev, *op. cit.* IV, p. 190; a *skazka*.
[3] Chadwick, *op. cit.* p. 67; tr. Rybnikov, *op. cit.* I, p. 16; a *bylina*.
[4] Afanasev, *op. cit.* p. 196; from another *skazka*. In another version Nightingale also howls like a dog. Rybnikov heard this *bylina* from no less than eight *skaziteli*, which shows its great popularity.

This occurrence exasperated Ilya of Murom...
He cut off his head, and he cried:
'You have caused enough fathers and mothers to weep,
You have widowed enough young wives,
You have orphaned enough little children.'[1]

This extraordinary and fascinating tale certainly gives the imagination food for thought. Was Nightingale an ogre, or some strange hybrid monster, and whence came the deadly power in his voice? The name is in some strange connection with his nature, which is no longer the case with Volga or Svyatogor, if it had ever been so. But it is difficult to say why a nightingale's whistle should have been so deadly. The ancient *byliny*-singers were perhaps aware of this anomaly, and may have added the bestial roaring, hissing and howling in an attempt to rationalise the tale. If the whole tone of the *bylina* were not against it, one would be tempted to see in his 'nest' a Russian *Venusberg*, and in his fatal song that devilish power which medieval monks believed the nightingale to possess, luring the listeners to sensuality and sin. But this conception of the nightingale will not fit in with the more ogreish than amorous nature of the villain.

How far Rilke realised the anthropomorphic character of Nightingale is open to doubt. He wrote to his wife in 1906 when he was remodelling *The Tsars*:

The nightingale has become different too; the part about the nine oaks is a Russian legend; it is called Solovéj in Russian and is a gigantic animal in those most ancient times, powerful and great, with an incomparable cry, resting on nine trees. The legend says 'oaks' explicitly as far as I remember. My new version brings all this out more clearly; it is mightier and more prehistoric.[2]

In his extremely 'psychological' version of the *skazka*: *Ilya and the Snake*, which he called *The Dragon-Slayer*, Rilke made his own individual use of two interesting motifs. In the *skazka*, Nightingale the Robber is overthrown by Ilya on his way to deal with the dragon who is sucking the life-blood

---

[1] Chadwick, *op. cit.* pp. 72 f.; tr. Rybnikov, *op. cit.* I, p. 22.
[2] *B. 1902–1906*, p. 298; to Clara Rilke from Meudon, February 5, 1906.

from a beautiful princess. Afanasev added a note to this story:

Popular belief ascribes to fiery dragons not only the sucking of maidens' blood, but also unchaste relations with them, the fruits of which are magicians and vampires.[1]

Rilke dwelt poetically on a mystical affinity between the maiden and the dragon; and brought in, not Nightingale the Robber, but a nightingale's song 'strong and mighty, like the voice of a gigantic bird, whose nest rests on the summit of nine oaks'.[2]

Ilya was not mentioned by name in *The Dragon-Slayer*, whose hero shares nothing in common with the 'old Cossack' but the actual legendary deed. There is no individual hero at all in the poem, and the nightingale has lost the human, or semi-human attributes of the *byliny* and *skazki*. Rilke transformed Nightingale into an almost disembodied symbol of the elemental, demonic, sinister and insidious forces of nature. His story takes place in prehistoric times, in a land full of gigantic, menacing birds and of phosphorescent dragons guarding treasures in forests and ravines. But lads are growing up, and men are anointing themselves for the contest with the nightingale:

> Which in the summit of nine oak-trees dwelling,
> Like to a monstrous beast within its lair,
> At nightfall sends abroad its clamorous yelling
> Which to the confines of the world goes swelling;
> The whole night long its call goes up from there.
> Oh night of Spring, more terrible than legions,
> And harder far, more fearful to withstand,
> No sign of foes in the surrounding regions,
> Yet everything surrendering in the land;
> Casting itself headlong and wildly calling
> To that fell Something of the ruthless grip,
> Trembling in every limb, sinking and falling
> Submerged at last, much like a foundered ship.[3]

---

[1] Afanasev, *op. cit.* IV, p. 201.

[2] *E.u.S.* p. 434. The two tales are well worth comparing as outstanding examples of extreme simiplicity of mind and extreme sophistication.

[3] *G.W.* II, pp. 98 f.

Only the superhumanly strong, the poem goes on, survived that terrible night, and were not destroyed by the well-nigh irresistible call bursting out volcanically from a myriad throats. They who endured came to understand the terror of April nights as they grew older, and led others through fear and sorrow to better, happier days, when walls were built, and cities founded, and the hitherto untamed beasts came forth from their lairs and laid themselves at the feet of these elders.

To rationalise the struggle with Nightingale the Robber into the conquest of primitive nature by mankind is to deprive the legend of its sinews and bones. There *is* something rather boneless about the last two verses of the poem, which remind one also, and to their detriment, of Schiller's *Eleusinian Feast*. Poetical histories of civilisation tend to become didactic poetry, and Rilke's poem began to slither in that direction before the end. His nightingale's song, however, haunts more eerie regions of poetry and romance. Yet the old tale is truer:

> Farther, farther upon the open plain waves the feather grass in the breeze, and there upon the open plain, among the old folk, mothers and men, rode the Old Cossack, Ilya of Murom, and the horse he rode was like a fierce wild beast and he himself was like a bright falcon.[1]

They are gone from Rilke's poem: the open plain, the valiant rider yelling to his steed, and the 'robber-dog' has vanished with them. That heroic encounter between a mythical hero and a chimerical monster in the 'great forest in Central Russia, once impenetrable and always legendary',[2] which took place by the glorious cross of Levanidov on the glorious river Smorodina (neither of which has ever been identified), seems far more real than the spring night of Rilke's imagining, when a band of consecrated warriors withstood the nightingale's song. The transformation of Nightingale the Robber into a fell unearthly songstress symbolises the aesthetic metamorphosis which Russia underwent in

[1] M. C. Harrison, *Byliny Book. Hero Tales of Russia*, Cambridge, 1915, p. 33. Told for children.

[2] L. A. Magnus, *Russian Folk-Tales*, London, 1915, p. 262 note.

Rilke's mind. The poetical crystallisation of his experiences combined the height of sophistication with the depth of decadence. Rilke's future God, Ilya of Murom and the nightingale are all evident efforts at mythological creation, but the atmosphere in which they have their being is more occult than mythical. The same may be said in a general way of all his aesthetic evocations of a country whose inhabitants were represented as experiencing in prehistoric times those insidious temptations and those evil lures which one associates with the black arts. Its legendary young virgins wrestled in their dreams with a perverted passion for the dragons which desired them. Small wonder if ages later an insane tsar went mopping and mowing through the oriental magnificence of the Kremlin, in which eerie palace his degenerate son achieved a mystical union with the Madonna. A strange God fittingly brooded over this strange land, still in the process of becoming and meanwhile suffering numerous fantastic and even grotesque incarnations. Laughter was unknown to the inhabitants, whose souls had been seared before the dawn of their history by the shattering cry of a monstrous nightingale more terrible than the sphinx.

This was the secret playing-ground of his soul, the fourth-dimensional country which Russia had revealed to him, and in which, as he said twenty years later, his real spiritual freedom began, his liberation from the pressure of reality.[1]

2. *Worpswede*, 1900–1901

Retrospectively it seems more like predestination than mere chance that Rilke should have spent some weeks in Worpswede in December 1898 at the invitation of the artist Heinrich Vogeler, whom he had met in Florence; for this apparently unimportant visit was not only to determine the external trend of his future life, it was also to modify, and fundamentally modify, his mentality and outlook. It brought

[1] *B. 1914–1921*, pp. 354 f.; from the letter to Sedlakowitz about the military academy.

into his personal life his deep, instinctive dependence on the plastic arts; and it strengthened his lifelong reverence for 'things', already apparent in 1898. Indeed his brief glimpse of the artists' colony in Worpswede impressed him so much that he made a particular point of visiting Abramzevo from Moscow in 1900, because it was 'a kind of Russian Worpswede'. And he returned straight as a homing dove to the German edition when he got back. He stayed there for five weeks, during the fag-end of August, the whole of September, and the first days of October. It was only a short visit; but it is impossible to exaggerate its importance or the interest of the published diary covering the period. This journal, which runs from November 3, 1899 to December 22, 1900, opens with a series of sketches and short stories, and continues with German verse and poems, interspersed with French verse, a few short reflections, and notes on his reading. One brief entry and a short poem were written down during the second Russian trip, which he summed up in Worpswede under the date September 1, 1900, commenting adversely on its effect upon his poetical powers. The diary proper then begins, interrupted very frequently by poetry, and much more rarely by prose sketches.

A great many of the poems published in *The Picture-Book* in 1902 (nearly all of which were retained in the enlarged edition of 1906) were first written down in this journal, which therefore reveals Rilke as a poet, as a prose-writer and as a young man. The difference between the poetry and the prose illustrates that strange dualism in Rilke apparent in the early works and strongly brought out in *The Book of Monkish Life* and *Tales about God*, where it almost amounted to a cleavage. The poems which were selected for *The Picture-Book*, and also the large body of rejected verse, give the same impression of effortless ease which characterised his poetry from the moment he began to write. At times this degenerates into facility; but, however nebulous the ideas, however loose the construction, however careless the manner or meaningless the matter, it is throughout evident that in writing rhythmically Rilke was writing naturally, speaking his mother-tongue.

The strong musical compulsion behind every line of this very unequal verse lifts even the most paltry stanzas into a somnambulistic region where chiming melodies drift unhindered through the mind. This was the very reverse of Rilke's conscious aesthetic aim; since everything within him was trembling to create, to fashion, to form, he stated at the beginning of the journal, under the sway of plastic ideals. But his poetry flowed out and flowed on, serenely indifferent to the poet's wish; and although he often made it flow into a form, it was far too fluid a medium to be shaped. He was not yet like the Brahmin's wife of Goethe's Hindu poem, whose heart was so pure that she could carry water from the well, formed into a crystal ball by her innocent hands. Rilke's mind was still too clouded to perform this magical feat. The horror left in it by the military academy was gradually silting down into his unconscious, but the process was not complete, and the sediment, far from petrified, was still easily stirred up. His instinctive feeling that prose was the vehicle for reality and verse the medium for visions and dreams, caused him to represent reality in his stories, that is to say the horrible element in life, for this was his notion of reality; in *Tales about God* and in some of the prose sketches in the journal he also tried to bend this recalcitrant medium towards vision; whereupon in *The Last Judgment*, written during the same period, horror rushed into his verse.

He was tormented at night with the feeling that he 'ought' to write a novel about the military academy, an emotion which was considerably less urgent in the day-time, when it dwindled to a mere literary scheme, and one moreover for which he felt insufficient skill. It would be necessary and frightfully difficult to show that society of boys in all their barbarousness and degeneracy, he said. But he made a beginning in *The Drill-Class*, a short story in which the unhappy Karl Gruber dies from over-exertion during drill; the brutality of the N.C.O. and the callousness of the boys were delineated realistically and with restraint. The same cannot be said of *Frau Blaha's Maid*, a nightmare fantasy in which a feeble-minded kitchenmaid is raped, strangles her baby at birth, wraps it up in her blue apron and bundles it into the bottom of her trunk. She then goes about her duties as if nothing had happened; but the thwarted maternal instinct compels her to buy a puppet theatre. This attracts the children of the neighbourhood, who crowd into the underground kitchen to watch Annuschka manipulating the dolls. One day she goes off to fetch the 'big doll' they are so anxious to see; the children take fright whilst she is out of the room and run away; an eerie harlequin-puppet they had not noticed among the dolls before was responsible for their alarm. Annuschka, finding the kitchen empty, breaks the theatre and splits open the heads of all the dolls, big and little. The horrors of child-birth, the frustrated effort to find a substitute for it in aesthetic creation and the dire result tell a dark story of Rilke's feelings about the lot of women, the hostility between life and art, and the uncanny similarity between their creative processes. It is a truly ghastly tale, and *The Grave-Gardener* is only a whit less horrible with its gruesome description of the plague; whilst the *Fragment*, later incorporated in that story, and of which more will be said in a moment, is perhaps the most dreadful of the three. All of them mingle girlhood, love and death in very disturbing proportions, and throw a lurid light on the nature of the shock Rilke had sustained in Italy. It was clearly a much more serious matter than the persistent memories of his school-days; and it had a queer fascination for him, as was to become even more apparent during the Worpswede period.

Situated deep in the moor and fen country near Bremen, Worpswede had attracted to itself a group of artists who had created quite a stir at the Crystal Palace Exhibition in Munich in 1895 and now included a painter of real genius, Paula Becker, who married a fellow-Worpswedian, Otto Modersohn, in 1901, and became famous as Paula Moder-sohn-Becker. She it was who later criticised the factitious peasant life they had tried to lead, saying that it had erected a partition between herself and the world. It was a barrier after Rilke's own heart, since it separated him from the dark side of reality. Worpswede offered that very rare gift, creative solitude combined with opportunities for intellectual and spiritual intimacies. It surrounded him with spacious horizons, gleaming waters and a wide, wild sky. Here, if anywhere, nature and beauty, art and what seemed like real life, were ideally combined. Here too was the possibility of studying a technique diametrically opposite to his own. Rilke's admiration for the powers of dispassionate observation and disciplined attention of the Worpswedian artists was intense. He felt that he was learning something of vital importance from them; and indeed both his letters and diary abound in landscapes, still-lifes and interiors. One even gets a little weary of his ecstatic repetition of the word 'gaze', not to mention the word 'things', which he used in a peculiarly up-lifted manner for natural objects, for works of art, for petri-facts, for artifacts, for objects which could give rise to works of art, in short for every kind of object. As for the rather self-conscious simplicity of the artists' lives, he took it enthusi-astically at its face-value. And indeed, who was he to throw stones at an artists' colony; he, who had gone gathering mushrooms barefoot in Russian dews, and had wormed his way into *izbas*? But far and away the most precious gift Worpswede had to offer Rilke was the presence of those 'girls', as he always called them; the fair-haired painter, Paula Becker, and Clara Westhoff, the dark-brown eyed sculptress. If one wished to put it unkindly with 'apt alliteration's artful aid', one might distinguish the Rilke of *Frau Blaha's Maid* from the Rilke of the Worpswede diary by the epithets ghoulish and girlish. Nor, in using the latter adjective, would one be saying anything about the young poet which he had not said himself:

> I'm with you both, I'm gratefully around you
> Who are as sisters to the soul of me;
> For my soul wears a maiden's dress, you see,
> And her hair too is silken to the handling.
> . . . . . . You know her better
> Than I myself . . . . . .
> You are the sisters of my bride,

Be good to her,
And love her well, your fair-haired sister.[1]

These verses, written shortly after Rilke's departure from Worpswede and sent to Paula Becker, were addressed to both his soul's sisters, and thereby hangs a tale. It reaches back into the past and very far forward into his future. It did not end, even when a string snapped and a shower of pearls scattered round Rilke's feet, never to be re-threaded.[2] He said of them then that they had no clasp; and I incline to think that they were cultured pearls; but during the greater part of his life, the shimmering string of girlhood was the rosary of his affections. Young girls had chanted the *Maidens' Songs*; and the belief that love spelt death to that fragile, innocent, embryonic state had been given a strange expression in *The White Princess*. The ghoulish monk and the girlish sister were both puppets in that play, which was in the nature of a curtain-raiser.

The episode of Rilke and the girl artists at Worpswede is a crucial act in the drama of his chaplet of pearls; it had a tragic, not to say a horrible, ending, but it opened idyllically and was full of exquisite humour. Not that Rilke aimed at producing the latter effect: far otherwise. His diary is prose poetry, when it is not actually verse, from start to finish. This first published autobiographical fragment of his is one of the most curious documents of poetical adolescence that exist: consciously self-adulatory, it is unconsciously far from flattering to the author. Sentimentality, at times almost sickliness, relieved by an occasional gleam of spite; intellectual snobbishness and spiritual priggishness; occasional ghoulishness— none of this is quite so disturbing as the wilful unreality which pervades these pages, and which proves that Rilke was indeed the son of that mother whose 'unreality' he disliked and even

[1] Cf. *B.u.T.* pp. 374 ff. for the whole poem under the date of October 28, 1900 in the diary; and pp. 70 ff., a slightly modified version, sent to Paula on November 6, 1900.

[2] Cf. *G.W.* III, pp. 470 f., *Perlen Entrollen*, dated by Zinn between 1913 and 1914 and *B.u.T.* p. 93, which reads like a prose draft of the poem; although here Rilke used 'pearls' for Paula's words. It was generally used as a synonym for girls; cf. *G.W.* II, p. 14.

feared so much.[1] Yet one is far from disliking *him*, in spite of his pretentiousness, affectation and *marivaudage*. It is impossible to feel seriously out of tune with anyone so incredibly young, engagingly ludicrous and tremulously happy. Moreover in spite of his style, or perhaps even because of it, he has given to that Worpswedian idyll a peculiar charm, which reminds one again and again of *Werther*. The proportions of poetry and truth are almost the same in both stories; but Rilke's self-revelation was poetical self-assertion.

One would give a good deal to have been present at one at least of those Sunday parties held regularly in Vogeler's white music-room, which generally lasted until Monday's dawn and were the great event of the week. They were always attended by the girls in their white party frocks, which harmonised with Vogeler's Empire furniture, white walls and mural decorations. The latter was not only a painter, he also went in for arts and crafts, landscape gardening and interior decoration; so that his house at least was not very much like a peasant's. The evenings were devoted to music (Paula's sister Milly sang songs), to enthralling conversations about life and art, and God and death; and best of all to Rilke's poems read to the circle by the solemn young author himself. Vogeler's wife said of these readings after his death: 'A great solemnity pervaded everyone in his presence. His poems lived their strongest life when they were read by candlelight and roses and silver bowls, or when women were present.'[2] For 'women' read 'girls' and the setting was exactly as she described it; a poet could hardly ask for a better one; nevertheless these parties had their ups and their downs. Unluckily for the young man's peace of mind, Carl Hauptmann, the brother of the dramatist Gerhard Hauptmann, and also a writer, was in Worpswede at the time, and joined the parties. Not only that, but he also read *his* effusions out loud. Being twenty-three years older than Rilke, he had certain advantages over him; it is evident that he irritated the young

[1] Cf. *B. 1892–1904*, p. 441.

[2] M. Vogeler in *Rainer Maria Rilke. Stimmen der Freunde*, ed. Buchheit, Freiburg im Breisgau, 1931, p. 83. Otto Modersohn also testified to the great impression Rilke's readings made, *ibid*. pp. 48 f.

poet unbearably and got on his nerves at the very first party, from the very word 'go'. Both Clara Rilke and Otto Modersohn in their reminiscences of Paula Becker speak of Carl Hauptmann as if his presence and his conversation and poetry had been as great an asset to the Sunday evening parties as Rilke's.[1] And to judge from the entry Paula made in her diary after Rilke's first Sunday in Worpswede, she considered Hauptmann a good deal the more interesting of the two:

> Dr Carl Hauptmann is here for a week. He is a great, strong, wrestling soul, who does not weigh light. High seriousness and great striving after truth are in him. He gives me much food for thought. He read extracts from his diary: *Reflective and Lyrical Poetry*. The German was hard, the style heavy and rigid but deep....Rainer Maria Rilke on the other hand has a subtle lyrical talent; he is delicate and sensitive, with small, pathetic hands. He read us his poems, delicate and full of divination. Sweet and pale. The two men could not at bottom understand each other. Conflict between realism and idealism.[2]

Emotional and professional jealousies were at work, probably in both of them, and certainly in Rilke, who was naturally annoyed, when Hauptmann took it upon himself to criticise Rilke's poem *The Fiddler* and to suggest that it would be better without the final mysterious line. Needless to say, Hauptmann's own contributions to the evening's entertainment ('saws, maxims and verses') received a slashing critique in the journal; 'unlyrical, philosophical, abstract'. There followed an elaborate analysis of Hauptmann's temperament, and the report of a duologue between the two later on, at midnight, when the candles on the piano were burning low. Rilke spoke like a poet about Kramskoy (he had been showing some Russian pictures and *ikons*), and Hauptmann answered like a philistine; he was obviously the sort of person to write down folk-song jingle in his diary, which would certainly be bound in pigskin.[3]

---

[1] R. Hetsch, ed. *Paula Modersohn-Becker*, Berlin, 1932, pp. 26, 46.

[2] P. Modersohn-Becker, *Briefe und Tagebuchblätter*, Berlin, 1920, pp. 123 f.; dated September 3, 1900, Worpswede.

[3] Otto Modersohn remembered very vividly the critical conflicts between Rilke and Hauptmann; cf. *Stimmen der Freunde*, p. 49.

So that there was a fly, rather a large fly, in the ointment. And there was another thing which sometimes ruined the parties for Rilke; those exuberant young artists were terribly fond of dancing. Rilke was unspeakably wretched whenever this occurred. He crept into a corner, 'smelling the beer and inhaling the smoke' at a harvest festival dance which took place the day after his first Sunday party. It was not a gathering of the peasants, alas, no; evidently a reunion of the lower middle classes in a tent,[1] with a sprinkling of artists; the fair-haired painter who had been so serious the day before, and the sculptress with her dark vivacity and power; also Vogeler, looking like a remote, ancestral portrait in a lumber-room; also Fritz Mackensen and his brother, to whom Rilke was introduced; but he could only sit and gaze at them dumbly. Hauptmann was there too, feeling just as shy and just as much out of it as Rilke, which was something of a bond; and the lonely walk home at night put the party where it belonged, absolutely nowhere at all.

The rest of the week passed in a dream; long rambles over the heath with Vogeler, who confided in Rilke all about his approaching marriage with Martha, a simple peasant girl; and who also told him about many previous Worpswedian excursions and adventures; a happy evening spent in Paula's studio, where Clara dropped in later; and Sunday was once more with them. Another party was in full swing in the white room. It had its moments. The arrival of the girls all in white was a good beginning; Paula smiling under an enormous Florentine hat; Clara in an Empire robe, with flowing brown locks. She was the queen of the feast, and especially beautiful when she was listening and not talking; for then the rather too striking characteristics of her face became less noticeable. Happily she had every opportunity for listening at some length, since Rilke read *The White Princess* to the party, getting a strong impression from it himself of music and power. The intolerable Carl Hauptmann, however, ruined the

---

[1] Fritz Mackensen, in his reminiscences of Rilke at Worpswede, rather maliciously emphasised Rilke's discomfort and inadequacy in the primitive society of a fisherman's hut; cf. *Stimmen der Freunde*, pp. 43 f.

whole thing in retrospect by his endless, pointless theorising
which began as soon as the reading was over. The girls, who
all believed in the White Princess, did not join in the argu-
ment. Even before this Hauptmann had made himself
obnoxious by getting Milly Becker again and again to sing a
song with ghastly words beginning: 'O gracious Art, in
many a darkling hour.'[1] But worse was to come. Unhappily
some wine was brought up from Vogeler's cellar ('it is
always a pity when gatherings end with wine'); and Hauptmann had the nerve to ask Rilke for a drinking-song, and to
keep on repeating that one day the young man would realise
what a chasm yawned in his art, because he had not written
one. Hauptmann then tried to sing one by Dehmel, but could
not remember a single line. By this time Rilke was evidently
steeped in sulks; for Milly went to sit by him, asked him
questions about Leopardi and repeated beautiful, sorrowful
words from an Italian song. But of what use was that, when
everyone else was dancing? That oaf Hauptmann with Miss
Westhoff ('Miss' shows how deeply Rilke disapproved of her
at that moment), whirling round and round until he got giddy
(can it have been the wine?), and then leaving her *plantée là*.
There was a great deal of laughter, all the words running in
circles round the revellers, none of them coming to Rilke;
a poem was composed to the absent Vogeler; and the author of
The White Princess, feeling incredibly lonely, surveyed from
an incalculable distance all this deplorable ragging, 'the
hideous *finale* of German sociability'. Rilke would never have
been able to say with Keats: 'But let us refresh ourselves from
this depth of thinking and turn to some innocent jocularity—
the Bow cannot always be bent.'[2] The party, from the poet's
point of view, was now in ruins, since they were all enjoying
themselves wildly and completely out of hand. In desperation,
he flung wide the window and door, a masterpiece of poetical
diplomacy, for they sobered down at once. The girls in white
went to lean on the window-sill and look out into the night,

[1] Cf. R. Hetsch, *op. cit.* p. 46, where Clara Rilke mentions this song of
Schubert's as being one of Hauptmann's favourites.

[2] John Keats, *Complete Works*, ed. Forman, Glasgow, 1901, iv, p. 25; letter to
Jane and Mariane Reynolds, from Oxford, September 5, 1817.

where the moon was silvering the poplars. They brought back the mystery of their girlhood and their artists' souls from that contemplation; and Rilke felt grateful to them for their beauty, in strong contrast to their jarring presence when they had been 'distorted by gaiety' and he had wished them away. He was now able to take warm farewells of them, and to write a poem, *About Girls*, in which the insufferable Hauptmann was well snubbed between brackets:

> ...from afar, he hears your voices sound
> (midst those men he wearily avoids).[1]

That 'great, strong, wrestling soul' seems, like the Snark, to have gone 'bellowing on to the last'. But Rilke's magic-casement mood was proof against the echoes of his voice. It was all like a fairy-tale; thus he summed up his final impressions of that rather chequered evening. Here he was, living in this white gabled house, lost in gardens, amongst beautiful and noble things redolent of Vogeler's atmosphere, sitting in his dreaming chairs, reflected in his mirrors, listening to his clocks, waiting alone for six days; and receiving on the seventh in the white music-room by the light of twelve candles in tall silver candlesticks the most solemn men of the district (Hauptmann with his ragging was now as though he were not) and lovely slender girls in white who played to him and sang to him and grouped themselves together in delicate Empire chairs, becoming the most distinguished pictures, the most precious luxuries and the sweetest voices of those whispering rooms. Yes, he was certainly living in a fairy-tale, and (what is rare enough in such circumstances) he knew it at the time.

Still, it had been rather a strain that Sunday, very much a matter of touch and go; and one is surprised that Rilke felt himself equal to another party at the Overbecks the following day. It was preceded by a visit paid to him by Paula (during which he showed her Russian books and portraits) and was a much quieter and more peaceful affair. Probably everyone was tired out. Rilke, sitting beside Paula, found Hauptmann,

[1] *G.W.* II, p. 15.

who entertained the company with one of Kleist's eerie tales, in a sympathetic mood. When they broke up, the young poet walked all the way back to Westerwede with Clara, who was wheeling her bicycle. Once more the landscape closed round him like a dream; and wandering through it, he gazed and gazed again for days on end in uninterrupted solitude until Vogeler returned. Then, having come to the conclusion that he got much more out of people singly than at parties, he called, first on Otto Modersohn, and then on Paula Becker. There is no mention in her diary of what was to him an epoch-making visit. She had just finished reading his *Advent*, and he felt in the ensuing conversation, and still more in the silences which interrupted it, that they were being drawn gently but irresistibly very close together. In fact there came a moment, he said, when during an eloquent silence the very stones spoke and they were together in eternity, before the gate behind which stands God. Rilke rushed away over the heath, and celebrated his moment in a poem. Had he remained alone, he believed that he might have gone through the gate; but daily life intruded; lassitude and disillusion followed. Next day, however, he was back again in Paula's studio.

This second visit to the 'lily-studio' deepened the sense of intimacy produced by the first. Words and silences seemed equally significant, and mystery grew all round them as they talked of Tolstoy, death, life, the beauty of all experience, the ability and the desire to die. Her hair was like Florentine gold; her voice had silken folds; never before had she seemed so delicate and slender in her white girlhood. And then a great shadow fell into the room, first over him, next over her; yet no one was passing the window, and the sky was serene.

Sunday, with its possibilities of comic relief for the reader, now dawned again, heralding a very weird party, and an extremely long one. Rilke came home after the milk; for it dragged on from hour to hour and from studio to studio in a thoroughly artistic way. Fortune had rid the young poet of that turbulent knave Carl Hauptmann. He was absent in Hamburg superintending the forthcoming production of one of his plays, and Rilke, who had magnanimously dispatched him a solemn and flowery telegram in verse wishing him luck only the day before, enjoyed every moment of a remarkable night, which was untroubled by dancing and unpolluted by drink. He read a great many poems to the assembled artists, and felt such sympathy emanating from them, that he ventured on the Michelangelo and ghetto stories from *Tales about God*. The first produced a most gratifying impression. Rilke found himself trembling when he spoke God's words: 'Michelangelo, who is in the stone?' The 'dark, grateful ones'[1] uttered never a word; they left him alone to follow them to supper at the inn, and altogether almost spoiled him, he said, with 'their subtle gratitude, not menaced with words'. They were probably very much bewildered and possibly oppressed; but their natural gaiety reasserted itself during supper, and since it was not contaminated by Hauptmann's dreadful jocularity, Rilke welcomed it, was indeed very glad to see it; and was altogether very happy, babbling away to Paula on the way back to Vogeler's house about how he was going to live here and now in the present, and be transformed by it; and how he had made a mistake to think he could belong to the past in Worpswede (verse); and he even spoke rather slightingly of the Russian journey, and was so much uplifted, that he read them all 'just one more' tale when they got back to the white music-room. After this, they all went round to Paula's studio, and made coffee, and the two girls went out to milk the goat in the stable by the light of a petroleum cooking-stove, and came back with suppressed giggles and a bowl of black milk. And it only shows how unreal Rilke made everything sound, that it is hardly possible to tell from his comments, whether or not he realised that this was due to smuts from the stove; whether he was serious or joking:

The milk was black. Although we were all surprised, no one dared to mention his discovery, and each one of us thought: 'Well after all, it's night. Never yet have I milked a goat at night. Evidently their milk gets darker and darker from twilight onwards,

---

[1] Dark also means mysterious; it is always a term of praise when used by Rilke.

and now, two hours after midnight, it's still quite black. But don't let me think of that now. Everyone of us will have to face that fact alone. To-morrow.' And we all drank of the black milk of the twilight goat, and became strangely wakeful after this mysterious beverage.[1]

A more disconcerting incident occurred in Clara's studio, where Vogeler's brother Franz and Rilke went next. After sitting for some time in her vine-covered arbour and later in her sitting-room, where she talked about Paris, and Franz fell asleep, they decided to break open her studio door as the people who had the key were asleep. They therefore seized the sculptor's hammer and assaulted the lock. This made such a ghastly noise that Clara suddenly put her left hand over the lock to ward off the next blow, with the inevitable result. If Franz were still asleep (which seems barely possible), Rilke may have been wielding the hammer, although this would not be very characteristic of him. But if those 'small pathetic hands' were behind the blow, that would account for the fact that Clara was not maimed for life. As it was, she bled a good deal, and was rather severely injured. Rilke described the accident in some detail. He was correcting the proofs of *Tales about God* at the time. The injured hand was a sculptor's hand. Surely the bleeding of God's right hand originated in Clara's studio? Personally I cannot believe that, if the incident had been written first, Rilke would have said nothing about what was in that case a most uncanny coincidence. His book appeared at Christmas, the scene I have just been describing was recounted under the date September 21; I should like to believe that the episode in the story was not the fruit of his unaided imagination; and the evidence at least is not against me.[2]

First aid having been rendered, and the pain wearing off, Clara's studio at length came into its own, and her work was carefully examined. Rilke held forth at some length about

---

[1]　*B.u.T.* p. 317.

[2]　On the other hand, Rilke may have invented the studio incident under the influence of the story; but this seems less likely. Nevertheless, in *All in One* the hero begins to carve his own hands.

Rodin to Clara, who was Rodin's pupil, and all three then
went to visit Modersohn. They ended up in Paula's studio,
where Rilke read to the girls his definitely ghoulish poem
The Last Judgment. Then off bright and early next morning
for a little archaeological expedition; for late nights do not
injure the young!

The next communal social event was the trip to Hamburg
to witness the first night of Hauptmann's play. They all drove
together in a carriage as far as Bremen, except Clara who
went on her bicycle, having deposited an enormous heather
wreath she had made for Hauptmann on Rilke's knees. He
was facing Paula and her wonderful Paris hat, 'on which
tired dark red roses unemphatically rested, as if they had just
been laid aside by a lonely hand'. And he watched her eyes,
noticing that they were beginning to unfold like double roses,
like them becoming warm and soft as they opened, holding
those soft shades and delicate lights which can be seen on the
shoulders and breasts of little curling petals. Sitting opposite
this remarkable hat and still more remarkable eyes, he felt the
simple strength of Clara's sculptural hands in the wreath, and
something mild and humble but courageous too flowing to
him from the sweet face of the other. Far indeed from Rilke's
mind was the unworthy desire for 't'other fair charmer' to
remain away. Quite apart from the fact that he always
thought of girls in the plural, he liked these two mutually
devoted friends in the dual; and if perhaps he hankered more
after the one, the other interested him more greatly. There is
no doubt that Clara interested him very much indeed. Not
only did he write down at some length in his diary her youthful reminiscences and her experiences in Paris; they made
such an impression on him, that he retold them to her later in
his letters. She also interested him as an artist; he thought
very highly of her work; and she interested him vitally as a
pupil of Rodin. Sculpture was beginning to fascinate him
more than painting; Lepsius had initiated Rilke into Rodin's
art as early as 1897; Michelangelo in *The Book of Monkish
Life* and *Tales about God*, and the divine sculptor of the stories
may have been partly modelled on Rodin, whose work and its

significance Rilke had estimated to Clara the Sunday she hurt
her hand. She was Rodin's pupil, and therefore near the rose.
She also attracted him physically by her vitality, exuberance
and strength, qualities in which he was deficient himself.

His attitude to Paula Becker was different. He hardly knew
her work then, and did not realise her genius, or he would
certainly have included her in his monograph on the Worpswede painters. She was reticent about her art, and he was too
shy to ask to see her pictures, or so he told her later; adding
that he had generally been with her in the evenings when the
light was bad, and that her words had monopolised his
attention. He introduced her to Rodin in 1903 as the wife of
a very distinguished German painter; whereas her reputation
has survived her husband's. Rilke's indifference to Paula's
art is all the more remarkable because she was much nearer to
him in genius than any of the other Worpswedians. She also
shared his attitude towards life. In their passionate love of
their art, in their unremitting pursuit of it, Rilke and Paula
were much alike. Both were ruthless to themselves, and
could be ruthless to others in its service. Her letters and
diaries bring out this similarity and underline the differences.
Paula was much more spontaneous and warm-hearted, natural
and simple than the excessively complicated person who had
just made up that simile about her awakening eyes. She
aroused little or none of the lively interest he felt for Clara;
few of her conversations were reported in his diary; but he
spoke to her with complete unreserve of the things nearest to
his heart; every interview with her produced one or more
poems, whereas Clara generally inspired descriptive or
narrative prose; he referred to the latter freely by name, and to
Paula by a poetical paraphrase. If Clara's beauty almost overwhelmed him at times, Paula's melted him. She was the more
girlish of the two to judge by his descriptions; and that
perhaps is the final word.

And so they went driving off to Bremen, Rilke irresistibly
recalling Werther accompanying Lotte on their way to that
fateful dance. I am not going to dog the footsteps of these
'bewildered children of the heath', through the 'great town'

of Hamburg; but it is pleasant to think of them supporting Hauptmann at the first night of his play, which went off well, and was duly adorned by Clara's magnificent wreath. Rilke surpassed himself by his speech at supper, which amazed the outsiders, amongst them a critic 'of the worst sort', from Berlin. These 'few terribly simple words', addressed to an omnium gatherum of actors, Worpswedians and others, described at some length the 'landscape' of the play, and the impression this had produced upon the speaker. Getting ever more solemn Rilke continued to instruct his audience to the effect that death meant life, and work meant resurrection, throwing off these impressive but not 'terribly simple' notions in very flowery language. True to his poetical character, he presented the girls with masses of red roses next day, during which every member of the party wore or carried a rose, so as to be easily recognisable in the crowd should one of them get lost in dreams. Rilke walked about, caressing his closed eyes with one of these blooms, a gesture which would have turned the poet in *Patience* green with envy, and withered the lily in his medieval hand. The discovery of this 'new caress' and the memory of Paula's flowering eyes dictated the peculiarly distressing *Fragment*, which found a place in his journal sandwiched in between descriptions of Hamburg. It is a fantasy about a dead girl, whose virginal body death does not touch, taking the life that is still in her from her face. Unable to bear the sight of her pinched features, the hero lays two frosty red rosebuds over her eyes. They open and blossom; and at the end of the day George has two great red roses in his hand, heavy with the life of one who had never given herself to him. Considered objectively, this is merely a piece of literary bad taste; taken in conjunction with Paula and Rilke, it is disturbing indeed, reminding one of Faust's evil vision of Gretchen on the Brocken, a wish-dream that was to be fulfilled. The desire behind Rilke's story is even less straightforward.

In the poem *About Girls* he had implored them never to give themselves to the poet, even if his eyes should plead, for he could only conceive of them as maidens. He now went further. Girls must die, one way or the other; better far that they should die in their girlhood, and not be ravished by men; let them blossom after death. One remembers with some relief that only the evening before he had assured a whole supper-party that death meant life. It is even more of a relief to read his account of Otto Modersohn's well-meant efforts to bring joy into the life of a spider, as recounted by that philanthropist the same evening in Hauptmann's rooms. Rilke's commentary, brief and witty, is a little jewel of sympathetic humour; something so new and unexpected, and such poles apart from his sinister rosebuds, that one marvels how the same mind could elaborate both fantasies in the space of a single day.

Returning to Worpswede on September 26 or 27, Rilke made up his mind to stay there throughout the autumn and winter into the spring, a decision certainly influenced by Clara's description of the first autumn and winter she had spent in the country as a child. He was in a state of abnormal receptivity, even for him, just then, and continuously ecstatic. Vogeler's sketches of the Annunciation and of the Nativity produced an almost blinding vision of angels, inspired a magnificent piece of prose, and some less remarkable verse. Another visit to Paula Becker, and her enthusiastic praise of Clara, led to a rhythmic outburst and another song about girls. Whilst the sight of Clara herself walking over the hill to the inn next Sunday rendered him dumb at the moment but eloquent on paper afterwards, when he deliriously compared her with the Madonna and wrote some verse about her. It was the most uplifting and sublime of all the Sunday parties. The music was glorious; never had the girls looked so lovely as when listening to his *Last Judgment*; and Rilke was in such a state of exaltation that, on accompanying the party out of doors to say farewell, he distinctly heard a heavenly choir singing 'Glory to God in the highest'; and knew beyond the shadow of a doubt that this song is always being sung, and can be heard by those who have ears to hear when they see singing profiles against starlit nights, a clairaudient reminiscence of Vogeler's sketches.

Rilke was tremulously solemn with Clara next day, speaking of the Worpswedian circle as a sacred shrine, which must be guarded from would-be entrants. And the following evening, spent, apparently alone, with Paula Becker, produced a monologue about God, on the lines of *The Book of Monkish Life*. His imperfections, injustice and inadequacy were ascribed to his state of evolution; and Rilke then went on to say that he himself had perhaps been entrusted with a kind of priesthood; alien from humanity himself, he was intended to approach another human being from time to time, solemnly, as if issuing from golden gates. But only such would be able to see him as dwelt by golden gates themselves. Christ, on the other hand, was a great danger to young people, since he obscured God from their view. This evening in the 'lily-studio' was followed by a positive spate of poetry, some of it very sad; and then, suddenly, Rilke was gone from Worpswede, and gone for good.

Was it really Russia calling to him, as he told everyone to whom he wrote? Was it the eleventh-hour realisation that he was forgetting his poetical mission to Russia, let alone the fact that he was divorced from teachers and books in Worpswede? Was that why he abandoned the 'little house' he had rented for the winter, realising that Worpswede (a real home and a true home for the artists) was not his own, which was situated under farther skies, many many rivers away; realising too that he must have no 'little house' of his own just yet, but that waiting and wandering must be his portion? It may have been true, or it may not. Rilke was too unreal just then, and more particularly so about Russia, to be sure himself. It was a sudden decision, made either before or after his departure for Schmargendorf, ostensibly to collect books and other necessaries for the winter. He left a manuscript book of his poems behind with an undated note to Paula, in which he spoke of his hopes of a speedy return. His last entry in the Worpswede diary was dated October 4; his first letters from Schmargendorf were written on October 18; the diary was reopened on October 28 with a string of poems, headed by the *Strophes* to Paula and Clara, from which I quoted earlier. It is

possible that the rumour of Paula's engagement to Otto
Modersohn, which was an open secret by October 28,
prevented his return. Paula told him the news early in
November; before this communication his letters to her are
exactly what one would expect from the diary; caressing,
yearning, poetical, often overflowing into verse, sometimes
consisting of nothing but verse; he certainly showed no sign
of being aware that his correspondent was engaged to be
married.[1] But Rilke's exquisite manners, a constant feature of
his conduct, would account for such camouflage, if camouflage
it were. The sudden gap in his diary (whether originally there
or made by his literary executors) points to a shock of some
sort; it is less plausible to explain it by the insurgent voice of
Russia, which Rilke would almost certainly have recorded and
which the editors would not have deleted, than by an emotional
upheaval. And the news of Paula's engagement would have
been a shock to him, whenever and however he heard it. Not
that Rilke wished to marry Paula Becker; far from it, she was
a symbol of girlhood, and marriage spelt death to that
mysterious, unconscious, beautiful state. He had seen, and
seen as something very desirable, a dead girl with rosebuds
opening on her eyes; that girl was obviously Paula, whom he
loved, mysteriously and poetically, because she was a girl, and
whom he would no more have thought of marrying than of
murdering; preferring indeed to kill her in his thoughts.
Acutely sensitive as he was, he may have become aware
during the trip to Hamburg of the marital danger threatening
her from Otto Modersohn, who, to make it worse, was a
widower; he may even have felt that she was in danger from
himself when he wished a virgin's death on her in the
Fragment.[2] For it was a very deep and a very queer feeling
which he had for her, and which received a mortal blow,
either in October or in November, the date is of little account.

[1] The diffidence about mentioning her name remained. He generally called
her 'Liebes Fräulein' or 'Liebe Freundin'; addressing Clara as 'Liebe Clara
Westhoff'.

[2] He thought well enough of this fantasy to include it in *Der Totengräber*,
1903, where indeed it is thoroughly well placed. Cf. *B.u.T.* pp. 336 ff. and
E.u.S. pp. 461 ff. *Der Totengräber* was reprinted in *Der Inselschiff* in June 1921.

The wound bled inwardly; his letters were almost as intimate after the news as before; his poetical 'blessing' almost as spontaneous as those *Strophes* in which he recalled his happiness in Vogeler's white music-room. And if, from now onwards, the letters to Clara were rather more frequent, this was partly accounted for by Paula's presence in Berlin that winter, and her Sunday visits to Rilke. The time for reproaches and recriminations was not yet. He even forgave her for not liking 'quite all' the stories about God. To the extent of writing her a really charming letter about her private diary and correspondence, which she allowed him to see; it was being written and kept with an eye to future publication, and appeared after her death. This letter was dated January 24, 1901. Before the twenty-third of March Rilke's engagement to Clara Westhoff was announced; their marriage took place on April 29, 1901, before the 'fair-haired painter' became Paula Modersohn-Becker.

The idyllic Worpswedian relationship did not survive married life, and could hardly have been expected to do so; but it was probably Paula's fault that there was something very like a three-sided quarrel between the young Rilkes and herself. Warm-hearted and hot-headed, she fancied herself neglected by Clara, to whom she was, and remained, devoted. The two girls had been intimate friends before Rilke swam into their ken, and the readjustment of their relationship clearly caused Paula real grief, though the accusations she made in a foolish letter to them both in February 1902 were probably unfounded. She reproached Clara with trampling her heart underfoot, and Rilke with dominating his wife spiritually and keeping her in golden chains. It is an affected letter, written in a high-flown style, and the praise of her own simple, faithful, German heart must have particularly exasperated the young couple. Rilke's answer comes as a shock after the perusal of the Worpswede diary and letters. It is surprisingly, disconcertingly adult, dignified and extremely aloof; written with a great show of reasonableness, but calculated to make her smart. More in sorrow than in anger, he reminded her that artists need solitude for their work; that Clara was going through an important phase of her aesthetic development; and that Paula was lacking in love and understanding not to realise that and humbly await developments, as he was doing.

Thereafter love and life, so different from anything the young Worpswedians had imagined, continued to weave the warp and woof of the emotional relationship between all three. If they were not capable of loving each other passionately and purely under the shadow of Beethoven and Boecklin all their lives, as Paula had piteously implored them to do, nevertheless art was also entangled in the web which alternately drew them together and pulled them apart. Rilke continued to write long, friendly and admiring letters to Otto Modersohn, for whose art he had a genuine and exaggerated respect.[1] Poor little Paula continued to hanker after Clara.[2] The Rilkes were now in Paris, and on hearing that Paula was coming over too, the husband wrote in his name and his wife's imploring her to make it up, to forgive them both and to come and see them. This was in January 1903, almost a year after the quarrel, and nothing could have been nicer or more appealing and soothing than his letter.[3] It thawed the recipient slightly, and all three saw a certain amount of each other whilst she was in Paris that spring; but Paula was critical now. She found the couple in low spirits, and very poor company, far too much taken up with themselves to be interested in her affairs. Nor was she much impressed by the monograph on Worpswede; and will she have been really grateful for that letter of introduction to Rodin which labelled her as the wife of a very distinguished artist?

But she melted towards Clara in the winter of 1905, when she painted her portrait in Worpswede, a compliment Clara returned with a sculptured bust of Otto. In spite of everything, so Paula wrote in her diary during this period, she still preferred Clara to everyone else. And her heart must have warmed strangely to Rilke too when he appeared for Christ-

---

[1] Cf. for instance *B. 1892–1904*, p. 293.

[2] Cf. Modersohn-Becker, *op. cit.* p. 170, the details of her attitude to the Rilkes are taken from the same work.

[3] Unpublished; dated from 3 rue de l'Epée, Paris, January 29, 1903.

mas, saw her recent work, recognised its originality, boldness
and ruthlessness, and her strange affinity with van Gogh.
Rilke was more competent to judge such matters now than
he had been in 1900 or when he excluded her from *Worpswede*,
so that his belated praise must have been all the more welcome
and encouraging.

When therefore she appeared in Paris the following
February in need of help, Rilke was the first person she
turned to. The marriage with Otto, a well-meaning but
mediocre man, had proved a disillusioning experience, and
worse than that; it was strangling her creative powers and
suppressing what she felt to be a great uprush of inspiration.
She hardened her heart against the laments of the worthy
widower (now threatened with another kind of widowhood)
and cut loose. Rilke met her train, welcomed her with beautiful flowers, and lent her 100 Marks, which she repaid the
following June. He also saw her occasionally after she was
installed in Paris, rendered her some small services, and
applauded her upward progress unaided and alone. But he
would not spare the time to sit for her, and he refused at least
one invitation to meet her owing to pressure of work. He
also discouraged her from joining him and Clara on their
family holiday in Belgium, and sent her a list of suitable places
in Brittany instead. It would seem that the tenuous threads
which still bound them together were now being spun by her
and not by him. He had warned her in 1902 when he wrote
his handsome apology that he was no longer the same person
she had known in Worpswede. The courteous manner in
which he now tried to disentangle himself may have had
something to do with her next step. For Paula, who felt in
May 1906, when she and Rilke were meeting fairly regularly,
that she was 'becoming something', and experiencing the
most intensely happy time of her life, withdrew her bid for
freedom and returned to the marital fold. Otto, who had
never ceased to plead and pester by post, finally came to Paris
in September and threw himself on her mercy. She withstood
him for a time; but the united pressure of her husband, her
family and her friends proved too strong, and she capitulated

in November. Rilke was in Germany at that time, and probably heard the news from Clara; but did not refer to it in a letter he wrote from Capri in February 1907, accompanying some reproductions of ancient paintings, a gift from himself and his wife. She answered by what seems to have been a very confidential communication, in which she probably also told him that she was with child, a piece of news which she broke curtly and dryly to her delighted family on March 9. To judge by the tone of her letters after the reunion with Otto, she was far from happy in her sacrifice, and by no means rapturous at the idea of her approaching motherhood; indeed, she was longing with her whole soul to be in Paris for the Cézanne exhibition just before her confinement. The letter, which Rilke answered on March 17, therefore, while probably courageous and cheerful, caused him uneasy feelings. Although he spoke of the happy and reassuring news she had told him, echoing her hope that it would all be for the best in the end, he also reproached himself for having failed her when she needed him by dissuading her from coming to Belgium in the past autumn; he assured her emphatically that his great expectations of her art would certainly be realised in the future, and circled rather warily round the subject of Otto and the prospective child:

And if the external circumstances have turned out differently from what we thought at one time, still only one thing is decisive: that you should bear them bravely and should achieve all that freedom in the existing circumstances which is necessary to that within you which must not perish in order that it may attain to the uttermost of what it can become.[1]

Friendly and kindly as is the tone of this letter, it shows a complete reversal of the Worpswedian situation; it was now Paula the artist who interested Rilke vitally, and the woman who left him untouched; and, if she had dealt him a blow by her engagement to Otto, this gentle withdrawal from her confidences must have struck quite as piercingly home to her. It was followed by one of those little pin-pricks which can so utterly explode delicate and fragile hopes. Paula left her

[1] *B. 1906–1907*, p. 225; dated from Villa Discopoli, Capri, March 17, 1907.

Paris furniture at Rilke's disposal when she returned to Germany, and he completely forgot that she had done so until he had been back in Paris for a month. His charmingly expressed apologies, his abortive efforts to sell the furniture for her, and his friendly offer to give her 20 francs in compensation will have rubbed a good deal of salt into the wound. She heard from him last towards the end of October, when he offered to pay her this sum. He was on a lecturing tour in Germany when she gave birth to a child on November 2 in Worpswede. He was in Venice on November 21, when she died suddenly exclaiming: 'What a pity!'

For a long time Rilke was silent on the subject of Paula's death, as far as one can tell by the published letters; but it would have been all the more disturbing to him if, as one critic shrewdly surmises, his eyes had just been opened to the full significance of her genius by the Cézanne exhibition she had been unable to witness, and which proclaimed the similarity between them.[1] That she was much in his thoughts is proved by his reference to a bust of the eighteenth dynasty in the Louvre which he declared resembled her closely.[2] But no such proof is needed in view of the *Requiem* which he composed in her memory in November 1908, and of the revealing letter he wrote to her brother in the spring of 1913 on the publication of her letters and diaries. Here he spoke most movingly about the freshness and grace of her personality, of her ardent creative spirit, and of the shock and sorrow her death had caused him:

You know, dear Dr Becker, how much the destiny of her passing away shook me to my inmost depths. There may have been other circumstances which played their part in this, nevertheless that she, who was so extremely lovable in her heart, should have left us so early, and in so shattering a manner: this was probably the cause that for many years death outweighed life for me, was greater, more in the right, and more urgently my concern than the plethora of

---

[1] G. Scheibel, *Rainer Maria Rilke und die bildende Kunst*, Giessen, 1933. This theory is supported by Rilke's descriptions of Paula's still-lifes of fruit in the *Requiem*.

[2] *B. 1907–1914*, pp. 45 f.; to Clara Rilke from 77 rue de Varenne, Paris, September 4, 1908.

earthly incitements which generally occupy our minds so readily. Forgive me, I am talking a lot about myself, but it struck home to me.[1]

It was not only Becker who was privy to the terrible shock which Paula's death caused Rilke. Katharina Kippenberg, who first met Rilke in 1910, knew all about it, and often heard him speak of her as one who had made the magnificent effort to achieve a unity between the woman and the artist within her. And he would add with sorrowful eyes, that she was the only one of his dead friends who troubled him. He interpreted her death to this listener as the final answer to a final question, a terribly bitter answer; for the woman who strove to attain this dual creativeness was unique among her sex as an artist, but was chastised with death before she was ready to die by the hand of a wrathfully denying God because she also wished to achieve motherhood.[2]

Tenderness for her reputation coupled with admiration for her genius led him to refuse to edit her unpublished private papers in 1917 and to advise against their publication; because they gave no adequate idea either of her personality or of her art and were not truly representative of that figure 'so fatefully destroyed'.[3] Yet Rilke abandoned without much regret his plan of going to see an exhibition of Paula's work in Bremen two months later, merely because he was not feeling very well and dreaded the journey from Berlin.[4] In December 1923 he came across the fifth augmented edition of her letters and diaries, and fell under their charm again, telling Clara that he felt he ought to place *Duino Elegies* and *Sonnets to Orpheus* in a niche dedicated to her memory, so that she might now forgive him his melancholy and everything else.[5] Yet only ten months later when Hermann Pongs asked him what

---

[1] *B. 1907–1914*, pp. 285 f.; to Dr Kurt Becker, dated from Paris on Easter Monday, 1913.

[2] K. Kippenberg, *Rainer Maria Rilke, Ein Beitrag*, 2nd ed., Leipzig, 1938, p. 46.

[3] *V.B.* p. 267; to Kippenberg from Westphalia, August 10, 1917.

[4] *B. 1914–1921*, p. 164; to Hertha Koenig from Berlin, October 13, 1917.

[5] *B. 1921–1926*, p. 218; he used the word *Unfrohsein* quoting from P. Modersohn-Becker, *op. cit.* p. 183; she said *Freudlosigkeit*.

personal impression he had received from her later pictures, he replied baldly and curtly that he knew little of the works produced in 1906 and later and was still unfamiliar with them.[1] This was the final word, and it was inaccurate. The *Requiem* for Paula shows that Rilke was well acquainted with her last pictures: self-portraitures in the nude. He referred to these explicitly in the poem, mentioning the amber necklace which figured in the paintings.

It will be seen from this sketch that the emotions Paula aroused in Rilke were strangely mixed. Worship for her girlhood mingled with wish-dreams for her death; enthusiastic acclamation of her genius contrasted queerly with the refusal to aid and abet it whole-heartedly on its course; remorse, relief and regret fought for supremacy when Paula returned to Otto; the shock of her death was sublimated into a glorification of that state, strangely at odds with his bitter resentment against her fate; finally he could canonise her as an artist-martyr and deny that he knew her work. From the very outset there had been something cloudy and equivocal in his feelings for her; this rose to the surface in November 1908 and formed itself into the strange poem he wrote: that almost frightening elegy, *Requiem for a Friend*, one of the curiosities of literature, and a very painful poem.

It ranks with his letters to Sedlakowitz about St Pölten and to Pongs about Tolstoy as a proof of the tenacity of his mind and of his grudge-bearing quality. A much more terrible and also a much subtler proof, in which abnormal emotions and very strange thoughts achieve an eerie union. The basic ideas of this poem, to be found in his other requiems, are the glorification of death as the beginning of real life; and the notion, which he probably owed to Jacobsen, that a personal death, our own particular death, is allotted to each one of us, and that our highest duty and happiness is to die that death and none other. It was a cardinal point of his belief; in his elegy on Kalckreuth of the same period he deprecated suicide because it interrupted the slow ripening of death; and he would only take opiates sparingly during his last illness so as to die, not a

[1] H. Pongs, *op. cit.* p. 108.

typical patient's death, but his own. This philosophy underlay his *Requiem for a Friend*, a philosophy all the more uncompromisingly held because it represented a hard-won and precarious victory over the terror of the grave.

The virgin's death Rilke had prefigured for the fair-haired painter in his *Fragment* was closely bound up with this creed. As she symbolised girlhood for him, he concluded that her destiny was to die untouched. The shock which her marriage had dealt to him reverberated in this lament. By returning to Otto and bearing him a child, she had incurred the further guilt of treachery to her art. It was this betrayal which Rilke pitilessly laid bare in his requiem, leaving his more irrational, deeper-seated horror unexpressed. He sublimated the tragedy of Paula's lost girlhood into the tragedy of an artist's self-mutilation. He had come to believe in her genius, and now acknowledged it unreservedly, the better to scourge her for wasting it. Nevertheless, the first cause for his physical and spiritual repugnance to her marriage and motherhood derived from his abnormal attitude towards girls and belongs to the same stratum as the *Fragment*. His nausea at the idea of her child-birth is part of the emotional complex from which the poem sprang; it dictated some merciless lines, in which the unclean nature of Paula's sacrifice and the squalid manner of her death were ruthlessly insisted upon. The cruelty of this poetic vengeance is heightened by the fact that the elegy is a dramatic monologue addressed to Paula's ghost, a poor, feeble, frightened spirit, who had been terrified of dying and was now frightened of the great kingdom of death which she had rendered herself unfit to inhabit by refusing to fulfil her death-destiny, and by failing to accomplish her artist's mission on earth. She was therefore haunting the earth and haunting the poet, losing a part of her eternity, frittering it away in a region which was not truly real, and where nothing actually existed. The poem is one long effort to exorcise that ghost. On the face of it overflowing with compassion and loving-kindness, it is in reality the most terrible indictment, and is almost intolerable until Rilke turned from the wife to the husband who had dragged her back into sexual slavery after

she had escaped. These lines contain a skilful allusion to an
incident in her married life which Modersohn had told Rilke
himself. Paula had once insisted on walking along a half-
submerged pier in a violent storm, and he had been unable to
restrain her.[1] Balefully ingenious, Rilke now turned this
tale against him:

> But now I will accuse:
> Not the one man who from yourself withdrew you,
> (I cannot find him out, he's like all others)
> All others I'll accuse in him: the male.

> If anywhere, unknown, deep in my breast,
> My having-been-a-child is rising in me,
> Perhaps the purest essence of my childhood,
> I will not know it. But I'll shape an angel
> From that same spirit, and with looks averted
> I'll fling it out into the foremost row
> Of screaming angels who remembrance God.

> For overlong this suffering lasts already,
> Nor can be mastered, being too hard for us,
> This complex suffering false love brings about;
> Which, building on antiquity and custom,
> Calls itself right and battens on injustice.
> Where is the man who has a right to own?

>   .   .   .

> As little as a captain can enchain
> The glorious Nike to his vessel's prow
> When the mysterious lightness of her godhead
> Wafts her away to meet the pure sea-wind,
> As little as that can one of us recall
> The woman who no longer sees our face,
> But on a narrow strip of her existence
> Wanders as by a miracle unhurt,
> Unless indeed he's made and lusts for guilt.

> For that is guilt, if anything is guilty,
> Not to increase the freedom of a loved thing
> By all the freedom we can find within us.[2]

---

[1] Cf. Hetsch, *op. cit.* p. 48; recounted by Clara Rilke in connection with this
poem.

[2] *G.W.* II, pp. 330 ff.

The virile denunciatory tone of this savage personal attack comes as a welcome relief after the previous purrings and snarlings of the tigerish elegist over his ghostly kill; and the passionate denunciation of the love of men for women, uttered with all the stridency of the screaming angel he invokes, at least brings the breath of the outside world into the stifling atmosphere of the poem. Purified by this cathartic outburst, Rilke drew more gently onwards to a reconciliatory conclusion, in which his own dire sufferings in the 'ancient hostility between life and great works' finally melted him towards Paula.

Many later motifs are intertwined in this extraordinary and elaborate elegy on the death of the 'fair-haired painter' whom Rilke had platonically adored in Worpswede; but the roots of the poem lie in that idyllic past and even farther back. All the elements which seemed so utterly harmless, so beguilingly ludicrous at the best, at the worst so youthfully morbid, in the Worpswede diary were present in this formidable poem, terribly transformed. Even the unreality was there, lurking in the grim pretence that Paula's dishonoured spirit was walking the earth; that the fair-haired painter was now a stained and deflowered ghost, reaping what she had sown. And the girlish poet with his visions and dreams, the ghoulish young man who had played so thoughtlessly with edged tools, killing a maiden in his thoughts, 'cruel only to be kind', now turned like a poetical sadist on the stricken living and the helpless dead. The symbolical rose was present too, flowering on Rilke's desk—wrongfully, like Paula's spirit; since it should have remained in the garden 'unmixed with me', or should have vanished away. Overpoweringly present, Rilke's genius, which had flickered through the pages of the diary like a will o' the wisp, permeated every line of the long and complicated poem in which the nature of Paula's disastrous sacrifice was pitilessly revealed.

The emotion behind the *Requiem for a Friend* is none the less genuine because the reason for it is so strange. From the *Maidens' Songs* through *The White Princess*, *Frau Blaha's Maid*, the *Fragment*, *Alcestis*, *Orpheus*, *Eurydice*, *Hermes*, and this requiem down to the *Sonnets to Orpheus* (another *In Memoriam* for another young girl), the lot of maidens and matrons was a constantly recurrent theme, in which women, 'the great lovers', were always glorified above men. But the indictment of Paula Modersohn-Becker is unique of its kind in Rilke's work, from which personal wrath, scorn and resentment are almost totally absent. One can only deduce some strong and embittering passion which transformed him for the space of this poem into an inexorable accuser, who conjured up the spirit of the 'fair-haired painter' to tell her what he thought of her marriage, of her motherhood, and above all of her nauseating death. Well might a great shadow have fallen over them both as they sat talking together in their innocence and youth about the very subject which was to inspire this elegy; for rarely indeed can an idyllic relationship have had so cruel an end.

3. *Westerwede*, 1901–1902

Schmargendorf, October 23,
1900.

Dear Clara Westhoff,

On that evening, when we were sitting together in the little blue dining-room, we also spoke of other things. There would be a light in the little cottage, a soft shaded lamp, and I would be standing by my stove preparing supper for you: a nice vegetable or a dish of porridge. Thick honey would be shining on a glass plate, and cold butter as pure as ivory would make a peaceful contrast with the gay colours of a Russian table-cloth. Bread must be there of course, strong granular whole-meal bread, and rusks, and on a long narrow dish some pale Westphalian ham, streaked with white fat, like an evening sky with long drawn-out clouds. The tea would be standing ready to be drunk: golden-yellow tea in glasses with silver saucers, exhaling a faint perfume, that same aroma which harmonised so well with the Hamburg roses, and which would also blend with white carnations or a fresh pine-apple.... Large lemons cut into slices would sink like suns into the golden twilight of the tea, their radiant fruit-flesh glimmering through it, whilst its clear, smooth surface would shudder as the sour juices mounted. Red mandarines

should be there containing a summer tightly folded, like a piece of
Italian silk packed into a nutshell. And there would be roses all
round us: tall roses bending down from their branches, and strewn
roses gently lifting their heads, and others wandering from hand to
hand, like maidens in a dancing-game. Thus did I dream. Premature
dreams. The cottage is cold and empty, and my rooms are cold and
empty too. God knows when they will be habitable. But nevertheless I cannot believe that reality is never to have any relationship
with my dream. I sent you a sample packet of an excellent oatmeal
yesterday. Directions for use on the envelope. But it is better to
let it boil rather longer than the stated fifteen minutes. When
serving, add a piece of butter, or eat it with stewed apples. I like
it best with butter, and eat it every day. The whole dish is ready in
fifteen minutes. That is to say, the water must be boiling first; the
oats are then put on to boil, and should boil for fifteen to twenty
minutes. If you order the patent double pot called Do-All from any
big household firm, you will hardly even need to stir, for the risk of
burning is almost negligible then. Try it, and tell me what you think.
The great Californian firm has other preparations. I will send you
their catalogue shortly.—By the way you realise, don't you, that I
imagined an industrious day to have preceded that rich dream-
supper?   Your
                         Rainer Maria Rilke.[1]

This letter, written the day after a yearning poem to Paula,
goes far to illuminate Rilke's feelings for the woman he was
to make his wife. The gift of a sample packet of Quaker oats
balanced a present to Paula of the works of Jacobsen. Yet
Clara had no cause to feel slighted. There is a wholesome
reality behind the precious still-life supper he described. The
ham must have been a concession to Clara, for Rilke did not
like meat; the roses, which could well be spared, were a
tribute to romance. But the longing for the simple comforts
of domestic life, for a truly German cosiness, the strong
desire for a little house of his own and a companion to share
his evening meal were as fundamentally normal and natural
as any bank-clerk's matrimonial aims. It is reassuring to
discover that the author of the chlorotic *Fragment* could cook

[1] *B.u.T.* pp. 56–58.

a dish of Quaker oats, and liked them best with butter. The fact that he was anxious to teach Clara the tricks of the trade is significant; and the whole letter shows, what his previous engagement to Vally also proves, that Rilke had no inherent distaste for marriage. It would have been a spiritual sin with Paula because of her essential girlishness; but not so with Clara. Writhing under the intellectual superiority of Lou, he had declared that child-birth was for women what aesthetic creation was for men, something similar but inferior. In the *Requiem* for Paula he was later to stress the incompatibility of the two and to contrast them violently: the first was ignominious, the second was sublime. But when no sense of inferiority or of injury was involved, he took a different view of the matter:

In my opinion a child is the completion of a woman, and her enfranchisement from uncertainty and apprehension. It is, spiritually as well as physically, the sign of maturity; and I am filled with the conviction that a woman-artist, who has had a child, and has it and loves it, is capable in just the same way as a mature man of reaching all the summits of art.... In a word I believe a woman, in whom profound artistic striving lives, to be the equal of a man from the moment of her completion and maturity.... I am saying this only in order to be able to add that the meaning of my marriage is to help this dear young fellow human-being to find herself, her greatness and her depth, in so far as anyone is ever able to help another.[1]

Rilke, indifferent to Paula's paintings in Worpswede, expected from Clara's genius 'the highest things imaginable'; one is justified therefore in concluding that his bitterness in the *Requiem* was aimed, less at Paula Modersohn-Becker the artist, than at the woman who should have lived and died a girl.

Clara Westhoff's vigour, energy and strength were not exactly girlish. She struck later acquaintances as more masculine than her husband. Rilke would therefore experience no supersensitive shrinking against doing violence to her girlhood by marriage; and her great personal beauty, her

[1] *B.u.T.* pp. 188 f.; to Julie Weinmann from Schloss Haseldorf, Holstein, June 25, 1902.

spontaneity and warmth appealed strongly to his natural man. The engagement which took place early in 1901[1] was the first practical step undertaken by the poet to establish contact with reality.

He had probably come to realise that it was a desperately needful step. In the winter of 1900 he went through a period so dark and desolate that he may well have feared to face such another alone. On November 7 he tried to describe his mental torments in verse, *Fragments from Lost Days*, a series of harrowing similes, elaborate, far-fetched and reeking of the grave. The eruption of despair in the diary on December 13 is even more striking. It is a supreme expression of the absolute misery of spiritual defeat, and enumerates all the pernicious symptoms of a prolonged attack of hopeless mental impotence. Rilke's description of this ghastly No Man's Land of the mind (as he called it) shows how acutely he had suffered:

...such days do not belong to death any more than they belong to life. They belong...oh No Man's Land, if there is a No Man's Spirit, a No Man's God above you, then they belong to him, this concealed and sinister being.

So this is what he wants. Hopelessnesses such as these, suffocations of the soul. And what if one day they did not give way, did not stop, did not retreat and did not suddenly become untrue?...What is one then? Who knows how many of such who are infected with the air of No Man's Land do not live and go under in mad-houses? And it is terribly easy to go under....Of what use are the efforts one makes increasingly nervelessly, laboriously and with less and less interest, like contradictions growing fainter, as disgust overwhelms one?... One becomes dreadfully humble, nastily humble, humble like a dog with a bad conscience....One flatters cravenly, crawling to meet every incident of the day, welcoming it like a visitor awaited for weeks and fussing over it; then disillusioned by its empty grimaces, one tries to hide one's disappointment....One accepts everything

---

[1] The published diary ends on December 22, 1900; except for a post-card in February there is a gap in the correspondence (almost certainly an editorial gap) between January 24 and April 21, 1901, by which time the marriage had taken place. The events leading up to the engagement and marriage are therefore obscure.

that happens, and all the petty, ugly, daily events scream at one like drunken policemen. One associates with menial thoughts, one drinks and gets drunk on filth; one wallows in the mire, and then walks defiled in the company of precious memories. One drips dirt on to holy ground, and takes things, hitherto honoured and untouched, into one's sweaty, swollen hands, and makes everything common, common to all, valid for all.... God is over life and death. But he has no power over No Man's Land. It exists despite his power and presence; it has neither space, time nor eternity; but it is filled with the beating of unspeakably sad and terrified hearts... whose beating is no more real or true than the speech of accession delivered by a madman in his strait-jacket before coarsely-laughing warders and frightened lunatics....

I had to write this as a sign to myself. God help me![1]

This confession occupies a crucial position in Rilke's private and epistolary self-communions. Compared with his account of the meeting with Tolstoy it shows a startling change in the determination to face the reality of humiliating personal facts. It seems at first sight as merciless a piece of self-accusation as could be found, impregnated with all the inconsolable anguish and despair with which saints recount their spiritual sins and backslidings. It was written for the purpose of castigation, and began in a matter-of-fact and forthright manner: 'It is terribly humiliating for me to write down the names of the last few days here; but I am going to do it for that very reason.' But Rilke could not hold this unimpassioned note, nor keep to the every-day level. The confession soared into generalisations, the passages I have omitted being particularly indefinite. Abstract nouns were put into the plural in the interests of greater vagueness: 'hopelessnesses, suffocations'. Fanciful conceits gave an added unreality to the situation. The use of the indefinite pronoun for the first person singular produced an effect of anonymity. Hard facts became similes. Naked truth was muffled in a mantle of poetry. Pegasus had been brought to the very brink of the waters of reality, but had refused to drink. So that aesthetic catharsis took the place of spiritual

[1] Cf. *B.u.T.* pp. 404 ff.

castigation. The fiery scorpions with which Rilke lashed himself were literary phrases. Nevertheless, this last important piece of self-revelation before his marriage shows an altered attitude towards unflattering or unpleasing truths; no longer ignored, they were heightened and intensified, sublimated into poetry. There remained a final step to take: to meet reality in daily life and accept it for what it was.

Rilke was preparing himself for this effort, which he had long known to be essential to his art. The poem *Prayer* which he wrote immediately after his release from his gehenna contains a realistic autobiographical conclusion in the diary which was not included in *The Picture-Book*.

> If I'm to speak out plain: this shall it be
> That I shall henceforth daily call my life:
> .   .   .   .   .   .
> Some craft or trade to occupy my hands,
> A fellow human-being who understands
> That I unnoticed and alone would be,
> Remote from others, living for her and me.
> Fruits of the earth and homely bread my fare,
> Soft sleep, all dreamy, as if death were there;
> And tired with toil, yet every night a prayer
> At the sun's setting.[1]

From the germ of a supper-party in his own little house, the idea of a life shared in common with Clara had grown with the tranquil inevitability of organic things. His use of the word human-being here and elsewhere for his chosen mate shows that he thought of her as a friend and a fellow-artist as well as a woman.[2] The simple married life he hoped to lead with her, near to the soil and following his trade in peace, sprang from the same source which had made him dream of becoming a Russian peasant; but the Germanised ideal was so modest and so capable of realisation that even the Weird Sisters could hardly withhold such a boon. Grimly they granted it. Before

---

[1] *B.u.T.* pp. 407 f.; dated December 13, 1900 at midnight.

[2] Cf. *B.u.T.* pp. 188 f.; and pp. 165 f., where his use of *Mensch* for Clara misled Angelloz into believing that he was complaining to Paula about Clara's treatment of him: J.-F. Angelloz, *op. cit.* p. 127.

the end of May Rainer Maria and Clara Rilke were settled in a cottage in Westerwede.

A dream had come true. During the first year of his married life Rilke repeatedly told Clara that now he no longer needed Russia.[1] Worpswede had sapped his allegiance to his spiritual home; Westerwede conquered it. His Russian studies were now pursued with a utilitarian end in view; dreams were ministering to reality. The reality itself was sufficiently like Russia to make the transition easy. The flat, seemingly limitless country, the loneliness and remoteness, the approximation to peasant life, the *samovar* and the 'Russian corner' all contributed to the illusion of life on the Russian steppes. But there was something snug and sheltered about the first few months in Westerwede which was more Teutonic than Slavonic; much more like a fairy-tale by Grimm than a *skazka* or a *bylina*. The little road that led nowhere, and the cottage they laboured to make 'warm in winter and cool in summer and safe all the year round'[2] had a reassuring and protective quality the reverse of wild or weird.

The road led nowhere in more senses than one, and the cottage was never really weather-proof. The two young artists, whose ideal of married life was leisure to work, each partner acting as the guardian of the other's solitude,[3] had a hard row to hoe when it came to the details of practical life. Rilke's only talents for this were the ability to cook simple patent foods and the gift to arrange rooms to his own liking. Before he had been married three months, all kinds of horrid little sordid cares were bestraddling the path to the future.[4] They were temporarily driven back, but Rilke was all too well aware that his wage-earning capacity was practically nil, like that of 'all those who are born out of due time'.[5] His efforts to

[1] Mövius, *op. cit.* p. 75; based on a communication made to the author by Carl Sieber, Rilke's son-in-law.

[2] Cf. *B.u.T.* p. 118; to F. v. Reventlov from Westerwede, November 12, 1901; and the tale of the three little pigs.

[3] *B.u.T.* pp. 107 f.; to Emmanuel von Bodman from Westerwede, August 17, 1901.

[4] *B.u.T.* pp. 109 f.; to A. Holitscher from Westerwede, August 26, 1901.

[5] *B.u.T.* p. 120; to F. v. Reventlov from Westerwede, November 12, 1901.

turn his knowledge of Russian into a marketable commodity were not crowned with much success; his proposed 'Maeterlinck evenings' dwindled down to one; and his casual reviewing was financially negligible. There was some hope that Clara might achieve a one-man exhibition in Bremen, and sell some sculptures. She had been very busy during the summer, but was now hampered by pregnancy and gave birth to a little daughter, Ruth, on December 12, 1901. The infant was rapturously welcomed by her young parents, who hardly realised at first that she was an added financial burden. They had been living so far almost entirely on the allowance Rilke's father made them, which just sufficed to keep the wolf from the door. Towards the end of December or the beginning of January Rilke was warned by his father that the allowance would have to cease after the middle of 1902.

The letters Rilke wrote after this bomb-shell had shaken his confidence are extremely interesting.[1] They were dictated, as he said, by terror which stood whispering just behind him, so that he could hear every word. This panic of the financial waters rising round all three and threatening to drown them was so great that he threw reticence to the winds and revealed the whole piteous truth of his financial insecurity; importuning his correspondents (as he put it twice) much as one would waken a sleeper roughly if the house were on fire or if someone were dying. For the imminent catastrophe resembled the gutting of his cottage, which he hardly felt that he could survive. He was in a state of spiritual panic at the prospect of losing the emotional security of his life with Clara in their lonely little house on the moors, where he was protected from the sordid side of reality because he was isolated from it, far from the squalor and turmoil of towns and the ugliness of crowded humanity. This miniature fortress was not built to withstand the assaults of real life. The garrison, already half starved out, would have to surrender unless some desperate

[1] Cf. particularly: *B.u.T.* pp. 135–138, 138–146, 146–153; letters written early in January 1902 to Carl Mönckeberg, editor of the Hamburg journal *Lotse*; to Gustav Pauli, director of the Bremen art-museum; and to Pol de Mont, Dutch professor and editor of *Kunst en Leven* (*Art and Life*).

sortie were made. This was the cruel situation. If Rilke was to
keep his home together, he must leave it for an indefinite
period and go out into the world; abandoning the refuge he
had only just discovered, that ideal combination of companionship and solitude, of creative leisure and a natural life
which were the daily bread of his art. All this he must barter
away for a mess of pottage.

It was the second time that life had appeared to Rilke in a
definitely hostile guise. He had evaded its cruelty at school
first by escaping into Christianity (an action of which he was
later very much ashamed) and then by illness. Neither refuge
could avail him now, since both would have injured his
genius, which like a wild creature caught behind iron bars
went pacing and padding, twisting and turning desperately
this way and that among schemes, hopes, plans and possibilities, vividly revealing the nature of the problem with
which artists are perpetually faced: their human need of daily
bread, their unfitness to procure it, and their downright
incapacity to live by bread alone. Hence those urgent letters
Rilke sent to friends, acquaintances and even strangers in
Hamburg, Bremen, Berlin, Holland, Paris and Prague in his
frantic endeavours to make money.

The only stipulation he made was that the work should
have some connection, however slight, with his gifts. He
refused stridently to consider his father's suggestion of a
clerkship in a bank in Prague. This would mean the end, a
killing frost, the annihilation of his art. He would rather
starve to death, and his family with him, than sell his soul
outright. But what could he do? His books, he inaccurately
declared, had so far never brought him in a penny;[1] and now
he could find no publisher to lend him money in advance of
royalties. With a sinking heart one reads his various impracticable proposals and suggestions. What hope was there
that Rilke could save Westerwede by translations from the
Russian; by contributions to aesthetic journals; by a series of
public lectures; by dramatic criticisms, or by acting as an

---

[1] Cf. *B. 1892–1904*, p. 51, for his statement in 1897 that *Larenopfer* alone
had already brought him in 160 Marks.

assistant in an art-gallery or a museum? These were his highest hopes; Hamburg and Bremen his chosen localities; for if Clara could take pupils at home until Ruth was weaned, and then open an art-school in Bremen, they would at least be fairly close together, and need not break up their home. These various 'ifs' and 'ands' remained hypothetical. The faint possibility of a post as art-correspondent to a Viennese paper never materialised; and the net result of Rilke's endeavours to find work was a commission from the publishers Velhagen and Klasing to write a monograph on the Worpswedian artists. He eagerly and thankfully accepted a task for which he was peculiarly well fitted, and which he conscientiously discharged; but the writing of *Worpswede* ('half pleasure, half hack-work') had not progressed very far before his feeling about Westerwede changed.

The whole thing was becoming too difficult; he would have to let home-life go and strike out for himself. He may have been influenced in making this decision by the prompt response he met with when, instead of begging for work, he asked straight out for money. On January 23, 1902, he appealed for a loan to the secretary of 'Concordia', an authors' society in Prague of which Rilke had been an active member and to which he still belonged in an honorary capacity, having been allowed to discontinue his subscriptions in 1899. Almost by return of post he received a bursary of £20 or thereabouts.[1] It was not very much, and was certainly no solution to his problems; but there were other sources to tap, a better way out of an intolerable situation than undertaking hack-work at home. On May 1, 1902, he wrote almost jubilantly to a friend that he and Clara had decided to emigrate to Paris, leaving Ruth with her maternal grandmother, and devote themselves entirely to their art. Clara wanted to be near Rodin; Rilke needed the libraries if he were to make literary capital out of his Russian studies; she hoped to obtain a studentship; he would manage somehow; and, as they would

[1] Information gathered from five manuscript letters from Rilke to Heinrich Teweles, secretary of 'Concordia', in the possession of Professor Fiedler of Oxford, who has kindly allowed me to see them.

live separately (she in a studio, he in a furnished room), there would be no household to keep up, which would be a great economy. Not a word of regret for Westerwede, no hint of repining for the home-life, the loss of which he had dreaded so much. As for his precious solitude, he would find plenty of that in Paris, he assured his correspondent. It was a complete right-about-turn: domesticity and country-life, the 'daily bread' of his art, no longer figured as necessities, although in subsequent letters he duly bewailed their loss.

They had proved too dear at the price demanded by life, and they had not provided that refuge for his genius which he had expected from them. The decision to live a bachelor's life in Paris 'for the sake of economy' was probably not easily made; but once made, it fascinated him with the promise of untold possibilities awaiting him beyond the Rhine. Foremost amongst these was the presence of Rodin, who drew both husband and wife towards him, as they gradually drifted apart. In later life Rilke complained to mutual friends, that Clara wore him out with her vitality. Had they continued to live together at close quarters, their relationship might have lost in mutual respect and affection what it gained in intimacy. They were still united in complete confidence, a situation which survived their partial separation for many years to come, and never came to an abrupt or painful termination. She was his principal correspondent until 1910, and his letters to her are amongst the most natural, confiding and delightful he wrote; they are penetrated too with an exquisite sense of humour, a quality of mind he showed to very few on paper, and to none in such profusion as to her. His love for Clara seems from the outset to have been deeply humane rather than strongly passionate. And now their different temperaments, his devotion to his own art and his respect for hers, were renewing a friendship which their brief experience as lovers had hardly interrupted. Humanly speaking, the semi-detached existence they were to lead in the future was the perfect *modus vivendi* for both; socially speaking, Rilke's conduct as a husband and father was unorthodox in the extreme. He was burning his social boats behind him, the

better to grapple with his art. Circumstances had forced him
to look for work in Westerwede; but very much against the
instinct which had prompted him to declare in 1897 that no
great art is the product of leisure hours.[1] His recent experiences had now convinced him that the concentration
necessary to works of genius was incompatible both with
professional or salaried occupations and with family life.

Economically as well as matrimonially he could only exist
outside the social pale; and, since he could not earn his daily
bread, he must clearly stoop to beg for it. On June 25, 1902,
he wrote to Julie Weinmann imploring her to help him. She
had shown him hospitality and kindness in Munich; and,
being the wife of a councillor of commerce, was probably a
wealthy woman. This letter, a moving plea for the subsidising
of poetry, is also the best *apologia* that could possibly be
written for Rilke's subsequent life:

I realise that I need help, if I am to continue onwards along my
path. I need the possibility to learn and absorb quietly for a year or
two without being forced to write.... I want to go to Paris in the
autumn, in order to work in the libraries under the guidance of the
Vicomte de Vogué, the Russian critic. I want to collect my thoughts
and to write something about Rodin, whom I have loved and
revered for a long time. This is the external side of what I want to do
immediately, a small part of that profound urge towards my work
and its continuous realisation.

What can a man say, who desires such things, without prostituting them and vaunting himself? In a case like this every word
has a jarring sound and lowers the thing it means. One can only say
that one comes more and more to protect this inclination towards
essential, deeply-hidden things; and that one wishes with increasing
sincerity and whole-heartedness to direct all one's strength and
love towards it, to undergo anxiety for its sake alone, and not to
waste oneself on those carking little cares of which a life lived in
poverty is so full. I am very poor. I do not suffer under poverty,
because it deprives me of nothing fundamental. But last winter for
the first time it stood before me like a spectre for months on end, and
I lost myself and all my cherished aims, and all the light went from

---

[1] *B. 1892–1904*, p. 40.

my heart. I was on the verge of accepting some petty clerkship, and that would have meant: to die, and embark on a rebirth full of homelessness and madness.—At the eleventh hour I refrained and clung to those things which even in my childhood I had obscurely and wistfully begun to long for.... Will you help me to attain them, dear Mrs Weinmann? Will you and your husband make it possible for me to develop myself this year in Paris, quietly, collectedly and free from this perpetual fear which whispers in all my thoughts and in the silent places of my heart? I do not wish to be freed from poverty, only from fear, and only for one year....[1]

Only a heart of stone could have refused such an appeal; and although the outcome of this particular letter is not known, Rilke's lot was not to be cast among the stony-hearted. He was even now a guest at the castle of Prince Schönaich-Carolath whom he had known in Munich, hunting in the library for likely subjects to write up, entertained and made much of for six or seven weeks. The ravens who were to minister to him at intervals throughout his existence had already visited him more than once. Vally had financed his first book of poems; his relatives had seen him through his prolonged university career; his Russian travels assuredly did not come out of his own pocket, and he had married Clara on his father's allowance. Society, or rather leading individuals, would continue to see to it that his genius had its way. He was to escape the economic slavery he dreaded so much and go on living from hand to mouth without visible means of support until he began to make money by his poetry. In 1908 he referred vaguely to a succession of bursaries which had kept him going; munificent hospitality and private allowances also played their part. At the moment, however, his plans all in the melting-pot, he was still hoping to capitalise his knowledge of Russian art and literature, and to find congenial work, if not in Paris, then in Germany on his return, if necessary by means of taking a university degree. For at times he believed that he needed some regular occupation to anchor him to reality as well as to earn him an independent livelihood; and he often regretted later the lack of a profession

---

[1] Cf. *B.u.T.* pp. 187–194 for the whole of this important letter; dated from Castle Haseldorf, Holstein, June 25, 1902.

or even a trade which would have kept despair at bay during the agonising periods of creative impotence. More than once he deplored the fact that he practised poetry and not medicine. But he knew himself too well on the whole to believe that this was his true destiny; or that he possessed sufficient vitality to work for his living and write for posterity. From now onwards he lived with only his poetry in view. The conflicts, torments, victories and catastrophes of his life took place, if not exclusively in the spiritual sphere, yet always under the dictatorship of his ruling passion. When he arrived in Paris on August 28, 1902, his long poetical adolescence was over, as was also his brief career as a husband, father and citizen. His genius had now assumed complete control of his actions.

Looking back over his youth and early manhood, however, one realises that this had always been so; and that the modest and pitiful young man, seemingly so ineffective, who asked nothing more of life than to live in a cottage with a sculptress, to have a real home, a real wife, a real child and yet to be a poet, was in fact a sufficiently fierce and ruthless person to condemn them all to starvation rather than himself to drudgery. Behind his gentle language and his timid airs, lurked an iron determination to let nothing and nobody stand in the way of his genius. He had believed to foster it by marriage; once convinced that this was a delusion, marriage went by the board; but so compassionately, so considerately, so regretfully that it is difficult to realise even retrospectively that it was a case of genius, like a thunderstorm, coming up against the wind, as Kierkegaard would have phrased it. Talking tenderly about Clara, declaring he was doing it more for her sake than for his, but gently making it clear that Ruth was her responsibility, he slid almost imperceptibly away; not abandoning her, for she was to follow him, and yet unobtrusively leaving her in the lurch. He was flying from that petty clerkship; but even as he flew, the son of Phia Rilke paused to exhibit himself as a poet to his sympathetic and admiring friends:

For my verses, for the health of my soul from which they spring, I need the open country, wide ways, barefoot wanderings on soft grass, on hard roads or pure snow, deep breathing, listening, silence and the hush of evening. Deprived of that: shut up in an office with other people and stale air, condemned to senseless and mechanical tasks, I should never again venture to write down a single word, distrustful of the disguised voice of my sluggish, ill-used blood, deaf to the dearest words of my soul, whose truth I would no longer be fit to feel or to live.[1]

Rilke would find few opportunities in Paris for those barefoot wanderings he declared to be so essential to his spiritual health, and to which he was always much addicted; but his genius was strong enough to survive an almost completely urban existence for years on end. What would undoubtedly have annihilated it was the deadly drudgery of office routine. No family was worth a sacrifice of that nature; nor was the last of a long line, as Rilke so often described himself, the right person to found a house.

The retrospective significance of Westerwede in Rilke's poetical life is less obvious than that of Russia and Worpswede, which each in their different ways conditioned the development and direction of the two great poetical themes to which Italy gave birth. Russia inspired his conception of the nature of the emergent artist-god; Worpswede, or rather the 'fair-haired painter', deepened and intensified the complex of emotions which had produced *The White Princess*. Westerwede, continuing the trend towards Rodin earlier perceptible, was altogether a transitional period in which reminiscences and glimpses of the future intermingle closely.

Published in 1902 but written between 1898 and 1899, the collection of tales called *The Last of their Line* is merely a hangover from his worst prose period. Mystery-mongering about art; pallid sentimentality about love; a Freudian situation played out to the death between a mother and son; these tales, together with *Reflexes*, 1902, and the sophistically eerie *Dragon-Slayer*, 1901–1902, are all more or less on a par with his previous stories. *Daily Life*, hissed off the Berlin stage in

[1] *B. 1892–1904*, p. 232; to Friedrich Huch from Castle Haseldorf, July 6, 1902.

December 1901, showed the persistence of Hauptmann's influence together with Rilke's longing for simple every-day love, and is therefore biographically interesting. *Worpswede*, published in 1903 and dauntingly discreet, fails, as it was bound to do, to make five mediocre painters seem important; whilst the all too fluent, poetical style does less justice to the country round Worpswede than the more spontaneous descriptions in the diary. Indeed, the introductory portion of the monograph reveals a thoroughly urban mind, which could only achieve contact with nature through art. This book was begun as a labour of love, but it assumed the character of a pot-boiler before it was finished. Rilke himself thought very poorly of it later, and refused to include it in his collected works.[1] Since it made no mention of Paula Modersohn-Becker (the chief, indeed the only glory of the school), one can hardly blame him. It procured him a commission for a monograph on Rodin; and this is its most important aspect in the story of Rilke's development.

The Book of Pilgrimage, written in Westerwede from September 15 to 25, 1901, bears obvious traces of its place of origin; but the inspiration still came from imperfective Russia. The love that drove the monk forth to seek his God was strikingly described as the love of a father for his son. This ingenious metaphor echoed the central simile in the first part of *The Book of Hours*, where God was compared to a vast cathedral still in the process of building. It has been plausibly conjectured that the profound effect Hauptmann's tragedy *Michael Kramer* made on Rilke in December 1900 was responsible for his choice of metaphor.[2] Since it was an artist's tragedy, this is not unlikely; nevertheless, the vision of the coming God was revealed to Rilke in Russia; and if the landscape of the poem recalls Westerwede in the storms of autumn, at the moments of highest intensity the steppe-country emerges again.[3] The key to *The Book of Pilgrimage*

---

[1] Cf. Andreas-Salomé, *op. cit.* pp. 26 f.

[2] Cf. Mövius, *op. cit.* pp. 79–82; *B.u.T.* pp. 409–418 and *G.W.* ii, pp. 235–237.

[3] Cf. *G.W.* ii, pp. 239, 248 (the troika), 250 f., 252 f. for Russian allusions; pp. 232, 235, 244 for the notion that God is being created by the poet; pp. 235 ff., 252 for his futurity.

lies in the Tuscan diary; the ecstasy experienced in Russia was
still the main source of inspiration, but no longer so overwhelmingly strong. It was obliterated at times by night
terrors and day-time panics of a machine-ridden, gold-
worshipping age. The gruesome episode of the epileptic monk
belongs to the same dark region as the earlier *Last Judgment*;
it also harks back to *Tales about God*; for the Ancient of Days
is blind to the frenzied worship of the epileptic until he strips
himself naked. In spite of moments of intense vision when the
union between God and the pilgrim trembles on the verge of
consummation, the main impression of the poem as a whole
tallies with the penultimate lines:

> Ah, but 'tis fearfully long, the road to thee,
> And lost, for none have travelled it of late.[1]

Much might be said in detail about the first edition of *The
Picture-Book*, 1902, which shows an increase in emotional and
intellectual vigour over *In my Honour*, although the themes,
the moods and the general attitude are not outstandingly
different. But two remarkable poems in this collection seize
and hold the attention even more strongly than the strange
evocation of a drifting host in *Angels* and of a ruthless taskmaster in *The Guardian Angel*. An indefinable glamour surrounded *The Son*, the central symbolical poem in the collection,
which came to Rilke on two successive occasions. On April 12,
1900, a few weeks before his second journey to Russia, he
began a rather wooden versification of some not very
original ideas on the lot of teachers of humanity, whose
thankless task was best undertaken, he maintained, by withdrawing into silence and solitude. Labouring in this fashion
over the problem of his own poetical destiny with the pen in
his hand, inspiration stole over him, transforming the halting
doggerel and the platitudinous notions (both of which strongly
recall Hans Sachs) into a queer musical incantation:

> Thus dreamy fiddlers we became,
> Who softly through the door go spying,
> For fear some neighbour should be prying,
> Before they venture out to pray.

[1] *G.W.* II, p. 265.

And only when all those have vanished
Whom the last evening-bells have banished
Uplift those songs behind whose singing
(Like windy woods behind fountains springing)
Is heard the fiddle's sombre lay.
For then alone have voices wings
When they midst silences go soaring
And noises like blood's muted roaring
Accompany the fiddle's strings.
And times are meaningless and boring
When behind vanity's outpouring
No stable empire rules all things.

Patience, the clock-hand's turning slowly,
And what was promised, that shall be.
Whisperers we, he's dumb and holy,
Meadows before that grove are we;
Wherein is heard much mystic humming
(Many the voices, choir there's none)
Preparing for the silence coming
In deep, dumb, sacred groves anon.[1]

The dreamy fiddlers softly playing at nightfall, the precursors of the one who is silent, are heralding the future God; yet the words and the rhythm seem to be murmuring 'death'; seem to be suggesting that true life, the artists' life, begins 'where, beyond these voices, there is peace'. The spell-binding and spell-bound quality of the lines (which cannot be rendered or even imitated in a translation), taken in conjunction with the prosaic opening, is a symptom of that trance-like state in which poetical ideas are born without being clearly apprehended. And it is my belief that there occurred whilst Rilke was writing this strange little charm the first fusion of his ideas about creative art and the mystery of death. Certainly the verses which have no definable significance by themselves were both inspired and inspiring. Six months later a lustrous pearl was found embedded in this poetical matrix, the legendary ballad of an exiled king from over the sea. His

---

[1] *G.W.* II, pp. 93 f.; cf. *B.u.T.* pp. 255 ff.; with the exception one line deleted, one epithet altered, and some changes in punctuation and spacing, the two versions are identical.

son's royal circlet is brought by an ambassador who recognises the young prince by the colour of his hair, and then rides off into the wind and the night. Lonely, exiled, without hope, the banished king listens night after night to the heir to the throne who whispers to him of the far-off land, of the values that obtain there, of the granite town or the tented field where their subjects watch for their coming in vain. This prelude to the song of the 'dreamy fiddlers' combines the simplicity of language of archaic ballads with great subtlety of diction and rhythm and shifting echoing rhymes. The subjective genesis of the theme of exile merges into the universal fate of poets, banished from their kingdom but facing towards it, minstrels and heralds of an order which is behind and beyond all life. The very title, *The Son*, links this poem with *The Book of Pilgrimage*; and since both parts were written before Rilke had seen *Michael Kramer*, one can well understand why that play had such an effect upon him. The emotional colouring of the whole ballad, but more particularly of the strange conclusion, shifts the glorious future, of which he had cherished virile if fantastic hopes in Italy, into a region which is only accessible after death and from which the poets of this world are unhappy exiles.

It is perhaps in this development of his idea of creative art deathwards that Rilke's main evolution in Westerwede is to be found. Another realm, a more mysterious one than Russia, had been chosen for the site of a revelation which he believed it was his poetical mission to prepare. Two months later, inspired by a letter from Clara about the death of her friend Gretel, he produced his first great *Requiem*, in which death was greeted as something greater than life, and therefore a preferable state:

> Life is only a part... of what?
> Life is only a note... in what?
>
> . . . . .
>
> Life is only the dream of a dream
> But the state of awakeness is elsewhere.[1]

---

[1] *G.W.* ii, p. 164. According to Rilke's own statement in the diary, he was merely versifying Clara's letter of which he gave a prose account covering most of the poem, but not including the idea of death as greater than life, nor the notion of 'personal death', nor yet the queer exultation; cf. *B.u.T.* pp. 393 f.

Glimmerings too of the notion of 'personal death' beckon from the lines of a poem more strange than beautiful, in which morbid exultation (another young girl saved from worse than death), macabre imaginings and actual fear contend together. Well might the mind that could contemplate the ivy wreath made by Clara entering Gretel's dead body, the leaves like rows of nuns strung together by a black rope, shudder in a natural recoil from such visions. For the shrinking from death, real death, remained. The poet who was to be famous as the apologist and rhapsodist of that unknown state feared it to the end.

Glimmerings too of the notion of "personal death," beckon from the lines of a poem more strange than beautiful, in which morbid exultation (another young girl saved from worse than death), macabre imaginings and sexual fear counted together. Well might the mind that could contemplate the ivy wreath made by Clara entering Gretel's dead body, the leaves-like rows of nuns strung together by a black rope, shudder in a natural recoil from such visions. For the shrinking from death, real death, confused. The poet who was to be famous as the apologist and rhapsodist of that unknown state feared it to the end.

Chapter III

LATIN LESSONS, 1902–1914

1. *Rodin*, 1902–1906
2. *Paris*, 1906–1910
3. *Playing Truant*, 1910–1914

CHAPTER III

LATIN LESSONS, 1902–1914

1. *Rodin*, 1902–1906

Until Rilke went to Paris, the main impression produced by his letters, diaries and poetry is that of a mind in love with unreality and of a man evading as far as possible the insurgent claims of real life. Neither of these two deeply-rooted tendencies, both of which he inherited from his mother, was ever quite eradicated from his poetry or ceased to affect his behaviour. But the bewildering richness of his mind and the intensity of his inner life are what one chiefly remembers after living through his outward and inward experiences from 1902 until the outbreak of the war. And this is so, in spite of the fact that Rilke's volubility does much to dilute his personality. Beneath the reckless generosity with which he poured out the treasures of his mind to his correspondents, there lurked the determination not to give himself away, but to use language, and a great deal of it, to conceal his essential self. His letters, whether descriptive, confessional or self-communing, were part of his creative life (a great deal of *Malte Laurids Brigge* was first written in letters, to Lou, Clara and others); but he never openly revealed the purpose of his art, until he believed that his life-work was done. Yet his need to express himself and confess himself was so great, that almost everything else came tumbling out, sometimes openly, often camouflaged, and always beautifully arranged. The great difficulty the reader has to face is to keep his mind open and alert beneath this torrent of mellifluous words; whilst only a superhuman memory could retain all the striking, fascinating and poetical things which Rilke said in his letters. Some of them nevertheless were reiterated so often and with so much force, that they cannot be forgotten; and it is on this mere skeleton of the multitudinous happenings in Rilke's mind that the rest of this biography is written.

The revelation of Paris was the first great experience Rilke underwent on his arrival, and it was to prove fateful. It terrified and fascinated him from the outset, although undoubtedly fear and dismay outweighed every other emotion at first. The lifelong relationship between the poet and this city was so deep and so strange as to throw into vivid relief the relative unimportance of his Russian romance.

Rilke disliked and distrusted modern life; he feared and despised its strident industrialism, its mechanisation, its sensationalism and its tawdry pleasures. For this reason he felt a deep aversion for big towns which create most of these phenomena and maintain them at their highest pitch of intensity. Yet the great modern city *par excellence* put a lasting spell upon him. He nearly escaped for ever in July 1903 after undergoing his terrible initiation; but Rodin pulled him back in September 1905; and after that, whenever he broke away or was forced away by circumstances, he pined to return; and either reproached himself bitterly for having left, or lamented the lot which kept him away. There are few 'oughts' in Rilke's vocabulary; so that the recurrent phrases: 'I ought to have stayed in Paris', or 'I ought to go back', have a special significance. Paris stood for whatever of continuity there was in his life, and therefore for something which the many strange and beautiful places he visited could not supply. There was more in it than that, however. In spite of all Rilke's subsequent experiments to find the ideal environment for his creative life, he was uneasily aware that he had found it in Paris, which was personally so overwhelming to him that again and again he cut short the flow of inspiration and sought relief in prolonged and frequent absences, which generally did him more harm than good.

Paris nearly broke him at first by forcing him to contemplate and assimilate the appalling misery and inhumanity of existence as a whole. It was a disintegrating experience, for it threatened to destroy the illusion of tragic solitude which had upheld him since his school-days; and which had not been really dispelled by his fancied brotherhood with Russian peasants or by his marriage-lines. He now experienced a terrifying feeling of solidarity with the submerged millions of life; and he felt for Paris, which was the medium of the revelation, something which might be likened to nostalgic horror of a bottomless abyss. The spiritual drama engendered by this dual emotion played havoc in his mind; now one, now the other aspect had the upper hand, but they rarely came to terms.

Hardly had he arrived before he received the full impact of an impression totally different from the effect which great, crowded, bustling cities generally make on the newcomer. He was struck by the presence of the numerous hospitals in his vicinity; they seemed to him the most conspicuous feature of the town. Everywhere he looked he saw sick persons either walking or driving to a hospital. He saw them staring out into the street from the windows of the Hôtel-Dieu. And suddenly he awoke to the realisation that Paris harboured 'regiments of sick, armies of dying, and nations of dead'.[1] It was a lasting impression, to which he constantly referred in later letters; for it was the first time any city had affected him in this way, as he also emphatically declared. It bred an obsession so great that the wish to fight it was atrophied; but at the same time an intuition that if he could begin to work in Paris, he would get very deep down indeed; that this 'abyss of ruthlessness, frivolity and artificiality' with its death-dance gaiety was pulling him down, down into his work.[2] When he left in July 1903 with no definite plans to return, he said that it had been like the military academy all over again: an inexpressibly terrifying experience of the 'unutterable confusion of what is called life'.[3] But he also realised that he had been torn out of himself into the lives of the suffering and the poor, 'through all their lives, through all their burdened lives'.[4] Further, the ugliness and pain, because of their very

---

[1] *B. 1902–1906*, p. 24; to Clara Rilke from 11 rue Toullier, Paris, August 31, 1902.

[2] *Z.B.*; to Oskar Zwintscher from 3 rue de l'Abbé de l'Epée, Paris, October 18, 1902, not paginated.

[3] *B. 1902–1906*, p. 97; to Lou Andreas-Salomé from Worpswede, July 18, 1903.

[4] *B. 1902–1906*, p. 102; to the same correspondent in the same letter.

greatness, had affected him like beauty, so that they 'became a world in a great, eternal space, and there was no turning away from it, just as there is no turning away from life'.[1]

Nevertheless, had it not been for Rodin, it is doubtful whether Rilke would have been able to endure all this at first. The sculptor was sixty-two years of age when the poet, aged twenty-seven, made his acquaintance in September 1902. The thirty-five years which separated them caused Rilke to regard Rodin almost as an octogenarian, an attitude singularly at variance with his descriptions of a hale and hearty genius in the very prime of his powers, but marking the excessive reverence of the younger man. Born of the people and endowed with that strong sanity and sense of reality of those whose life is conditioned by poverty and hardship, Rodin's existence had been one of stubborn endurance and heroic labour. This was now being crowned by achievement and rewarded by a renown perilously bordering on notoriety. It had been ushered in by storms and even hurricanes of hostility and abuse, aroused by the reckless sincerity of his outlook and the remarkable originality of his technique. The Balzac affray, which ran the *affaire* Dreyfus very close in popular interest and even became involved in it, had hardly yet died down when Rilke came to Paris. And that other 'affair', the tragic passion of Rodin's life, was not yet and never was to be eradicated from his heart, although his refusal to sacrifice Rose Beuret had brought it to a tragic end. In feeling himself to be indissolubly bound to the woman who had shared his whole life with him, he gave proof of that moral beauty and rock-like strength of character which radiated from him then. Serenity, goodness of heart, simplicity, patience and humility seemed also to be outstanding characteristics; nevertheless, he could be hard, imperious, even tyrannical to his intimates, for the years of colossal struggles and conflicts were beginning to tell. But his complete absorption in his art, his 'work' as he preferred to call it, favoured an apparent imperturbability which even the agitated, nervous, wildly jealous and irrational Rose

[1] *B. 1902–1906*, pp. 134 f.; to Arthur Holitscher from Villa Strohl-Fern, Rome, December 19, 1903.

could not often shake. This had its unyielding side; for, as Rilke quoted in his monograph on Rodin, 'the hero is he who is immovably centred'. In dramatic contrast with the phenomenal patience and calm which produced his works are those works themselves, in which passion and movement abound, and which are endowed with intenser energy and more dynamic life than ordinary human beings possess.

Rilke, who had come to Paris chiefly in order to write the monograph on Rodin which Richard Muther had commissioned from him, was predisposed to worship the sculptor and his works on trust, for he had seen very little of his art. It is not too much to say that the revelation of Rodin's personality and achievement enslaved him. He prostrated himself and adored week after week, month after month and year after year. Clara received almost daily epistles at first, filled with ecstatic descriptions of his idol. Rodin's letters to Rilke were unfortunately lost during the war; those which he received from the poet are of greater biographical than intrinsic interest. Rapturous and humble in tone, they are rather monotonous and suffer from being written in an alien idiom which Rilke took years to master. He found the foreign language a great bar between himself and Rodin. Not only was it a strain to follow what the Frenchman was saying; but, strain how he might, Rilke could never really say what he wanted to express. Nor could he communicate his own art to the sculptor, who knew no German, and remained in contented ignorance of the work of the poet who was so deeply inspired by his own. Kindly, benevolent and well-disposed, Rodin showed Rilke a good deal of hospitality during the latter's first few months in Paris. He allowed him to spend whole days in Meudon contemplating the statues assembled there, and reading newspaper files about his work; he was also willing enough to talk to him, but one rather doubts whether he was really aware of him:

After lunch...I went into the garden with Rodin, and we sat down on a bench with a wonderful wide view over the park. The little girl (I think she must be Rodin's daughter) had come out with us, though he paid no attention to her. Nor did the child seem to expect it. She sat down on the path not far away from us, and began searching slowly and sadly for curious stones in the gravel. Sometimes she came up to us and looked at Rodin's mouth if he was speaking, or at mine if I happened to be saying anything. Once too she brought a violet. Her little hand laid it shyly on Rodin's; she wanted to insinuate it somehow into his or to secure it there. But the hand was like stone. Rodin only glanced perfunctorily at the violet and then looked away from the timid little hand, from the flower, from the child, from the whole short moment of love with looks absorbed by those things which seem to be continually forming themselves in his mind.[1]

A closer parallel than the one between Rodin's early attitude to Rilke and his behaviour with the child and the violet could hardly be found. Utterly absorbed in his own creative life, the master barely noticed the gift of devotion proffered by this timid disciple. He neither accepted nor rejected it; he let it lie, and went on dreaming his sculptural dreams. This detachment was probably salutary for the young poet who was staggering under the impact of the pavilion at Meudon, which housed 'a century of achievement, an army of work'.[2] Whilst he was assimilating this strange new world, a more emotional attitude on its creator's part would have added greatly to the strain. As it was, Rilke could contemplate the master as if he were one of his own works.

He believed that he recognised two great guiding principles in Rodin's life, one of which confirmed him in his own convictions, and another which completely revolutionised his attitude towards aesthetic creation. Surveying the discomfort of the household at Meudon, where friction was by no means rare, and remembering Tolstoy's still more volcanic homestead and his own domestic difficulties, Rilke found the highest sanction for having abandoned his home. He did not see far enough into Rodin's very human and deeply affectionate feelings for Rose; he knew nothing about the great passion which had been sacrificed, not to art, but to the stable and

---

[1] *B. 1902-1906*, pp. 32 f.; to Clara Rilke from 11 rue Toullier, Paris, September 5, 1902.

[2] *B. 1902-1906*, p. 28; to Clara Rilke from 11 rue Toullier, Paris, September 2, 1902.

permanent relationship which continued unbroken through many vicissitudes until the sculptor's tragic end. Paying scant attention to Rodin's statement 'il faut avoir une femme', he deduced from the words, 'les amis s'empêchent. Il est mieux d'être seul...il faut travailler, rien que travailler', the maxim that artists must sacrifice their human relationships to their art:

Either happiness or art....Great men have all allowed their lives to be overgrown like a disused path, and have put everything into their art. Their lives have become stunted like an organ they no longer need.[1]

His daily life and the people which belong to it are there like an empty river-bed through which the stream of his life no longer flows; but there is nothing sad about that, for near by is to be heard the great rushing and the mighty course of the river which refused to divide itself into two arms....And I believe...that this is as it ought to be....For should we not be like rivers which do not flow into canals and bring water to meadows? Should we not keep ourselves intact and go rushing onwards? And perhaps when we are very old, just once, at the very last, we might give way, spread out and flow out in a delta.[2]

Although Rodin, like all other great artists, put his work first, his virility, vitality and exuberance were such that they overflowed and fertilised his human relationships too, even if these were restricted to a small circle of intimates. Rilke, far less creative, had far less to give; the maxim he deduced from Rodin's words was one after his own heart, since it was true in the main, as he said of himself at the time, that there was much more reality in his poems than in any of his relationships or affections, and that he was only real when he was creating.[3]

But so sweeping a statement needs considerable modification. Far from living in an aesthetic void, Rilke was extremely dependent on human beings. Clara was still a downright necessity to him as his letters witness; and at the moment it

[1] *B. 1902–1906*, pp. 36 f.; to Clara Rilke from 11 rue Toullier, Paris, September 5, 1902.

[2] *B. 1902–1906*, pp. 115, 117; to Lou Andreas-Salomé from Oberneuland, August 8, 1903.

[3] *B. 1902–1906*, p. 115.

would be hard to imagine his existence without Rodin. He would have been glad in the past to hitch his wagon to Jacobsen's star, but that potential master was dead. He had realised with mortification later that there was no room for him in Tolstoy's life. His rapture was all the greater when he found in Rodin a paternal protector as well as a great master, a living inspiration and an incarnate rule of art.

For the second guiding principle which Rilke discovered from his observations of the sculptor's life and from his conversations with him was to rely on work rather than inspiration. The idea that hard, patient, laborious toil could take over the function and hasten the appearance of inspiration was an entirely new notion to Rilke, who had hitherto never dared to write unless the mood was on him. He had done everything he could think of to induce inspiration except to work for it. He now believed that he had discovered the secret to progress surely, steadily, genuinely in his art, and to avoid the despair which had in the past made his sterile periods such a torment to him. Rodin's example and achievements were paralleled by the great Gothic cathedrals of France, which were at least as much the fruit of patient labour as of inspiration. With many relapses in practice, but none in theory, Rilke stuck manfully to the guns of work until 1910. If he did not spend all day and every day at his writing-table (and during frequent periods this was his actual practice), he was consciously at work in his mind, or through his eyes, day by day, week by week, month by month; learning to look and observe; learning the nature of things, watching them, contemplating them, assimilating them after the fashion of Rodin. He was naturally aware of the great advantage which the manual labour associated with the plastic arts offers to the devotees of patient, unremitting toil; and he was shortly to bewail its absence from the technique of poetry; but at the moment he accepted Rodin's maxim as an attitude of mind, a golden rule of conduct, which would found his future achievements on the rock of reality he had once despised so much.

Meanwhile, if both Paris and Rodin were ministering to his genius, the problem of his daily bread was still unsolved and

was almost as urgent as it had been in Westerwede. Ruth
was off his hands, it is true; but Paris was dearer than he had
anticipated. The monograph on Worpswede had been well
paid; but the essay on Rodin only brought in 150 Marks; and
Rilke was still facing the cruel dilemma of prostituting or
renouncing his art. But his instinct for self-preservation was
already developing into an almost uncanny flair for potential
saviours and benefactors; and he was not slow to recognise
the possibilities latent in the enthusiastic interest felt for him
and his writings by the Swedish author Ellen Key. She had
succumbed utterly to his *Tales about God* which had appeared
almost simultaneously with her *Century of the Child*. Born in
1849, she was twenty-six years older than Rilke; philan-
thropic and warm-hearted; a sentimentalist of the deepest dye,
an ardent champion of womanhood, motherhood, childhood
and love. Having heard through mutual friends of the situation of the young Rilkes, she eagerly began to suggest
arrangements by which Ruth might live with them in Paris,
the notion of the child being separated from its parents
shocking her profoundly. Neither husband nor wife wanted
Ruth at this juncture, however, both being utterly absorbed
in their work, and rightly of the opinion that Paris was hardly
the ideal environment for infant life. It was this aspect of the
situation which Rilke mournfully stressed in his answer to
Ellen Key's unwelcome proposal, pointing out the undesira-
bility of her plan for all three, but at the same time drawing
such a pathetic picture of their poverty and homelessness as
might induce her sympathy to flow into more practical
channels. It was a wistful, clinging letter, followed by others
in the same vein in which he also underlined the affinity with
the North inborn in Clara and himself and made her privy to
the wretched state of his health.

He was indeed so much enfeebled by the strain of Paris,
Rodin's overwhelming personality and repeated bouts of
influenza that he fled to Viareggio in March 1903 to submit
himself to the healing powers of the sea. His monograph on
Rodin was published during his absence and placed in the
master's hands by the author's wife. In answer to a graceful

10-2

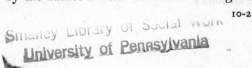

acknowledgment Rilke declared that the sculptor's good-will was his fatherland, and that he must never lose it, for he would need it all his life.[1] This was by no means a mere phrase, as is shown by his tribute to Rodin in a letter to the young poet Kappus at the same time:

If I am to say from whom I learnt anything about the nature of aesthetic creation, its depths and its eternity, then there are only two names I can name: that of *Jacobsen*, the great, great poet, and that of *Auguste Rodin*, the sculptor, who has not his equal among living artists.[2]

Nevertheless, the letters from Viareggio, refreshingly full of the sun and the sea, of sun-bathing and bathing, of winds and storms, and containing allusions to Jacobsen and the Bible, no longer betray the previous obsession with Rodin. Perhaps the publication of the monograph had cleared the air a little; more likely still it was the much-needed absence and the sound and sight of the sea, which he loved passionately, which had accompanied the *Maidens' Songs* and *The White Princess* with its murmurings, and which now rose and fell and ebbed and flowed, whilst Rilke, exalted and inspired, wrote down in seven days (April 13–20) *The Book of Poverty and Death* in exactly the same manner as he had written the first two parts of *The Book of Hours*: neither laboriously, nor patiently, but in the throes of poetic inspiration, for which on this occasion he neither toiled nor span.

Rilke might well be peculiarly open to inspiration on the subject of poverty. The shoe was pinching him abominably; and unless someone came to the rescue the petty clerkship, still hanging Damocles-fashion over his head, would fall and end him. In an immensely long confessional letter to Ellen Key, he indulged himself in a positive orgy of self-pity, obviously hoping for relief from her. His pitiable childhood, his unmaternal mother, his loving but uncomprehending father on whom he was still financially dependent and who was urging him to enter that bank; his dire distress, and his

---

[1] *L.R.* p. 29; to Rodin from Hôtel Florence, Viareggio, April 25, 1903.

[2] *D.B.* p. 16; to Kappus from Hôtel Florence, Viareggio, April 5, 1903. The italics are Rilke's.

need for a human being who would understand his desperate
straits and yet not think him a beggar; his certainty that it
was not the voice of 'real life' which was calling him to
surrender the things of the spirit for the things of the flesh;
all this was poured out with an eloquence which throws the
earlier begging letter to Julie Weinmann quite into the shade;
and is all the more irresistible because Rilke did not ask
outright for money, but for sympathy, encouragement and
advice.[1] In this he was well-inspired; for Ellen Key, by no
means a rich woman, was parsimonious in the extreme; and
though this letter did not fail of its effect, nothing occurred
immediately to put poor Rilke at ease. He was, therefore, by
no means out of the wood when he returned to Paris in May.
Of the two months which this second visit lasted little is
known, except that Rilke's health was not re-established by
Viareggio, and that both he and Clara suffered greatly from
the heat. She had joined him in Paris in the autumn of 1902,
but had not accompanied him to Italy; and they now both
decided to leave Paris earlier than they had originally planned.
Rilke wrote to Rodin on June 23, announcing his departure on
July 1, and asking for several favours. He begged Rodin to
visit them in Clara's studio in order to see her work, and to
listen, although he would not be able to understand them,
to some of Rilke's poems. Finally his help was wanted to
procure for Clara a bursary from the Bremen senate, merely a
formal statement that she was a suitable person to receive
such a grant to aid her in the pursuit of her studies. I do not
know whether or not Rodin answered this letter, came to the
studio or wrote the testimonial; but it is not unlikely that he
felt slightly pestered when he received the letter. Reading
between the lines of Rilke's effusions, one gets the impression
that Rodin was benevolently disposed to both young people,
especially to Rilke, but that he was not at all interested in the
gifts or the career of his sometime pupil Clara. Rilke was
continually trying to create an interest where none existed:
writing in the name of his wife, and begging Rodin to notice
her, to encourage her, to look at her work, or simply recalling

[1] *B. 1892–1904*, pp. 328–342; to Ellen Key from Viareggio, April 3, 1903.

her to his memory. It was all done gracefully if not guile-
lessly; but it was strange behaviour to persist in despite
Rodin's evasiveness. Rilke's continual harpings upon Clara's
hopes, fears and desires with regard to Rodin came perilously
near to badgering; and, considering the effect the sculptor's
countenance would have had on Clara's reputation, one
cannot altogether absolve Rilke from the charge of trading on
his friendship with Rodin. The old lion may have shaken his
mane and growled out a refusal on this occasion, for he was
perfectly capable of it, or he may have ignored the letter;
certainly a whole twelvemonth elapsed before Rilke wrote to
him again. Nor did he return to Paris until two years and
more after this letter. He seemed indeed to have broken with
Paris for good, although he proposed a flying visit of a week
or ten days in September 1905. He was therefore a voluntary
exile from the 'fatherland' of Rodin's presence, and did
nothing for a whole year to ensure the continuance of his
good-will. He may have been attempting to keep outside the
zone of an influence he felt to be dangerously strong; he may
have been incapable of facing the horrors of Paris; or his
absence may be attributable to both motives. But he was
evidently chary of asking Rodin for any more favours just
then; he apologised to the artist Oskar Zwintscher in July
1903 for not having approached the sculptor on Zwintscher's
behalf, saying that Rodin had been so much overwhelmed with
business that he had rarely seen him.

In the long recuperative pause during the summer of 1903,
first in Worpswede and then in Oberneuland, Rilke kept in
touch with Ellen Key, but wrote his most significant letters to
Lou Andreas-Salomé, to whom he was wont to turn when he
was violently troubled in spirit. The first of these letters,
recording his impressions of Paris, makes painful reading; it
shows that *The Book of Poverty and Death*, the third part of
The Book of Hours, written in Viareggio and dealing with the
horror of great cities, had not relieved Rilke's mind, but had
been the poetical sign of an incurable obsession. The letter to
Lou, on the other hand, was the first step in an agonising self-
analysis which culminated in *Malte Laurids Brigge*, and was

used almost *verbatim* in the book whose cathartic aim is indubitable. Recapitulating to his mother-confessor what Paris
had taught him during the first few months, Rilke began with
the disintegrating shock that had opened his eyes to grinding
poverty, foul diseases and squalid deaths. He then turned
away from this subject to consider the 'superhuman impression' Rodin had made on him, the only protection he had been
given against the 'thousandfold fear that came later'.[1] His
correspondent, who knew him through and through, saw
beyond the ecstatic gratitude and fervent admiration to the
conflict, the turmoil and the fear Rodin's art and personality
had produced in his disciple. She deduced that Rilke had
suffered without knowing it from the proximity of something
too hard, too rock-like and too great in the sculptor and his
work, a suffering due in the last resort to the incompatibility
of two different worlds of art. Rilke could not but accept this
accurate reading of the situation, but how to escape from the
consequences was another matter.

During his prolonged absence from Paris, it was not Rodin's
personality, it was the very nature of his art which came
between Rilke and his rest. All his problems would have been
solved, if he could but have followed in the footsteps of his
master and built up his own art on a craft or a trade. Discipline and regular habits of work would then come of themselves. Give him but the tools of his craft, and he would make
real things. But where, he vociferated wildly, was the chisel
of poetry? Could it be language itself? Strangely enough, he
seemed to think this suggestion rather preposterous and
hurried on to consider other possibilities, floundering helplessly among them, much as he floundered, according to his
own account, among the books on library shelves. Incapable
of study, completely uneducated, as he seriously believed
himself to be, distrustful moreover of knowledge gained in a
laborious and roundabout way, he yet wondered desperately
whether the pursuit of a special branch of learning, or the
acquisition of general information would supply him with the

[1] *B. 1902–1906*, p. 109; to Lou Andreas-Salomé from Worpswede, August 1,
1903.

craft he needed and the solid reality he pined for. He was now in his twenty-eighth year and, according to himself, had not even begun to write. This is strange language from the author of *The Picture-Book* and *The Book of Hours*; but the victorious reality which he saw in the smallest fragment of Rodin's work had completely undermined his faith in himself. His present search for the philosopher's stone of poetry betrayed such fetishism and blind belief in plastic methods, that one is irresistibly reminded of Goethe declaiming in Italy that he would in the future *make* his works in the sculptural manner and eschew all other forms of composition. Both he and Rilke, faced with the achievements of sculpture and architecture, denied the validity of poetical inspiration in favour of a close imitation of reality.

Rilke took his problems and perplexities with him to Rome, where he lived through the late autumn and winter of 1903, and the spring of 1904, chiefly in the garden-house of the Villa Strohl-Fern which had been placed at his disposal by a friend. Clara, whom Rodin had advised to study here (so he may after all have written that testimonial), lived in the neighbourhood; and although the husband and wife did not meet every day, they found their mutual proximity helpful to their work. It was here that Rilke began to write *Malte Laurids Brigge*, and he was later to look back on his residence in Rome as a fruitful and important period. At the time, whilst succumbing to the charm of Roman fountains and staircases, he greatly deprecated the prevalence of museums and the museum atmosphere, and had nothing but scorn for the flamboyant nature of the Italian spring. Rodin's pupil was making some progress. He noted triumphantly towards the end of this period that his methods of work and observation had changed fundamentally; he would probably never again, he jubilantly announced, write a book in ten days or even ten nights, but would need on the contrary an incalculably long period for each. He also considered that his critical attitude towards the spring was a step in the right direction; his calm, dispassionate, botanical contemplation of the exuberance all around him had revealed the essential poverty underlying the

flaunting riches of trees and flowers. This wilful self-disen-
chantment was a wholesome corrective to facile enthusiasm,
it is true, and was founded as well on his greater spiritual
kinship with the North; but it was carried to lengths which
make one doubt whether he were not misapplying Rodin's
methods:

The nightingale here is really only a lecherous little bird with an
insipid song and a longing easy to assuage. Two nights suffice to
become accustomed to its call; and one listens with an inner reserve,
as if one feared to spoil one's memories by giving way to sympathy
—those memories of nightingale-nights which are so utterly
different.[1]

Allowing for the nordic strain in Rilke, and for those
delicate susceptibilities of his which were easily wounded by
shrillness and ostentation, his withering contempt for the
southern spring was partly due to the mental disarray induced by his efforts at cold contemplation carried to extremes.
Throughout these months in Rome, when he neither wrote to
Rodin nor referred to him except incidentally, the wearing
struggle to find a poetical counterpart to the handicraft of
sculpture went on in Rilke's mind. Something like a solution
was found in taking up again and completing his earlier
translation of *The Lay of the Band of Igor*; but even during
this congenial task, which brought Russia back into the forefront of his thoughts, he felt that he was hindered in this as in
every other Russian scheme by his lack of solid knowledge;
and that he would have done better to devote himself to
medicine than to poetry. Then at least he would have been
real, and would have been able to tend the Russian victims of
the war with Japan, the news of which disturbed him profoundly.

But though Rilke almost doubted his reality as a poet
during this period, he did not doubt the superiority of art
to any other form of human activity. He still believed it to
contain those possibilities of transforming and re-creating the
world which he had described in the Tuscan diary, and which

[1] *B. 1902–1906*, p. 152; to Lou Andreas-Salomé from Villa Strohl-Fern,
Rome, May 12, 1904.

he recurred to again in an unpublished fragment almost certainly written in Rome. It was a rhapsody on loneliness, one of his articles of faith, much in his mind just then, and probably intensified by the upsetting presence of his mother in Rome that spring, a dire interruption to that 'strengthening of two neighbouring solitudes' which was his engaging description of the present relationship between Clara and himself. The whole passage is violently antagonistic to all external happenings and communal undertakings, and ends thus:

If there has ever been a creator anywhere (and I speak of creators because they are the loneliest of all) who in days of unutterable concentration created the world of a work of art; can it be, that the progress and distance of this life should be lost to us, because time has shattered the form of his work and we do not possess it? Does not on the contrary the most confident inner voice assure us, that the wind which was present in the work as it grew has had its effect beyond its own limits on flowers and beasts, on dew and rising mists and on the birth-throes of women? Who knows whether this picture, or that statue, or that lost poem was but the next and the nearest of many transformations which the power of the creator accomplished in its hour of ecstasy? The cells of far-away things ordered themselves differently perhaps under the compulsion of new rhythms. The cause for new species was given; and it is not impossible that we have been conditioned by the might of a lonely poet who lived hundreds of years ago, and of whom we know nothing. . . .

The main difference between the Rilke of the Tuscan diary and the Rilke who bewailed his poetical impotence in Rome is that he had temporarily lost confidence in himself owing to Rodin, although probably to a far lesser degree than his letters to Lou would lead one to believe; for he always put the case (whatever it might be) very high when writing to her. Moreover, after 'that lost poem' stood a revealing clause which he then struck out: 'the reason for it being that my cells are ordered differently'; so that he obviously had himself in mind when speaking of great, lonely, creative poets. And that he had not lost the arrogance which such an opinion inspired is also proved by his answer to Ellen Key's question about his belief in immortality:

Immortality? I believe that nothing *which is real can perish*. But I believe that many human beings are not *real*. Many human beings and many things.[1]

It was also more than three parts economic necessity which made him feel so ineffective and humanly speaking so futile. He was beating his brains perpetually to discover a means by which his work might be made to support him; and was very much inclined to believe at the moment that this could be brought about by further developing his mind at some suitable university. He was certainly in deadly earnest, as is shown by those impressive, methodical and pathetic lists he made of tasks to be undertaken and carried through in the immediate future:

1. The 'prayers', which I intend to continue (*The Book of Hours*).
2. My new book (*Malte Laurids Brigge*).
3. An attempt at a drama.
4. Two monographs: The poet Jens Peter Jacobsen. The painter Ignacio Zuloaga.[2]

So much for the creative list, only one item of which was ever undertaken. A far more strenuous programme was elaborated to consolidate his knowledge:

1. I will read scientific and biological works and listen to lectures which stimulate to read and learn about such things. (I will look at slides and watch experiments.)
2. I will learn how to handle archives and historical documents, in so far as this is technical work and a handicraft.
3. I will read Grimm's Dictionary and also medieval poetry.
4. I will learn Danish.
5. I will continue to read Russian and to undertake occasional translations from Russian.
6. I will translate a book of the poet Francis Jammes from the French.

---

[1] *B. 1892–1904*, p. 436; to Ellen Key from Rome, April 2, 1904.

[2] *B. 1902–1906*, p. 155; to Lou Andreas-Salomé from Villa Strohl-Fern, Rome, May 12, 1904.

And I will read the following books attentively: Michelet's scientific studies and his history of France, the eighteenth century by the brothers Goncourt etc.[1]

Luckily for him and for us this strenuous and not exactly enlivening programme was rendered temporarily unnecessary by the good offices of Ellen Key. To the unconcealed dismay of Rilke, she had made another energetic effort to throw Ruth into the arms of her parents in Rome; it being then neither the time nor the place for the three to be together as he piteously assured her. Was this the only form her gratitude was to take for his flattering request for a preface from her for the second edition of *Tales about God?* If so, it was as unwelcome as the preface proved to be, which had to be courteously rejected when it came; because, partly composed of his letters to her, it threw altogether too much light on the book, banishing what Rilke called its 'obscurity', and what he believed to be its mystery; it was also far too prophetic of things still to come from his pen not to steal his own future thunder. The book was, therefore, re-issued without a preface, but with an affectionate and solemn dedication to Ellen Key. That excellent creature, no whit rebuffed by having two potential favours scorned, was meanwhile giving enthusiastic lectures about Rilke to Scandinavian audiences, causing the subject of her eulogies no little alarm; for he was already beginning to shrink from her 'enlightening' approach to his works; to the extent of denying categorically, in answer to a question of hers, that the black brother of mercy in *The White Princess* had any definable meaning whatsoever. Rilke's life-long desire not to be understood made the idea of Ellen's intelligent interpretation of him extremely distasteful. He took a different tone about her lectures, however, when faced with the gratifying and opportune results: several invitations to Sweden by literary personalities of the day. He gratefully and promptly accepted them and sped away from Rome. The little villa there had been emptied of its borrowed furniture since the middle of April; what is more, he had been paying

[1] *B. 1902–1906*, pp. 162 f.; to Lou Andreas-Salomé from Villa Strohl-Fern, Rome, May 13, 1904.

rent for his lodging, and had been finding his board as well. The costs of the journey to Sweden would be amply defrayed, since he would no longer be living at his own expense.

He was six months in the North, from July to December 1904; mostly in Sweden as the guest of the writer Norlind in a castle in the province of Skåne, and then with a family called Gibson, friends of Ellen Key. But he was also in Denmark, in Copenhagen and Charlottenlund. His letters from Scandinavia are chiefly remarkable for magnificent natural descriptions of the sea and its storms; of boisterous autumn winds and skies; of winter and sledge-drives in the snow. The northern climate and scenery, which he had been pining for in Rome, really revived him, and renewed some of the emotions he had experienced in Russia. Whilst still longing for Russia as his home, and for the right to feel its present sufferings, to be part of the sorrow of that sorrowful land, Rilke's self-knowledge had nevertheless increased to the extent of a confession to Lou that he was not strong enough for the great spaces of the Volga, and indeed had not been strong enough for them in the days when they were given to him. But the plaintive note of self-depreciation was heard more rarely from the North than from the South. Rilke complained to Lou, but much less volubly, of his continued inability to work, and of the lack of solid ground beneath his feet; but to Clara he tremulously and modestly owned that he seemed to be building at some invisible something; not building, he hastily corrected himself, but clearing the ground for a future erection. Actually he wrote the second version of *The White Princess* in Sweden, *Evening in Skåne, Orpheus, Eurydice, Hermes, Harlots' Graves* and *The Birth of Venus*. The last three poems were included later in *New Poems* and are extraordinarily interesting. Rilke called them 'poems in prose' in 1904, so that they may have been put into blank verse later; but even he was satisfied with them at the time, and considered them the most mature and spacious he had written. The months in Sweden, if not prolific, were, therefore, far from sterile. The new *White Princess* alone would mark this as the period of recovery Rilke felt it to be, after the exhaustion which Paris and Rodin had occasioned.

It must have been stimulating too to be among people who took a lively interest in his poetry. Tongue-tied and poetically dumb with Rodin, he was obviously pleased to renew those literary evenings which had been such a happy feature of his life in Worpswede. Before enthusiastic audiences of from forty to over two hundred listeners, he read the educational tract *Samskola*, the Michelangelo story from *Tales about God*, and selections from his poems, old and new. The study of Danish, in which he progressed rather slowly, tentative efforts to document his proposed monograph on Jacobsen, the pleasures of a simple country life, varied by meetings with Scandinavian notabilities, such as the Danish critic George Brandes; all this contributed to an existence which was free from the spiritual panic of Paris and the appalling perplexities which had beset him in Rome. For all this, thanks were due to Ellen Key, who had brought him to the notice of the Swedish intelligentsia by her lectures. These, now printed in essay-form and translated orally to Rilke by Norlind, caused the poet great pleasure at the time, and made him particularly eager to meet in the flesh the patroness of the second edition of *Tales about God*. She was then fifty-five years of age, full of harmless but irritating mannerisms, and probably approximating in her personal appearance to the contemporary English blue-stocking. Once he had seen her, Rilke hardly ever referred to her otherwise than as 'the good Ellen'; and the tone of his letters to her after they had met was less enraptured than before. Still, he signed his letters to her 'Your son', and remained on excellent terms with his nordic godmother.

Returning to Germany to spend Christmas with Clara and Ruth near Bremen, Rilke may well have asked himself what next? For the six months' hospitality at Ellen Key's instigation (if not at her expense) had after all led nowhere, and the same dreary situation remained to be faced. All had gone, courage and strength, he moaned to her early in January; and the next that is known of him is the fact that he was undergoing a cure in a sanatorium near Dresden from March to April 1905. Most people would be seriously out of pocket and

probably much the worse in every way for such an outlay; but
Rilke was born under a poetical star; his sojourn at the White
Stag made him acquainted with the Countess Luise Schwerin,
evidently one of those delicate-minded, open-handed and
sympathetic ladies whom Rilke's personal magnetism attracted
to him in shoals. She clearly took a great liking to him in
Dresden, and a great interest in him; he kept it alive by
exquisite, graceful, plaintive letters which earned him an
invitation to her country seat Castle Friedelhausen that
August. This visit was a turning-point in his life, for it
introduced him to a whole circle of future friends and benefactors: Alice Faehndrich, sister of his hostess, the Baron and
Baroness Uexküll, Countess Kanitz-Menar, Baroness Rabenau,
Countess Solms-Laubach, Countess Mary Gneisenau, Edith
Bonin, and that truly princely Maecenas Baron Karl von der
Heydt and his wife Elizabeth. The *Almanach de Gotha* lay
open before him to use whenever he liked. It was no new
thing for Rilke to stay in castles and mingle with their inmates. He had been the guest of Prince Schönaich-Carolath
before leaving Germany for Paris; and he had but just
returned from a castle in Sweden; but this positive spate of
wealthy aristocrats was a new factor in his life, and one which
was to modify it greatly. That time, however, was not just
yet. Stronger than the wiles of fair women and brave men was
the pull of Paris and of Rodin. Rilke and Clara had written
him a joint letter from Düsseldorf on their way back from
Rome; it contained, with much homage charmingly expressed,
not an excuse, but a reason for not having written before. This
drew from Rodin a kind little note, for which Rilke thanked
him warmly from Sweden. Further greetings were exchanged,
and emissaries from Germany were charged with devoted
messages to Rodin. The latter was finally moved to write a
warm and encouraging letter enclosing some kind words for
Clara, and altogether showing so much friendship that Rilke
replied by return announcing his intention to visit Paris for
ten days in September, so that he might see Rodin again at
last and breathe the divine air of his masterpieces. This was in
July 1905. A month later, having received no reply, he wrote

again from Friedelhausen to find out if Rodin would be in Paris at the beginning of September. After a welcoming telegram, Rilke received a letter, inviting, indeed urging, him to stay with Rodin at Meudon, 'pour pouvoir parler'.

I believe that he was almost more frightened than pleased. He was overcome with the honour, and told Clara, rather tremulously, that it was Rodin's will, and would, therefore, be all right. But he stipulated for a visit of a few days only in the first instance, fearing to inconvenience 'Madame Rodin' on account of his delicate health. Then he set off, timorously but gallantly, for what was undoubtedly the great adventure of his life. He had braced himself for an ordeal; he was received in a manner that put all his fears to rest. It would be wearisome to summarise those many rapturous accounts with which he almost daily regaled Clara from Meudon, and which differ but slightly from his earlier descriptions of the sculptor, his art, his life, his surroundings, and his divine kindness to Rilke. If the latter were so much relieved to find this kindness still functioning so freely, the former had possibly shown on a previous occasion that it was not always available. Be that as it may, nothing could have exceeded the warmth with which Rodin welcomed Rilke to his home; and the proposal he made about ten days later that he should stay on as his secretary seems also to have proceeded from pure kindness of heart. Rilke himself said later that Rodin had wished to help him financially in this manner, allowing him to earn his keep (it is not clear if he earned more) by the trifling sacrifice of two hours' secretarial work a day. As Rilke's written French was far from perfect (he said himself that there must be a purgatory for it somewhere), it really looked as if Rodin's benevolent regard for his young admirer was solidly founded and likely to endure. But he was not making a bad bargain. Rilke's French might be faulty, but his devotion was extreme. He poured it out into this labour of love, and flew off on wings of the same radiant fabric to lecture about Rodin in Dresden and Prague in October 1905, and again in March 1906 in Berlin, Hamburg, Bremen and Weimar. One good turn deserves another. Not only was Clara invited to Meudon too, staying there before and during her husband's first lecturing tour; but Rilke was also given two weeks' leave of absence in order to spend the Christmas of 1905 in Worpswede with Clara and Ruth. Then back fluttered the moth to the candle in January 1906.

A bruised and rather battered moth by now. Already in November 1905 Rilke had begun to sigh, more for Rodin's sake than his own, over the mountainous correspondence to be dealt with; two hours were totally inadequate; the whole morning hardly sufficed. After his Christmas holiday, he was faced with an accumulation of work which included, besides the letters, speeches to be concocted and edited from Rodin's fascinating but chaotic notes. Piteous complaints of overwork now formed the *leitmotiv* of his letters. Then came his second lecturing tour, his father's death on March 15 whilst Rilke was in Prague; a host of business to be done on that account; the belated return, and more letters than ever to be coped with in French. This was all the more burdensome, because there was stirring within him at the time the first steady, consecutive flow of inspiration he had experienced since Viareggio in 1903. Poems were urgently pressing against the doors of a mind doomed to grapple in the most elusive of languages with someone else's letters. Rilke was eloquent to his friends on the martyrdom he was enduring; presumably the inmates of the Villa des Brillants will not have been altogether unaware of his sufferings. The 'quiet inward patience' with which he was bearing his lot may have irritated Rodin, who had been seriously ill with influenza, and who suddenly rounded on Rilke and turned him out of doors on May 11, 1906. The poet had made some exasperating muddle, and probably it was not the first of its kind. He had answered a letter off his own bat which he should have shown to Rodin; and had further aroused the latter's suspicions by embarking on a private correspondence with one of the sculptor's friends. Trivial though these lapses from secretarial etiquette were, they seemed monstrous to Rodin at the time, and after a violent scene, Rilke found himself dismissed like some thieving domestic, as he truthfully put it. Sympathy has always been entirely with Rilke in this matter; for his innocence is as palpable as Rodin's irascibility is notorious. The latter was indeed to turn savagely, irrationally and suspiciously on many a friend in the future, as his hidden physiological trouble became more acute. His friend and biographer, Judith Cladel, tells me that after 1906 he was easily roused to wrath. As far as I can discover, however, the scene with Rilke was the first of its kind to have taken place with such singularly slight provocation. It should also be noticed that Rilke was particularly struck by Rodin's look of radiant health and his appearance of serene confidence in the autumn of 1905. The epithets calm, patient, cheerful, placid recur continually in his descriptions of the man whom he also characterised at the time as unchangingly, unalterably the same. This appearance was undoubtedly deceptive. Rodin's herculean labours, the formidable strain he had undergone about his *Balzac* and the difficulties he had had to face over his exhibition in 1900 had aggravated his latent malady and undermined his self-control. Then came that most demoralising of complaints, influenza, on the top of overwork and overstrain, and the harmless, devoted secretary bore the brunt of it all.

One could interpret the events like this, more sympathetically to Rodin than is usual, and yet keeping Rilke's blamelessness intact. But the only documents available, Rilke's letters from Meudon, tell a rather different tale. For some time before the rupture, he stated plainly to his friends that he wanted to go, because the work was too hard. He had felt convinced at one time, that he would welcome, in the interests of his art, any post which would offer him some security,[1] and had accepted with rapturous gratitude Rodin's seemingly ideal and congenial work. But the secretarial duties had increased alarmingly, and now took up the whole of the day. Rilke was probably too meticulous and fastidious to be a quick worker, quite apart from having to write in French. It was at this juncture that Baron Heydt came forward with the glamorous proposal that Rilke should live at his expense for a year or two on one of his properties, Volkardey. The unhappy poet

[1] *Z.B.*; to Oskar Zwintscher from Oberneuland, August 11, 1903.

naturally felt that he was committed to Rodin, and could not leave him just then to better himself, since his employer was overtired, overdriven, and really dependent on his services. It was in this sense that Rilke wrote to Heydt a few days before the thunderstorm; and from letters to other correspondents too, one gains the strong impression that Rilke was consciously hoping for the end, although not of course for the manner in which it came about. Exhausted as he was and chafing to be free, with a prospect of liberty and leisure dangled tantalisingly before him, his attitude and his mien probably betrayed his weariness and impatience with his once beloved task. His independence of mind, completely submerged hitherto in the presence of Rodin, was reasserting itself. He wanted to live his own life again, to think his own thoughts, and to write his own things. What had once been the proudest of privileges was now mere drudgery, and the erstwhile willing slave had become a martyr to duty. Such a situation never lasts long, and always ends in notice given and received in mutual exasperation. Rilke's self-pitying letters arouse a sneaking sympathy with Rodin. A plaintive, martyred Rilke trailing dismally about the house and fulfilling his secretarial duties inaccurately must have been rather maddening, and Rilke himself believed that Rodin had noticed his sufferings:

It was probably inevitable, and it came of its own accord. After all I had borne everything, even the last few weeks, in mute, reserved patience; and I suppose that I would have gone on bearing it in the same way for another month or two. But the Master must have felt that I was suffering.[1]

Rilke's previous idolatry must have had its irritating side. There had been something leech-like in his adherence to Rodin, from whom his genius derived sustenance and was seeking its own ends. So few people ever wanted to get rid of Rilke; it was so often the other way round, that his capacity for clinging too close was rarely in evidence. Rodin may have shaken him off roughly in the summer of 1903; but

[1] B. 1902–1906, pp. 321 f.; to Clara Rilke from Meudon, May 11, 1906, the day of the rupture.

if so, he repented in 1905 and summoned him back. For the young man who had stayed on at Yasnaya Polyana after Countess Tolstoy had shown him the door had an insinuating way with him and generally got what he wanted. He percolated through Rodin's defences to the extent of obtaining entrance to the sculptor's studio when Bernard Shaw's bust was being modelled in April 1906. Now Rodin never allowed anyone but the sitter (and in this instance the sitter's wife) to see him at work. It is highly entertaining to learn that the dynamic dramatist and the diffident poet both got round the adamant sculptor on this occasion. For it was such a sacrosanct law that Shaw refuses to believe that Rilke was there. He cannot remember his presence in the studio, he assures me (though he remembers Rilke perfectly well), and fails to see how it could have been justified. Rodin undoubtedly allowed it, however, much as he allowed Rilke the dangerous privilege of his intimacy; and the result was a fascinating description of Rodin's methods in a letter to Clara.[1] Almost until the very last, Rodin's kindness to Rilke was therefore extremely great. The latter's reputation for exquisite delicacy, about which all his friends and acquaintances are vocal; the very fact that this quality was so extraordinarily conspicuous and so often put grosser mortals to the blush suggests that some fundamental human delicacy was lacking. Rilke's passionate self-pity in the service of a man to whom he owed, as he believed, his spiritual life is a glaring symptom of this deficiency. Rodin cannot have enjoyed the spectacle of his sometime worshipper surreptitiously withdrawing himself, still humbly on his knees. His actual suspicions were grotesque and wide indeed of the mark; but he had some cause to harbour suspicions against his disaffected secretary. For, secretarially speaking, Rilke was disaffected. His admiration was as strong as ever; but his own genius was now demanding its due; and his feeling for Rodin was not, and never had been, of that kind which 'bears it out even to the edge of doom'.

His dismissal was undoubtedly a terrible shock; but it did not break him as it might have done during his early days in

[1] *B. 1902–1906*, pp. 314 ff.; to Clara Rilke from Meudon, April 19, 1906.

Paris. Rodin's brutality and cruelty probably if paradoxically softened the blow, since this behaviour put him so clearly in the wrong, and Rilke in the right. The latter had obviously nothing tangible to reproach himself with, and came out of the ordeal with flying colours. His letter to Rodin shows dignity, fortitude, magnanimity and a sense of proportion governing the feelings of injury, grief and loss. It is a model of what such a letter should be, except that the plaintive reference to Clara strikes an importunate note:

I am desolated that you should not have thought of her when you dismissed me, not by a single word; although she—who needs you so much—has not offended you. Why must she share this fate of being in disgrace, which has overtaken me?[1]

The adieu, however, was extremely fine:

I shall see you no more—but, like those apostles who remained behind, saddened and alone, my real life begins now, the life which will celebrate your great example and will find in you its consolation, its justification and its strength.[2]

Reticent even to Clara (as far as one can judge from the published letters) about the details of his dismissal, Rilke gave proof to her and to his other correspondents of the same high philosophy, courage and magnanimity. He was not now and never was to be rancorous about Rodin through all the vicissitudes of the relationship still to come. It is this behaviour which has given rise to the belief that he was incapable of harbouring resentment or even of showing proper pride. Secretly he was much too arrogant not to be far above the necessity of exhibiting the latter quality. He had also no vital cause to feel resentment against Rodin; on the contrary, deep and enduring gratitude for the past and hidden thankfulness for his release. His genius had gained inestimably by his friendship with the sculptor; and nothing which benefited his genius could materially injure Rilke. Human relationships were always of very secondary importance to him; and he read the whole situation like a book; telling Rodin that he

[1] *L.R.* p. 61; to Rodin from Paris, May 12, 1906.
[2] *Ibid. loc. cit.*

understood how the wise organism of the sculptor's life must inevitably reject anything injurious to it, and that this was the real reason behind his dismissal, a statement even truer for Rilke, whose genius could be no man's drudge and no man's slave for long. The poet gained more than he lost by the rift, winning his freedom at the very moment when he had learnt all that the master could teach him. As for the human aspect, superficially regarded, it would almost look as if the hard old giant had been dallying with a pigmy, had then tired of the dalliance and had irritably shaken the pigmy off. But Rilke had counted for something in Rodin's life; something which at one time he had wanted near him 'pour pouvoir parler'; and Rilke had found for a time in Rodin the most fatherly of friends.

Rilke wrote two monographs on Rodin, the first completed in 1903, the second and more interesting one in 1907, based on the text of the 1906 lectures. They remind one of those pamphlets, flowery in language and hushed in tone, in which literary men, bewitched by an incommunicable magic, have attempted to convey the impression made on them by the Taj Mahal. It cannot be done. There is a fine passage on the statues in the Louvre and on French cathedrals in Rilke's first essay; and a striking exposition of his own doctrine of things in the second; but neither of them approximates to a direct communication of the effect Rodin's works produce. Written idolatrously in rhapsodical prose, they are shot through here and there with vision and penetrated by Rilke's enthusiasm; they give interesting evidence too of the new attitude to life and art which he owed to Rodin. But the descriptions of the works are mere 'literature', whilst the personal notes are hagiographical. Like all uncritical enthusiasts Rilke over-reached himself in these monographs, which are more likely to create an irrational prejudice against the author and his hero than to interpret Rodin's art to the reader.

A more impressive tribute to the master was the unpublished poem which originally closed *The Book of Poverty and Death*, and which, after lamenting the disarray, aimlessness and feebleness of modern singers and seekers of God, turned to make an exception for Rodin:

> There's only One, a man alert and mellow,
> A giant speaking to himself in stone.... [1]

But this poem was deleted when it came to publication, for *The Book of Poverty and Death* owed its existence to Paris and not to Rodin.

Not nearly so problematical as *The Book of Monkish Life* and *The Book of Pilgrimage*, this third part of *The Book of Hours* does not depend on knowledge of the Tuscan journal, nor on Rilke's conception of the Russian God for its interpretation. The divinity addressed in this poem has lost the imperfectiveness of the first two cycles. Endowed with the definite attributes of deepest poverty, misery and wretchedness, compared to a homeless stone, to a leper, to a starving dog, he is still no orthodox deity; but his futurity has disappeared. He has been banished out of time, it is true, because he was too great and heavy for everyday use; but he is there in eternity, exiled by humanity and howling in the storm. In a word, he is death, whom human beings have refused to recognise as part of their lives. In *The Son*, the poets were represented as straining towards the kingdom of death whence they had been exiled. In this poem death is portrayed as having been banished from life; and the task of the poets or artists is to reinstate him as a God. This is linked up with the first definite statement of Rilke's glorification of personal as against impersonal death. Our real destiny, he maintained, is to die our own death, the death that belongs to us, that we have carried within us since childhood, and matured like a fruit. The greatest indignity that can be done to us, or that we can do to ourselves, is to die a common death, an anonymous death, a death which anyone might die and which thousands in great cities are forced to die, mown down as they are, willy-nilly, by a single sweep of the scythe. The first draft of *The Book of Poverty and Death* was written down on the blank sheets at the beginning of the Reclam translation of Jacobsen's

[1] Mövius, *op. cit.* p. 242.

Six Short Stories which Rilke was re-reading in Viareggio, and the Danish writer undoubtedly begat this strange and puzzling notion in Rilke. 'Everyone lives his own life and dies his own death', Marie Grubbe said to Magister Holberg just before her end; Niels Lyhne 'died the death at last, the hard death' (of a sceptic); no one but Ulrik Christian Gyldenlöve in *Marie Grubbe* could have died quite as he did; and indeed all the deaths (and they are numerous) in Jacobsen's works are strange and individualistic. Rilke, therefore, received from Jacobsen the germ of one of his leading metaphysical ideas. But only the germ, wrapped up in what seemed a mere platitude. It grew, threw off its outer husk, and took on a strange power over the mind of the poet. What Jacobsen had stated as a self-evident fact and illustrated copiously, Rilke set up as a mystical code of conduct; judging individuals —more—reviewing whole civilisations according to their success or failure to achieve a personal destiny in death. The conception loses some of its mystery when it is seen as an aspect of Rilke's dislike of modern life and its levelling standardisation, which forces millions of individuals into stereotyped moulds, and allows them so little scope for choice or personal development, that their lives and their deaths have the soulless similarity of factory goods. Rilke sublimated the sociological problem and made it metaphysical, by shifting the emphasis from life to death. In *The Book of Poverty and Death* his passionate prayers to God to grant present-day humanity the grace of personal death rose to a culminating entreaty for the coming of the Death-Messiah, the man who would bring forth this death and fulfil a greater dream than that of the virgin giving birth to God. Rilke represented himself as desirous of dancing before the ark of this covenant or of playing the part of John the Baptist to the new Messiah in a passage which rings out rather hysterically; and his laboured description of the conception, bearing and delivery of death into life by a man fringes the grotesque. He was never quite happy when touching on sexual subjects; and especially when prowling uneasily round the phenomenon of childbirth, as he frequently did, he is apt to set one's teeth on edge.

Here he was betrayed into bathos by his anxiety to make it clear that men (that is to say artists) would redeem the world, and that the birth of Christ had not done so. Until this deed was performed the lives of men, and especially of the poor, in the bottomless pit of great cities, would continue to be tragic indeed. For in these appalling towns everything that once made life gracious and valuable has gone. The reality, pageantry, power and glory of the rich have disappeared; and the fragrance has gone out of the lives of the poor. For Rilke's ideal of poverty, which had found expression in *Tales about God*, was that touching, simple, humble poverty, which Maeterlinck was also preaching; that closeness to nature and nearness to God, of which St Francis is the symbol. This same ideal had in the past led to Rilke's enthusiasm for the Russian peasants; it gained much emotional vitality by the contrast in this poem between such idyllic poverty and the appalling squalor and misery of the lives of the poor in modern towns. An invocation to St Francis closes the poem, in which God or death has a special and definite function as the archetype of poverty, misery, sickness, desolation, loneliness and homelessness. The fine apostrophe to him as the divine beggar which occurs in the middle of the poem is made to soften his heart to the poor on earth, so that he may show mercy on them, delivering them out of the maw of great cities to nature and the earth.

The third part of *The Book of Hours* forms the junction at which reality flowed into Rilke's poetry, and the waters of two different kinds of inspiration began to mingle freely. *Tales about God*, *The White Princess* and *The Last Judgment* are typical representatives of the kind of interpenetration Rilke had attempted before; poetry in prose, reality confronting beauty, horror in verse; but no true fusion had hitherto taken place. Reality had merely been seeping insidiously into his poetry, heavy with the impurities of the stagnant reservoir in which it had accumulated. It now burst through the artificial dam he had erected against it, and poured its waters into the dreaming river of verse flowing melodiously along; this now swept onwards with a fuller sound and a stronger movement. It is possible that Rodin was responsible for the bursting of the dam. But the source of inspiration was Paris, and its *modus operandi* the same as before.

The thirty-seven new poems included in the second edition of *The Picture-Book* in June 1906, some of which were written in Meudon, some earlier, and some after the rupture, are all echoes from the remote or immediate past. Young girls' voices chimed out again in *The Lover*, *The Saint*, *Catechumens*; the God of *The Book of Hours* raged through *Storm-Night*; individual voices chanted sombre variations to the main theme of *The Book of Poverty and Death*, in *Voices*, *Madness*, *The Neighbour*, *Pont du Carrousel*; the autumn winds of Scandinavia blew through several poems; while others, such as *Lonely*, *Loneliness*, *Memory* and *Presentiment*, echo the melancholy subjective lyrics of earlier days. The power to enter into the mind of his sitters (human beings, all of them, in these new poems) was growing apace, and showed signs of a new objectivity, due almost certainly to the more dispassionate method of contemplation he had learnt from Rodin. This widened his range, as is evident in *Voices* and *Aschanti*. But it is in the last four poems of *The Tsars* that signs of a different technique are most manifest. Rilke had remodelled the whole cycle at Meudon, and had found it a most inspiring occupation as is shown by his letters to Clara on February 1 and 5, 1906, and also in a magnificent passage in another letter to his wife on May 3 about a nightingale near Meudon. This is almost like a paraphrase of the second poem in *The Tsars*, and recalls strongly too the description of the nightingale's song in *The Dragon-Slayer*. It would be of the utmost interest to compare the final versions of these poems with the first sketches; for here, if anywhere in *The Picture-Book*, one would deduce the influence of Rodin and the plastic ideal; but in the absence of such proof, one can only assume that the remodelling included technical alterations. The whole cycle probably underwent the kind of transformation which *The White Princess* suffered in 1904—great increase in power, both in the suggestion of mystery and in the terrifying description of the plague, into which the notion of personal death was retrospectively introduced.

The Son dominated the first edition of *The Picture-Book* by mystery. The poems about Ivan the Terrible and his son Fedor in *The Tsars* dominate the second by their mastery. The voices of the beggar, the blind man, the drunkard, the suicide, the widow, the idiot, the orphan, the dwarf and the leper in *Voices* waver and die away before the tragic dumb show played out in *The Tsars*. There is a fearful fascination in the meticulous description of external details which reveal the inner states of mind of these two entirely different but equally decadent tsars. It is challenging portraiture and stark psychology all in one, and it represents a unique moment in Rilke's poetical life: the hail and farewell between Russia and Rodin. They met and saluted in these poems, and then went their separate ways. Slavonic mystery, music and mysticism for one miraculous moment took on plastic form, as if under the compelling gaze of Latin realism which probes into the depths for truth and thereby discovers beauty. It would have been impossible to serve two such different masters for any length of time. Rilke was halting between the two in 1906; yet gradually gravitating away from the limitless steppe to the walls of the granite town.

2. *Paris*, 1906–1910

Bracing and liberating in effect, the mode of Rilke's parting from Rodin nevertheless threw the shadow of a sorrow over his studious days in the rue Cassette. Nor was it the only shadow lying across his path just then. Luise Schwerin had died early in February 1906, taking with her a personality of great charm and also the sense of protection, refuge and security which her existence had seemed to offer to his. Then there was the loss of his father to be overcome, no easy matter for Rilke who had been devoted in an instinctive, almost elemental fashion to the parent who had really loved him and done his feeble best to provide for him. How little his mother could be counted on to fulfil her maternal obligations is all too clear from his references to her in letters to Clara, Lou and

Ellen; and also from the tone in which he wrote to her about his father's death, conveying what comfort he could, but expecting none, and gently keeping her at arm's length.[1] This is the simplest and most direct of all the letters to be found in his published correspondence and it clearly reveals the lack of a filial relationship with his mother. They were perhaps too much alike, that nervous, slender woman, who wished to be thought young, suffering and unhappy, and the poet whose spiritual needs were grotesquely mirrored in her disconcerting passion for unreality. It was one of those shaming family likenesses under which the younger generation often suffers acutely. Rilke never acknowledged it openly; but the letters he wrote to her so fluently in her own language betray the kinship. Although he continued all his life to cherish an elegiac affection for the parent who was now gone beyond recall, it cannot be said that Rilke was fortunate in his filial life. Tolstoy, whom he had chosen as a spiritual father, was agonising in Russia without the faintest recollection of the young poet's existence. Rodin, once so benignly paternal, was lost from sight in a cloud of wrath, and his real father had never understood him, facts which may well have cast a gloom over his super-sensitive mind.

It was, therefore, emphatically not the moment for the bustling arrival of Ellen Key, to whom the news of the recent rupture had to be broken immediately, as she was counting on him for an introduction to Rodin. Rilke, revising the *Cornet* for publication and preparing the second edition of *The Picture-Book* for press, was unwilling to see even Clara at this juncture; far less did he feel any enthusiasm for interminable sight-seeings with good Ellen Key. His exasperated descriptions of these outings are so vivid and comic that Ellen will be born and live again whenever they are read; but only Max Beerbohm could do full justice to the story of that distressing fortnight, during which Rilke lived in a poverty hitherto unknown to him, since Ellen saw to it that he lived within his means; waiting at innumerable street-corners for the most diverse omnibuses; snatching hasty meals at fourth-rate

[1] Cf. *B. 1904–1907*, pp. 121 ff.; to Phia Rilke from Berlin, March 20, 1906.

establishments, whilst Ellen kept a stern eye on every franc she spent, determined to have full value for her money. But this rather pathetic miserliness, for which her early struggles were accountable as Rilke compassionately saw, was far less intolerable than the way she organised their expeditions down to the last detail, fussing unnecessarily, always on the go, and voluble to a degree. Worst of all were her sentimental raptures before great works of art. Cynically Rilke listened to her gushing away before the haughty and withdrawn Monna Lisa, whilst the Venus of Milo seemed to be waiting her turn. Poor, unenlightened, unattractive old maid; and yet so disarmingly, so appealingly good; she went off at last; and Rilke nobly accompanied her to Fontainebleau, which they saw together at exhausting length; but release came in the end; and as they stood on opposite platforms waiting for opposite trains, gazing at each other across the rails, Rilke rightly felt the moment to be extremely symbolical.

The good Ellen completed in Paris the disenchantment which had begun in Sweden. Rilke's recoil revealed an unwilling sense of similarity with this robust, plebeian, caricatured female edition of an earlier and less distinguished self. His letters prove that her mind had really called to his before he came to Sweden; he had even spoken of telepathy; and he had been extraordinarily impressed by her 1904 essay about him, declaring that every word of it was true, and that much of it had been personally enlightening. He felt very differently now; and her proposal to publish this same essay in German and in a book caused him mental anguish. He owed his reputation in Scandinavia to Ellen Key, to say nothing of all those months of hospitality; and it looked like the blackest ingratitude to implore her to refrain. Yet he did so, not once but twice, in the most piteous manner. That enthusiastic interpretation now set his teeth on edge. He had grown far beyond the stage where she had understood him. The mixture of childhood and godhead in *Tales about God* was a potion, alas, which might have been brewed expressly for her, and which was the chief ingredient in the essay, but it nauseated its author now; so that when, in spite of his pleadings, *Rainer*

Maria Rilke: a God-Seeker appeared in 1911, he was really disgusted with the writer.

Poor Ellen Key will have seemed all the cruder in 1906 because of the fastidious and discriminating circle of admirers which was now at Rilke's command. After the rupture with Rodin, the bevy of barons and baronesses, of countesses and counts began to affect Rilke's life noticeably. His correspondence with them had begun in Meudon; and from 1906 until his death, the poet was surrounded at a greater or lesser distance by graceful, cultivated, munificent beings; beckoning fair ones, princely patrons, sensitive soul-sisters and noble admirers; whilst Kippenberg of the *Inselverlag* assumed from November 1906 until his client died the delicate and onerous duty of providence-in-chief. Rilke's attitude to these many and various benefactors was at this period confined to a grateful but wary acceptance of boons. This at least is the impression derived from his letters to them, the correspondence with Mary Gneisenau being an extreme instance of his general evasiveness. The sickly elegance, the high-flown courtesy, the flowers of flattery, the intangible preciosity with which he masked his graceful withdrawal from her graceful advance are typical of his elusive behaviour to those who approached him to succour him, but nursing other hopes as well. It can never be said that Rilke flung himself at the head of his lady-patronesses. He put out tentative feelers, it is true, and could be persuaded to accept favours; but at the slightest hint of possessiveness he shrank back into a mist of poetry. All that he really asked of life in 1906 after his exhausting experiences with Rodin was the completest possible solitude in Paris. His poetical life had been conditioned by Russia until 1902, and by Rodin until 1906, two successive manifestations of an external fate. Now it was Paris, to which his genius tenaciously, even desperately clung, although circumstances often tore him away.

Rilke lived in Paris for three periods between 1906 and 1910 after he left Meudon; from May to August 1906; from June to November 1907; and finally from May 1908 to January 1910; first at 29 rue Cassette, then at 17 rue Cam-

pagne-Première, and lastly at the Hôtel Biron, 77 rue de
Varenne. It will be noticed that the periods were increasingly
long; they were also increasingly productive. It was a
strenuous, solitary and austere existence which he led in the
French capital; shutting himself up to work every day,
whilst the weeks melted into months, he still adhered to that
almost religious method of life to which we owe *New Poems*
and *Malte Laurids Brigge*, and in which he found a perfect
compromise between poetical inspiration and Rodin's daily
routine:

> I have absolutely decided to shut myself up daily for a certain
> number of hours for the sake of my work, wherever I may be and in
> whatever external circumstances, and whether I am able to work, or
> merely make appropriate but fruitless gestures... I will kneel down
> and rise again, daily, alone in my room, and will hold sacred what-
> ever may happen to me there: the failure of inspiration, the dis-
> appointment, and the sense of being abandoned too.[1]

It worked like a charm, as indeed it deserved to do. The
second edition of *The Picture-Book* and the inception of *New
Poems* marked the first period in Paris. And then Rilke was
forced to leave. He once said in a letter to Clara that she
knew as well as he those moments when Paris tried to shake
one off, like a horse attempting to throw its rider. It would
become unmanageable, giving faint warnings at first and then
much clearer ones; whilst the traitor in Rilke's own breast
would begin to murmur about holidays and a change of scene.
But if Paris became restive at times and Rilke restless, there
was another factor at work in his frequent and prolonged
absences from the one place where he really wished to be. It
was economic necessity which drove him to accept the offers
of hospitality showered upon him by those many emissaries of
providence who seemed to be appointed to cheat him of his
fate. So that Paris, Rilke himself, and his generous hostesses
and hosts were in league against the rebellious genius time
and yet again. On the present occasion the conspiracy was
insidiously disguised as a necessary, even imperative, period

---

[1] *B. 1906–1907*, p. 41; to Clara Rilke from 29 rue Cassette, Paris, June 29,
1906.

of rest; and was further camouflaged as a natural desire on Rilke's part to see his wife and child; but it was ten whole months before he struggled back to Paris which he had left for such innocent, indeed laudable, purposes. In quitting it, however, he had broken through the magic circle of his destiny and exposed himself to adverse influences, all the more difficult to recognise as such because they were clearly benevolently disposed. There was Heydt generously paying for the family holiday in Belgium in August 1906, and then entertaining them all three at Godesberg; there seemed to be nothing sinister about that; nor in the kind invitation from Frau Alice Faehndrich to Castle Friedelhausen, where she acted as their hostess in the place of her departed sister, Luise Schwerin. And yet the summer and autumn wore unproductively away, and ended uncomfortably in Berlin, where Clara and Rilke discovered themselves to be extremely unsettled about their plans for the future, and in very low water financially. Clara was hoping for commissions from her aristocratic friends; and Rilke was trying to insinuate to Heydt that the spirit of the late Countess Schwerin agreed with Rilke in thinking that he ought to go to Greece. He said later that there had been a possibility of being financed in Paris just then (I believe through the offices of good Ellen Key), but that he had lost this chance through his own fault. Heydt was evidently not enthusiastic about Greece; so that there was nothing for it but to accept with a rather heavy heart Frau Faehndrich's invitation to spend the winter in her villa on the island of Capri. He was without the means just then to support himself in Paris, as he piteously confided to Ellen. For this was the sinister aspect of the providential interventions of his friends. They would (or they could) only help him, it would seem, if he kept away from Paris. Obviously they could not transport their castles or their villas to the banks of the Seine and entertain Rilke there; but why he could not ask Heydt (who had offered him two years' financial freedom at Volkardey, had paid for his holiday in Belgium, and seemed capable of being approached about Greece), to finance his frugal life in Paris, is a mystery. One way and another, the trend of providence was adverse to Paris. Its instruments lived elsewhere, and hankered after Rilke's society; they were perhaps hardly to be expected either to understand the importance of Paris to the poet, or to pay him to leave them; nor would it be easy for him to suggest it.

Capri was, therefore, very much of a *pis aller* for Rilke, and its beauty, of the obvious flaunting kind he had so much disliked in Rome, was as dust and ashes in his mouth, until he discovered Anacapri in the spring and surrendered to its greatness and Greek aura. But even this could not compensate him for Paris, nor soothe his remorse for having left it in the summer of 1906, and then failed to seize the chance to return that winter. In February 1907 he declared that he had so far written nothing in Capri; and although this state of affairs did not continue unbroken until he left for Paris at the end of May, the chief product of the visit was the translation of Elizabeth Barrett Brownings's *Sonnets from the Portuguese*. Rilke complained steadily of his incapacity to combine work with any kind of social life, however sympathetic and considerate the people who composed it might be. Their very intention not to disturb him was discomposing; and every half-hour of conversation resulted in dissipation of mind. Complete solitude, more, invisibility, was his only desire.

This is strong language, but not, I believe, exaggerated. Human relationships were, from 1903 onwards if not before, one of Rilke's major trials. It was during the winter in Rome that he first began to show unmistakable signs of suffering under the strain of loving, or trying to love, Clara; although he believed that he had solved his marriage problem by calling it 'the strengthening of two neighbouring solitudes'. But his rhapsodies on the beauty and necessity of loneliness and two letters of the same period, one to his brother-in-law, and the other to young Kappus, elaborating the same subject, are enlightening; and more so still his views about love communicated to the same two men. Here for the first time he announced his doctrine of the extreme difficulty of loving,

and of the manifest unfitness of young persons for such a
strenuous and responsible undertaking. He did indeed make
it all sound so hard, laborious and hopeless as to show that
the spontaneous, irrepressible and dynamic nature of love was
a lost secret to the writer. He may have known it once, and he
probably recaptured it for brief periods; but on the whole it
eluded him; and his incessant and strident strictures on the
incapacity of men for love were hidden self-reproaches. There
were a great many women in Rilke's life, 'offering love for
all their lives', and many passionate interludes in which his
own feelings became involved; but when it came to simple,
unselfish, devoted loving, when any kind of sacrifice loomed,
his emotions immediately dried up; or rather were deflected
into their true channel. On the other hand, he was abnormally
dependent on sympathy and understanding. The most important and enduring friendship of his life, his connection with
Lou, shows that; and the same desire was satisfied to a
greater or lesser degree in nearly all his relations with older
women. He brought to his rarer friendships with men something of the same clinging, twining quality; whereas he
impotently wrung his hands over the tragic fate of Paula
Becker. In apparent contrast to all this dependence and helplessness was his habit of exhorting, consoling and advising
young men and maidens in beautifully written letters; com-
municating with his disciples by post, a modern epistolary
prophet. But he kept such connections as far as possible out of
his real life. Like the Holy Men of India, he was dependent
on a different type of disciple for the material conditions of
existence; and unlike them, he stood in almost daily need of
comfort, counsel and succour.

It would be madness to expect of such a man that he would
make an ideal husband. But, until Rilke's departure for Capri
in November 1906, he managed to retain Clara as his dearest
friend whilst keeping her more or less at bay. Circumstances
rather than his own desires had aided and abetted their
separation; and it was probably not until they were both
invited to Capri that he realised how much this freedom meant.
He had spent all the summer and autumn with Clara, and

could not face the winter too. It was also true that one of them at least ought to be earning money, and that the mother's place was near her child. These two last were the reasons Rilke used to persuade Clara to stay quietly in Berlin and go on with her work; maintaining that it would be something like an evasion of her nearest duties if she accepted Capri. She gave in and stayed behind, a situation to which she was by now becoming accustomed, and with which she was to be more familiar still. A flying visit to Furuborg was all that she had seen of her husband whilst he was in Scandinavia; and during the years 1902 to 1910, not more than three all told were spent in his vicinity. After the first few months in Paris, they only slept under one roof when they were fellow-guests in the same house, or sheltered by the same hôtel on their increasingly rare holidays together. As for Ruth, Rilke visited her when he was in Germany, which was not very often, wrote to her fairly regularly, spoke of her fondly and even sentimentally; but seemed as totally unaware of his responsibilities as if he were an astral body, tenderly surveying some human child, whose destiny was no concern of his. He was often poetical about her, but hardly ever paternal. His kinship with Clara was decidedly closer. They had their brief romance, their devotion to their art and their feelings for Rodin in common. Their aesthetic hopes and fears, their schemes and plans also bound them together. Rilke was a cool enough absentee husband; but he was a warm and communicative friend. His affectionate concern for her welfare, a curious blending of devotion and indifference; his admiration for her artistic gifts; his determination that Rodin should admire them too; his cheerful acquiescence in their frequent prolonged separations; his complete irresponsibility, made him unique among husbands. He liked Clara so much, he cared for her so little. He took her claims as an artist so seriously, he was so utterly heedless of her claims as a wife. Hitherto she had not urged these upon him; but the Capri incident seems to have rankled, and she would have been less than human if it had not. She evidently confided in Lou, and certainly repeated in a letter to Rilke the former's strictures on his unsatisfactory conduct as a husband, father and citizen. His reply is very illuminating, both in matter and in manner. In those evasive, pleading and impassioned terms with which those who are being dunned emotionally offer stones for bread, Rilke wrote an apologetic masterpiece about his married life. It may have been cold comfort for Clara; but one sees retrospectively that he was in the right. There are two letters involved.[1] In the first he took his stand on his poetical mission, and its stark incompatibility with the duties of a breadwinner. He had only married for the sake of his art, he confessed, although in veiled and flattering terms; but his married life was part of his art, and he was still doing his utmost to ensure the continuance of what had been founded at Westerwede—spiritually however, and not in a grossly material manner:

> By committing myself too hastily to what in the name of 'duty' would like to overwhelm me and make me useful, I might certainly exclude from my life some uncertainties and the appearance of perpetually wishing to evade responsibilities; but I feel that by the same act I should also exclude those great and wonderful assistances which have hitherto intervened in almost rhythmic succession, and which would have no place in a recognised and ordered existence lived under the leadership of energy and consciousness of duty.[2]

He was right, as he always was; providential interventions play no part in self-supporting lives; and it was Rilke's determination not to lower his poetical flag that attracted so much interest. Nevertheless, when he went on to assure Clara that a house still sheltered all three, a real house which only lacked a visible symbol to be apparent to the whole world, one recognises the language of the stone-giver, of the emotionally broken reed. Such reeds, however, are broken to some purpose. Rilke was, humanly speaking, but a 'poor, dry, empty thing' to Clara; but he was the vehicle of a 'piercing sweet, blinding sweet' voice.

---

[1] B. 1906–1907, pp. 131–137, 140–147; from Capri, December 1906.
[2] B. 1906–1907, p. 132.

He was also a brilliant special pleader; and the claims of his poetical mission showed up the demands of Clara and Ruth for what they were, very small beer indeed. Nevertheless, sounding brass and tinkling cymbals echo loudly in the second letter, written from Capri to Clara to read on the first Christmas Day they had spent apart since their marriage. Rilke's sentimentalities about Christmas were always rankly luxuriant, though his feelings for Christ were frankly hostile; and his Christmas epistles are among his less attractive letters. On this occasion he outdid himself, retrospectively transforming the snug little house in Westerwede where his bonny little daughter had been born into a stagey nativity-scene, drowning in this bucket of prose-poetry the feeble stirrings of remorse which Clara's reproaches and the festive season had combined to engender in his mind. The hopeless unreality of the Christmas missive evokes such a fantastic picture of Rilke as a paterfamilias, that one can only applaud his refusal to play the part in real life. The more so as his other letters to Clara were generally so genuine and frank. Push him too far, and he would begin to utter streams of meaningless words. Deeds must not in any circumstances be asked of him, for he was totally unable to perform them. He was an instrument for the voice of a God.

These letters put into grandiloquent words the marital situation, undefined until then, or ascribed to economic pressure. Clara now knew where she stood in Rilke's life; but the friendship between them survived the matrimonial liquidation. She remained Rilke's most important correspondent and friend until 1910, although his letters to her were not quite so confessional as those to Lou. The indisputable reality of his feelings for Clara is even discernible in the two high-flown, self-exculpatory letters of the Christmas crisis, which was as accidental or as incidental to their friendship as their love and marriage had been. Absolve him from marital responsibilities, and Rilke would do his duty by Clara, as was evident in his behaviour with Rodin. And, if blood could not be wrung from his petrified heart, the rock could be cloven, and sparkling, refreshing waters would gush out.

The extraordinary charm of his personality, vouched for by innumerable friends, the exquisite delight which his conversation afforded to his intimates, are nowhere more credible to those who did not know him than in the letters to his wife. No one but she, to judge by the correspondence, was privileged to see him in undress and to hear him speak absolutely informally. She and she alone in 1906 was made privy to his rueful, humorous, exasperated yet self-reproachful feelings about Ellen Key. And when the reward of virtue crowned her sacrifice in spending the winter of 1906–1907 in Berlin, no one could have been more genuinely delighted than Rilke. To readers of the correspondence, it cannot but seem the neatest piece of poetic justice ever executed. Left desolate in Germany to angle for commissions whilst her husband was wafted to luxurious idleness on the island of Capri; left alone with Ruth over Christmas to hold the baby in more senses than one, Clara suddenly received a dazzling invitation to Heluan near Cairo, where she was to stay with a Baron and Baroness Knoop and execute a commission into the bargain. She and Rilke met at Naples both on her way out and on her way back, and she stayed for a night or two on the island of Capri on both occasions. Rilke's generous delight at her good fortune shows that he grudged Clara nothing but his own society. The aesthetic bond between them working on his poetical imagination produced some startlingly intuitive pages about Egypt, the Nile, the desert and the Sphinx which he described to her almost as if he had seen them. He even proposed to collaborate with Clara in a book about Egypt, which would certainly have been interesting to read.

Otherwise the letters from Capri are rather distressing epistles, although less carping in tone than the so-called conversations with Leopold von Schlözer, which the latter, a fellow-guest at the Villa Discopoli, printed with Rilke's implicit approval.[1] The precious type chosen is all too symptomatic. Querulous about modern life, supercilious about the tourists (always easy game), these highbrow talks do poor justice to Rilke, even to the Capri Rilke. For Rilke on

[1] L. von Schlözer, *R. M. Rilke auf Capri*, Gespräche, Dresden, 1931.

the island of Capri was so different from Rilke in Paris as almost to suggest a dual personality. And indeed, according to whether he was in the hands of fate or the clutches of providence, his letters reveal either a sensitive and highly original poet, or a self-loving *poseur*. Such letters as the Christmas epistle to Clara from Capri, or the incredibly affected effusion to Mary Gneisenau about a yellow rose in the same month, were never written in Paris, which liberated and sustained his genius. But genius will out; it flashed forth and transformed him at times even in his bad periods, as for instance in his clairvoyant letters to Clara about Egypt, which reconcile one momentarily to the 'other' Rilke, as he sometimes called himself. And how much he was the 'other' Rilke in Capri is shown by the letter purporting to come from our dismal old friend, Ewald the cripple, to Rilke himself. It was written to oblige the Baroness Gudrun Uexküll; because her little daughter Damayanti wanted to pray 'differently' from the other children. One hardly knows whether to be more vexed with the baroness for the petition to exhume Ewald's corpse, or with Rilke for galvanising it. But only on the island of Capri, I maintain, would he have been guilty of this; only in the care of providence would he have embalmed a yellow rose with so much unction, transformed Westerwede into Bethlehem or resuscitated Ewald. On the other hand, could he ever have written *The Rose-Bowl*, that exquisite piece of preciosity, anywhere else? Or have become so deeply encoiled in the emotions of Marianna Alcoforado, or have written *Alcestis*, or translated Elizabeth Barrett Browning's sonnets? The providence which watched over Rilke in Capri had a decidedly female aspect. The genius which brooded over him in Paris was essentially male. Was this the reason why the much-dreaded visit of Ellen Key to Capri in March 1907 went off so well on the whole? She nearly outstayed her welcome, it is true, though she was there for only five days. But Rilke felt all his old affection for her returning, and declared that they had understood each other again, as they had been incapable of doing in Paris. He attributed this to the more reposeful condition of Ellen; I believe myself, that

she jarred less on him in Capri than in Paris for the reason
suggested above.

Be that as it may, she once more lived up to the epithet he
had bestowed on her. He had probably felt unable to accept
any favours at her hand the previous winter, being so critical
of the benefactress. But now, when she opened the door
again, Rilke made all haste to slip through and return to
Paris, formidable but inspirational, leaving Capri, beautiful
but banal, without regrets:

Paris...is so much a thing apart, and one which has no desire to
share one with anyone else. It is a jealous town. If one is living in
it and begins to think of another...then Paris is quite capable of
making herself extremely disagreeable. I could tell tales about
that....But everything I ever said about Paris is true...nowhere
else has life become so real as here, so genuine in all its manifestations, in the best and most distressing ones. One dare not say evil,
faced by this completeness of phenomena and events, not one of
which should be absent....A human landscape emerges here; the
heavens form a canopy over this city, the real heavens in all their
vast expanse, as they do over the sea.[1]

Italy seems so far away already: Capri with its pleasant, monotonous, sheltered days, with the house, surroundings, everything
one did or thought or dreamt, so that deeds, and thoughts, and
dreams became something mild, and nearly noiseless...—all that
is so far distant now.[2]

Ellen Key had evidently not made a very lucrative arrangement for Rilke, since he told Clara on his arrival in Paris that
he had been doing accounts and quite failed to see how he
could afford either to stay or to leave. Ellen's ideas about
money differed very widely from his own, as he already knew
to his cost. But he nevertheless settled down and began to
work at once. He finished *New Poems I* in July, which month
also saw the final form of his second essay on Rodin, based on
the lectures of the years 1905 and 1906. Other poems were

---

[1] *B. 1906–1907*, pp. 274 f.; to Countess Manon zu Solms-Laubach from
    29 rue Cassette, Paris, June 20, 1907.
[2] *B. 1906–1907*, p. 273; to Baroness Julie von Nordeck zur Rabenau, from
    29 rue Cassette, Paris, June 20, 1907.

also being written, and *Malte Laurids Brigge* was beginning
to occupy him again. He was once more back in the creative
rhythm, frugal, solitary and content. A great aesthetic
experience, the discovery of Cézanne in the autumn exhibition, revealed and confirmed his own destiny. It is of very
minor importance to note the marked progress Rilke's
technical knowledge of plastic art had made since he wrote
about Rodin in 1903. This made him diffident about embarking on a monograph on Cézanne, and dissatisfied with his
second essay on Rodin. But connoisseurship in the arts,
stimulating and pleasurable though it is, has no more necessary
connection with poetry than an acquaintance with the natural
sciences. Greater self-knowledge was the real gift Cézanne
bestowed on Rilke. Rodin's objectivity had held in solution,
or so it now seemed to Rilke, a cloudy residuum of love for the
object created. Cézanne's paintings, on the other hand, merely
said: 'This is.' The love he had felt for the object created had
all gone into the creative act, no disturbing judgmatic element remained. This was the way which, all unconsciously,
Rilke had been going himself in his recent poems, and which
now became clear to him. To put it briefly: Rodin's pupil
and disciple identified himself with Cézanne, whilst by no
means denying his master. Not that he thought anything he
had yet written to be comparable with Cézanne's masterpieces; but he felt that his feet were on the same path, and that
there was the strangest similarity between their lives, their
temperaments and their fates.

The letters to Clara about Cézanne in October 1907 are
amongst the most fascinating he ever wrote, even to her. He
drew an unforgettable sketch of the old painter who had died
two years earlier. Rilke was then thirty-two and only just
beginning, he believed, to find his true poetical bent; certainly
only just beginning to work, in the sense he now gave to that
term. Cézanne had been in a similar position at the age of
forty, when Pissarro had converted him to the gospel of work.
For the last thirty years of his life, he had done nothing else.
He had no joy in what he was doing, for he lived in a perpetual
rage with his achievements, since none of them attained in his

eyes to that reality sublimated into indestructibility at which he aimed. Old, sick, exhausted nearly to fainting-point at the end of the day, jeered at by urchins, and generally considered to be mad, he went on working grimly, desperately, and so obstinately that he would not stop even to attend his mother's funeral, dearly though he loved her. He hated his increasing fame; he was revolted by Zola's misinterpretation of him to the extent of refusing to read another line about his own work; and he identified himself with the hero of Balzac's *Chef d'Œuvre inconnu*, with that artist who went under in his struggle with an impossible task. A close spiritual parallel obviously exists between Cézanne and Rilke. All the incidents he detailed about the painter had a counterpart in his own life. For Cézanne and Pissarro read Rilke and Rodin; for Cézanne and his mother, Rilke and Clara; for Cézanne and Zola, Rilke and Ellen Key; for Cézanne and Balzac, Rilke and Cézanne. They were also alike in their refusal to read criticisms about their work, in their distrust of fame, and in their passionate dislike of modern life. It was an extraordinarily inspiring discovery for Rilke to make at a moment too when he was dedicating his life once more wholly to his work.

But if he believed that the parallel would hold for the rest of his days, he was tragically mistaken. Both these great artists lived for their work, and for their work alone. But Cézanne, even more monomaniacal than Rilke, was of tougher spiritual and physical fibre and had a far lower standard of living. As Rilke's 'room-summer' waned into autumn, he began to be assailed by longings for a holiday which he could ill afford, and for a sight of Venice, which seemed financially quite out of the question. He said that he hated fame; but, whether for economic or other reasons, he accepted invitations to several towns in Germany in order to give recitals of his poems and repeat his lectures on Rodin. The desire to see Clara and Ruth again was also beginning to make itself felt; providence in a word was beckoning, and Paris let him go. He left at the end of October 1907, and did not return until the following May.

The lecturing tour, which included Prague, Breslau and Vienna and about which Rilke was extremely witty, was rather a frost on the whole; but he was genuinely indifferent to that, so scornful was he of his audiences. The four Cézannes he saw in Prague would have been quite enough to compensate him for the sight of the same old hags he remembered in his childhood; but a friendly letter from Rodin which he received there, followed by a really warm one in Vienna, made leaden listeners, boring receptions and violent nose-bleeding during a recital matters of little moment. Rodin was obviously remorseful; he also needed Rilke's help over a forthcoming exhibition of his in Vienna; but more than that he seems to have wanted to be reconciled with his ardent young disciple: 'Venez quand vous êtes à Paris me voir...Nous avons besoin de la verité, de la poésie tous deux et d'amitié',[1] he rather touchingly explained. So that Rilke went off ecstatically to visit the musician Signorina Romanelli in Venice (the hand of providence again), and enjoy a well-earned rest. It was during the ten days of this visit, that Paula Modersohn-Becker died in Worspwede on November 21, 1907.

Most of the ten letters available between this event and Rilke's return to Paris in May 1908 contain plaintive references to his shocking state of health, and his consequent nervous exhaustion and misery. He was with Clara and Ruth in Oberneuland from December 1907 until February 1908; he then gave in and accepted another invitation to the island of Capri, where he spent six weeks as Frau Faehndrich's guest; after that, halting for a few days in Naples, Rome and Florence, he crept back, rather like a beaten dog, to the city which owned him still. Although he had been away for six months, providence had not had it all her own way during this period. The Baroness Sidonie Nádherný had flung wide the gates of Castle Janowitz to him after his recitation in Prague; Signorina Romanelli had sheltered him in Venice; and Frau Faehndrich had once more lured him to Capri. But Rodin's

---

[1] *B. 1907–1914*, p. 23; quoted in a letter to Clara Rilke, from H. Mayreders Hôtel Matschakerhof, Vienna, November 11, 1907.

letters looked like a direct intervention of fate; and the death
of Paula, cut off for ever from her life's work by the circumstances which had forced her away from Paris, sounded a
warning from those regions where providence is powerless
and fate alone holds sway. Arrived in Capri, Rilke did not
surrender himself to circumstances; he did some hard thinking
and then wrote an important letter to Anton Kippenberg. The
Inselverlag was by now deeply interested in Rilke and anxious
to secure the publishing rights of his future works. Kippenberg had written to that effect in November 1906. The connection, which had begun with *Tales about God* in 1900, had
proved a fairly good investment from the publisher's point of
view; a second edition had appeared in 1904, and a third was
now imminent. *The Book of Hours,* published in 1905, had
sold out its first five hundred copies by 1907, and was now
being republished in an edition of eleven hundred copies.
Further, *New Poems I* had appeared in December 1907, and
Kippenberg was also in possession of the finished manuscript
of the translation of the *Sonnets from the Portuguese.* Rilke
was, therefore, justified in hoping that the financial independence he needed might be obtainable through his books,
if Kippenberg could be persuaded to make him a regular
allowance in advance of his royalties.

This seems at least to have been in his mind when he wrote,
but he made no definite proposals, and as Kippenberg's
answers have not been published, and nearly all references to
business matters have been deleted from Rilke's letters, one
is naturally rather in the dark. Rilke's general wishes are
perfectly clear, however. He stated that he was at a decisive
point in his poetical development, and that he needed his
whole and undivided powers to enter into the possession of
his heritage. He therefore wished to assure himself for one or
two years of those propitious conditions under which *New
Poems I* had been written:

...that is to say, I intend whatever happens to return to Paris as
soon as possible from this hospitable villa where I am now con-
valescing; to go back to the tested work-solitude to which I am
looking forward with pleasure, confidence and determination, how-

ever hard it may sometimes be in detail. Up till now a series of grants has made it possible for me time and again to indulge in a similar retirement. A state-subvention for which I was hoping this year seems unobtainable at the moment, and I must therefore try to discover if my past and future writings and the increasing reality of my work do not already offer me some sort of guarantee.[1]

The answer was satisfactory, and seems to have embodied some generous proposal; it was thankfully accepted by Rilke, who from now onwards always turned to Kippenberg when he was in financial straits. The arrangement was undoubtedly to their mutual benefit; for not only did Rilke's books sell fairly well, but his name shed great lustre on the *Inselverlag*. It was extremely far-sighted of Kippenberg to have realised what a great poet he was dealing with; but his kindness was even more remarkable. Not only does he seem to have given him very favourable terms at the outset, but he went beyond the letter of their bond again and again; advancing considerable sums whenever they were asked for, and behaving with a generosity, delicacy and tact which are rare indeed in business relationships. He was Rilke's friend, his banker, his lawyer and his publisher all in one. Although he often played providence when Rilke was playing truant from fate, he was sometimes an agent of destiny as well; and never more clearly so than in March 1908, when he made it possible for the poet to return to Paris in May. The initiative however came from Rilke, whose one desire just then was to accept the fate which had governed the life of his spiritual brother Cézanne.

For Rilke was painfully aware that the agents of providence were not completely disinterested, but expected some emotional return for the bounties they showered on him:

Your conception of the relationship with an artist (he wrote to a lady who seems to have assisted him) is more than merely magnanimous, it is just. You can have no idea how rare it is, or how much everyone wants to interrupt the aesthetic worker, to deflect him and to hinder him from inner absorption; how everyone condemns him when he desires to cultivate and perfect his inmost world.

---

[1] *V.B.* p. 32; to Anton Kippenberg from the Villa Discopoli, Capri, March 11, 1908.

. . . And even friends who watch such a spiritual existence without begrudging it, how often they fall into the error of demanding a spiritual return for their gifts from the creator, beyond what he gives them in his work.[1]

As if to safeguard him from such situations, death removed Frau Alice Faehndrich from his path in July 1908, and the Villa Discopoli, as far as Rilke was concerned, was no more. His former benefactor, Prince Emil Schönaich-Carolath, had also died in the preceding May; Paula had vanished; and a promising young poet, Count Wolf Kalckreuth, an intimate of the Worpswedians, had shot himself in October 1906, at the beginning of his period of military service; sobering, shocking, terrible, but inspiring events. Seated at his desk in the rue Campagne-Première, and later in the rue de Varenne, Rilke gave substance to poems which were positively besieging his mind: the second part of *New Poems* was finished by the middle of August 1908; the requiems for Paula and Kalckreuth were written at the beginning of November; last of all *Malte Laurids Brigge* achieved completion.

It was on September 1, 1908, that Rilke moved into the Hôtel Biron, 77 rue de Varenne, now the Musée Rodin. His wife, who was temporarily leaving Paris, allowed him the use of her studio there during her absence; and when she returned, he got other rooms in the building. De Max the actor and Jean Cocteau were also inmates, and made the night uproarious with their parties; Isidora Duncan had hired one of the galleries in the pavilion (now demolished) for dance-rehearsals; and Rodin, at Rilke's instigation, was shortly to set up a studio there too. It was therefore full of interesting people, with whom, however, Rilke had very little contact. Gerhard Ouckama Knoop, a cousin of Clara's host in Heluan, visited him here in April 1909, and wrote an interesting description of his rooms in the Hôtel Biron, which his wife has kindly allowed me to use:

I came to a big old house in the faubourg Saint-Germain which had belonged to a great noble before the revolution. I approached

---

[1] *B. 1907–1914*, pp. 58 f.; to Frau Rosa Schobloch from 77 rue de Varenne, Paris, September 24, 1908.

a door with a notice on it: 'On est prié de frapper fort'. Then I went
in: a large, lofty, square, unfurnished room; in one corner, lost and
looking very small in this wide space, a bed and a washhand-stand.
Opening out of it a large round room containing two book-shelves,
a writing-table and two chairs. There was a view out of the window
of an old, spacious, lovely garden. He told me that the house used
to be inhabited by nuns who were chiefly occupied with education.
After the last anti-clerical laws, the state seized the house, and now
it will probably be demolished; for the rich who could buy it, have
no feeling for ancient dignity and cannot live without the most
modern comforts.

In these surroundings Rilke wrote the requiems and *Malte
Laurids Brigge*; these works and *New Poems II* are the story
of his life from May 1908 to January 1910; for it was a period
devoted almost entirely to his work. It was sometimes interrupted by ill-health, sometimes by visitors; he left Paris once
or twice for a week or two in the summer of 1909; he saw
something of Clara when she happened to be there (she left at
the beginning of June 1909 and did not return); but on the
whole the triumphant exclamation: 'I am seething with
work'[1] was the *leitmotiv* of these intoxicatingly creative
months. For greatly though Rilke suffered during his sterile
periods, when inspiration came at last it came vigorously and
smoothly, so much so indeed that he rarely had any corrections
to make to the first drafts of his poems.

The years 1908–1910 were one long flow of inspiration;
they also marked a pause, almost the first of any length he
had ever had, from unstable and unsettled conditions. Owing
to Kippenberg he was financially secure, and his daily routine
became firmly fixed; his various human relationships were
quiescent; nothing really concerned him at this time but
his poems. Like most artists in similar situations, he was
immune from external disturbances. How invulnerable he
was just then is shown by his attitude towards Rodin. Far
from bearing him any grudge, Rilke's deference, admiration
and gratitude were as warm as ever; but they were rendered

[1] *V.B.* p. 72; to Anton Kippenberg from 77 rue de Varenne, December 11,
1909.

to the sculptor as from equal to equal. Rodin now seemed the more anxious of the two for the other's society. He pressed Rilke to return to Meudon for a visit; Rilke made graceful gestures of acceptance, but stayed away. It would be indeed a miracle, he wrote to Clara in September, if Rodin should come to need him now a thousandth part as much as he and Clara had needed the master in the past. Yet, although he urged Rodin to establish his studio and museum in the Hôtel Biron and welcomed him warmly there, he declared himself to be too busy to accompany him on his walks. In a long and fundamental conversation with him about women and love, he eloquently upheld his own convictions against Rodin's, which he would never have done in the past. Nevertheless, he dedicated *New Poems II* 'A mon grand ami Auguste Rodin', and sent him a copy with an extremely handsome acknowledgment of the great debt he owed him. But when Rodin wished to mark the occasion by a gift of one of his sketches, Rilke was too much occupied to come and choose it for some time. Rodin, who was now allowing Clara to work in his studio in the rue de l'Université, further sent Rilke hampers of fruit and flowers from Meudon; and was altogether so anxious to make amends for the past, that Rilke was emboldened to borrow a writing-table from him, which was immediately sent; and then to ask for the loan of 400 francs to tide him over a financial crisis. Luckily a cheque from Kippenberg made Rodin's help unnecessary; for hardly had Rilke made the request before he regretted having placed himself with regard to Rodin in a position similar to the one which had ended so disastrously. He therefore not only sometimes denied himself to Rodin, including him in the general category of interruptions to be avoided at all costs; but when he emerged from his seclusion, it was often to ask for some favour to be shown either to himself or to another. In June 1909 he pleaded with Rodin again to inspect Clara's work before the latter left for Germany. A six months' gap in the correspondence seems to suggest that history had repeated itself on Rodin's side too. When Rilke next wrote at the end of November to thank Rodin for a note, he commented on the fact that it was a very long time since he had seen him last, and continued:

...but to tell you the truth, I have now only a very imperfect notion of time. I have gone down further into my work than ever. It is sometimes as dark down there as at the bottom of the sea and the pressure of the currents above me is very strong. Happily there are phosphorescent ideas in these depths which shed a little of their own light around them. They float by very opportunely at times, when I am at the end of my strength; and their passing, however rapid it may be, allows me to guess that I am surrounded by beautiful things, things which are very real, but almost unknown and little exploited.[1]

Ill-health forced Rilke to the Black Forest at the beginning of September, and he spent the rest of the month in Avignon; but neither of these removals from Paris was in any sense a flight. He returned to plunge so deeply into his work as to be almost unaware of what was happening round him. The most significant letter of this period is neither to Clara, nor to Rodin, those two beings who were after all still nearest to his heart in 1909; it was to one of his Capri acquaintances, the Baroness Elizabeth Schenk-Schweinsberg, a poetical sermon on the text of the duty of parting from those we love, so that love may become perfected. Rilke's emotional austerity, not far removed from aridity, evident in this letter, was probably intensified by the disillusioned pity with which he watched the all too human Rodin in the clutches of Madame de Choiseul; but it was inborn in him. What he preached in this letter as a spiritual duty to all who love was first and foremost a duty he owed to himself, the highest kind of pleasure, since it was the very condition of his art. So much so, that he was even placing his poetry between himself and his artist-god, the better to love and serve him. He resisted, and resisted rather violently, in September 1908, Clara's attempt to make him read *The Sayings of Buddha*, which had just been translated into German, preferring to study Bettina's letters to Goethe:

---

[1] *L.R.* pp. 125 f.; to Rodin from 77 rue de Varenne, Paris, November 29, (1909).

You (he wrote to Clara) are at the moment directly approaching the divine; more, you are flying straight towards it, irresistibly surmounting all obstacles. But I have been there, always, even as a child, and am returning thence on foot. I have been sent back, not to proclaim it, but to be among what is human, to see everything and reject nothing, not one of those thousand transformations in which the absolute disguises itself, vilifies itself and makes itself unrecognisable. I am like a man gathering fungi and healing herbs among the weeds, who appears to be bent and occupied with small things whilst the tree-trunks around him stand and pray. But a time will come when I shall prepare the potion. And yet another when I shall mount upwards with it—this potion, in which everything is distilled and combined, the most poisonous and deadly elements as well, because of their strength. And I will take it up to God, so that he may slake his thirst, and feel his own glory running through his veins.[1]

This dual aim, to represent life or the world without direct reference to the creator; and to assimilate into art that element of disharmony where, except to the penetrating senses of the artist, divinity is least manifest, informed *New Poems*. The first had already been recognised as a duty in *The Book of Monkish Life*, but had been overshadowed by the consciousness of the poet that in doing this he was helping to build the great cathedral, God. The second was also not new; but it had been brought into the forefront of Rilke's mind by Baudelaire's *Charogne*; from which he learnt the lesson that art cannot be universal, and is therefore no true art, unless it accepts the whole of life, and sees that whatever is, has value, however terrible and even horrible it may appear.[2] And Rilke, always an extremist, aimed now at nothing less than to transfigure the whole world and all life into art, thus giving it indestructibility.

New Poems, therefore (under which title I include both parts) must be considered, not as a collection of poems but as an artist's vision of the world, an impression which they

---

[1] *B. 1907–1914*, p. 48; to Clara Rilke from 77 rue de Varenne, Paris, September 4, 1908.

[2] Cf. *B. 1906–1907*, pp. 393 ff.; and *G.W.* v, pp. 89 f.

certainly produce after living with them for a time. If the
poems which indicate the climate and atmosphere, the landscape and horizons of that world were collected together, no
more fitting title could be found for them than *The Sense of the
Past*. The great medieval cathedral which dominates the first
part, the dreaming parks which enclose the second, communicate almost mesmerically that emotion which seized upon the
hero of Henry James' unfinished novel when he committed
himself to an adventure whose ending he could not foresee. It
is the sense of the past, not the past itself, which Rilke evoked
in these bewitched and bewitching poems. For he combined
the life that had gone with the life that remained in his vision
of a cathedral, of a tower, of a square, a quay-side, a convent,
a procession, a fountain, a pavilion, or the great staircase at
Versailles. By penetrating to the ultimate reality of these
things, and extracting their spiritual essence into verse, he
caused the past to filter through into the present, a desolate
present, a haunting and spell-binding past. Many of us have
been haunted in reality as Rilke haunts us in his art. We have
sat in those spacious empty squares whence the life that once
flooded them has ebbed, and have wandered through parks and
palaces melancholy with the splendour of by-gone days. We
have gazed giddily at those formidable cathedrals towering
above the huddle of frightened hovels beneath them, and have
cautiously closed the door behind us and tiptoed away from
some ruined but watchful pavilion. Rilke's poems add something to these experiences which few of us can supply of ourselves. Like the rose-window in his description, they seize
upon the beholder and drag him in. This is the strange and
almost frightening effect of many of the poems. The poet is
not outside the object described; he is not contemplating it,
although he has contemplated it; he is in the object itself, and
at a given moment he pulls the reader in as well. What was in
our previous experience a dreamy, perhaps rather tentative
reaching-out to the spirit of a landscape or a monument, is
reversed; they are reaching out for us. It is this active
spiritual energy in such poems which differentiates them
sharply from descriptions no less faithful, imaginative or

13-2

beautiful. It is magic, fraught at times with a strange, imperious message, such as the one which radiates from the
Archaic Torso of Apollo: 'Thou must reform thy life.'

For objects, and especially works of art, were all animate in
Rilke's eyes, and lived their own life, a conviction which
found its definite expression in *Auguste Rodin II,* and is
indeed the great glory of that essay. In *New Poems,* it is very
largely to things that the atmosphere owes its strange and
disturbing quality; the landscapes are all related to buildings
or monuments, and gain their true significance from them.
The impression that the objects described are radiating life
makes landscapes, townscapes, monuments, statues and
objects unfamiliar and new. Rilke undertook no very distant
journeys in *New Poems;* Paris, Chartres, Bruges, Furnes,
Ghent, Naples, Rome and Venice; hundreds and thousands of
tourists have seen them all; and the works of art and other
objects treated are at the service of any sightseer: statues of
the Buddha, of Apollo and of Artemis; marble chariots,
Tanagra figures, lutes, sundials, sarcophagi, fountains, portraits, family daguerrotypes, merry-go-rounds; scarabs, play-
balls and old lace; they are not hard to come by, and might
even be criticised as a job lot. Their value for Rilke was their
penetrability, their transparency for him. This was often, but
not always, in direct proportion to their aesthetic value. But
all objects endowed with a life of their own were significant, and
embodied, as he suggested in *Lace,* the real justification of life,
which could only be understood by penetrating to the meaning
of such objects and rendering them transparent for others. In
this sense the things he describes are hard to come by indeed.

The world reanimated in this fashion by Rilke contains no
country in which human beings as we know them could ever
find a home. Rilke's cities, landscapes and horizons either
belong to the past or else to foreign regions which can be
visited, but not for long. The stranger in the poem of that
name stands for the author and reader of *New Poems;* both are
travellers, completely subdued by the fascination of the dreams
and emotions evoked by flashing past landscapes and castles;
or by loitering through strange streets; by pausing for a

moment before leaving yet another town behind them where they will never stay; by driving through villages which will never shelter them; by the memory of sights, people and places who will not remember them; but the transient vision of which will forever affect the travellers' lives.[1]

The whole fascination of travelling is in this poem; travelling rather like a ghost along paths trodden by others, which take no imprint from the stranger's foot. And indeed the world of *New Poems* is unaware of those who come to it; it exists for its own sake; but it has bestrewn the modern world with fragments of the past; works of art, unconsidered trifles, pearls of great price, dried and withered flowers, shattered vases, skeletons and bones. Like *Harlots' Graves* the modern world was for Rilke a dried-up bed through which the river of life no longer flowed, but which was filled to the brim with significant remnants of former times. This vision of life hardly allowed of natural descriptions, which are very rare in *New Poems*. The few but exquisite flowers which bloom with such arresting loveliness here and there have been transformed into works of art. The seductive roses, the sophisticated blue and pink hydrangeas, the embroidered heliotrope, the baneful poppy have the transparency of egg-shell china, and are destructible by no natural process; they have been removed from the influences of life. In the same way the animals are either caged or cut off from normal existence in a poetical Jardin des Plantes. The panther pads noiselessly behind bars, encased in crystal-clear, but sound-proof glass. It is not only the flamingoes which seem to be stepping delicately out into unreality; the exquisite gazelle, the stately swan, the enchanting dolphins, the sinister snake, the baleful black cat, the baffling dog, all seem to be undertaking the same journey; and appear like the miraculous unicorn, to be heraldic or legendary beasts.

The joint-author of *New Poems* is the adventurer; the stranger traverses landscapes and passes by monuments which suck him in to themselves and back into the past. The adventurer enters into a similar relationship with the men and

[1] *G.W.* III, pp. 231 f.; *Der Fremde.*

women of *New Poems*. Rilke's adventurer is an enigmatic
Don Juan who has intercourse with the souls of those around
him, with the living and with the dead; he can lure them to
him and live their lives for them; they will come when he
beckons; and he need only pass by the vaults of those who are
gone for the fragrance of their possibilities to be on the air
again.[1] Such spiritual adventures are the essence of the
dramatic art, and had already been undertaken by Rilke in the
past, in *Maidens' Songs*, *The White Princess*, *Voices*, *The Tsars*
and other poems. His range was now greatly widened and he
penetrated farther than before. Warily, compassionately, as in
the past, he approached the mystery of childhood, the tragic
transition between nature (things) and the world (men and
women). He continued to express the nebulous expectancy of
young girls; the tremulous surrender of young lovers, fraught
with reverence and awe, brought this conception a step
further; and older women, fading, barren, sick, or blind,
formed a pendant to the beggars, the despised and rejected,
the delinquents and the madmen of Paris, who also people his
world. In considering men like the stranger, the adventurer,
the poet, the bachelor, a lonely man, a reader, a man imprisoned in his mind, another accepting a hard but glorious
mission, Rilke was looking into his own heart; and it may be
said of all these lads, girls, men and women, that in spite of
the delicate originality of Rilke's psychology, they belong to
the world of common experience. There are others who have
their being in a remoter sphere, inhabiting a past or a present
separated from life by art. Counting slowly up to seventy
before signing a death-sentence, the young king, hemmed in
by his aged counsellors, is the human counterpart to the
panther. The standard-bearer, the Count of Brederode, the
snake-charmer, the Spanish dancer, the courtesan, the emperor
in *Falconry*, and the lady before the mirror have mystifying
gestures, and belong to a world of inner reality, once removed
from the beggars of Paris. They are people not so much comprehended and interpreted by Rilke as fashioned by him from
the very stuff of dreams.

[1] *G.W.* III, pp. 208 ff.; *Der Abenteurer*.

Rilke's dreams often had a nightmarish quality, strongly impregnated with macabre elements, evident in his early prose and in such poems as *The Last Judgment*. His visions of the heroes and prophets of the Old Testament bordered on the horrible at times; notably the poem about Abishag and David, and the lament of David for Jonathan; and even in the poems dealing with Elijah, Joshua, Saul, Samuel and Jeremiah the fierce Hebrew prophets speak and act feverishly, almost neurotically. This is particularly noticeable in the second part, which in addition to the biblical subjects portrays another Last Day, quaint and grotesque this time; a dance of death, the temptation of a saint, a leprous king and St Simeon Stylites, from most of which persons and events Rilke distils unbearable physical horrors. He was experiencing from within the perilous spiritual torments of his prophets and saints; and represented ruthlessly and realistically the savage resistance of the flesh to the wildly struggling spirit. Here he was on his own ground and more successful, even if more painful, than with his Old Testament heroes. But his real achievement in biblical interpretation was undoubtedly his Prodigal Son. As he groped his way into the spiritual processes of this particular representative of humanity, first recognition, and then identification took place; and the souls of all those who have ever gone forth from home into homelessness were given symbolical form. No less original were his versions of Christ on the Mount of Olives, and Christ on the Cross, two compassionate if inexorable revelations of the sufferings of one who did not endure to the end; and Christ's return from the dead to teach Mary Magdalene to hold herself aloof from her beloved strikes a familiar Rilkean note. The God who broods over the whole is rarely mentioned, although his presence is felt in the biblical and medieval poems: the terrible Jehovah of the Old Testament, and the formidable God of the Middle Ages give gigantic proportions to the deeds and the works which glorified them. But it would almost seem as if God had withdrawn himself completely to-day and left humanity to the mercy of his austere, radiant and commanding angels, who visit Don Juan, the saint and the prophet-poet in *Mission* with imperious mandates and crucial tests.

The wings of another angel are often heard in this book. Death in many shapes and forms visits the inhabitants of *New Poems*, and always with the same effect of opening a door into another and a more real world just beyond our line of vision:

> But when you went, and from our stage were banished,
> Reality itself, a shimmering patch,
> Came filtering through the chink through which you vanished,
> Real green, real sunshine and real woods to match.[1]

If the men and women in these poems are less complete, less assured and triumphant than the objects and works of art around them, than the animals and flowers, this is because they are out of their real element, the water of death:

> This weary striving on through things undone,
> Heavily burdened and as if we're bound,
> Is like the clumsy waddling of the swan.
> And our death, this agonising sliding
> From our daily-trodden, well-worn ground
> Resembles much his anxious downward gliding:
>
> Into waters which receive him sweetly,
> And happy seem, and in their passing, featly
> Withdraw themselves beneath him, wave on wave.
> Whilst he, now sure and calm beyond all telling,
> His majesty each moment more compelling,
> Serener ever deigns the floods to brave.[2]

The glorification of this death at the expense of the untimely end of girlhood by marriage and love was the theme of Rilke's reinterpretation of the legend of Alcestis, which he modified profoundly, transforming it in a manner which none of its modern exponents (Racine, Alfieri, Goethe, Verrall and Browning among them, not to mention Hofmannsthal) have outrivalled or even equalled. Boldly breaking with tradition, he placed the action of his poem before the marriage of Alcestis to Admetus was consummated, making the messenger-god appear with his fearful command at the wedding-feast

---

[1] *G.W.* III, p. 63: *Todeserfahrung.*   [2] *G.W.* III, p. 51: *Der Schwan.*

itself. 'Admetus is to die, now, in this very hour.' In the horror, confusion and panic of the moment, Admetus prays for a reprieve, even for this one night, but the inexorable God denies him. The young man then turns, first to his parents and then to Creon his friend, imploring them to die for him, so that he may live his life with Alcestis. But it is already too late. She has taken his fate upon herself, and is speaking to the God:

> No one can ransom him from death but I.
> But I can do it. None is at end
> As I am now. For what remains to me
> Of all that I am here? 'Tis this:—I die.
> Did not the goddess tell you when she sent you
> That yonder couch within, waiting for me,
> Belongs to the underworld? I've said farewell
> Again and yet again.
>
> No dying man ever took farewells so.
> I'm here for this:—to be buried 'neath the man
> Who's now my husband, to be dissolved away.
> So lead me forth. It is for him I die.
>
> .   .   .   .   But just before she went,
> He saw Alcestis' features turned towards him
> Radiantly smiling, holding out the hope
> (A promise nearly) to return to him,
> The living, from deep death, a woman grown.[1]

The idea behind the primitive vegetation-myth, that all change is a form of death, and that the fundamental events of conception and birth take place in the underworld, fused in Rilke's mind with the horror Euripides had felt at the cruel sacrifice men demanded of women, and with the realisation that 'each man kills the thing he loves' into a striking symbol for the fate of girlhood as Rilke conceived it and as he made Alcestis express it. This poem closes on a note of reconciliation with that destiny. More greatly tragic is his interpretation of the legend of Orpheus and Eurydice, whose framework he did not alter, but from whose data he wrung a meaning and a poignancy entirely new. He did full justice to Orpheus'

[1] *G.W.* III, pp. 105 f.: *Alkestis.*

feelings; but it was Eurydice who was the focus of the poem.
He represented in her person the utter impossibility of a real
return from the underworld, and more—the ruthlessness of
the attempt. Eurydice's deadness was such, that there could
and should be no weaning her from it. She was already partly
given back to nature; any idea of resurrection was as cruel as
it was blasphemous. She had entered on the further and the
better state. Yet the human aspect of the situation, the hopeless passion of Orpheus, was not forgotten either. In this
poem Rilke achieved a balance between the two worlds which
he rarely attempted, and showed an unusual sympathy for the
man's point of view. In spite of the strange and mysterious
setting, the psychological insight has the subtlety of Ibsen,
and something of his ruthless realism too:

> But she was walking by the god's left hand,
> Her foot-steps hindered by the clinging grave-clothes,
> Groping and gentle, not impatiently.
> Withdrawn within herself, filled with high hope,
> She thought not of the man who went before them,
> Nor of the road ascending into life,
> Withdrawn within herself; filled to the brim
> With that great fulness of her having died.
> Full as a fruit with sweetness and with darkness
> Her great death filled her; and it was so new,
> That comprehension failed her utterly.
>
> She was within a second maidenhood,
> Untouchable; her sex was closed
> As a young flower its petals folds at even.
> Her very hands, estranged from marriage-rites,
> Felt the light god's gentle and guiding touch
> Repellent, as too intimate and close.
>
> She was no longer now that fair-haired woman
> Who sometimes sounded in the poet's songs,
> No longer the broad couch's scented island,
> Nor yonder man's possession any more.
> She was already loosened like long hair,
> And given far and wide like fallen rain,
> Distributed like blessings manifold.

A root already.
And when her steps were stayed
Abruptly by the god, who called out sadly:
'He has turned round', she did not understand,
But softly questioned: 'Who?'

But in the distance, dark in the brilliant opening,
Someone was standing, features in the shadow,
Not to be recognised. He stood and saw,
How on the narrow pathway between meadows
With melancholy looks the god of message,
Silently turned to follow that same figure
Already moving back down the one pathway,
Its foot-steps hindered by the clinging grave-clothes,
Groping and gentle, not impatiently.[1]

Written a little later, the requiem for Paula elaborated
with a fiercer intensity the destructive nature of love, the
victim in this case being a woman-artist. But the personal
anger made it less great than these two Greek poems; and
far less humane than the contemporary elegy on Kalckreuth's
suicide, another sin against another latent 'personal death',
which however Rilke understood and interpreted more truly.

These two great elegies, although entirely in key with the
ideas expressed in *New Poems*, were rightly excluded from
the collection, since they were manifestoes from the real
world, highly personal poetry, not plastic works of art. Their
intense subjectivity throws the almost superhuman imparti-
ality of *New Poems* into vivid relief. This quality makes the
latter as mysterious and remote as the nebulous island lost in
the North Sea so magically described by the author.[2] They are
not misty, however, but crystal clear in cut, the fascinating
objects and monuments stirring with life, the exquisite
flowers and beautiful beasts which adorn a country whose
enigmatic inhabitants are all going one way: deathwards;
while the landscapes and towns are all facing backwards to the
past. The experience of entering this country is comparable to

---

[1] *G.W.* III, pp. 101 f.: *Orpheus, Eurydike, Hermes*; the translation is partly
based on J. B. Leishman, *Rainer Maria Rilke, Poems*, London 1934, pp. 42 ff.

[2] *G.W.* III, pp. 93 ff.: *Die Insel (Nordsee)*.

the strange adventures of travellers to Mars or the moon. It is a country to which we are not sufficiently acclimatised, and far from well-adapted, the legendary land of art.

And Aaron shall cast lots upon the two goats; one lot for the LORD, and the other lot for the scapegoat.... Then shall he kill the goat of the sin offering...and bring his blood within the vail...and sprinkle it upon the mercy seat.... And Aaron shall lay both his hands upon the head of the live goat, and confess over him all the iniquities of the children of Israel, and all their transgressions in all their sins, putting them upon the head of the goat, and shall send *him* away...into the wilderness: And the goat shall bear upon him all their iniquities unto a land not inhabited....[1]

The hero of *The Note-Books of Malte Laurids Brigge* is one of those poetical scapegoats of which Werther is the great prototype. Both Goethe and Rilke (and how many other poets?) put all their emotional and mental torments upon the head of a creature made in their own likeness, and sent him away into the wilderness, bearing all their iniquities 'unto a land not inhabited'. The parallel holds in another respect. The suicide of Jerusalem, and the death of the young Norwegian Sigbjörn Obstfelder, provided the two high priests of poetry with the second victim, whose blood had to drench the altar. These are modern instances of art arising from ritual, and still impregnated with its magical function. Ceremonial purification became poetic catharsis in *The Sorrows of Werther*, and the sacrificial victim was transformed into the hero of an immortal novel. For if the emotional need for a scapegoat was the same which was felt in Aaron's day, the mind and the heart, the sins and the sufferings of the victim became the focus of interest for Goethe even before the self-purification had begun to take effect. The relation between art and autobiography, between confession and creation in *Werther*, a difficult critical problem, is actually the relation between ritual and art; certainly the novel was due to an instinct for purification, as much as to the creative impulse.

[1] Leviticus xvi.

Read in this fashion, and we have Rilke's authority for
doing so,[1] *Malte Laurids Brigge* loses much of its incoherent
character, although the transformation into art is by no means
so complete as in *Werther*. Quite apart from the style, whose
laboured irony, mannered prose and purple patches compare
ill as a confessional medium with Goethe's lyrical, spontaneous and natural language, Rilke somehow fails to convince
the reader of Malte's separate reality. Poetry and truth, far
from being inextricably mingled, relieve each other throughout the book whenever it suits the author. Straight autobiography alternates with pure fiction; at times too Malte
leads Rilke's life; at others Rilke leads Malte's; and these four-
fold changes are not aesthetically fused. Malte's poetical
existence often hangs by a hair; nevertheless, it can be saved
by accepting him as Rilke's double and scapegoat; whereas
all is lost aesthetically if one attempts to make either the
author or his hero responsible for the book as a whole. It is
extraordinarily miscellaneous. Goethe used real letters in
Werther and copied out a whole passage he had earlier translated from Ossian, perhaps instinctively impelled by the
guiding ritualistic motive to attach to his literary scapegoat
something that had belonged to himself. Rilke positively
plundered his own correspondence as well as paraphrasing
many of his poems. Indeed, if he were not known to be a
highly conscientious artist, one would accuse him outright of
book-making. For, although the letters and passages from
letters he incorporated in *Malte Laurids Brigge* were written
with this end in view, the reminiscences from Jacobsen, Bang,
Hofmannsthal, and André Gide seem almost like plagiarism
with their strong verbal similarities. So that, what with these
passages and the pages devoted to renderings of Froissart,
Commynes and other writers, an investigation of the sources
of *Malte Laurids Brigge* is not unlike retrieving objects from a
magpie's nest. But they were assimilated to an extent that
made them completely Rilkean, even the doctrine of non-
possessive love which he owed to Gide. As for the pages on
French history in the fourteenth and fifteenth centuries, he

[1] Cf. for instance, *B. 1907-1914*, pp. 53-55, 147-148.

treated them as he had treated the torso of Apollo in *New Poems*, as material for his art; and the fragmentary nature of the confessions is compensated for completely by the all-pervading colouring of fear. This gives emotional unity to the book, and is the decisive factor in its aesthetic effect.

The pendulum of the action swings backwards and forwards between Malte's present life in Paris and his childhood in Denmark in a natural if rather monotonous fashion during the first part of the book. In the second, although recollections of his youth and impressions of Paris still intrude at intervals, a large proportion of the total space is given to chronicles of historical events which Rilke felt to be symbolical of his main theme. The deaths of various outstanding persons of the period of the Avignon papacy are meticulously described; and obscure allusions are made to a number of people and events now almost totally forgotten. This allusiveness is an outstanding instance of Rilke's indifference to his readers. A phrase here and there and a proper name now and again were all that was needed to rivet attention and to reveal the strange mental processes Malte was undergoing. Rilke defeated his purpose by assuming specialised knowledge of the period in his readers, who inevitably become restive and bored under so much almost unintelligible knowledge retailed with a long-windedness which betokens a grave lack of aesthetic *savoir-faire*. This is the reverse side of that sense of the past which gave such magic to *New Poems*; but even so it throws a tragic light on the mental tortures of Malte, the part aesthetic, part cathartic aim of the book.

Death is the centre of the circle round which the thoughts of Rilke's double frantically revolve; the emotions to be cast out are fear and love, the greater of the two being fear. Paris brought to the surface and supplied symbols for a terror so omnipotent in Malte's mind that the secondary emotion could hardly maintain itself beside it. The hospitals, the sick, the dying, the poor of Paris inspired him with such dread, such intimate horror, that he fought vainly against the sensation of being pulled down into that underworld and of losing himself for ever. It was an ascending scale of panic; fear of the abject

poverty he saw all round him and whose pinch he was
experiencing himself in his daily life; fear of the horrible
squalor lording it over the streets and houses and cynically
revealing itself in the unthinkable defilement of a disem-
bowelled house; sympathetic fear with a man suffering from
St Vitus' Dance, and with the mental torments of room-neigh-
bours; night-terrors, supernatural terrors, fear of losing his
own identity; fear of illness, of the fever-fantasies and deliriums
he had known in childhood and which were beginning to
recur; and lurking behind all these the fear of death; of his own
death, of the multiple death of the underworld; and a fascinated horror for those great individual deaths he had heard or
read of. Panic was paralysing his soul.

To escape from these many and torturing obsessions, Malte
would look back at intervals to his childhood and re-live it in
his thoughts. Forced inexorably to live through Rilke's life in
Paris, he was spared the bitter cup of the poet's past, and given
a fictitious existence in Denmark created for him from Rilke's
memories of Scandinavia, from some episodes of his childhood, and from the atmosphere of Jacobsen's novels. The total
effect is extremely weird. Beginning with the appalling death
of his paternal grandfather, Malte recollected a series of
persons and events, generally grotesque and often incredible
in the sense that they seem completely unreal. This is perhaps
because Rilke was haunting the more than half-fictitious past
of his spiritual double; a situation in itself so occult, that the
supernatural element introduced is something of an anti-
climax. The ghosts of Christine Brahe and of Ingeborg; the
spirit of the burnt-down house materialising inexplicably,
are by no means the most hyperphysical part of Malte's
reminiscences, in which all the characters seem to be ghosts
from Jacobsen's novels, and the delicate, sensitive, frightened
child the only creature of flesh and blood in a world of
eccentric shades.

Particularly shadowy is Malte's young aunt Abelone with
whom he fell in love when he began to grow up. She symbolises that second emotion whose purification was one of the
aims of the book. Rilke confided later to one of his friends

that the only human beings who could really communicate
themselves to him were women-lovers and those who had
died young.[1] The fragile Abelone was the only charm the
unhappy Malte had against the horrors of Paris and the terror
of death; she had introduced him to Bettina's letters to Goethe,
and inspired his panegyric on the selfless devotion of women-
lovers, giving him an ideal of love never attained to by men,
and which he saw realised in the lives and writings of Bettina
von Arnim, of Sappho, of Marianna Alcoforado, of Gaspara
Stampa, the Countess of Die, Clara d'Anduze, Louïze Labé,
Marceline Desbordes-Valmore, Elisa Mercoeur, Aïssé, Julie
de Lespinasse, Marie Anne de Clermont and Clémence de
Bourges. This long literary list diminishes the human interest
of Abelone; who, with her comet-tail of loving sisters,
illuminates at intervals the dark heavens of the second part of
the book, in which death broods heavily, nauseatingly at
times in the personal deaths of Christian IV of Denmark, of
Felix Arvers, Jean de Dieu, the false Demetrius, Charles the
Bold, and Charles VI of France. The influences of Capri and
Paris were at war here; and seemed to be fighting it out in the
Bibliothèque Nationale; an inconclusive and rather wearing
struggle which continued almost until the end of the book.

The wan Abelone then made a final, effective appearance,
singing a song to Malte in a Venetian drawing-room, a song
which represented the lesson of relinquishment of love, which
he had learnt from her. This song accompanies another fear
which rears its tragic head at the very last: the fear of being
loved. The fear of possessing, which some of the male lovers
in *New Poems* experienced, was in reality in the poet's heart
the fear of being possessed. Malte looked his last on Abelone,
and expressed the emotion behind her song in his interpretation of the parable of the prodigal son. André Gide's *Retour
de l'Enfant Prodigue*, published in 1907, which Rilke was
shortly to translate into German, had caused him to ponder
deeply the mentality of voluntary outcasts from love. He
gave a version not unlike Gide's in *New Poems*, where the
departure of the prodigal son was due to spiritual aspirations,

[1] *B. 1907–1914*, pp. 175 f.

confined and cramped by human closeness. Gide showed how these aspirations were thwarted and finally tamed by dangers and hardships. Rilke believed, on the contrary, that the man who had fled away from love, and taught himself the hard lesson of loving selflessly; who then, despairing of a human lover, had turned to God, was finally convinced that the distance between them was too great. He nearly forgot God over the hard labour of approaching Him. Part of this labour was to live through his childhood again, and make good the failures and omissions he had been guilty of then. What was his horror when he returned to find his family making gestures of love towards him. They had misinterpreted his motives; but this lack of comprehension relieved him of his worst terror. It was clearly not he whom they loved:

What did they know about him? He was terribly difficult to love now, and he felt that one alone was capable of it. But He was not yet willing.[1]

These words close the confessions.

Rilke's tragic scapegoat had to live through the horror of Paris without the assistance of Rodin. Nor, with the exception of Aubusson's tapestry of *La dame à la licorne*, did he find relief in art. The Louvre was too full of the confraternity of the underworld, warming their feet over the hot-air gratings and grinning as they watched their renegade brother pretending that he did not belong to them. The Bibliothèque Nationale was a safer asylum, for the reader's ticket kept out his derelict kith and kin. The literary allusions in this book are as numerous and varied as one would expect from an inexperienced but sophisticated reader who had no guide but his own curious and capricious fancies. Francis Jammes, Baudelaire's *Charogne* and Ibsen inspired some of the finest passages in the book, which the wonderful descriptions of the Duse and of the theatre at Orange counterbalance in the second part.

A certain Russian current flows through the novel. Grischa Otrepyov's death, which may have come from *Boris Godunov*,

[1] *G.W.* v, p. 300.

is much more vividly described than the episodes from French history. The room-neighbour in St Petersburg, Nikolay Kusmitch, with his rather spuriously Russian obsession about time, recalls the manner of Dostoyevski; whose emotions are also reflected in Malte's feeling of solidarity with the insulted and despised. But I agree entirely with Edmond Jaloux in his acute remark that *Malte Laurids Brigge* might have been written by one of Dostoyevski's characters, but not by the novelist himself. The vast canvas, the abysmal knowledge of the human heart owned by the Russian writer were not within Rilke's scope. The haunted mind, the panic fears, the egocentric torments of Malte are saturated with nordic gloom; Jacobsen and not Dostoyevski is the prevailing influence in these confessions.

The impression of reading *Malte Laurids Brigge* is almost identical with the one produced by *Niels Lyhne*, *Marie Grubbe* and *Mogens*—a general feeling of minute observation and meticulous description; of delicate lights and shades; of highly sophisticated, even decadent, emotions. The historical learning behind *Marie Grubbe* is reflected in Rilke's accounts of French history; the number of curious deaths described is also in the tradition of Jacobsen. Rilke even borrowed the phrase 'he died his hard death' and applied this comment on Niels Lyhne's end to the appalling demise of Christoph Detlev Brigge; and he further filled the gallery at Urnekloster with portraits of persons in *Marie Grubbe*. By making his scape-goat an aristocratic young Dane, he proclaimed his kinship with the north rather than with the east of Europe. Dostoyevski was hardly more than a room-neighbour, a disturbing and problematical influence, which only made matters worse for Malte, and which was eventually removed.

And indeed, as the book draws to a close, Malte's isolation becomes such, that one cannot imagine it being broken, even by the presence of someone next door. More and more his mind was thrown back upon itself; after he had recollected his childhood and early youth, he had no other occupation than to revive memories of life from books, since of personal life there was none: it had been swallowed up by fear. Lovers and death rose to confront him from the printed page: unhappy lovers, unthinkably ghastly and brutal deaths. The illusion of love could not protect him from the onslaught of death; he tried to exorcise it in the parable of the prodigal son; then he crumpled up and disappeared. He left a silence behind him which seems still to be ringing with his terrified outcries. The scapegoat had been driven forth into the wilderness; but one has the uneasy impression that he might return again; and that the ritual act of purification lacked some essential feature.

Rilke's prolonged monologue with his own reflexion in *Malte Laurids Brigge* is not great art. The scapegoat Malte is not an aesthetic creation, but a pallid looking-glass image, mutely repeating Rilke's gestures and expressions. He disappeared or 'went under' when the latter finally moved away from the mirror. His existence in the world of art is tenuous; the part he played in his author's life was of greater importance.

The novel obviously marks a crisis in Rilke's attitude to God, a crisis which might be hailed as the loss of a delusion, or deplored as the loss of an ideal. The future artist-god had never been more than a sublime hypothesis, deriving from Rilke's belief in the creative and transforming powers of art. Metaphysically he had represented a goal to which to approximate, although so remote, such aeons removed from us in time, as to be practicably unattainable. Nevertheless, Rilke had believed him to be capable of mythological treatment; and it had been his supreme ambition to represent this divinity in his works, much as the Hindus portray the next and final avatar of Vishnu, the god Kalki on his milk-white steed. But either Rilke's inspiration was at fault, or his conception of the deity. He could be invoked, he could be sought; but ransack the apparent world for similes as Rilke might, he could not represent him, not even when he identified him with death, which proved to be merely begging the question. Death was just as nebulous and amorphous and resisted aesthetic creation quite as stubbornly as the 'Russian' God. Incapable of representing his godhead, Rilke began to transform life into art. What he learnt during the process is what every artist has to face sooner or later, the realisation that life is much more creative than art. So that his mythological dream, the apotheosis of art, appeared to be founded on a delusion. Either art was not as creative as he had thought, or he was not such a great artist. Both these doubts were paralysing, and quite sufficient to account for the terrible apprehension present in every line of *Malte Laurids Brigge*. For this scepticism struck at the roots of his reason and justification for existence. Either he was the prophet of a new religion, or he was nobody and nothing.

Rilke had been hoist with his own petard. He had used in a private and narrow sense a word with the widest and most colossal connotations. It was steeped in unfathomable mystery, heavy with antiquity, and shining with the resplendent visions of the mightiest minds in the world. The word was too much for him, for the word was God. It had been a double-edged tool from the very start; for Rilke could no more free himself from its magical power than the most superstitious savage. Again and again he had involuntarily used it in a purely religious sense; and he had now come to the parting of the ways. He must abandon this term (that is to say he must abandon God), and create his artistic mythology by other means. He must find an adequate substitute for the emergent aesthetic deity.

3. *Playing Truant*, 1910–1914

Yesterday I nearly changed my rooms. I discovered in the Boulevard Saint-Michel, towards the upper end, near the Observatory, a small and very charming hôtel, with electric light everywhere, very clean and white inside, and with rooms on the third floor, one of which would just have done for me, and the other for you. They were both smaller than my present room, which is really large, though very low, and they had the advantage of a wide perspective and space before the windows. In spite of the cleanliness, that was nearly the most attractive thing about them; for however many other faults my present hôtel has, the biggest of all as far as I am concerned is the narrow street with the windows opposite.... And

when you think that all those twelve windows which I overlook
from my writing-table are not merely frames, but have eyes as well
bracketed onto my life, then it is sometimes hardly tolerable. I sat
down on a bench in the Luxembourg Gardens and thought and
calculated. The light staircase of the Hôtel de l'Observatoire
wrestled with the dark dragon of my present staircase like St
Michael. My wretched, wavering, ill-smelling oil-lamp contended
in my thoughts with the lovely, abundant, ever-ready electric light.
...But at last, I said to myself, that I was thinking on the old lines,
from which I wish to free myself, the lines of the 'rich', and I went
humbly and timidly back from temptation to my room [which he
left four days later].[1]

I came down to breakfast. The waiter asked for my order in
German, and German was being spoken at the next table. Well,
that might have been a coincidence. But German was being spoken
at the second, third and fourth tables as well, in the hall, on the
stairs, and in the street. I was up to the neck in German words, and
what words too....This gave me a notion of what the Italian
Riviera really is. But worse was to come. In the train nothing but
Germans, and German blossoming in abundant conversations. I hid
behind a big French newspaper....The hôtel was cram jam full,
and so were all the others; full, need I say it? of Germans....In
Viareggio...a little dining-room, unluckily with round tables.
I was put with an old Scotchwoman, who insisted on talking, first in
Italian and then in French. It was ghastly. I kept on underlining
my silences heavily, but in vain....I had supper in my room next
evening...and as soon as one of those old hags from England
leaves, I will get a table to myself in the dining-room and repel all
advances.[2]

Alas, that I have no family country-seat; nowhere in the whole
world a room of my own with a few old things and a window opening
on to great trees....[3]

The showman's spirit, which is so characteristic of the city, is also
the main feature of the Roman spring. It is a spring exhibition, and

---

[1] *B. 1902–1906*, pp. 50 f.; to Clara Rilke from 11 rue Toullier, Paris,
September 28, 1902.

[2] *B. 1902–1906*, pp. 68 ff.; to Clara Rilke from Hôtel de Florence, Viareggio,
March 24, 1903.

[3] *B. 1902–1906*, p. 149; to Ellen Key from Villa Strohl-Fern, Rome, May 9,
1904.

not spring itself. And of course the tourists enjoy it and feel flattered, like petty sovereigns in whose honour everything has been decorated. To these respectable Germans Italy must always have been a kind of royal progress with triumphal arches, flowers and fireworks.[1]

Then I went to my friends in Sweden, who gave me everything that the most generous hospitality can offer; but they were nevertheless not able to give that limitless solitude, that whole life in one day, that merging of oneself into everything, in a word that feeling of unlimited space in which one stands encircled by countless phenomena.[2]

It is absolutely appalling to behold what humanity has made of this lovely island. . . . But when have human beings ever produced pleasing results in the name of pleasure, recreation or enjoyment? Neither bull-fights, nor music-halls, nor any other place of entertainment, from ball-rooms to beer-gardens downwards, are, or ever have been, either beautiful or agreeable.[3]

I simply must write to you before I start packing again, although enmity already reigns among my things, who are bruising each other's head and treading on each other's heels. There are letters waiting to be put in order, and all those things which take a positive pleasure in getting in one's way perpetually until one wants them, when they vanish like smoke and watch one from some hidey-hole vainly searching for them all over the place instead of wishing them further. There are all those remarkable configurations caused by gutting one's rooms, those bastards sprung from the co-habitation of impossible objects: in a word misery and hell; you know all about it. And one plays at providence, and imagines that one can take heed and select for an uncertain future. . . . Well, I must go on struggling with my things. Some of them are on my side, and are lying there as good as gold, behaving like model pupils; but most of them are naughty and are having fun behind my back.[4]

---

[1] *B. 1902–1906*, pp. 152 f.; to Lou Andreas-Salomé from Villa Strohl-Fern, Rome, May 12, 1904.

[2] *B. 1902–1906*, p. 309; to Karl von der Heydt from Meudon in the spring of 1906.

[3] *B. 1906–1907*, p. 120; to Elizabeth and Karl von der Heydt from Villa Discopoli, Capri, December 11, 1906.

[4] *B. 1907–1914*, pp. 7 ff.; to Clara Rilke from 29 rue Cassette, Paris, October 26, 1907.

I will write a proper letter soon. It is impossible here. The table in my room upstairs is minute; and here in the writing-room pens scratch so loudly that one can do nothing but listen to them, unless one is too much irritated by the American who cannot find a place for his legs and keeps squinting across to see if he can't put them up on the writing-table yet. This whole journey has really brought me nothing but the complete realisation that Italy is impossible during these months unless one has friends who hide one in their houses and guard one as the apple of their eye from foreign bodies.[1]

Did you know that I spent last winter in Algiers, Tunis and Egypt? Unluckily in circumstances so very unsuitable to me, that I lost my seat and the reins, and finally only kept up like someone who has been thrown from his horse and is being dragged along by the stirrups.[2]

This year I am a guest here in this old fortified castle (at the moment quite alone), which holds one rather like a prison; it can hardly do otherwise with its immense walls. And at least it will help to straighten out the disorder in my financial affairs....[3]

Now this would really be the place to live like a Spaniard, if it were not for the winter and my own apathetic aversion from involving myself in any but the most unavoidable inconveniences... and besides the devil has inspired the English to build a really excellent hôtel here, in which of course I am living neutrally and expensively as many another would like to live, and am shameless enough withal to spread it abroad that I am living in Spain.[4]

So that I arrived here rather short of funds, and had to sit about for days on end unable to begin settling in, except that I became aware, as I calculated and counted, that a great deal had to be done: my furniture to be got out of store, the move to be made, urgent purchases—blankets, towels, everything the lack of which made going away easier is now vitally necessary and had to be procured. I've been to the Bon Marché and have had the paper-hangers and carpenter here, so that I shall be able to settle into my new rooms in a few days.

[1] *V.B.* pp. 85 f.; to Anton Kippenberg from Hôtel Regina, Venice, May 1, 1910.

[2] *B. 1907–1914*, p. 151; to Lou Andreas-Salomé from Castle Duino on the Adriatic, December 28, 1911.

[3] *B. 1907–1914*, p. 152.

[4] *B. 1907–1914*, p. 257; to Marie von Thurn und Taxis-Hohenlohe, from Hôtel Reina Victoria, Ronda, December 17, 1912.

I wish for nothing, nothing, but that I may be able at last to return to quiet achievement in them, to that modest, regular life that was possible in this same house before the days of the rue de Varenne.[1]

I am sick to death of Paris, it is a city of the damned. I always knew that; but in the old days an angel interpreted their torments to me. Now that I have to explain them to myself, I can find no decent elucidation, and am in danger of making what I once conceived of greatly, petty and mean. If God has any consideration at all, he must let me find a couple of rooms in the country soon.[2]

These dissolving views of Rilke during the years before the war show that his truancy from Paris (by no means confined to the present period) was rarely a success. They also show increasing demands on life, and ever increasing discontent. If he had gradually solved the acute financial problem of his existence in an industrial world, the much greater question of how and where to live still awaited an answer. Between the years 1902 and 1914 the name of the towns Rilke visited is legion, and the ten different countries which contained them (France, Italy, Germany, Austria, Denmark, Sweden, Belgium, Africa, Egypt and Spain) average out at almost a country a year. But he was not really happy in any of them, and even Paris was often intolerable and began to pall. He was looking for an 'ideal home'; and although he sometimes talked longingly about Russia, it was clearly not exactly what he needed, since he never returned there. Highly fastidious and sensitive, unmodern in some ways, very much of his times in others, he wanted what seemed to him bare necessities, and was really crying for the moon in asking for solitude, cleanliness, beauty and spaciousness; luxuries which to-day are hardly to be bought with gold.

Rilke faced the horror of packing and unpacking, moving and settling in again and again; he joined the stream of continental tourists, and also adopted their habits of thought

---

[1] *V.B.* p. 165; to Kippenberg from 17 rue Campagne-Première, Paris, March 6, 1913.

[2] *B. 1907–1914*, p. 317; to Marie von Thurn und Taxis, from Paris, December 27, 1913.

and behaviour. Some of his letters echo the complaints of
nearly every traveller one meets abroad. Furious at the sight
and sound of his countrymen, hating all the other nations as
well, superciliously sensitive in his efforts to avoid his fellows,
he became one of the mighty army of tourists who, lured into
beautiful or famous surroundings, spend their time and
exhaust their energies in seeking for absolute solitude in
popular and populous resorts. His health was too delicate, his
standard of cleanliness too high, and his temperament too
unenterprising and helpless to allow him to strike off the
beaten track. There was nothing for it but to bewail his lot
and creep round corners when he wanted to sun-bathe in the
nude; for he was one of the pioneers of a movement the prevalence of which would probably distress him to-day, since he
hated all communal pleasures. Luckily for him, the castles and
villas of the great were often ready to shelter him when he
went abroad. He was not slow to learn, however, that the
most considerate of hosts and hostesses are sometimes in the
way; and, even when they vacated their houses for him, it was
not like being in a home of his own. In truth, he was hard to
please; and never more so than during this period, when the
hold of Paris was slackening, and his mind was in an uproar
too.

For, if Malte was driven out into the wilderness at the end
of the book, a similar lot overtook his creator, upon whom also
a great silence fell. He put the finishing touches to the confessions under one of the many hospitable roofs which so often
sheltered his head. Providence, weary, not of well-doing, but
of waiting to do better still, snatched at Rilke's request to
Kippenberg to find him a German typist in Paris, and lured
him across the Rhine. Rilke needed someone to help him with
the transcription of his notes; let him then come and stay with
his publisher, who would provide a competent amanuensis and
every other facility. It was far too good an offer to refuse;
high time too for Rilke to see Clara and Ruth; and the poet
had worked himself to a standstill. He left Paris in January
1910, stayed for a night or two with Heydt at Elberfeld, and
arrived at the Kippenbergs' on January 13. He was very

warmly welcomed both by the publisher and his wife Katharina, whose book about him shows her to have been almost idolatrously affectionate. As yet another woman to adore and mother him, she opened the new year in a truly providential way, ably seconded by her husband, whilst already in December 1909 a still more potent auxiliary had been found. The Princess Marie Thurn and Taxis-Hohenlohe had made Rilke's acquaintance in Paris, and had fallen under the spell of his personality. She herself was obviously a woman of great charm. Highly cultivated, an amateur of the arts, she combined delicacy and tact with active sympathy. Rilke's forlornness and homelessness made a strong appeal to her heart. She opened wide its doors, and also flung apart the gates of the magnificent Castle Duino on the Adriatic, as well as those of Castle Lautschin in Austria; whilst her mezzanino in Venice was henceforward at his disposal as a refuge from the more oppressive hospitality of the Palace Valmarana. All these snares of providence were well and truly laid before Rilke returned to Paris in May, having spent his time with the Kippenbergs in Leipzig, with Clara and Ruth in Berlin, in Rome by himself, at Castle Duino with the princess and then in Venice. Nor were his old friends abandoning the absorbing sport of luring the poet from his lair. Heydt was as hospitable as ever; the Baroness Sidonie Nádherný was always glad to see him at Janowitz; a new huntswoman, Frau Oltersdorf, was waiting to pounce on him in Paris and carry him off to Africa and Egypt, where Baron Jacob and Baroness May Knoop were ready and willing to harbour him in Heluan.

All this hospitality had a financial rather than a romantic significance for Rilke, whose life was more parasitical than paradisical among these providential lords and ladies who beset his path. It was a disintegrating existence he led between castles, luxury liners and palace-hôtels; and his movements between January 1910 and the outbreak of the war are so bewildering, that one can only just keep track of them by means of a date-sheet divided into weeks, months and years, and by marking maps. Even so, it is not always possible to find out why he should be at Cologne, or Munich, or

Prague on any given day rather than anywhere else. Paris is the only clue to guide one through the maze of his movements; no longer the sun maturing his works, it was at least the moon which erratically controlled the ebb and flow of his tides. In the tug of war for Rilke's person between providence and fate which now set in, providence seemed to be winning hands down; but fate and Paris never let go.

Arithmetically considered Paris scored very low. Of the four years and a half involved, one year and two months only were spent there, the longest of the seven sojourns being four and a half months, whereas the longest absence lasted nearly a year and a half. But Rilke's visits to Paris were numerically more frequent than those to Duino, the great antagonist of Paris during this period, and one which had much of the inspiration of its adversary. Translated into round figures and taking Paris as the starting-point, the broken and irregular rhythm of this epoch shows oscillations of varying lengths between that city and other places on the globe, oscillations which became quicker and feebler towards the end. From January 1910 until August 1914 this is how the rhythm ran:

PARIS:

Four days present; four and a half months absent.
Two months present; four months absent.
One month present; four and a half months absent.
Two and a half months present; three months absent.
Three weeks present; a year and a half absent.
Three months present; four and a half months absent.
Four and a half months present; one month absent.
One month present; one month absent.
Two months present; departure for Germany, where he was
    caught and held by the war.

Nearly two years of the time spent away from Paris were accounted for by hospitality of one sort or another. The year 1910 saw Rilke in Germany, Rome, Duino, Venice, Paris, Lautschin, Germany, Austria and Paris again. In November he then set off for a voyage to Algiers and Tunis, which was

extended after a halt at Naples to Egypt, the valley of the
Nile, Cairo and Heluan. Back in Paris in April 1911, he was
away again at Castle Lautschin, Janowitz, Leipzig and Berlin
during the late summer and early autumn. After a short three
weeks in Paris, he left it for Castle Duino, where he lived,
with the exception of two brief visits to Venice and one
longer residence there, until October 15, 1912. There followed
a journey to Spain, to Toledo, Cordova, Seville and Madrid,
whence he returned to Paris at the end of February 1913. He
then swayed backwards and forwards between Paris and
Germany and Paris and Italy until his last visit to Germany in
the summer of 1914.

Even allowing for the hospitality showered upon Rilke,
particularly during the year at Duino and the voyage to
Africa and Egypt, his life, involving as it did so much
travelling and so many hotel bills, was an expensive, not to
say an extravagant one, all the more so as the best hotels
were now only just good enough for Rilke; a fact which
caused some wry smiles from those benefactors who met him
staying in first-class establishments, when they were putting
up at second-rate hostelries. But one has to pay dear for
relative quiet, unobtrusive service and spotless cleanliness.
Luckily for him, the sales of his books were increasing
rapidly. In August 1914, *The Book of Hours* was in its
seventh edition, and forty thousand copies of *The Lay of the
Love and Death of Cornet Christopher Rilke* had been sold. *New
Poems I* and *New Poems II* were in their third and second
editions respectively, the former having sold six thousand
copies, whilst *Auguste Rodin* had ten thousand to its credit.
Tales about God, which went like wild-fire, was in its fourth
edition; the *Inselverlag* had bought *The Picture-Book* from
Juncker, and had already printed a second edition of their new
property; the two *Requiems* were selling well; *Malte Laurids
Brigge* ran through the first edition in the year of its publication; the third edition printed in 1918 was numbered six to
eight thousand. Apart from the various translations Rilke
published with the *Inselverlag* between the years 1910 and
1914, *Early Poems*, collected and brought out in 1909, was

reprinted for the third time in 1913; and *First Poems*, which appeared in 1913, seems to have been fairly successful, as a second edition was needed in 1918. All this must have represented a considerable sum in royalties. But there were other sources to tap. In May 1910 Rilke received 600 Kronen (about £175 in contemporary currency) from the Austrian government through the good offices of A. Sauer; and in September 1911 Heydt, Kassner, Count Kessler and Kippenberg clubbed together to make him an allowance for the years 1912, 1913 and 1914 over and above whatever royalties he might receive. The sum is not mentioned; but Heydt's presence among the contributors suggests that it was handsome. Nevertheless, Rilke was always in financial straits and perpetually appealing to Kippenberg for more money. He was cleaned out after the voyage to Egypt and again in Spain. Kippenberg sent him £25 for the journey back to Paris; only to receive an urgent telegram for more funds to defray the costs of installation. I have been told privately that his publisher did in fact give Rilke at one time and another a good deal more money than his books brought him in; and the letters to Kippenberg with their reiterated expressions of gratitude bear out this opinion. However that may be, his complete inability to settle for long in any one place made hay of his financial affairs.

Those retired and studious habits which had produced *New Poems* and *Malte Laurids Brigge* now suffered so many and such prolonged interruptions, that they had little chance to prevail. This was due, at first, less to the temptations with which providence bestrewed Rilke's path so liberally, than to the mental and emotional exhaustion produced by the sustained creative effort of the previous years. But the spiritual aridity persisted long after the reaction might be expected to have worked itself out, and had so far not had its equal for hopelessness and seeming finality in Rilke's life. He himself did not attribute his complete loss of inspiration to *New Poems*. It was with *Malte Laurids Brigge*, he always maintained, that the virtue had gone out of him. He looked upon it as a desperate feat of strength which had probably enfeebled him for good. Sometimes he believed that it marked the end of one poetic epoch and the beginning of another and a greater one; a watershed, separating the waters of inspiration flowing into two different beds; at other times this double-edged simile was used to denote the flowing of the waters of inspiration down a slope and away from him for ever. After *Malte Laurids Brigge* nothing remained for him to write, he often declared, and he reverted to his earlier desire to become a doctor, if it were still possible. In 1911 he elaborated an exacting and fantastic programme, in which medicine, Egyptology, riding-lessons and walks were to fill a life avoided by the muses. In reality it was by travel that he both sought to distract himself and to court inspiration. The power he had attributed in earlier days to the plying of some trade or craft, he now expected from sightseeing and globe-trotting: that it would let loose the dammed-up flood of inspiration.

The first considerable effort in this line, the voyage to Africa and Egypt, was something of a fiasco. Although the letters to Clara, especially one from Luxor, show enthusiasm and a poetic response to the overwhelming greatness of Egypt, they are not to be compared with the televisionary descriptions of the country he had sent to her from Capri. The fact that he stayed at Shepherd's Hotel in Cairo serves to make this tour indistinguishable from those undertaken by so many literary men of his day and ours, a fact which he felt keenly himself.[1] In his letters to other correspondents during and after the trip he was far more eloquent about the discomforts of the journey and the wretched circumstances in which it was undertaken than about its inherent interest. Even retrospectively, as Lou Andreas-Salomé pointed out, he could not regard it humorously. He often lamented to the Princess Thurn and Taxis that the whole expedition had been a failure. His travelling-companions were uncongenial, and various distressing mishaps occurred, about which he was singularly reticent. But he was also thoroughly out of tune with everything, harassed, nervy and unwell; so much so that

[1] Cf. *B. 1907–1914*, 2, p. 126.

when a yellow dog bit him in Kairwan Rilke felt that the
animal was in the right to do so, because he himself was so
utterly and completely in the wrong. The most that he could
say for the journey was that it had added to his experiences,
and might bear fruit in the future. Safe in the shelter of the
Knoops' house in Heluan, he was delighted to be done with
the whole undertaking. It had been merely an evasion to go
at all, he maintained, and it took him a long time to recover
from it. Later he showed real interest and enthusiasm for
things Egyptian. He even contemplated accompanying Professor Steindorff on an archaeological expedition to the Nubian
desert in 1913, with the Kippenbergs and Lou Andreas-
Salomé. Luckily perhaps for Steindorff, but unfortunately for
posterity, this plan did not progress beyond talk. An
excavating-party including Rilke would have added an item to
the annals of archaeology which lovers of the human comedy
would have certainly enjoyed. Anyone less likely to undergo
the hardships of that type of expedition cheerfully would be
hard to find; and the exasperation he would have caused the
fellow-members of the party can readily be imagined. The
idea was fantastic but significant, and later still the vision
which had lain dormant whilst he was in Egypt shed radiance
over *Duino Elegies* and *Sonnets to Orpheus*.

At the time Africa and Egypt intensified alarmingly the
prolonged and painful crisis Rilke was undergoing. The effect
of the refuge in Duino was more complex. The mistress of the
castle has given such glorious descriptions of it and such enchanting accounts of Rilke's life there, that one is almost
dazzled by the fortune which wafted this tormented poet to a
haven so sublimely situated, so beguilingly furnished, whose
presiding genius understood him so well.[1] She made his
visits a feast of reason and a flow of soul by providing for
short periods the most stimulating and enlightened companions, and organising romantic entertainments and expeditions. But more than that, she gave him for months on end
the complete solitude and independence he desired, leaving

[1] Marie von Thurn und Taxis-Hohenlohe, *Erinnerungen an Rainer Maria
Rilke*, Munich, Berlin, Zürich, 2nd ed. 1933.

him to a bevy of discreet and devoted servants whilst she betook herself elsewhere. A curious little scene was played out before she went which might be taken as a sign that, even in these circumstances, Castle Duino struck Rilke as far from ideal. Having discovered a disused and entirely uninhabitable pavilion in an ancient oak-grove on the estate, Rilke pleaded passionately to be allowed to live there instead of in the castle. The ruined pavilion with its columns and veiled statues, the romantic silence and desolation surrounding it, were made for poetry and dreams. A few sticks of furniture, or even one old leather arm-chair, would be enough for him, he childishly maintained. Water, servants, cooking facilities, all these were inessentials. The princess and her house-keeper, in despair but determined to humour him, began to make what arrangements they could for his comfort. Finally even Rilke saw that it would not do. But his irrational eager-ness to put the plan into execution reflects a critical attitude towards the castle as well as enthusiasm for the mysterious aura of the pavilion.

For Rilke was hostile to Duino during the long period he spent there, mostly alone, from October 1911 to May 1912. He looked upon his residence in the castle as having much to recommend it from an economical and disciplinary point of view; but he repeatedly compared it to a prison, deplored the austere and menacing character of its surroundings, which sometimes also seemed to him deadly monotonous and hate-fully Austrian; and he wailed over the trying nature of the climate, which jangled and jarred his nerves. But the grandeur and sublimity of Duino, a hard task for him to face, called out something from him which only Paris had done until now. Nevertheless, when he left it for Spain in October 1912 he did not return again until April 1914, and then only for a week. Something else within him fought against it, as it had fought against Paris; and even resisted the outrushing of inspiration which in January 1912 and immediately after produced the first two *Duino Elegies* and some further fragments. It was a visitation such as he had never known before; and Rilke, far from encouraging the return of this mighty spirit, buried himself in the study of Venetian history the better to keep it at bay:

I have a sort of instinct (he wrote at this time to the princess) to beware of creating at the moment. The spirit rushes in and out so violently, comes so wildly, and absents itself so abruptly, that I feel as if I were being physically torn to pieces.[1]

This was the only time in his history that he denied himself to the spirit which his whole life was led to serve; and for a strange reason; it was a shattering and exhausting visitant. *The Book of Hours* had come so easily; *New Poems* had so obviously been the reward of virtue for hard spiritual endeavour; this was something so different as to be almost sinister, he felt. Perhaps his recoil was a symptom of bad mental health, of something so gravely wrong that it seemed as if nothing could right it. The glorious solitude of Duino had resulted in the uprising of that inspiration whose failure had been the subject of such tragic laments; and behold, it was more than he had bargained for, and hardly to be borne.

His abysmal melancholia in Duino was such that he kept on remembering Capri, and longing to be back there again. It was one example among many of the delayed action of happiness in his mind. Happiness was nearly always retrospective for Rilke; his yearning descriptions of the Villa Discopoli and of its deeply loving, strangely moving inmates were none the less genuine because they came so late, and were made to the disadvantage of Duino. The gehenna he was undergoing there might well make the disgruntled moods on Capri appear retrospectively the acme of bliss. Eloquent about his sufferings in his letters, he was the most charming, courteous and grateful of guests at close quarters. All his hostesses delighted in his visits, and believed that they were making him happy. As he catalogued her treasures for her, the princess was overjoyed by his interest. Yet the mind of this great poet was living in hell as he went hunting throughout the castle of Duino for rouge-pots and other *petits objets*

---

[1] Thurn und Taxis, *op. cit.* p. 43; from Duino, n.d.

pour la femme with which to adorn a show-case in the red drawing-room.

A much more positive symptom of his mental disarray was his deliberate dabbling in the occult. Rilke's imaginative gifts (psychic or mediumistic if you like), which brought him into direct spiritual contact with persons and things outside and beyond himself, were the very basis of his art in *New Poems* and elsewhere and are indeed the stuff of which poetry is made. Unable to achieve similar evocations in prose, he fell back on the grosser effects of ghosts and materialisations in *Malte Laurids Brigge*, translating his experiences into the kind of language which inevitably vulgarised and trivialised them. The occult tales in his confessions can be capped by almost every reader, and are familiar to thousands who would be incapable of undergoing at first or even at second hand the spiritual processes he was symbolising. The spate of psychic gossip purveyed at tea-parties, drawn from those overheated parlours which enshrine murky mediums, dingy crystal-gazers and shady *clairvoyantes*, flowed into and contaminated a book which, except for the unfortunate ghost-stories, had absolutely nothing in common with it. Poetically speaking, it was a step downward after *New Poems*, and it is painful to watch Rilke slithering down it in person whilst he was at Duino. He was aided and abetted therein by his fairy-princess, who was irresistibly attracted, as such leisured and cultivated *dilettanti* often are, by the mystery of inexplicable phenomena. The actual experiences recounted by him to her, or witnessed by her, are on the whole credible, with the exception of one or two. Only one man in a thousand can be entirely straight about horses, it is said; hardly one human being in a million can be completely truthful about the occult; and Rilke probably belonged to the majority. As for the presumably genuine experiences, they are nearly all of the stereotyped kind, with which most of us have been far too often regaled: a strange feeling that supernatural influences were at work in Rilke's meeting with the princess; psychical shudders in an eerie deserted part of Venice, which could never be found again; the ghosts of three dead women,

Theresina, Raymondine and Polyxène, invisibly haunting
Rilke in the castle; the sensation of being out of time and in
eternity under an ancient olive-tree, and of fearing to go back
there, lest he should never return. The author of *New Poems*
had dealt magically with kindred themes; but his occult
experiences in Duino and in Venice were far less important
than the spiritual life led by this or any other great poet during
periods of inspiration. Nevertheless, since to the episode
under the olive-tree we owe the sketch called *An Experience*,
one of the most haunting evocations of Rilke's sense of the
past, it would be churlish to regret it. But this, and similar
experiences, made such an impression on Marie Thurn and
Taxis, that Rilke, or so I believe, began to fake others after
the fashion of professional mediums in order to enhance his
prestige. How else to account for that too-opportune bunch of
violets, discovered by Rilke and the princess in one of those
very places where the poet's child-lover, Amélie, used to
leave such posies for him years and years ago? The long arm
of coincidence may have been having a night out; but Rilke
seems to have led the princess to the nosegay very much as if
he had planted it there. The suspicion is corroborated by the
tale he told of Amélie's spirit appearing by his bedside at
school when she became a nun; and of the ring which she then
returned to him, and which he professed to have still. When it
came, inevitably, to *planchette*, something of the same sort
may have occurred, although the conditions certainly pre-
cluded any kind of manipulation, unless Rilke and Pascha
(Marie's son) were in collusion; and one hardly sees Rilke
going as far as that. The poet stood at some distance from the
table and wrote down his questions in silence; the princess
and her son sat together at the board, and Pascha held the
pencil. The answers, given by an 'unknown woman', were so
extremely Rilkean in style and subject-matter, that Marie
Thurn and Taxis deduced the influence of the poet's subconscious mind, a reasonable and charitable interpretation.
Rilke was on tiptoe to visit Toledo at the time, so that the
'unknown's' transparently urgent injunctions to go there
probably emanated from him; but whether consciously or un-

consciously is the vital question. Uneasily one remembers in this connection the insinuations made to Heydt in 1906 that the spirit of the departed Countess Schwerin was suggesting a journey to Greece. Was he practising telepathy now, either to reconcile the princess to his departure from Duino (an ethereal form of blackmail), or in order to create yet another sensation? Such unworthy and possibly unjust suspicions hover round amateurs of spiritualism, which has not yet emerged from the swaddling-clothes of superstition and charlatanism. But even if the messages of the 'unknown' were genuine psychical manifestations, one's heart sinks to see a poet like Rilke using this grotesque and clumsy method of approach to a kingdom which was his by right divine. At the moment, it must be remembered, the gates were barred against him by the glorious but terrifying Duino angels. Efforts to force an entrance led, not only to spiritualistic experiments, but also to a frantic search for the predestined place where inspiration and revelation awaited him. The hopes thus harboured were not far removed from fetishism. The longing to inhabit the pavilion at Duino was hardly rational; and the same may be said of the violent desire to betake himself to Toledo, where he was convinced that something of the utmost importance would happen to him. The rapture with which the first sight of this magnificent city and of El Greco's paintings inspired him seemed to justify his premonitions. Spain was responsible for some remarkable poems, among them the greater part of his sixth elegy.[1] But although his soul was stirred and shaken, the climate proved too trying for him, and he left it after a month. Journeying farther southwards through Cordova and Seville (which he hated) to Ronda, a profound depression overmastered him; and he declared that, unless he himself could become fundamentally different, all the miracles in the world would be of no avail.

The successive disillusions and defeats which he experienced in Egypt, at Duino and in Spain were so bitter, that he must have despaired completely, had it not been for his

---

[1] For the influence of Toledo and El Greco on Rilke, cf. H. Gebser, *Rilke und Spanien*, Zürich, New York, 1940.

continued belief in the power of Paris. This upheld him during his absences from it, and for a time whenever he came back and found the old spell beginning to work again. As late as March 1913, he spoke of it to Kippenberg on his return from Spain as the most remarkable, the most significant and formative of places, and of the incomparable joy of being back. It was nothing new for him to bewail its hardness and menace, as he did to Lou in the following October after she had with difficulty persuaded him to return; but a different kind of criticism to the princess that December showed that the might of Paris over Rilke's mind was at last beginning to weaken. He was utterly sick of this city of the damned, he declared in this letter; it was dirty and morose, he added to another correspondent, and he no longer cared for it; partly because it was becoming americanised, and partly because he needed it less. Similar allusions occur in January and February 1914; nevertheless, the charm began to work again during this period, for in the winter of 1913 to 1914 he composed the third elegy and other fragments. In the following June he blamed himself bitterly for having gone away from Paris at a time when inspiration was just beginning to stir again. The fact that the two first elegies were written at Duino and the sixth in Toledo seems to suggest that Paris was no longer vitally necessary to Rilke. On the other hand, not even Toledo had replaced it in the poet's mind. He was beginning to be off with the old love, perhaps; but he was not yet on with the new.

This must have contributed its quota to the appalling misery, compounded of melancholy, restlessness, fatigue and depression, which continued almost unbroken from 1910 to 1914. He felt like Raskolnikov after the murder, he stated in 1910 on the completion of *Malte Laurids Brigge*. In 1911 he compared himself to a man who spent his time buttoning up a coat-button which always came unfastened again. His state of mind in 1912 was such that he nearly decided to undergo psycho-analytical treatment. In 1913 he lamented that his heart was extinguished and full of cold ashes; and in 1914 he represented himself as looking wanly out into the world through a small hole in the wall of his apathy. These are only a few similes, chosen at random and greatly condensed, from innumerable lengthy and desperate outbursts, revealing an almost incurable despair, which the Princess Thurn and Taxis also witnessed and described.

Rilke, however, did not merely wail. His positive efforts to escape from the vicious circle of apathy and restlessness were unremitting. Not only did he journey through Europe and beyond in search of a new self; not only did he have recourse to spiritualism and dally with the thought of analysis; not only did he embark on various avocations and pursuits, the most important being his translations; he also undertook many spiritual adventures into minds hitherto unexplored by him. A vital and sustained interest in literature is manifest during this period. In his callow youth, Rilke had come under many poetical influences and succumbed to them all, almost to the point of plagiarism. Then Jacobsen had affected him fundamentally; and after that he had felt for Russian writers a strong but superficial enthusiasm. During the years 1902 to 1910 his reading had been desultory and capricious. He had made some literary finds, such as Baudelaire's *Charogne*, and had amassed a heterogeneous collection of authors rather after the fashion of a jackdaw; but his real interest had been all for plastic art. The position was now reversed. Kippenberg aroused Rilke's enthusiasm for Goethe, whom he had hitherto avoided and instinctively disliked; his knowledge and understanding of Dostoyevski greatly increased during this period; and his interest in Ibsen grew deeper. More than this: Cervantes, Strindberg, Dante, Marlowe and Shakespeare (in translations); Kleist, Hölderlin, Hofmannsthal, George, Werfel, Dauthendey; Proust, Gide, and a good many other contemporary writers now became a living reality to Rilke, whose comments and criticisms, penetrating and constructive, show what a sensitive and intellectual mind was feeling its way into the poetry of past and present ages.

His efforts to escape from himself did not end there. His personal relationships show a more adventurous disposition than before. Towards the dead and gone, towards Tolstoy and

Paula Modersohn-Becker, a deepening comprehension, a greater magnanimity in the letters reveal the fact that his mind was still actively occupied with them, and that the spiritual relationship between them had not been cut off by death. But the connection with Clara was growing slacker. He spent only five months all told in her vicinity from January 1910 to August 1914, and the former steady stream of letters dwindled almost to nothing. There are none from January 18, 1911 until August 21, 1914 in the published correspondence; although there is evidence that letters did pass between them during this period; and, as they met in Paris in the summer of 1913, and saw something of each other then, they were obviously not estranged. Rilke told Kippenberg that he would like to help Clara and Ruth financially when he received the allowance from his four friends; he also began to show a rudimentary sense of responsibility and anxiety about Ruth's future. Slender though the bond between Rilke and his wife now appeared to be, it was nevertheless strong enough to play a part in the final rupture with Rodin.

His affection for Clara was dying from inanition; his friendship with Rodin long survived the feelings which had brought it into being. Until October 1911 Rilke went on living in the rue de Varenne, where he was a neighbour of Rodin's whenever they were both in Paris; and after he had removed to the rue Campagne-Première in 1913, he continued to keep in touch with him. The initiative, as far as one can judge from the letters, now came once more almost wholly from Rilke, but in a fashion which is open to some criticism. No longer dependent for inspiration on his sometime master, he bothered him unmercifully to show smaller or greater favours to others. He was for ever asking Rodin's permission to introduce this, that, or the other person to him; or begging him to grant interviews to amateurs; or to encourage some struggling artist. All this at a time when the sculptor, old and enfeebled, was beginning to lose his powers of endurance; and was so much overwhelmed with business that it was cruelty to add to his burdens. Considering how

jealously Rilke guarded his own solitude, his frequent interruptions of Rodin's were the reverse of considerate. He
seemed more fearful of disappointing friends and even indifferent acquaintances than of harrying the old artist with his
petitions. There were, on the other hand, occasions when he
could not help himself; as for instance when German collectors
or directors of museums used him as an intermediary in
acquiring Rodin's works. Such negotiations were always
attended by irritating difficulties and delays owing to Rodin's
growing unreasonableness. The bow between them was,
therefore, bent to breaking-point when Dr Wichert, director
of the Mannheim Museum, conceived the unfortunate notion
of commissioning a bust of Rodin from Clara Rilke in 1912.
Her husband's influence was absolutely necessary to obtain
Rodin's consent to this proposal, and he rose manfully to
the occasion, writing a suitably diffident letter of an extremely persuasive kind. This was in August 1912. In
October, having received no answer, he tried again; and
Rodin gave a modified approval, something like a half-promise
to give Clara 'a few moments' next spring. But when, in
March 1913, Rilke announced the impending arrival of Clara
in Paris to claim this promise, Rodin changed his mind and
refused to sit for her. Rilke's consternation was naturally
great, and Clara's disappointment must have been cruel. One
cannot help feeling however, that, considering their relative
positions as artists, it had been too much to expect or to ask
for. Obdurate in this matter, Rodin seems to have been kind
to his former pupil when she appeared in Paris; for the last
letter Rilke wrote to him, dated May 13, 1913, is a paean of
thanksgiving for a sublimely happy morning spent with
Rodin by the pair of them. This meeting would have made a
fine curtain to the drama of their friendship, which unhappily
was rung down a few days later on a scene of recrimination.
Rodin, who had given permission for certain photographs of
his works to be produced in a new edition of Rilke's *Auguste
Rodin*, withdrew his consent without rhyme or reason at
the eleventh hour; the author seems to have protested; the
sculptor seems to have flown into one of his rages; the final

result was a breach between them which was not to be healed again.

It was perhaps a pity that the first violent quarrel had ever been patched up. There was something tragically right about that, conspicuously absent from the wranglings over sittings and copyrights which parted them for ever, and in which Rilke played the part of a well-intentioned but maddening gadfly to Rodin's infuriated bull. When the latter savagely shook himself free, Rilke was correct in saying that the relationship between them had gone bad because the greatness had gone out of it. The poet had been a shrinking witness of Rodin's mental and moral deterioration; it had been pain and grief to him to see the transformation of an immortal god into a piteous human being. Rodin's callousness about the bust and the photographs completed his disillusion. The master, on the other hand, may have been so intractable about these matters because one way and another Rilke had asked for too much. The game of friendship was no longer worth the candle for either in May 1913, and the flame was extinguished for good.

The gap in Rilke's emotional life made by the gradual fading out of his feelings for Clara and Rodin was partly filled in by the strength with which his even older friendship with Lou Andreas-Salomé put out new and vigorous tendrils between his heart and hers. They seem to have been out of touch with each other for some time after December 1906, when Rilke had probably resented her interference between Clara and himself. But he wrote her a marvellous letter about Orange and Les Baux in October 1909; and she visited him during his Malte-period at the Hôtel Biron. In December 1911, he wrote to her from Duino, resuming his confessional letters; he also visited her in Göttingen in the summer of 1913 and they were in the Riesengebirge together. Real affection, absolute trust and confidence informed his attitude to her even more strongly than before. He poured out all his troubles to her with spontaneous sincerity; he confessed his failings to her; he revealed his desperate mental and emotional straits; and he devoted a long letter to an enthusiastic appreciation of her *Three Letters to a Boy*. She was capable of understanding, advising and comforting him. No one else ever quite took her place in his affections or in his life; and no one else ever drew from him quite the same accents of absolute sincerity as she. But she was not the only one of her kind. Both Katharina Kippenberg and Marie Thurn and Taxis, particularly the latter, enjoyed much greater intimacy with the poet than such former benefactresses as the Countess Schwerin, Frau Alice Faehndrich or Mary Gneisenau. He was on happy and easy terms with the princess; and altogether it may be said of his relations with his numerous women-correspondents that a greater warmth and friendliness is noticeable in the letters of this period. He began to show them less elaborate courtesy and more human affection; relatively less and relatively more; for he remained exquisitely formal with women to the end of his life. Nor was there much solidity in his epistles to N. N., a young lady who turned to him for advice, and then began to cling. Rilke was expansive at first, and prodigal of counsel; but his letters became rapidly shorter, hastier in tone and more sparing of sympathy. He always found the rôle of poetical mentor alluringly easy to assume and irksome to support for long. A more obvious proof of fundamental goodness of heart is to be found in certain letters to Kippenberg. The trouble he took over Vogeler's illustrations of some early *Songs of Mary* of his; his real regret that the sketches were inadequate; the dedication of the new *Life of Mary* thus inspired to his old friend, of whose art he now had so poor an opinion; all this revealed delicacy, kindness and gratitude for the past. His active interest in the publication of Regina Ullmann's *Field Sermon* with the *Inselverlag* is another such instance. Rilke took the matter up energetically and was delighted to see it put through; he was most selflessly anxious to do the author a good turn and to encourage her to the utmost of his ability. He also spent much time and trouble over the unpublished verse and prose of his friend Gerhard Ouckama Knoop when he died in 1913. Rilke wished to do something for the memory of Knoop and also for the consolation of the widow; he achieved the publication of the poems in 1914; for it was owing to the representations of Rilke that Kippenberg accepted them.

In two other more outstanding cases, a positive desire to help replaced the negative acceptance of sympathy, protection and support which had formed Rilke's staple response to human stimuli in previous years. The little Parisian waif called Marthe, whom he half and half adopted, aroused protective, anxious and loving emotions which were rare visitors in his heart. He placed her with a Madame M. in 1912, in the hopes of educating her; and he seems to have loved her dearly, and to have been very much beloved. But neither he nor Madame M. was capable of disciplining his fantastic little *protégée*, part lover, part daughter to one of the strangest poets who has ever existed. She escaped from chaperonage in 1913 to live in a most bohemian fashion with a wild Russian artist, and to career through Paris with Rilke from cabaret to cabaret all night, dressed in Greek costume with a gold fillet twined round her hair; almost visibly slipping back into the underworld from which she had emerged to touch a heart which was difficult indeed to hold. For Rilke soon realised that he would not be able to help or to save that queer appealing little Marthe. He lamented his ineffectiveness to the princess, and attributed it to his lack of real love for the child, bewailing his emotional aridity contrasted with the riches of her temperament. The same impression of hopeless inadequacy overcame him in the presence of Eleonora Duse, whom he met in Venice in the summer of 1912.

She had filled his thoughts for many years. Even before he had seen her act, he had remodelled *The White Princess* in 1904 with the Duse in mind, and had dedicated it to her. In November 1906 he had seen her as Rebecca West and had unavailingly tried to get an introduction to her through Heydt. *Portrait* in *New Poems II* described the impression she had made on him; and a very fine passage was devoted to her in *Malte Laurids Brigge*. She was and remained for him one of the great portents of the age; an actress of such genius that no contemporary theatre or dramatist could exploit it, a fact which he considered a tragic comment on modern times. They now met at last, and spent three weeks in Venice very largely in each other's company. It was without exception the most hectic time in Rilke's life. Surrounded by the satellites great artists so often attract, the Duse was indeed a disturbing person to encounter. She was a tragic, ageing, desperate woman, torn by passions and desires, embittered and disillusioned; frantically but fruitlessly searching for the work of genius to bring her back in glory to the stage; and endowed in the very teeth of her sorrows and despair with superabundant, almost daimonic, vitality; with a great and sombre charm. In her train was Signora Poletti, many years younger than her distinguished friend. Energetic, capable and gifted up to a point, she was working furiously at an *Ariadne* which was intended to give the actress her heart's desire. But a hard streak in her nature assorted ill with the tempestuous temperament of the Duse. They had been bosom friends, and were now in the grip of those embittering and torturing scenes which mark the beginning of the end in such relationships. Hovering around them was the actor Moissi, the Duse's would-be impresario, all alight and aflame with Rheinhardtian ideas; whilst the brother of Marie Thurn and Taxis, an old and devoted friend of the actress, made an anxious and uneasy fourth. Rilke was soon keyed up to a high pitch of sympathy, all the more wearing because it effected nothing. *The White Princess* was early mooted between them; but, though the Duse herself was enraptured by the account of it and clamoured for a translation, Rilke had lost faith in it, and the princess from a distance was the reverse of encouraging. Before anything definite could be undertaken, the party was swept asunder by the emotional hurricane raging between the two women, who rushed away from Venice in opposite directions, leaving Rilke behind them in a state of nervous collapse. An expedition to one of the islands in the lagoon, during which a peaceful picnic-tea was rent in twain by the merciless screechings of a peacock which scattered the whole party in uproar and confusion, was symbolical of the three unnerving weeks during which Rilke danced attendance on the great tragic actress of his age. Quixotically attempting to mediate between the two women, he was exposed to the full force of their disruptive emotions, which bruised and battered his spirit, and exasperated them even more.

Although Rilke could be extremely comic about these episodes both orally and in letters, the emotion he felt for the Duse, 'that glorious sympathy with suns that set', was perhaps the noblest of which his letters give proof. It was far removed from the rather callow hero-worship he had felt first for Tolstoy and later for Rodin; it was much more deeply humane and far more active. He moved heaven and earth after he had seen her to get a Duse-Theatre founded, or failing that, some play produced in which her genius could set in splendour. He was not successful; but how different these urgent, almost desperate letters read from those well-balanced and benign epistles, full of mellow wisdom and tender charm, which were thought so beautiful and helpful by such recipients as young Kappus; but which, being largely self-communings, seem hardly more related to the correspondent than his equally famous letters of condolence which can surely never have brought much comfort to a grief-stricken heart.

Rilke was a real friend to the Duse, *in posse*, if not *in esse*; he really understood her, really felt for her, really grieved over her lot. It is one of the few relationships of this sort in his life. His friendships with such men as Kippenberg, Gide, Kassner, Verhaeren and Hofmannsthal lacked this kind of significance, being for the most part intellectual associations, stimulating and interesting, but making few demands upon him. But Rilke was a generous-minded as well as a delicate-minded friend; his enthusiasm for the gifts of these brother-poets and writers is one of his most pleasing traits, and was particularly apparent in his relationship with Kassner, whose mind and personality he almost helplessly admired. They met both in Paris and Duino, for Kassner was intimate with the princess; and Rilke never tired of extolling the other's mental and personal gifts. Kassner's slight and rather dry reminiscences of the poet show less fervour and are tinged with something like respectful spite. In this case Rilke seems to have met with concealed antipathy and an instinctive recoil, a response to his personality which one can readily imagine to have been often made by men. It is not, however, in such occasional animosities that the deep defeat of his personal life is to be found. It lay, or so he was convinced himself, in his own utter incapacity to love. One could adduce passage after passage in his letters in proof of this; it was one of his standing griefs, which became greater as time went on, and his 'stubborn heart' as he called it, continued obdurate; but let one particularly desperate outburst stand for many:

If during the last years I sometimes tried to flatter myself, that certain efforts to gain a more human and natural footing in life had failed because the people involved did not understand me and had, one after another, injured me, violated me and done me wrong, and had thus unnerved me, I have entirely altered my opinion now after these last months of suffering. This time I have been obliged to recognise the fact that no one can help me, no one at all. And even if he should come with the best and the most loving of hearts, and should prove his worth to the very stars, bearing with me however hard and stiff I might make myself, and keeping his regard for me pure and untroubled, however often I broke the ray of his love with the cloudiness and density of my submarine world; I would yet (I know it now) find the means to strip him of the fulness of his ever-renewed assistance, and to enclose him in a loveless vacuum, so that his useless succour would rot and wither and die a terrible death.[1]

Rilke was in a sad dilemma between his need for human sympathy and his craving for solitude; between an almost fatal gift for attracting love and an utter incapacity to feel it for long. He feared love horribly, and shunned the fascinating Countess de Noailles whom he met in 1909 as if she were the plague. He gave her the flattering reason that he was terrified of becoming her slave, and of losing his individuality in hers; but he was probably much more frightened of his

---

[1] *B. 1907–1914*, p. 357; to Lou Andreas-Salomé from 17 rue Campagne-Première, June 8, 1914; cf. also *ibid.* pp. 90, 149, 175, 236, 241, 258, 271, 282, 329.

own emotional impotence. It was another proof of this which dictated the despairing passage above, the tragic ending to a love-affair which had begun with an exalted correspondence and withered away under the stress of three months' personal intercourse. He confided this last crushing experience in the letter to Lou and also in conversation with the Princess Thurn and Taxis. He was in a desperate state when he saw the latter in April 1914, and almost raving about his inability to experience great love, about the sufferings, remorse, struggles and despair he had undergone in his erotic relationships, and his determination to consult only his own inclinations in the future, and be done with compassion and unavailing regrets. Kassner's unsympathetic comment on this outburst was to the effect that all these women were beginning to bore Rilke at last. It certainly showed that his sexual life gave him very little pleasure, and a disproportionate amount of pain.

It shows more than that, however, an insatiable hunger for love, a divine discontent with loving, a sense of something wrong with the very basis of human existence, which is the curse all artists labour under, and Rilke more greatly than most, since his moments of self-forgetfulness were so few and so short. His incapacity to love had not mattered much whilst he was under the sway of Rodin and completely absorbed by his art. But during the years of sterility, when his genius had been playing truant from fate, his general vagrancy had precipitated him into many and various passionate experiments, none of which had turned out well. A little waif like Marthe could put him to the blush when it came to loving; and neither the Countess Pia di Valmarana, to whom some highly emotional letters were written during this period; nor even the unknown woman about whom he wrote so desperately to Lou, and for whose sake he had been actually contemplating a divorce from Clara in the spring of 1914, could really hold him.

All these upheavals and his unassuaged longing for some place of his own in which to live and work, resuscitated the dream-vision of an ideal home shared by an ideal companion which he had communicated to Clara in the days before their marriage. He was now once more yearning to live in the country in some modest little cottage; but the standard he set for his female companion was both lower and higher than the fellow-worker and fellow-artist he had chosen in the past. He now needed some gentle unassuming sisterly woman, devoted enough to share his solitude, cook for him, watch over his creature comforts, understand him and make no claims upon him. Such a person, he acknowledged himself, did not exist; and should God create her on purpose, she would not grow up in time to be of any use to Rilke. Indeed, one can far more readily imagine him entertaining angels aware or unaware than a sisterly cook-housekeeper whose soul was in tune with his own. Certainly none such approached him, whereas angels had visited him in Duino, and had been very close to him in Toledo and Paris. In the spring and summer of 1914 they seemed to be winging towards him again.

It had not been quite in vain after all that Rilke had gone to ground in Paris and remained there for more than four months on end from October 18, 1913 to February 27, 1914. Hidden in the rue Campagne-Première, he had even dissuaded Marie Thurn and Taxis from coming to Paris, so that nothing might interrupt a solitude which was beginning to bear fruit. Then he had given way, probably to emotional pressure, not once, but twice, in the spring; going first to Berlin and Munich, and then to Duino, Assisi and Milan. On his return in May he confessed that never before in his life had he experienced so terrible a sensation of having literally destroyed himself, by undertaking these journeys at a time when inspiration was just beginning to flow freely. But the destruction was not as complete as he thought. The strange essay *Dolls*, charged with promise, had been published as early as March 1914; on June 20, a poem called *Turning-Point* and enclosed in a letter to Lou showed which way the wind was blowing; and *Thunderstorm* ten days later confirmed his hopes. Rilke was reading Hölderlin in Hellingrath's edition during these last months in Paris. He stated that the influence radiating from this supreme poet was 'great and magnanimous'. Hölderlin probably accelerated the release of inspiration which was breaking through of its own accord. The greater mental health which made this possible is manifest in Rilke's categorical refusal to read Schrenck-Notzing's book on spiritualism, and his determination to avoid mediums and crystal-gazers in future. That he nevertheless experimented with *planchette* when he was at Duino in April 1914 in order to re-establish contact with the 'unknown' is not inconsistent with his fastidious recoil (expressed with great wit and point) from the mediocre nature of the spirits who frequent most mediums, and the paltry things they say. He was in direct communication with his own spirit again, and needed no adventitious aids.

Looking back over Rilke's life since he first came to Paris, one sees that the poverty-stricken and half-baked young poet who had lived in an attic and worshipped Rodin had developed into a much more dominant personality, magnetic, exacting, restless; a danger to others and himself. First Rodin and then Paris had exercised and controlled his formidable genius, which ran wild when left to its own devices, coming perilously close to self-destruction in the process, but also coming within the confines of an inspiration greater than Rilke had known before. It tarried even more inexorably; it seized upon him more terribly when it came. Meanwhile he had exchanged his homely nordic godmother for a dazzling fairy-princess; and he was living dangerously, because he was on unfamiliar, perhaps on higher, ground and had not yet got his bearings, even in Paris. Yet such was the persisting power of that city over his mind, such the strength of its associations, that when he left France for Germany on July 23, 1914, to visit the Kippenbergs, it almost seemed as if Paris had effected the cure which years spent elsewhere had failed to effect. Then he innocently broke through the circle again, to meet a very different kind of fate.

During the last four years before the war, nearly everything Rilke published or prepared for publication had had its inception in Capri. It was here that he translated in 1907 the *Sonnets from the Portuguese*, influenced and assisted by Alice Faehndrich. It was here also, and much more fatefully, that his interest in the love-letters of the Portuguese nun, Marianna Alcoforado, was first aroused. He wrote a rhapsodical account of them for the *Inselalmanach* in 1908; and henceforward the writer symbolised for this strange poet all that was heroic and sublime, selfless and almost divine in the unrequited love of women. One has to take Rilke's mania for Marianna as one takes Goethe's youthful enthusiasm for Ossian (which however he outgrew), as a symptom of the times; and also as an instance of the changing nature of taste. Rilke raved about these unconvincing love-letters, which are probably not even genuine documents, and are certainly not real cries from the heart. He spent a whole evening declaiming about them to Rodin; and his letters give proof of the lasting nature of this perplexing passion. Undeterred by the monotony, feebleness and vapidity of the style; overlooking the torrent of reproaches and even abuse poured over the head of *cette bête Chamilly*; he took the hysterical ravings, the swoonings, the throbbing self-pity, all the romantic claptrap dear to an age which had forgotten how to love, as the purest and highest expression of this emotion. One begins unwillingly to believe in the face of such evidence he cannot have experienced it himself. This seems almost tragically clear by the awe-stricken manner in which he was wont to repeat the phrase: 'My love no longer depends on the way you treat me.' This alone, Rilke vociferated, would stamp Marianna as a lover-saint. It would be recognised as the merest truism by anyone in the know; and the far from saint-like Philine in *William Meister* went a good deal further than Marianna when she asked the recalcitrant William: 'And if I chose to love you, what's that to you?'

Rilke's wearisome obsession with Marianna and her unfortunate sisters occupied his mind during this period almost to the exclusion of anything else. After meeting the Countess de Noailles in 1909, he wrote an essay about her poetry, *The*

Books of a Lover,[1] impregnated with the same notions, which
also led him to translate in 1911 a French sermon, attributed
by some writers of the seventeenth century to Bossuet, called
The Love of Mary Magdalene. Rilke was enraptured by this
effusion of religious eroticism; and it was certainly grist to his
mill, since it preached renunciation and abnegation to earthly
lovers, and was eloquent on the selfless passion of Mary. In
the autumn of 1911 he also began, with the help of Marie
Thurn and Taxis, a translation of Dante's *Vita Nuova* at Duino.
This was never completed, and was lost with many other of his
papers during the war. In 1913 he finished his translation of
Marianna Alcoforado's letters from the French (the original
Portuguese letters have never been seen); and made a
rendering of the twenty-four *Sonnets* of Louïze Labé, published in 1918. In 1913 he also produced *The Life of Mary*,
ten poems which he wrote to replace the ten *Songs of Mary* in
Vogeler's possession, which the latter wished to publish with
his own illustrations. The ruling passion of the period further
inspired the unpublished fragment on God's love for us and
the first *Duino Elegy*. The translation of Maurice de Guérin's
Centaure in 1911, of André Gide's *Retour de l'Enfant Prodigue* in
1914, and the essay called *Dolls* in the same year complete the
sum of Rilke's published productions. With the exception of
the last three works women-lovers dominated the whole, and
also played a large part, it will be remembered, in *Malte
Laurids Brigge*. The mystical, unearthly, despairing love of
his prodigal son had been humanly speaking a confession of
defeat. Otherwise Rilke had concentrated on the sorrows and
sufferings of the other sex; it is perhaps but natural therefore
that his interpretations were in the main translations from
their language into his.

Rilke was a sympathetic translator, but not a great one.
His version of the *Sonnets from the Portuguese* reads more
smoothly than the original, and seems superficially more
poetical, but is actually not nearly such great poetry. The
arresting similes, the strange expressions, the powerful, at
times uncouth language, the occasional clumsiness of the

[1] Published in *Corona*, 1934, v, 2, pp. 165–168.

original were all toned down by him to the same level of gentle, musical, womanish laments. Rilke adopted a less exacting rhyme-scheme than his model and varied it when it suited him. The result is pleasant but minor poetry, containing some misapprehensions and giving a general effect of preciosity and languor. His slight knowledge of English, and the help Alice Faehndrich gave him, made his version a gentler edition of himself, and not very characteristic of his author. Nevertheless some of the poems are extremely successful.

The sonnets of Louïze Labé suffered a more fundamental change at the hands of Rilke. Their simplicity and directness, their archaic language, their haunting music disappeared from his highly wrought and sophisticated versions. German is a better medium for English poetry than for French, whose exquisite elusiveness baffles all efforts to reproduce it. Rilke was by now steeped in the French language, and translated Maurice de Guérin and André Gide extremely well; but, poetical though his renderings of Louïze Labé's sonnets are, better poetry perhaps than his version of the *Sonnets from the Portuguese*, they fail even more signally to evoke the impression made by the original. *The Life of Mary*, consciously retrospective, was yet another translation; this time made by Rilke the man from Rilke the youth; and again to the greater glory of the pure and selfless love of women, a theme which by now he had irretrievably staled by endless repetitions.

It was the Capri Rilke who found it so difficult to dispel the gentle feminine aura which had surrounded him on that island. But the real Rilke, the man of genius, was undergoing very different experiences from 1912 onwards, exposed as he was at incalculable intervals to a mightier influence and a more formidable type of inspiration. The first and the second *Duino Elegies* showed him almost blinded by a vision of terribly glorious angels. The sixth, written in Toledo, was a hymn to heroes; and the third, composed in Paris, revealed the dark mysteries of sex. More than that, from the spring of 1913 onwards strange, visionary, sometimes apocalyptic and often fragmentary poems broke violently through into his conscious mind, couched in a language of almost elemental spiritual force, many of them clearly inspired by Toledo and El Greco. They were too closely related to the main experience he was trying to recapture for publication, and he spoke of them to Kippenberg as mere fragments. Early in 1914 elegiac inspiration seized upon him again, and he almost completed that remarkably deep and beautiful poem about childhood and its terrors which was long believed to be the fifth elegy. In the middle of an attempt to recapture the uncanny relationship between childhood and dolls, the poet broke off almost on the word 'treachery', as the bitterness mounted in his heart, and he remembered things past and present, bethinking him of that 'larger than life-size silence' whose nature he had first learnt from dolls 'in a world in which fate and indeed God himself have become famous first and foremost on account of the fact that they keep silent towards us'.[1] This is the leading idea behind the essay on dolls published in March 1914; his greatest and strangest piece of prose. It is a highly intellectual and highly imaginative statement of the birth of disillusion, of the dawning realisation that it is impossible to establish contact with our own kind, or with the powers above us. Powerfully condensed, it is as subtle and as ruthless as Kafka's unforgettable allegory on the same theme in *The Castle*. Rilke chose dolls for his symbol, and recalled with loathing and shrinking the life in death he had led with dolls as a child, a description shot through with grim humour and irony, no longer really directed against those revolting, inanimate playthings, those inert and soulless travesties of reality, but against both the God who had mocked him and his fellow human-beings. It is one of the strongest expressions of his lack of contact with the world that he ever made; and it was made from the height of a conscious superiority to which he certainly had every claim. The direct experience he was pining for was partly no doubt the human passion which eluded him; but chiefly a recurrence of that shining angelic host which had visited him in Duino, only to disappear. For neither the sixth elegy, nor the third, nor the

[1] *G.W.* iv, p. 271: *Puppen.*

childhood elegy had brought them into focus. Unlike the
mystical artist-god of *The Book of Hours,* these glorious sub-
stitutes for an unapproachable divinity were real visions, for
whose reappearance the poet must wait in fear and trembling.
His position between stuffed and lifeless dolls and remote and
invisible angels was utterly and excruciatingly lonely. But
the poems which preceded and followed this essay showed that
it was yielding to the pressure of inspiration slowly rising to a
flood.

Chapter IV

WARS AND RUMOURS OF WAR, 1914–1921

1. *The Non-combatant, 1914–1919*
2. *The Refugee, 1919–1921*

CHAPTER IV

WARS AND RUMOURS OF WAR, 1914–1921

1. *The Non-combatant*, 1914–1919

I

For the first time I behold you uprising,
Rumoured, remotest, incredible war-god.

.   .   .   .   .   .   For, blazing, the god
With one sweep of the scythe mows down
The crop of the nation's roots, and the harvest begins.

Godhead at last! And we who so often failed
To hold fast to the peaceful god, are suddenly seized by the war-god;
Hurled is his brand, while over the heart full of home
Blood-red the heaven screams where thundering he dwells.

II

Blessed am I, beholding the possessed. Long, long ere this
Our dramas seemed unreal,
Nor did the symbols used make a decisive appeal.
Beloved, now speaks like a seer old Time
Blind, from the spirit of yore.
Hark. You ne'er heard it before. But now you're the trees
Which the most mighty of winds louder and louder streams through.

III

For three days, is it true? Am I really hymning the horror,
Really that god whom as one of the olden times,
Distant and only remembering, I was wont to believe and admire?
Like a volcanic peak he lay to the westward. Sometimes
Flaming. Sometimes a-smoke. Sorrowing, godlike.
Only perhaps some district near to his borders
Would quake. But we raised aloft our undamaged lyres
To others: to which of the future gods?

And now up rose he. He stands. Higher
Than standing towers. Higher
Than the inbreathed air of the days just gone by,
He stands. He transcends. And we? We merge into one together,
Into a new kind of being, mortally animate through him.
So too *am* I no more. Out of the general heart
My heart is beating in tune; and the general mouth
Is forcing my lips apart.
And yet in the night there blares like sirens on shipboard
In me a questioning, blares for the way, the way.
Does the god see it above over his lofty shoulder?
Is he a light-house beam cast over future storms
Which have long sought us? Has he foreknowledge?
Can he foresee and know, this rending divinity,
He, the destroyer of everything known to us? Long known
And lovingly, all that we trustfully knew. And now sprawl
The houses round us like ruins of his temple. Uprising
He scornfully thrust them from him and rose up into the skies.
Even now they were summer skies. Skies of summer. The summer's
Inmost heavens over the trees and us.
And now: who feels, who's aware of their boundless protection
Over the meadow-lands? Who
But has stared as a stranger into their limpid depths?
For we have been altered, changed to resemble each other.
Each one has received of a sudden
Into no longer a breast of his own, meteoric, a heart,
Hot, an iron-clad heart from an iron-clad cosmos.

. . . .

V

Up, and frighten this frightening war-god. Assault him.
War-lust had spoiled him of old. But now, let pain press you;
Let a new battle-pain press you and urge you
Even to dare his wrath . . . .
Are you not pain now, pain up in arms?[1]

Whatever else one might have expected from Rilke at the
outbreak of war, one would not have foreseen *Five Hymns*,
written in the white heat of the moment in August 1914. It
is hard even now to credit the fact that this shrinking,

[1] *G.W.* III, pp. 389–396: *Fünf Gesänge*, August 1914.

sensitive poet, so morbidly affected by every kind of pain and suffering, was the only one in Europe to fire a truly royal salute to the god of war, even granted that the ecstasy with which he performed the deed was mingled with awe, and that relief and terror contended in his mind. The language of Hölderlin, the greatest of modern rhapsodists, informed Rilke's magnificent war-hymns; and Hölderlin's sublime apostrophes to the gods of Greece re-echoed in Rilke's invocations to the god of battles returning in power and glory into modern life. For months, and perhaps for years, Rilke had been under the spell of Hölderlin; *Five Hymns* were written down in the fourth volume of Hellingrath's superb edition, which contained Hölderlin's last elegies and hymns, the highest visionary flights of all. And yet the experience which taught Rilke to speak with the voice of Hölderlin was that same appalling shock which struck civilised and imaginative people dumb. Rilke, who had nearly gone under in the sea of human misery in Paris, now acclaimed a cataclysm which would wipe out, wreck, mutilate and break millions of human beings. Not only that, but the cultured cosmopolitan poet, to whom the word patriotism meant nothing at all, found it in his heart to magnify and glorify a spirit which was raging against Russia and France, his spiritual fatherland and the country of his adoption. He was dazzled, it would be truer to say that he was blinded, by the greatness of the catastrophe which had overwhelmed Europe, and for a time his sense of reality, never very alert, seems to have lain dormant. It was enough for him that he felt himself to be surrounded by a world grown to huge proportions and towering inspirationally above him, a world from which pettiness, narrowness, materialism and artificiality seemed to be utterly swept away.

To this uplifting sensation was added a species of intoxication, aesthetic and emotional in one. During his short-lived exaltation he felt himself to be part of a mighty action which he could yet regard as a sublime spectacle; to be involved in tragedy, and yet to be personally immune from it. He was temporarily transformed into a choric spectator, interpreting and glorifying the heroic events unfolding themselves before his eyes. Nietzsche would have recognised in him one of those frenzied and ecstatic worshippers of Dionysus who behold a vision of their god. At such moments the iron bonds which enclose the imprisoned self are shattered, and the soul escapes from the duress of individuality to merge with the universal soul of humanity and the world. In this entranced condition union with the spirit of life engenders a vision, or a revelation, of the god. Rilke's *Five Hymns* strongly resemble those choric odes by which Greek tragic writers represented this ecstatic state of being. They are unique among his poems, because they are inspired by a feeling of solidarity with his fellows which amounted to the loss of his personal identity. Rilke's highly specialised, deeply civilised and strongly individualised personality had debarred him from sharing the emotions of mankind as a whole. He had escaped from the prison of the self in his solitary communings with God; he had also gone down in his mind among submerged existences, and had established strange relationships with the past, with creatures of his own imagination, and with inanimate things. But never before had he been exposed to the vibrations proceeding from humanity at large. Now for a moment, under the pressure of emotions surging wildly all round him, he was swept into the current and found himself worshipping with the crowd. To the shaken cry: 'Godhead at last!' was added the paean: 'Blessed am I, beholding the possessed!'

The exaltation did not last long. It faltered before reality in the third hymn; but the memory of it, mingled with the dawning of realisation, swept Rilke onward through that most magnificent poem. Inspiration began to fade in the fourth and had almost gone before the fifth came to its slightly didactic and moralising end. The choric singer, retreating from the ranks of his fellows, was dwindling into an individual; and, clinging to his function of interpreter, began to speak less like the leader of a Greek chorus and more like a prosaic modern *raisonneur*. In the short prose passage *An Apparition has been granted us*, also written in 1914, a limp white tunic is just visible beneath the black frock-coat of this dogmatic

personage, the schoolmaster of modern drama, whose un-
grateful task it is to teach the actors and the audience what
they ought to think and how they ought to behave:

No, you must not pretend to be familiar with it. You are not to
affix to it the epithets and appurtenances of previous wars. For,
though it is a war, you know nothing about it. When you were
shown pictures by El Greco, you owned that this was a hitherto unfamiliar experience. And if this war has a countenance, then you
must contemplate it as you would gaze on the features of Amenophis the Fourth, which were not there before. You must stand before
it as you recently stood before the fact that in a couple of horses
there dwells the presence of an indubitable spirit, unsuspected until
now. You must, all imperfect as you are, submit to the passionate
intercourse with death and return his intimacy. For what do you
know of his love for you?[1]

Rilke's belief in the talking horses of Elberfeld is on a par
with his attitude to war in this essay; neither is based on
reality. *Five Hymns* and *An Apparition has been granted us*
stand in the same kind of relationship to each other as *The
Book of Hours* and *Tales about God*; his vision of war, like his
vision of God, could not be translated into terms of real life.
The metamorphosis of God into a silver thimble has the same
kind of incongruity as the comparison between the spirit of
war and a pair of mathematical horses. In this essay Rilke
spoke of the war as something which (to quote Clive Bell in
Civilisation) he was 'proud and pleased to make other people
die for'; this is also true of the first two poems in *Five
Hymns*; but there he was speaking for all and with all, an enraptured dionysiac poet; here he was lecturing an audience
from a platform, striving to drum a little sense of reverence
and duty into civilians and soldiers alike.

Rilke never attempted any such feat again; nor was he ever
able to recapture his sense of solidarity with those around
him. As early as August 15 indeed he was already suffering

---

[1] *G.W.* IV, pp. 278 f.; the use of *ihr* and *euch* adds to the dogmatic tone of
this essay. I have translated 'ihr sollt als die, die ihr jetzt seid' by 'you must,
all imperfect as you are', which is perhaps straining the meaning of the phrase,
but it is in accord with the general manner of the address.

from his isolated position as a born non-combatant, physically, morally and spiritually unfit for any and every kind of war-service. Throughout the four dreary, devastating and crushing years which lay before him, he remained a passive victim. He spoke tentatively at the beginning of getting up his strength in order to bear his share in the vast common lot; he dreamt of becoming a doctor, of recreating a European commonwealth by his writings; but even these impracticable schemes soon ceased to occupy his mind as his vision faded. On September 17 he contrasted the universal emotion which had swept through him in August with the tragic recoil into his own individual abandoned heart; and on November 16 he confessed that the war-god he had glorified was no longer visible; the war was a visitation let loose by a god over the peoples, but not a god itself. Thus he brooded, whilst one after another of his young poet-friends were drafted off to the front: Thankmar von Münchhausen, Norbert Hellingrath, Paul Keyserlingk, Hans Carossa, Georg Trakl, Alfred Walter Heymel. Already two of them were ghosts. Trakl died in barracks in Cracow on November 3; and Heymel succumbed to consumption on November 26. He had been far gone in this disease when the war broke out, and he knew it, but he had enrolled in the cavalry none the less. Rilke, who had been undergoing open air cure for very slight lung-trouble, travelled to Berlin to be with Heymel in his last hours, exposing himself to the most painful impressions and the most harrowing scenes with no consciousness of virtue, much as he was wont to evade responsibility without a sense of guilt. This was the great strength of his character. Introspective to a fault, he nevertheless applied no standardised ethical judgments to his conduct, for he was barely aware of their existence. He was spared fruitless heart-searchings, unavailing regrets, stultifying remorse. He never felt the necessity to justify either to others or to himself his passive attitude to a war which was no responsibility of his. Had his mind been divided against itself on this issue, his life from 1914 to 1918 would have been tragic indeed; as it was, whatever torments he endured, he escaped the worst of all. During the war-months of 1914 his sensation of the greatness of the sacrifices and of the issues involved partly sustained him. If no longer carried along by the wildly rushing flood, he was still close enough to feel himself both uplifted and shattered by the spectacle, and to entertain a wavering hope of its cessation:

. . . one can hardly hear oneself live; it is as if one were standing day and night by the most thunderous waterfall; those at the front are in the great torrent of the rushing events; but a man like myself, who only stands beside it, waits and is silent, and hopes that at the end a word, a feeling, a realisation will mature in his mind that might prove of value when the exhausted war subsides into itself, leaving the colossal spaces it has filled to emptiness, to silence, to a future beginning anew. . . . When?[1]

The words and phrases used by Rilke about the war during the first months reveal his realisation of the great proportions of the disaster, and have an apocalyptic sound: 'thunderous waterfalls, seething abysses, dense mass of clouds; a terrifying jungle, one of the rhythmic convulsions of the universe; world-uproar, colossal, vast, monstrous, unspeakable'; the sonority and energy in his phrasing prove that he was shaken but not yet crushed. Stefan George was to say later that he himself had suffered too much before the war from the appalling brutality, ugliness and materialism of modern times not to have foreseen the catastrophe, and that he was therefore steeled against its horrors. Lou Andreas-Salomé believed that the same was true of Rilke; that he had anticipated the suffering of the war by the agonies he had undergone earlier in the realisation of what we human beings are. Rilke himself said something similar in November 1914:

The most that can be achieved at the moment is that the soul should survive; and misery and disaster are perhaps no more prevalent than before, only more tangible, more active, more apparent. For the misery in which humanity has lived daily since the beginning of time cannot really be increased by any circumstances whatsoever. But increase of insight into the unspeakable misery of being a

---

[1] B. 1914-1921, pp. 17 f.; to Prince Alexander von Thurn und Taxis from Pension Pfanner, Finkenstr. 2, Munich, October 4, 1914.

human creature is possible, and perhaps all this is leading to it: a great downfall to make space for a great ascension.[1]

This conviction accounts for the fact that Rilke was spared the violent shock which the outbreak of the war dealt to the sensitive and enlightened; but it impaled him on the horns of a depressing dilemma. For if, as he reiterated in June 1915, the sum of human misery is constant, and it was only the keener awareness of it which had called forth the greatness, fortitude, strength, heroism, sacrifice and devotion which he perceived all round him, how did it come about that a dismal and disastrous piece of human botchwork like the war could accomplish what poets, artists and dramatists had been powerless to do? Their function in life, he maintained, was to create opportunities for such transformations, and he had been tormented for nearly a year by the realisation that the war had succeeded where the poets had failed. Most artists in Europe were suffering under the seeming inefficacy of art in a world relapsing into barbarity, and they bewailed the defeat of imagination which had made the war possible at all; but few went as far as Rilke, who declared to Katharina Kippenberg in a dark moment, that art was superfluous, because it could not heal wounds, deprive death of its sting, console the despairing, feed the hungry or clothe the naked. But his deepest grief was caused by the victories of war. Life and death, those obvious yet ultimate mysteries, argent and sable on a field gules, were revealed directly to hundreds and thousands without the intermediary of art, and called forth qualities for which the word superhuman is not too strong a term. This rankled terribly in Rilke's mind. He rationalised the situation by declaring more than once that all the love, warmth, sacrifice, devotion, suffering, misery and despair made manifest sprang, not from individual human hearts but from some vast impersonal common stock of emotions, which was being used up in this emergency and passed round from hand to hand. If he misjudged the emotional capacity of his fellows by this interpretation, it was because he was judging

[1] *B. 1914–1921*, pp. 25 f.; to Karl and Elizabeth von der Heydt from Finkenstr. 2, Munich, November 6, 1914.

them by himself. 'Dumbness' and 'numbness' were the words he used most often in 1915 to describe his own state of mind. Acid criticism began to curdle the tragic realisation which had replaced the enthusiasm of August. Bitterly he censured the exploitation, profiteering, greed, hypocrisy and falsifications of the truth rampant around him. He denounced the low amusements, the cheap-jack literature, the despicable theatres, the unspeakable vileness of the press. Something great and incommensurable had been behind the war at first, he maintained; but now the world had fallen into the hands of men, who were befouling and degrading it.

An extreme idealist such as Rilke could hardly feel differently; and his tone was so bitter perhaps, because his own particular defeat was a tormenting aspect of the general failure of art. He was unable at this juncture either to write, or to speak, or even to think anything of any value to humanity. With a wry smile he watched that gallant young poem of his, *The Lay of the Love and Death of Cornet Christopher Rilke*, carrying all before it; appealing to every heart and mind with its glorification of heroism; whilst he lurked in the shadows of complete creative impotence, observing its meteoric career. He felt himself to be homeless and ageing in a world gone mad, whose values were the utter negation of everything he held dear. Yet he could not bring himself to say this publicly. The nearest approach he ever made to a manifestation of his opinions was his proposal in July 1915 to read *The Book of Hours* out loud to an audience of about two hundred people. He withdrew the offer in some trepidation when he realised that this would call for a preamble of some sort, which would certainly reveal his feelings about the war. These, he said, were not such as the censor could pass; and since it was beneath his dignity to consider the censor, it would be better to wait until the impulse to communicate had been transformed into art, whose incomprehensible and incalculable influence could not be arrested. Until that moment came, he preferred to maintain silence. It was probably less the fear of the censor which caused Rilke to refrain from the projected attempt to act on public opinion than the realisation, when he came to consider the preamble, that he had nothing positive to say. For, as he confessed to the Princess Thurn and Taxis shortly afterwards, he might a few years earlier have produced something which could have been at the height even of times like the present: a standpoint which might have confronted the incomprehensibility of the war with that spirit which passeth comprehension. He might have found what was so urgently needed, the attitude of the Old Testament writers, to whom the terrible and the supremely great were identical. Some such consolation he might in the past have been able to give. Now it was beyond him. He had misused and abused his heart, and it had become too lumpish and heavy to feel either bitterness or pain.

The war was creeping closer and closer up to Rilke. The castle of Duino, the birthplace of the elegies, was in ruins; everything he had left behind him in Paris, including precious books and papers, had been sold by auction; and now his personal freedom was menaced; the men born in 1875 were being called up, and a medical examination was imminent:

Can no one hinder and stop it? Why is it that there are not two, three, five, ten persons gathered together in the market-place and shouting: 'Enough!'? They would be shot down, but at least they would have given their lives to end the war; whereas those at the front are dying so that the horror shall go on and on, and no end can be seen to destruction. Why is there not even ONE who can bear it no longer, who *will* bear it no longer? No one could call him a liar if he screamed throughout one night in the midst of this unreal town hung with flags, if he screamed and refused to be silenced.[1]

Had Rilke been a saint or a martyr he would undoubtedly, feeling as he did, have testified against the war in the market-place and suffered the penalty at the incalculable price of *Duino Elegies* and *Sonnets to Orpheus*. Had he even been a normal compassionate human being, he would have volunteered for light hospital duty twelve months before and have found some measure of relief. But the author of those excruciating pages on Paris hospitals never learnt how to roll a

[1] *B. 1914–1921*, p. 78; to Ellen Delp from Widenmayerstr. 32/111, Munich, October 10, 1915.

bandage or to pad a splint. He was a pure poet, whose mysterious gifts were allied to a child-like irresponsibility. He had urged his compatriots to embrace death in the name of war in August 1914; he now demanded a similar sacrifice from civilians at home for the sake of peace. But that any such self-immolation should be expected of him appeared unthinkable. And as if to prove that he was right in this latter assumption, a sudden flood of poetical inspiration overtook him. It was favoured by a change of quarters to a quieter and more remote part of Munich. For it was not so much the war itself as its infectious spiritual unrest and the distracting external conditions it created which were so inimical to Rilke's genius. Temporarily isolated from its repercussions, he was able to forget it, and to abandon himself to the steady and rising stream of poetry which seemed to be carrying him far away from the noise and horror of war. His conscious poetical aim: the representation of the world, not from the human, but from the angelic angle, was indeed so utterly remote from the world around him, that when on November 24 he was found fit for military service and ordered to report at Turnau on January 4, he took the blow with surprising calm. Not only was he fairly certain that the second medical examination in January would reverse the decision of the first, as indeed it did; but he was also buoyed up by his own element: swimming, floating and swimming again on the rising tide of poetry:

So that I must abide by events. No one who knows in what relationship I stand to my work, and comprehends that in it I am powerful and glorious and utterly feeble outside it, will blame me for hoping that God may leave me at my work as long as possible, especially now when its taste is just on my lips again.[1]

This passage occurs in the last letter printed between November 26, 1915 and February 15, 1916, a gap which covers the crucial period of Rilke's military service. According to his passport he was enrolled in the infantry of the last

---

[1] B. 1914–1921, pp. 95 f.; to Marie Thurn und Taxis from 11 Keferstr., Munich, November 26, 1915.

reserve on November 24, 1915, and found unfit for active service on January 15, 1916. On December 13 he went to Vienna, where he stayed with the Thurn and Taxis, and obtained permission to serve in Vienna instead of Turnau. In January he reported for service (according to his own account in the infantry of the second reserve); then, for nearly three weeks, as he said, or for about ten days to judge from the passport, he underwent training in barracks and in the field. He was on the verge of a collapse when he was transferred to the ministry of war, where he remained until early in June, attending daily from nine to three, and lodging first with the Thurn and Taxis and then in the Park Hôtel. Owing to representations made to the authorities by Katharina Kippenberg, Rilke was officially demobilised on June 9, 1916; but he had already left Vienna before that date, and had obviously been allowed to do pretty much as he liked at the ministry of war from the end of March onwards, if not before.

Weeks of suspense, many days of hard labour and months of acute boredom were the component parts of the period during which Rilke actually if not actively served his country, 'buried beneath the landslide of the universal fate', to quote his own words.[1] What he suffered in barracks can readily be imagined; and his misery in the ministry of war seems to have been hardly less great. He could not and would not contribute a single item to the military propaganda which was being manufactured there, and of which he spoke with bitter contempt. But no reprisals of any sort were undertaken against him:

To the honour of Austria, it must be said, that Rilke was treated in a particularly kind fashion, especially in the ministry of war. Colonel Veltzé, a highly cultivated officer, knew exactly who Rilke was, and quietly spared him from anything that could be a burden to him. He was given a room to himself, and very light work which had as little as possible to do with military happenings. All the other officers there respected him particularly because of this treatment, and Rilke had no cause to complain.... The Austrian

---

[1] B. 1914–1921, p. 97; to Anna von Münchhausen from 11 Keferstr., Munich, February 15, 1916; written during four days' leave from Vienna.

authorities really treated him in a most extraordinarily humane way, and he always recognised this most gratefully.[1]

According to another eyewitness, Veltzé proposed that Rilke should merely spend his mornings at the ministry, and occupy himself with his own work. Rilke refused on the grounds that he was there to serve, and serve he would, not a very characteristic pronouncement; but the atmosphere of the war ministry would hardly have been propitious to poetry. In order to keep him occupied, he was finally set to rule lines on the pay-sheets, a duty he discharged with meticulous neatness, clad in a fancy-dress uniform.[2] Meanwhile he bewailed in letters to his friends the soul-destroying boredom of his inactive existence. It must have been a happy day for everybody when he left.

'The *poor* child, the *poor* child!' Hugo von Hofmannsthal exclaimed when he heard of this wretched predicament; it might well stand for an epitaph on Rilke as a soldier and a servant of state. It was lamentable that he should have been called up; yet, compared with the lot of thousands no less sensitive, there is an almost Gilbertian atmosphere about his war-service. But one man's mole-hill is another man's mountain; and the monticle of Rilke's military experiences crushed him quite as effectively as if it had been the landslide he called it. Had he been left alone towards the end of 1915, he would in all probability have escaped for longer or shorter intervals from the inferno of war into the kingdom of his own mind. Whether or not the sum of human misery is constant, Rilke's mental sufferings before the war, to judge by his letters, had been such that they were hardly capable of being intensified. He was recovering from a prolonged period of misery and sterility in the spring and summer of 1914. *Five Hymns, I will praise thee oh Flag* and *To Hölderlin* show that the outbreak of war accelerated rather than retarded his convalescence. He then relapsed into silence, as he began to assimilate the grim reality of the catastrophe and its effect on his own life. But he rallied far more quickly from this than

---

[1] From a private letter from Stefan Zweig to the author.
[2] Sil. Vara in the *Prager Tagblatt*, March 1, 1931.

from the despairing lassitude which had overwhelmed him after *Malte Laurids Brigge*. In November 1915 he was in full force of inspiration:

> You ask about my work. That's almost, no certainly, the worst part of all; because during the fortnight before the medical examination at which the lot fell, I was making a rapid ascent in my work and was in the midst of a veritable onset; several remarkable poems, the elegies as well, everything was rising and rushing, and the store of Michelangelo poems was increasing daily, far beyond anything I had done before. Never have I written such strong, accurate and clean-cut translations. I believed myself to be standing on the verge of the freest vision, when the thick grey military cloth blotted everything out.[1]

This was written during four days' leave in Munich in February 1916, when Rilke was in the kindly clutches of the war ministry; more than a year later, however, in April 1917, when he was as free as air, he was still unable to forget what had happened to him:

> I would prefer to wait before giving an account of myself, until I am in a better condition. Unluckily these heavy months have proved that I was right in fearing that the Vienna interruption would not be quickly overcome. Its fatal similarity with that hardest stratum of my life, the military academy, has done the same kind of thing to me, as I now clearly see, as would happen to a tree, if it found itself temporarily turned upside down, with its crown in the refractory and hostile earth, from which it had grown upward into the light after the most unutterable efforts, a tree-generation ago. To which must be added the fact that this crown, at the very moment when it was buried, was full of new sap, and ready to blossom and bear fruit as it had not done for years.[2]

Feeling as he did, it is not surprising that Rilke, totally unable to write poetry, also found fewer and less striking things to say about the war. Until the end of 1916 the letters,

---

[1] *V.B.* p. 249; to Anton Kippenberg from 11 Keferstr., Munich, dated February 15, 1915; this is an obvious error for 1916, as the address and the contents prove. The letter is also wrongly placed.

[2] *V.B.* pp. 262 f.; to Anton Kippenberg from 11 Keferstr., Munich, April 15, 1917.

when they touch upon this subject at all, do so almost exclusively in terms of its effect upon himself: 'Nervous inhibitions . . . apathy . . . dulness . . . completely diminished powers of communication. . . '; this now formed the matter for laments which had previously been uplifted more tragically for an incomprehensible universal lot. He was attempting to ignore the war as far as possible, to abstract his mind from it, to creep into some refuge and lick his sores.

But even this forlorn struggle suffered a check when Norbert Hellingrath fell before Verdun on December 14, 1916, since it brought Rilke into renewed personal contact with the devastating present; and he began to wonder if he were wrong in trying to forget about the war, whilst realising that it was almost a condition of his inner existence to do so, thus preserving his insecure balance on the edge of a bottomless abyss. During the first seven months of 1917 his situation remained essentially the same, and certainly did not improve. The numbness he was suffering from was so great that he declared the destructive, inhibiting times had been poured over him like lead; he also complained that he felt dull, opaque, indifferent and completely cut off from life; that the war had isolated and utterly disavowed him.

Yet Lou Andreas-Salomé stresses a point about Rilke, which is partly confirmed by his letters. In spite of his helplessness and frequent lamentations, she maintains, he had a fortifying effect upon others. He appeared to many as a counsellor, a guide, even a leader without whom a whole little community would have felt itself to be orphaned and deprived of its support. Presumably she was referring to the small circle of the intelligentsia in Munich, in which women naturally predominated. From 1914 onwards, although rarely, Rilke had occasionally struck a hopeful note about the future, which he maintained must be better than the past because of the lesson humanity could not but learn from the grim teacher who was chastising mankind. In 1917 and 1918 this optimism made rather more frequent appearances, generally in letters to women, mingled with those self-pitying laments which are a constant feature of the war period. He was almost bracing in August 1917 to Mary Gneisenau, whilst reserving for himself the part of one crushed and maimed by the war. In September he wrote a letter to Marietta Nordeck-Rabenau in which, though still bewailing his own frozen state in a narrow and hostile world, he uttered a prophecy about the future, which sounds ironical indeed to those of us who have survived to see it:

But when I think how much my spirit will be redeemed and lightened when the great healing of the world takes place, then... I also foresee the moment when in an irrepressible reaction of repressed humanity, one and all will again strive towards us and concur with us, more strongly, more passionately and more unconditionally than was the case in those strangely tense years before 1914.... I sometimes think that every single day the war continues to last increases the obligation of humanity to a great, common future, full of greater good-will. For what could be more compelling than the pain which has grown beyond all knowledge, which must surely make millions of human beings in all countries more united than before? Ah, then it will be possible to speak again, and every word of love or art will find a new acoustic, a more open air, and a wider space—I confess, that I can only continue to live on this assumption; without it all that is happening now would remain lying upon us like a mountain.... I have again and again had to conquer infinite hopelessnesses, but one may at last trust to be near to that conclusion by means of which the spirit will again be reinstated in its own special function.[1]

Rilke was as wrong in believing that Germany was on the eve of winning the war in the late autumn of 1917, as he was tragically astray in his prophecy of a better future. The wish was father to those thoughts of peace which were rudely interrupted by the news of Rodin's death. This reached him on November 19 and profoundly depressed him. It was hardly a personal loss; but it seemed terrible that it should have taken place beyond the unnatural wall of war, the horrible smoke-screen behind which both Rodin and Verhaeren had disappeared for ever;[2] when at last it was dissipated,

---

[1] *B. 1914–1921*, pp. 160 f.; to Marietta Freiin von Nordeck zur Rabenau from Böckel near Bieren, Westphalia, September 19, 1917.

[2] Verhaeren had been the victim of a railway accident in 1916.

neither of Rilke's two great visionary friends would be there to help in the reconstruction of the world.

The last year of the war found Rilke plunged in a defeatism too absolute even to be eloquent, and so apathetic that he only responded languidly to the eager friendship of the young poet and soldier Bernhard von der Marwitz. They met in October 1917 at a literary party in Berlin, of which both gave an account; but whereas Rilke did not mention Marwitz, the latter described him in some detail, and obviously had eyes and ears for no one else:

> I was immediately fascinated by the great 'Hyperion' Rilke, and as he knows very little about Götz [von Seckendorff], I showed him the lithographs and told him everything I could think of about his work and art. The little, small-boned man was enraptured with the powerful sketches. I invited him to come to Friedersdorf to see the rest of them, and he accepted. Then he recited a few of his own poems, they were the ones he prefers because, he said, they have most of the future in them: *The Harrowing of Hell, The Raising of Lazarus*, the one about the shepherd, and an apotheosis of Bellman, which he introduced with some fine explanatory remarks. His reading is impressive and conscientious, moaning and subdued, but his voice is queer and frightening, without warmth or modulation. Since the war, he says, he has been unable to work at all. The destiny of this war has disturbed him utterly, he cannot assimilate it.... We have become friends.[1]

Marwitz, to judge by his published journal, was one of those gallant, high-hearted, gifted and sensitive young men, whose loss is among the greater tragedies of war. He was full of mettle, chafing at inaction of any sort, fretting whenever he was attached in relative comfort and idleness to staff-quarters

---

[1] Harald von Koenigswald, *Stirb und Werde. Aus Briefen und Kriegstage-buchblättern des Leutnants Bernhard von der Marwitz*, Breslau, 1921, pp. 244 f. Götz von Seckendorff, the painter, Marwitz' most intimate friend, had already been killed in the war; cf. *B. 1914–1921*, pp. 162 ff. for Rilke's account of the party. He was clearly more interested in Seckendorff than in Marwitz. The poem on the Swedish poet Bellman is not yet published; and the 'shepherd' poem is almost certainly *Die spanische Trilogie* as Mr Leishman suggests. The three published poems are all impregnated with the influence of Toledo and El Greco.

and fervently patriotic. His journal, however, also reflects his spiritual torment during the war. He was at one time or another on the Russian, Rumanian and French fronts, meeting with perils, facing hardships and witnessing horrors, to which considerably less space is given than to his reflections on the sombre tragedy of war, to his grief at the loss of his twin brother and his intimate friend, the painter Götz von Seckendorff; and above all to descriptions of nature and the seasons, of the tundra in particular, which betray the poet. He was twenty-four when the war broke out, and twenty-seven when he crossed Rilke's path. The older man was then forty-one, and was not at the height of the other's enthusiastic idealism. In response to an eager request, he copied out *The Harrowing of Hell, The Raising of Lazarus* and the 'shepherd' poem into a little red leather book, which he sent with a charming but melancholy letter. Marwitz was delighted with it:

In the evening—it was more than a premonition, it was a certainty which made me wait for the post to-day—I received a loving letter from Rilke, so full of sincerity and friendship and the joy of communication, that these lines stir me profoundly....But there is a divine sadness in the letter.[1]

It was a profoundly hopeless letter, re-echoing Rilke's earlier conviction that art had failed humanity in the crisis of the war. But its friendliness captivated Marwitz, who begged Rilke to write again and to keep in touch with him at the front. Rilke did not exactly refuse; but he declared that this would result in plunging Marwitz into a poverty of spirit beyond his means to describe. The younger man was wrong in believing that there was any spiritual continuity at home; certainly Rilke himself was completely cut off from the source of his spiritual life:

The more I realised this, the more I tried to look around me at the occurrences of the times. But this very survey only made me increasingly wretched. For where is the visible manifestation for us at home of this terrible world? One feels as if (bowed down under

---

[1] Harald von Koenigswald, *op. cit.* p. 267; Rilke's letter was dated February 12, 1918, and contained apologies for having delayed to copy the poems for several months.

the prolonged consciousness of what is so disastrously happening in the world) one must in the end arrive somewhere where human beings are kneeling down and screaming. I should understand that. I would throw myself down beside them and utter my cry under the protection of theirs. But to take part in the visitation here at home means reading the newspapers.... Terrible though the war is in itself, it seems to me still more terrible that its pressure has no-where contributed to make men more recognisable, to urge them towards God, either as individuals or in the mass, which was the effect of great disasters in earlier times. On the plane which has meanwhile developed, and on which the newspapers are experts at giving an unscrupulous, word-made average of all events... on this plane a continual cancelling-out of all tension is created, and human-ity is taught to accept a world of news instead of reality.... I have never been a newspaper reader, and I cannot go on reading the papers. Enough. I have asked one of my friends to-day to allow me the use of a quiet room in the country where I need see no one and speak to no one.... I am afraid that I shall fall ill without some such change towards solitude, nature and the seasons.... From now on-wards I shall need a refuge of this sort continually.[1]

Young Marwitz, who had written in his diary during the first year of the war: 'Woe to him, who now lives according to his own aloof and arrogant mind', would not take no for an answer from Rilke. He felt strongly drawn to the great poet who was so utterly remote from the fierce and raging element of war. He wrote him a 'glorious letter' (the epithet is Rilke's) on August 9, which the recipient cherished but did not answer. This failure wrung his heart when he heard that Marwitz had died of wounds on September 8, 1918. Marwitz had been a real friend, and potentially a very close one, whom Rilke had not grappled to his soul with hoops of steel, and for whom he had not even performed those proofs of friendship which the situation demanded. Bitterly he blamed himself for his sins of omission; deeply he grieved for the loss of one of the very few men who had ever sought his intimacy. But his losses did not end with Marwitz. Paul Keyserlingk, another young poet, had been killed at the front in August; and Rilke's

[1] *B. 1914–1921*, pp. 181 f.; to Bernhard von der Marwitz from Hôtel Continental, Munich, March 9, 1918.

doctor, Baron von Stauffenberg, a kind and most helpful friend, had died early in 1918. Exhausted, frozen, barren, the poet looked out as from behind prison-bars at the life and death all around him. This was his parlous state of mind a month before the armistice, expressed in a letter to an intimate friend, the Countess Aline Dietrichstein, written to congratulate her on her approaching marriage. And yet in this very letter, inspired by the sympathy he felt for his correspondent and for the happiness upon which she was entering, he broke out into a very strong affirmation of his faith in life, its inexhaustible possibilities, its fulness, its essential kindness; and he even went on to assert that the precious things of life would emerge from all the destruction and annihilation of war, pure, undefiled and desirable.

The paean of thanksgiving one would have expected from the author of this creed when armistice was declared, was never uttered. Some relief Rilke undoubtedly felt, and some understanding too for the revolution in its early stages. He attended workmen's meetings, and experienced real sympathy with the speakers. But he was soon disillusioned like everyone else with the nature of the peace and the character of the revolutionary leaders. He tried to keep an open mind, not to condemn rashly, and to trust in the future; but he belonged, as he acknowledged, far too intimately to the old order of things, he was far too much bound up with his own past, to make common cause with the new ideas. His task he felt to lie in the continuation of all that had been precious to civilisation and to himself before the war; but this proved to be impossible during the turmoil, danger and discomfort raging in Munich in 1919. Involved in this chaotic aftermath, Rilke realised that, unless he escaped from it, he would go under. He did not even begin to recover from the war until he left Germany for Switzerland in June 1919; and he believed himself to be broken by it, for more than a year after it was over, as may be seen from the following confessions:

My dear dear Lou, oh how lost I feel. My innermost self has withdrawn and protected itself, and will give out nothing. My determination to ignore the external world altogether went so far, that finally not only the war, but even the most harmless and purest manifestations of nature had no effect on me. Never have I been so far beyond the reach of the wind in the spaces, of the trees, of the stars by night. Ever since I had to stare out at all this from the evil disguise of an infantry uniform, it has been alienated from me, and is maintaining that divorce into which I forced it, in order not to spoil it for myself later.[1]

I spent nearly the whole war in Munich, more or less by chance, waiting, and continually thinking that it *must* stop; not understanding it, not understanding it, not understanding it. It was not to be understood. Yes, that was my whole occupation these last years, and I can assure you it was no easy one. For me the wide world was the only possible world. I knew no other: what did I not owe to Russia—it has made me what I am; spiritually I derive from thence; the home of all my instincts, my inner origin is *there*. What do I not owe Paris, and shall never cease to thank her for it. And other countries too. I cannot and I could not take anything back, not for a moment, not in any direction can I reject, or hate, or make suspect.... My only part in the whole thing is suffering. Suffering in sympathy, suffering in prospect, and suffering in retrospect too. Soon I shall be played out.... I have done no work at all. My heart just stopped, like a clock. The pendulum had swung against the hand of misery, and was checked.[2]

In comparison with the war and its effect upon him, nothing else seems of great consequence during the five dismal years Rilke spent in Germany from July 1914 to June 1919. And indeed, gathering up the threads of his former existence and tracing their pattern during the war, one realises with no little surprise that the external upheaval in his material life was far less serious than one would have supposed. Stefan Zweig put the matter in a nutshell when he said, 'Rilke suffered terribly *under* the war, but not *through* the war'.[3] Yet at first sight it would appear that in losing touch with Paris, he was completely cut off from his past. But Paris had after all been gradually relegated from the position of his base or

---

[1] Andreas-Salomé, *op. cit.* p. 74; dated from Munich, January 13, 1919.

[2] *B. 1914–1921*, pp. 292 f.; to Leopold von Schlözer from Pension Villa Muralto, Locarno, January 21, 1920.

[3] From the same letter as the one quoted above, pp. 260 f.

headquarters to that of a *pied-à-terre*. And if the war disorganised his life, it must be remembered that disorganisation
had been the key-note of his existence for many previous
years. He travelled light, and this vagrant tendency now came
to his aid. It was nothing new for Rilke to live out of his
trunk for months and even years on end. He had so often left
most of his possessions behind him in Paris, and so often
bade a prolonged farewell to his room, that they were not
indispensable to him, grieve though he naturally did when
they became completely inaccessible, and mourn though he
must when he heard of the loss of his papers and books. But
he was willing to regard this lost property as the estate of the
late Malte Laurids Brigge and to start afresh. The inspiration
of Paris had been on the wane of late years. Rilke was too
completely estranged from Rodin to feel any further sense of
loss in that quarter. Verhaeren was the only French friend for
whose presence he seems to have passionately longed; whilst
the deaths of Verhaeren and Rodin, neither of them due to the
war, were the only ones from beyond the Rhine to which
reference is made in his published correspondence. Yes, Rilke
travelled light. Moreover many, indeed most, of his closest
friends were either German or Austrian. Lou Andreas-
Salomé, the Heydts, the Kippenbergs, the Thurn and Taxis,
Hans Carossa, Hugo Hofmannsthal, Gertrud Ouckama
Knoop, and many others, not to mention Clara and Ruth,
would have been cut off from him entirely had he been in-
terned in France for the duration of the war. On the whole he
must be accounted fortunate to have been surprised by the
catastrophe in Germany. A number of his intimates, including his wife and child, were in Munich for the greater part
of the war; and many friendships, previously slight, were
strengthened by the common disaster in which all were involved. Thankmar and Anna Münchhausen, Norbert Hellingrath and Alfred Walter Heymel were among these war-time
friends. To these were added a long list of new intimates and
admirers. Of the eighty-one correspondents in the 1914–1921
volume of letters, almost sixty bear names hitherto unrepre-
sented. Of the forty-nine women and thirty-two men who

make up the total number of addressees, more than twenty belong to the titled aristocracy; a discovery which recalls the saying: '*Plus ça change, et plus c'est la même chose*', and which strengthens one's conviction that the war affected Rilke's external life but slightly. As long as he had these powerful protectors, the wind would still be tempered to the shorn lamb. One of the most irrefutable proofs of his high degree of civilisation is the almost automatic fashion in which the aristocracy gravitated towards him. It was a natural affinity. Like will to like; and Rilke had many of those qualities which are fostered by birth and breeding. He was wrong in attributing these to a noble lineage, which he actually did not possess; but perfectly logical in deducing it, for he was civilised to an extent which almost amounted to a taint; and so nearly decadent that only his genius saved him. Super-sensitive as he was, over-fastidious, with exquisite manners and delicate tastes, graceful, fine and fragile, it was small wonder that great ladies cherished him, and that he slightly repelled most men. For the more virile virtues of the nobility were not conspicuous in Rilke, although they were not absent from his make-up. Gallantry and courage, even heroic endurance, played an important part in his creative life; but it was a subterranean part. They helped him to wrest spectacular poetical victories from his personal defeats; but this was behind the scenes; forlornness and helplessness were much more apparent in his bearing.

During the war Rilke's dependence on the society, succour and sympathy of cultivated women increased. Their lack of stridency, their civilised manners, their sensitive minds, their grace of living, all this soothed and fortified him. Lou Andreas-Salomé spent a great part of the war in Munich, watching over him. The painter Loulou Albert-Lazard made him free of her studio and shared his solitude in Rodaun in June 1916 after he had escaped from the war ministry. The poet Regina Ullmann was much in his company; and many others, like Gertrud Ouckama Knoop, were always unobtrusively at his service. A former Munich hostess of his, Elsa Bruckmann, invited him to attend lectures by Hellingrath and Schuler which were held in her house. Hertha Koenig put her flat at his disposal for four months in 1915; here he communed daily with Picasso's *Mountebanks*, which later formed the subject of the fifth *Duino Elegy*. When Hertha Koenig returned to Munich, Renée Alberti, wife of a counsellor to the legation, sheltered him in the Keferstrasse, which remained his Munich home until July 1917, and where he wrote the fourth *Duino Elegy* in the late autumn of 1915. Marie Thurn and Taxis did everything she could to make his war service tolerable, and offered him hospitality in Vienna. It was owing to Katharina Kippenberg that this period was so short, and that Rilke was demobilised. Isabella Hilbert invited him to Burghausen in the winter of 1916; and he was for several months the guest of Hertha Koenig in Westphalia in 1917. Apart from all this active kindness, the spiritual understanding and sympathy of women were as balm to his mind. This is especially noticeable in his letters to the Countess Aline Dietrichstein; but it is also visible in his writings to many others: to Marietta Countess of Nordeck-Rabenau, to Ellen Delp, to Anna Countess of Münchhausen (the mother of Thankmar), to Helene Nostitz, to Elizabeth Countess of Schenk-Schweinsberg, to Elizabeth Schmidt-Pauli and to Elizabeth Taubmann. The intimate parties in Munich, described by Katharina Kippenberg, of which Rilke was always the spiritual centre, and at which the war was sometimes forgotten in conversation among artists, poets and great ladies, were also a slight alleviation in his desolate life. Members of the aristocracy of birth and of intellect wove a fine and delicate web over the bottomless gulf of horror, a network less fragile than it seemed, since it preserved Rilke from being devoured by the flames licking greedily upwards. The providence which protected him from that fate was providential indeed. In the mechanised and industrialised twentieth century, amid the incomprehensible brutalities of war, there still remained in Germany and Austria enough gently born and nurtured ladies to protect a helpless poet and shed some glamour over his life, a seeming anachronism which was due to Rilke's magnetic charm.

Such domestic happiness as he was capable of enjoying was also within his reach. Clara and Ruth were in Munich for a great part of the war; and although Rilke declined Clara's invitation to make use of her house or flat, they saw each other at least once a week, and appear to have been on easy and comfortable if no longer on intimate terms. Rilke was punctilious about their birthdays; and though he omitted to visit them when they retired to Fischerhude near Bremen, he spent a whole day in 1917 looking after Ruth in Munich between trains, and escorting her to her destination.

His rapidly increasing fame was a source of solace and vexation combined. He was becoming the rage. It was enough for him nowadays to set foot in a town for some frantic admirer or other to insist on sheltering Rilke in his house, retiring to an hotel himself. One embarrassing gentleman appeared at the threshold of his door with a lighted candle several metres long. A shop-girl, catching sight of Rilke's name on a telegram, nearly swooned with delight on hearing that it stood for the poet of *Cornet Christopher Rilke*. That particular poem was indeed the reason for Rilke's widespread popularity. It had sold forty thousand copies in 1914; in 1919 it stood at a hundred and eighty thousand, being issued, re-issued and issued again every year of the war; sung, recited, set to music, and illustrated, as well as translated into many languages, it was universally beloved. Rilke was not a little exasperated with its success; but the steadily mounting sales of his other books must have pleased him. In 1918 *The Book of Hours* was in its ninth edition and had sold sixteen thousand copies. *Tales about God* was in its eighth edition; *The Picture-Book* in a seventh, *Malte Laurids Brigge* stood at six to eight thousand copies, and all the other books were moving. Eight, ten, fifteen, twenty-five and forty thousand copies were the satisfactory figures to which *New Poems, Early Poems,* the translations from Gide and Marianna Alcoforado, *Auguste Rodin* and *The Life of Mary* had mounted. Far from being ruined by the war, Rilke was actually one of the profiteers.

At the very beginning, when things looked dark financially, an anonymous testator left Rilke 20,000 *Kronen* in his will; and this was followed early in 1915 by another considerable gift deriving from an unknown young Maecenas who gave a large sum of money away to be distributed among poets. Rilke and Georg Trakl were chosen as the recipients, but the name of the donor is still unknown. Returning from the front at the end of the war, he made over all his money to the poor and became a village schoolmaster. It is possible that Rilke did not tell Kippenberg about the 1915 gift, for it is mentioned in none of the published letters to him. He certainly tried to keep the knowledge of the first windfall from his publisher. But the latter had also been notified of the will, and insisted on administering the sum for Rilke's benefit. Actually the whole capital had to be realised to keep Rilke going during the early years of the war. But by the end of December 1917 his books were selling so well, notably the despised *Cornet*, that Kippenberg was able to increase his allowance substantially. Rilke began to receive large monthly cheques, to be worried by the income-tax, and to make good resolutions about putting by for the future.

Besides his friends, his family, his income and his fame, he was also able to derive some comfort from other people's books, for it was not until the end of the war that he began to feel shut off from the communion of minds. Hölderlin, Strindberg, Montaigne, Flaubert, the Bible and in particular the Psalms; Werfel, Büchner, the Flemish poet Guido Gezelle, Hans Carossa, Yeats, Spinoza, Goethe, Jacobsen, Verhaeren, Tolstoy, not to mention Michelangelo whose poems he was translating; he could forget himself and his personal miseries in these writers; and the fact that he was able to read the foreign poets in the original added greatly to his sense of escape. His critical powers were sharpened if anything, and his power of appreciation certainly not diminished. His interpretation of Büchner's *Wozzeck* is one of the finest of his literary estimates; his account of Däubler's poems recited by the author is a little masterpiece of irony; his strictures on *The Saint and her Fool* keenly discriminating and acute; whilst his advice not to publish the complete diary and correspondence of Paula Modersohn-Becker reveals an exacting standard which saw beyond sentimental considerations to the duty owed to her fame. Finally, his letters as a whole during this period bear witness to the fact that, despite his poetic sterility, his power of self-expression was becoming an even greater force than before.

A disorganised and hand-to-mouth existence was nothing new to Rilke; nor was the painful experience of being unable to write; old friends rallied round him more closely than ever; new friends came forward and sat at his feet; Clara and Ruth were no more obtrusive in Munich than they had been elsewhere; every month that passed, if not adding to his output, greatly increased his fame; such are the blessings which a cool-headed biographer might enumerate for Rilke, and come to Zweig's conclusion, that he did not suffer much through the war. But there was one dismal feature of his external life at this period which was entirely new and very hard to bear. Rilke changed his address at least twenty-eight times between July 1914 and June 1919; living at numerous different places: Munich, Irschenhausen, Würzburg, Frankfort, Berlin, Vienna, Rodaun, Burghausen, Chiemsee, Westphalia and Ohlstadt In fact, he behaved in his normal, erratic, nomadic fashion. But he was like the panther he had once seen in Paris. Restlessly circling round his circumscribed cage, he could not escape into the open world. Iron bars, frontier bars hemmed him in. And hemmed him into a country where he had no wish to live. He had always loathed Austria. Do what Marie Thurn and Taxis would to reconcile him to it in 1916, she failed. This dislike was now not unnaturally extended to Germany as a whole and to Munich in particular. Munich was his headquarters during the war and the revolution; he associated it with captivity, wretchedness and misery. He had nothing more urgent on his mind than to escape from a city and a country where he had endured so much; and he began to scheme to get away. Fortunately for him an invitation to give lectures in Switzerland overcame the passport difficulties which were a feature of the revolution. Offers of hospitality poured in too, making the formidable rate of exchange a matter of little moment. His last letter from Munich was dated June 6, 1919; his first from Switzerland was written on June 22. He was never to see either Austria or Germany again.

The legend of Rilke, the saint and the seer, will hardly survive the publication of his war-time letters, which tell a tale of personal defeat and also of failure of vision. He behaved less greatly than many men like himself; less heroically than his brother-poets; less disinterestedly than the young pluto-crat who gave his wealth to the poor; less idealistically than those pacifists who testified to their convictions; less lovingly than Marwitz in their brief association; and one might almost say less selflessly than anybody. A saint, in a word, he was not, nor yet a genuine seer. I would be the last to deny that his poetical gifts made him a visionary, since poetry and vision seem to me interchangeable terms; but prophecy is far too definite a word to be applicable to his utterances as a whole; and when he attempted to foretell the future, he was invariably wrong. He was no true prophet about the war in *Five Hymns*, and utterly astray about the nature of the post-war world in his letters. But if he had no feeling for the future, he might still lay claim to be a seer, one who looks deeper into human hearts and world-events than his fellows. In much of his previous poetry he had given proof of this gift. But though it flashed out occasionally during this period, it failed him on the whole. He underrated humanity, and was also blind to a particular aspect of the war which no inspired seer could have missed—the consciousness of mortality and the revelation of godhead which it brought to a whole tragic generation. The famous letter about God and death which Rilke wrote in November 1915, contemporaneously with the outburst of poetry before his mobilisation, reads like an anachronism. He, like a different type of aristocrat, had learnt nothing and for-gotten nothing since he had inveighed in *Malte Laurids Brigge* against the crass ignorance and dense indifference of humanity on the all-important subjects of God, love and death. He could not conquer his amazement, he said in this letter, that these great question-dynasties still remained unanswered; and that human beings who had been associating for thousands of years with life and death (not to mention God) were still completely in the dark about them and content to remain so. Harking back to the idea first mooted in *The Book of Poverty and Death*, and stated again in *Malte Laurids Brigge*, he repeated his belief that God had been pushed out of life because he was too hard to live with. From the earliest days men had created gods to contain all the more terrible, menacing, annihilating and incomprehensible elements of life, so as not to have to face them. The history of God was therefore the history of that part of the human mind which has never been explored owing to the feebleness and cowardice of men. Rilke's constant belief that God was the creation of mankind is as old as the hills, and as firmly founded. It was brilliantly and beautifully stated here, devoid of the eccentricity surrounding his earlier notions of the future artist-god. What is distressing is his apparent belief that he alone since the beginning of time had not shirked the problem of the divine nature; that no one but he had the courage to face life's terrors (and this from Rilke in the middle of the war); and no one but he, and a genius here and there like Tolstoy, had the glimmering of a notion what death might mean. For humanity had also banished death from their lives; and for the same emasculate reasons:

And so, you see, the same thing happened with Death. Part of our experience, and yet incapable of being apprehended by us in his reality, always seeing further than we do, and yet never quite acknowledged by us; encroaching upon and surpassing the meaning of life from the very beginning, he too, was banished and relegated so that he should not continually interrupt our search for the meaning of life. And yet he is probably so close to us that the distance between him and the inner centre of our lives cannot be registered. But he was made into something outside us, something to be kept daily at a distance, something lurking in outer darkness ready to pounce on this man or the next, according to his malevolent selection. More and more the suspicion grew and spread that he

was the antagonist, the opponent, the invisible opposite in the air.
. . . But nature knew nothing of this banishment, which we had somehow been able to effect. When a tree blossoms, death as well as life
blossoms in it; and every field is full of death which germinates a
rich expression of life from its prone countenance. And animals go
patiently from one to the other, and everywhere around us Death is
still at home. . . . Lovers . . . are full of death, because they are full of
life.[1]

The plain biological truth about life and death ('Every
mother's son travels with a skeleton') was now wedded to a
more rational ethical conclusion than the categorical command
to die 'personal deaths' which Rilke had been wont to issue.
Humanity should at last recognise the organic connection
between the two, and not attempt to banish death from their
lives, thus impoverishing their whole existence and leading it
awry. Rilke was so certain that this lesson in *memento mori*
was needed, as to tell Kippenberg in January, 1919, that he
saw his poetical aim to lie in preaching it. He was determined, he said, to make death, never really a stranger, more
recognisable and perceptible as the silent witness of everything that lives. In *The Raising of Lazarus*, written in 1913,
he had represented Christ as overcome by wrath, because
human beings would distinguish between living and dying:

> But suddenly there burst from him a flame,
> Such mighty contradiction to their thoughts,
> To all the small distinctions they were making
> Twixt living and by death being overthrown,
> That every limb with enmity was shaking
> The while he hoarsely uttered: 'Raise that stone.'[2]

Rilke's poetry is so much greater than his prose, that these
few lines transport the reader into a different region from the
dogmatic letter to L. H. One remembers his comparison
between life and death in *The Swan*: the hard and clumsy
approach, the cautious descent into the waters, and the serene
and regal progress on the gently flowing element; and one

[1] *B. 1914–1921*, pp. 88 ff.; to L. H. from 11 Keferstr., November 8, 1915.
[2] *S.G.* p. 15.

becomes inarticulately aware of the essential difference between philosophy and vision. What Rilke said about death in the letter is neither new, nor revealing, nor yet touched with that sublime beauty of thought which moulded the *Phaedo* and Faust's second monologue. But quite apart from this, it shows a disconcerting ignorance of mightier minds than his and utter blindness to what was happening during the war. The revelation of the mysterious connection, the identity one might almost say, between life and death, which he was preparing to point out to his contemporaries, had been made to hundreds and thousands of men and women whilst Rilke mused apart. Young Marwitz, the truer poet on this occasion, knew that it was self-evident:

The past remains as dark and mysterious as the future. There is no wisdom about death; why then should there be any wisdom about life, since both spring from the same root?[1]

There is a refreshing absence of arrogance in this simple statement of a fact, which Rilke believed himself to be unique in perceiving, but which the very nature of war had revealed to his contemporaries. As the visionary discoverer of this truth he was too late in the field; and he did not realise it because he was out of touch with his fellows. The war had struck him blind, and everything round him was dark.

Civilians in Germany saw the most dismal, depressing and disillusioning side of the war. What the soldiers saw at the front no one but they will ever know; carnage unspeakable, courage unutterable:

The war, the mass-fate, in which the adventures and heroism of the individual signify nothing, the progress and operation of a force which is greater than the sum of all the forces which produce it; this, which differentiates the present from all previous wars, can probably never be described.[2]

Beyond good and evil itself, this terrifying force brought out all that was worst and all that was best in human nature, and its bewildering intensification proved that the good out-

---

[1] Koenigswald, *op. cit.* p. 124.   [2] Koenigswald, *op. cit.* p. 162.

weighs the ill in mankind. Rilke would never have been able
to say that human beings were lowering and degrading something great in itself, had he served, even for the space of a
week, in a hospital at the front. He was thinking of profiteers,
politicians and the press, who blocked his horizon at home.
A shattered non-combatant, vegetating wretchedly in Munich,
he had no conception of the quality shown by those of all
nations who were caught up in the maelstrom of war. 'The
world has fallen into the hands of men', he groaned in bitter
contempt of humanity. But the men who had fallen into the
hands of that world altered the situation. Heaven knows
what they went through in the trenches; rumour has it that
they bore themselves bravely there; certainly the British
in field-hospitals were remarkable, to put it midly. But one
has the impression that to define their qualities with high-
sounding words is to mar them with a literary taint. Only
very common nouns are robust enough not to sag beneath the
weight of grit, spunk, pluck, humour, decency and cheer,
which, projected against the apocalyptic background of war,
achieved a greater significance than the treachery, inhumanity, lust for power and gold, savagery and brutality
which had called them forth. Miraculously they were, thriv-
ing amid chaos and bestiality, indestructibly sane.

Rilke, who believed (I think erroneously) that nothing
could increase the sum-total of human misery, began by
hailing the war as a positive good, since (according to him) it
added cubits to the stature of man, and not one drop to the
ocean of sorrow. This was his position in *Five Hymns*, to
which he clung with less and less assurance for about a year.
It was the legacy of that mysterious revelation he had had at
the outbreak of war. But the memory of this experience was
gradually obliterated by the reality of a war-time world in a
civilian setting; it could only have been revived by contact
with the spirit at the front which it was impossible for him to
establish. In default of his earlier vision, he substituted an
irrational faith in the greatness of war in general, and blamed
his disillusion and terrible distress of mind on the particular
nature of the war in question and on the human beings who

were degrading it. He was surely wrong in this. War is an evil whenever, wherever and however it occurs. It generates far more evils than it destroys; it annihilates far more good than it creates. But the unconquerable greatness of the human spirit was made manifest by it in 1914–1918 none the less. Not in everyone by any manner of means. Hundreds were defeated by it, and Rilke was one of these.

He said some fine and impressive things about the war; he was shaken more than once by deep and selfless emotions; he struggled against his despair, rallied at times, occupied his mind, condoled with his friends, and even tried to sustain them. But the contest was too unequal. Rilke was among the most pitiable of the thousands of war-victims; not a saint, not a prophet, not even a martyr; but an unhappy man, spiritually maimed and mangled by three weeks in barracks and five months as a clerk. It cannot have been only his war-service with its similarity to the military academy that brought him to this pass. Behind his outcries one perceives the horror and confusion with which he recognised something greater than poetry and art, rising like a burnt sacrifice from such savagery and violence as he could not bring himself to face. He was forced to erect a barrier between himself and the war in order to survive at all, and this cut him off inexorably from the spirit which was the source of his life. And yet he was right. Rilke did not and could not live in the same world as the war. He was as utterly remote from it as that silvery, radiant St George whom he sketched in 1911, coming down from the morning clouds through which his steed in its shimmering armour ploughed a snowy path; coming down, not to fight a fierce and bestial dragon, but to irradiate a dreaming castle park. In this cruelly imperfect world St George is irrelevant without the dragon; but not in the world where Rilke's mind held sway:

> Fair as the swan
> On its eternity of unplumbed surface,
> So sails the god, and dives and guards his white.[1]

---

[1] *G.W.* III, p. 399: *So angestrengt wider die starke Nacht*; based on Leishman, *Rainer Maria Rilke, Later Poems*, London, 1938, p. 111.

The poet who wrote those exquisite lines did so from the height of conscious genius which made his spiritual isolation from his fellows bearable at least. The outbreak of war destroyed his sense of otherness at first, and although he soon recaptured that, he was to learn the bitterest lesson of his life, his own impotence, and the impotence of art in the face of this catastrophe; and worse than that, the realisation that the war was doing on a colossal scale what he had believed to be the sole prerogative of art, the transformation of humanity, its translation to a higher plane. This realisation he later denied, concentrating almost venomously on the moral degradation war induced. What else could he do? In a world gone both sublimely and bestially mad, there seemed no place for poets, and therefore no place for him. If it was the sensitive poet in Rilke who almost cringed before the horrors of war, it was the fierce egotism of genius which made him hate its spiritual victories to the extent of tacitly denying them in his arrogant letter about God and death. But he was far too great a poet to stop there. The curve of his spirit reflected in his letters and in his works shoots downwards comet-like from the radiant war-hymns to the fourth *Duino Elegy*, the nadir of his emotional despair. But, perplexing, painful and indeed agonising as this poem is, its tragic statement of aesthetic defeat is on a very high plane of Rilkean art. To say which is to say that in 1915 at least his genius was far from vanquished. Whilst the *Requiem for a Boy* shows even more clearly that it was not being deflected from its course.

Yet, in view of his poetic silence after his mobilisation, one is justified in wondering if even his spirit would have survived the war and its ghastly aftermath, had he not escaped into a country which had been practically unscathed by the catastrophe. The sturdy sanity of Switzerland was perhaps the only effective remedy for his deeply injured mind, and he somehow knew it. All his life had been led with a view to fostering his genius; the last few years had been solely occupied with protecting it. Now he was determined to save it. It is perhaps less in the few great poetic utterances of the war period than in Rilke's tenacity of purpose throughout that his genius is most manifest. Never for a moment did he contemplate seriously abandoning his method of life or betraying his poetical destiny. He stubbornly went on trying to work amidst the horror all around him. When inspiration totally deserted him, he still went on labouring at his translation of Michelangelo's poems. At the very edge of extinction, he resisted spiritual extermination; he was tough and endured. If there were any saint-like elements in that baffling and fascinating nature, they were certainly in abeyance during the war. But his genius, crucified on the cross of the world, was taken down at the eleventh hour and triumphantly survived.

2. *The Refugee*, 1919–1921

It is a pity that nature is so exaggerated in Switzerland, or so it seems to me. How pretentious these lakes and mountains are; there is always a bit too much of them.... The admiration of our grand-parents and great-grandparents appears to have collaborated in producing these regions. There they came, travelling from their own countries, where there was 'nothing' so to speak, and here they found 'everything' in an *edition de luxe*.... A mountain? Good gracious no—a dozen whichever way you look, one behind the other. A lake? Certainly, but a superfine lake of the best quality with reflexions of the purest water, a whole gallery of reflexions, and God to act as a guide, explaining each in turn; unless of course he happens to be busy at the moment, in his capacity of stage-manager, directing the spot-light of the sunset glow onto the mountains... I can't help it, the only way I can reach this assorted nature is through irony; and indeed I remember those happy days when, travelling through Switzerland, I used to draw the curtains in my compartment, whereat the other travellers in the corridor greedily devoured my share of the view. I feel sure that they left nothing over.... It is odd too that psycho-analysis (at least in Zurich) has assumed its most intrusive forms here. Nearly all these already clean and angular young people are being analysed. Just envisage the result; a sterilised Swiss, whose every corner has been swept out and scrubbed. What kind of an inner life can find place in his mind, which is as free of germs as an operating-theatre and as glaringly illuminated?[1]

Many a heart will beat as one with Rilke in his ironical dislike of the theatrical beauties of Switzerland and of the antiseptic virtues of its inhabitants. Well might he sigh over those happy days when he had arrogantly excluded Swiss scenery from his compartment. Anything obvious and too luxuriant (like the Roman spring) had always aroused his antagonism and drawn forth expostulations similar to the above. Indeed, it is a relief to find that he was still capable of them; and it rather wrings one's heart to discover in this and other letters conscientious enumerations of objects and persons of interest in such towns as Bern, which afforded that aesthetic satisfaction the natural scenery did not arouse. He was making the best of a bad business and virtuously counting his blessings; but as late as June 1920 he still regarded Switzerland as a waiting-room plastered with Swiss views. In this antechamber he nevertheless remained for the rest of his life.

Rilke once told Katharina Kippenberg in an outburst of bitterness that his destiny was to have no fate, and there was some truth in this statement. The external circumstances which moulded his life were often essentially irrelevant, and their action haphazard. Personal anchors he had none after the faulty cable snapped which had moored him to Meudon. Profuse, unusual and interesting as his friendships were, they only assumed real importance if they had a topographical aspect; the local habitation outshone the name. Things meant more to Rilke than persons; the background dwarfed the figures which animated it; countries, towns, landscapes and castles, these and not human beings really spelt his fate. But the letters which composed this word were always being accidentally or 'providentially' reshuffled, sometimes wilfully by Rilke himself. Russia, in spite of its long, strong call, ceaselessly re-echoing in his mind, never really possessed him. His marriage intervened at the psychological moment, and the

[1] *B. 1914–1921*, pp. 269 ff.; to Gertrud Ouckama Knoop from Soglio, Bergell, Graubünden, September 12, 1919.

Russian dream was later dissipated by Rodin and Paris, the creator of things and the great impersonal city. This latter loomed compellingly over twelve disrupted years; but numerous random interruptions alternated, with its inter-mittent sway, and gradually weakened its hold. Then Duino wrestled for the poet; but before the issue was fully engaged, Paris was lost and Duino was wrecked by the war.

Rilke had almost as little personal choice in the matter of his post-war refuge as he had had in his war-time incarcera-tion in Germany. There was practically nowhere else to go. Switzerland was accessible; it offered hospitality; it was willing to pay for the honour of hearing him read his poems; a passport could be obtained for it. It was safe and clean; respectable and conventional; tourist-ridden and picturesque; not the land for him (he declared haughtily in August 1919) with its 'abominable' aesthetic. But it proved impossible to keep this proud standard flying indefinitely. The atmospheric pressure all round him was too strong. To a person of Rilke's susceptibility and impressionability, the sight of the more blatant 'beauties' of Switzerland is such a shock, the frequented resorts are so strident, that the quieter, remoter and less obvious districts seem more beautiful than they would to an eye unused to the scenic vulgarities of the country as a whole. Rilke came to love and admire some parts of Switzerland greatly; but by that time his standard was at half-mast, mutely mourning for the mighty Volga and the mysterious steppe, for the glory that had been Duino, for the sublime Atlas mountains and for the tragic greatness of Toledo. They were gone for ever from his life; but they had not vanished from his mind. They were there in the shape of petrified inspiration.

Four of the ten *Duino Elegies* were already written, and there were considerable further fragments, including the first lines of the six uncompleted poems. The cycle as a whole was like a buried treasure, and Rilke's peregrinations through Switzerland resembled a treasure-hunt with no other clue to guide him but the words solitude and quiet:

'Or is your desire for real solitude and quiet?' Indeed it is, all day long, all night long, and for nothing else but this. Years ago, in the winter of 1912, I once had it: peace and loneliness, real loneliness and peace, for about four or five months. It was incredible. At the present time I am longing for one thing, and for one thing only: to embark once more on the great works I began then (you do not know any of them yet). But in order to do this I need the same kind of uninterruptedness and inwardness which a mineral has in the interior of a mountain when it is turning into a crystal. Only yesterday I said to myself, how can I deserve that from God? What does the dumb creature in the mineral do to be allowed that...?[1]

After the disorder and the ruthless interventions and interruptions of these last years, I need nothing so much as the calm of inner contemplation, something after the style which was granted to me in poor ruined Duino...I know that I shall not be able to take up my work again properly until such a refuge comes to my aid...and my work was always so much inspired by solitude that I am bound to wish for quiet, not from misanthropy, but for positive reasons, especially as so many inhibitions and fears have to be overcome.... But a refuge of this kind, with the stipulation of the most rigorous solitude, is hard to find.[2]

It proved indeed exceedingly difficult, in spite of the many offers Rilke received to shelter him and the numerous experiments he tried. The first was at the châlet of Countess Mary Dobržensky in Nyon on the lake of Geneva, where he stayed in June and October 1919 and again in August 1920, and which was always open to him. It would have had much to recommend it, if only his hostess could have vacated it; but in spite of her contemplated absence she was there all the time, except for a bare fortnight in England. Worse still, she filled the small house with other visitors, tucking Rilke away in a little room under the stairs, hardly as large as a cabin. Soglio, where he lodged in the Palazzo Salis, whose owners allowed him the private use of an attractive old library, was much more like a refuge, but not quite ideal. He regretted it when he left it, and might have stayed there longer, but for his lecturing tour which was arranged for the end of October and

---

[1] *B. 1914–1921*, pp. 279 f.; to Dory von der Mühll from Pension Villa Muralto, Locarno, December 24, 1919.

[2] *B. 1914–1921*, pp. 283 f.; to Prince Schönburg from Pension Villa Muralto, Locarno, January 12, 1920.

the whole of November 1919. This took him to Zurich, where
he probably first made the acquaintance of Nanny Wunderly-
Volkart; to St Gallen, Lucerne, Bern, Bâle (where two future
hostesses, Helene Burckhardt-Schatzmann and Dory von der
Mühll-Burckhardt, opened their doors to him); and finally to
Winterthur, where he made friends with Hans Reinhart and
probably stayed with him. I have been unable to discover
which poems Rilke read out loud to the 'dense, often arid,
hard-to-penetrate Swiss';[1] but he was pleased with his reception everywhere, attributing his success to the impromptu
introductions and comments with which he accompanied the
readings. Meanwhile, although the sale of his books went
rocketing sky-high in Switzerland, the refuge he needed was
still to seek.

After angling for and obtaining an invitation to inhabit a
garden-house near Ascona, Rilke discovered it to be completely
unsuitable, and was not altogether sorry; for the cranky inhabitants of Monte Verità (not yet under the present enlightened and munificent management) alarmed him; nudism
and vegetarianism were one thing; nudists and vegetarians in
the mass quite another. He therefore retired gloomily to a
pension in Locarno, where he was neither comfortable, nor
solitary, nor quiet, and whence arose many piteous cries of
'Whither?' The capital W, as he ruefully pointed out, also
stood for 'Woe'. Nor did Schönenberg near Pratteln in the
Bâle country, placed at his disposal by the Burckhardt sisters,
who vacated it for him, prove propitious to inspiration. He
was there from March to June 1920, and used it as his headquarters during that summer and autumn; but he spoke of it
as a 'kindly offered but inhospitable house', so that it cannot
have been comfortable. Locarno, so unattractive but so near
Italy, had unsettled him; urgently he implored the Princess
Thurn and Taxis to meet him in Venice, and gladly she consented. He was back again in the Valmarana Palace, surrounded by his old friends. But his plans for the future were
still completely unsettled. Soglio was so far the only place he

[1] *V.B.* p. 298; to Anton Kippenberg from Hôtel Baur au Lac, Zurich,
December 2, 1919.

had seen in Switzerland which even approximated to his ideal.
There were other possibilities outside that country, but there
was something against them all. The anonymous Countess M.
would have liked Rilke to come to the equally anonymous R.
The Kippenbergs suggested Leipzig; and Katharina had
further procured from Prince Egon Fürstenberg the offer of a
little house in a German castle park. But Rilke had no mind
for Germany, nor for becoming involved in new relationships.
The rate of exchange and the terrifying prices in Venice
(where he could not have stayed twenty-four hours, he said,
had he not been there as a guest) probably told heavily
against the asylum near Padua in the Euganean Hills which
the Valmaranas evidently offered him. As for Lautschin, now
and ever at his disposal, it was very far from being Duino;
Austria appeared to him more impossible than ever since the
war, and his long-established affection for the princess was
not strong enough to induce him to inhabit it. Nevertheless,
Castle Lautschin was the only serious rival to Switzerland as
the prospective birthplace of the *Duino Elegies*. More than
once Rilke's decision hung by a hair; but a prophetic instinct
(and this time Rilke, who had neither foreseen the war nor its
consequences, was a true prophet) kept on murmuring that
Switzerland it would be:

I am curious to see if Switzerland will be able to arrange once
more for the kind of conditions in Soglio; everything there was like
a promise of future events, like the pattern of a material which will
provide one later with a whole dress, a cloak and hood of invisibility.[1]

The visit to Venice added if anything to Rilke's perplexities.
He had hoped and prayed that the place he had loved so much
before the war would hold the same magic for him as in the
past. The prayer was granted, Venice was unchanged. But he
had not bargained for the eerie sensation produced by discovering that he too was unaltered, that everything was the
same. It was in the nature of a shock, and perhaps a salutary

[1] *V.B.* p. 296; to Anton Kippenberg from L'Ermitage, Nyon, Vaud, October 5,
1919.

one. Could he, he asked himself, be really seven cruel years older and yet without the slightest proof that he had undergone those consecutive spiritual changes which constitute being alive? Was this the result of the numbness he had purposely induced as the only means to protect himself against the universal attitude towards the war? The apparently exact repetition of the past he experienced in Venice took on the proportions of a nightmare; and when he heard that the Duse was on her way there he flung himself across the Swiss border rather than live through that episode again. Signs and tokens were not wanting that he had done well to leave behind him that haunted city of the past. Switzerland began to beckon him behind her flaunting scenes. He was shown Castle Berg on the Irchel, a foretaste of what was to come; the Valais country was spread out before him, and delighted his eyes. The town of Geneva discovered itself to him, and he fell in love with its Parisian climate and atmosphere. Finally a glimpse of Castle Hollinger near Bern showed Rilke what Switzerland could do:

The large old chestnut avenue of the approach; at the end, behind the iron-barred gate, the steep little castle, and sidewards beneath the row of trees, the long view over the horizontally-lit country— the tears came to my eyes again. An avenue like this, and a house like this, for the space of a year, and I would be saved. I felt that if only I could walk straight up to that house and into a quiet study awaiting me, I should start to work this very evening. (Is it an excuse? I am quite capable of deceiving myself, of being dissatisfied even in such circumstances, and of discovering inhibitions, interruptions, difficulties....) But nevertheless, why am I so much moved by such avenues?...You do see it, don't you? How tall it was, how protective, dark, solemn...I went close up to the park gate...and an evening bird was whistling in the park trees, a solitary bird; whistling as if it were asking if the silence was deep enough to feel its tone. It was.[1]

Nanny Wunderly-Volkart, to whom this outburst was addressed, must have felt even more strongly moved by its

[1] J. R. von Salis, *Rainer Maria Rilkes Schweizer Jahre*, Frauenfeld and Leipzig, 1936, p. 42; to Nanny Wunderly-Volkart from Bern, August 22, 1920.

heart-shaking appeal than posterity, since she knew and loved
the writer, who was in desperate straits and haunted by the
fear that he would have to return to Germany, or Austria, or
Czechoslovakia almost immediately. This prospect was all the
darker because his previous critical attitude towards Switzerland had been vanquished by the Valais and Geneva. Geneva
now seemed to him a second Paris, and as such desirable in
the extreme. Moreover it harboured two inspiring artists:
the painter Baladine Klossowska, and the Russian producer
George Pitoev, whose genius was such a revelation to Rilke
that he even felt a transient desire to act as Pitoev's secretary.
But Geneva was out of the question for financial reasons; on
the other hand, such hospitality as Switzerland had hitherto
offered was unacceptable to the poet. He was being edged
closer and closer to the frontier. But providence had another
shot in the locker; none other than Nanny Wunderly-Volkart,
yet one more of those friends in need who were friends indeed
to Rilke. The depth of their intimacy can be gauged by the
extracts from his journal-letters to her which form the material
on which Salis' book about Rilke's life in Switzerland is
based. Her feelings for him, to judge by a letter she wrote to
me, did not fall far short of idolatry, and she left no stone
unturned to give him his heart's desire. Castle Hollinger was
not within her gift. But she could and did procure for him an
invitation to Castle Berg on the Irchel from the proprietors,
Colonel Ziegler and his wife Lily. It was offered to him for
his sole use during the winter and spring of 1920–1921 with
the services of an admirable housekeeper called Leni, quiet,
devoted, unobtrusive and reserved. Rilke, who had already
seen and liked the castle, accepted this providential invitation
on October 17, 1920 from Bern, with what relief and gratitude
can be imagined. Then, his mind at rest about the immediate
future, he obeyed an almost irresistible impulse, and was over
the hills and far away almost before he knew it himself.

When he first escaped from Germany, he had spent whole
days reading the names Houbigant, Roger and Gallet and
Pinaud through the windows of perfumery shops. They represented freedom and Paris. Marthe, whom he had sent for

in September 1919 for a few days' reunion, stood for Paris and healing; and ever since Venice Rilke had felt more and more convinced that the return to Paris was the one possible, although dangerous, method of healing the wounds the war had dealt, an experiment which would either kill or cure. The week which he spent at the Hôtel Foyot, rue de Tournon, from October 22–29, 1920 rewarded his courage. '*Ici*', he wrote in the note-book he bought in the Odéon arcade, '*commence l'indicible.*' He had meant to keep a journal of his experiences in Paris, but he got no further than this one sentence. It is impossible to think without emotion of Rilke alone in Paris after the war, wandering entranced through the streets and gardens of the city he had loved more than any earthly thing. Persons can change and vanish; things endure and remain. Rilke made no effort to seek out his former friends. The strange, intimate relationship with Paris was what he wished to re-establish, and this was effected in the first hour, which gave him back the consciousness of the continuity of his life. Here, in the streets, buildings, monuments and museums, was the same fulness of existence, the same intensity, the same rightness even in wrong, which had been such a revelation to him in the past; the same indescribable influence to which, as he said, he had owed for nearly twenty years his best and most resolute states of mind. Could he but remain here, he would have all his life back again, all its dangers, all its bliss, his whole life, the life that had always been his. So he wrote to the Countess M. on October 27; and he told his mother two days later that he could think of nothing but to return to Paris as soon as possible, and to transplant his life back again into the soil and climate of his work. But he had already ruefully confessed to the countess that the rate of exchange made the scheme impracticable. It was the old dilemma: Paris and poverty, or foreign lands and dependence; which was it to be? Fate and providence waited for the answer, but gently and almost indifferently. It hardly mattered now. He had been healed and blessed by Paris, who had already surrendered the gift of solitude into the hands of providence. The Princess Thurn and Taxis had dispensed it in

1911 and 1912; it was in Nanny Wunderly-Volkart's gift in 1920; and it was the lode-star of the poet's existence. Where-ever it might be, there too the elegies, incubated at Duino, would finally be hatched out. They had been begun and would fittingly be completed under the auspices of providence. But external forces were no longer of paramount importance in Rilke's life. The personal fate whose existence he had denied to Katharina Kippenberg was now assuming the reins of government. Its workings, the workings of his genius, can be clearly seen in his purposeful search throughout Switzerland for a fitting refuge. If he was gravitating towards a pre-destined environment, this was because he was dictating his own terms. His choice of Berg rather than Paris seemed to turn in the old fortuitous way on questions of ways and means. But this was only partly the case. Had financial considerations been paramount, Lautschin would have prevailed over Berg, where lodging, heating and service were provided, but prob-ably not the board which the fairy princess would have lavishly spread. And had gratitude hampered Rilke at this juncture, Lautschin would also have had the first claim. He had always been a law unto himself, and kept himself free from ties, encumbrances and responsibilities; but this was negative freedom. He now began to act more positively, as the master of his own fate. Needing no advice, heeding no suggestions, but having weighed the consequences, he left Paris for Geneva without crippling regrets, travelled from there to Berg on November 12, and shut its oaken doors behind him.

A revealing symptom of his newly found mastery of life was his omission to bewail his departure from Paris, which seemed in no wise to weaken the miraculous effect it had had upon him. He also found nothing to criticise in Castle Berg but everything to be thankful for. Of all the many refuges thrown open to him in his life, this was the only one he ever accepted without murmurings or reserves. The Villa Strohl-Fern had been rendered hideous by the Roman spring and finally uninhabitable by the Roman climate. Borgeby-gård had failed to give him solitude; life at Meudon had involved him in appalling drudgery and had ended disastrously; Capri was crowded and vulgar, Duino terrifying and austere; there was something amiss with Castle Schönenberg, and no space at the Nyon hermitage. But neither whilst he was in residence, nor after he had left, did Rilke ever find any fault with Berg. From the beginning he adored the small sturdy seventeenth-century stone castle, solitary and remote; the tall beeches, the rather neglected park, the sheet of water with its slender murmurous fountain, the avenue of old chestnut-trees, and the garden which melted into the landscape, meadows gently sloping up to the foot of the wooded Irchel hill. The rooms within the castle were fine, spacious and full of pleasant objects; Leni was a pearl of great price; and, to put the finishing touch to his sense of secure isolation, there was an epidemic of foot-and-mouth disease in the village, necessitating a quarantine strict enough to confine him to the boundaries of his own park. It is something new to find in Rilke's correspondence a whole sequence of letters written in ecstasy and gratitude, in deep and abiding content. Again and again he gave thanks for Berg, coupling it together with Paris as a miracle; and openly announcing that his war-wounds were healed, and that he was completely cured. This frank recognition of release from stress and pain is the measure of his sufferings during and after the war and counterbalances his previous outpourings of self-pity. It is all the more remarkable, because inspiration tarried; and there lurked in his mind the haunting dread that he might fail to win from himself that victory for which all the circumstances were so extraordinarily propitious. If he failed to complete the elegies here, he believed that he would never complete them at all. Courageously he maintained in the face of this doubt that the fault in this case would be his and his alone.

Whilst he was in this frame of mind—joyful and fearful in one—he received a letter which put his recovery to a severe test. Sedlakowitz, a former master at the military academy and now a major-general, wrote to recall himself to his one-time pupil's mind, little realising that he was touching off a bomb which did indeed after some delay explode violently in his face. Rilke was convinced that his war-service had been so

destructive to him because of its similarity with the long
drawn-out misery he had undergone at St Pölten and Weisskirchen. The two experiences were indissolubly connected in
his mind because he never outgrew the first. A panic-stricken
lad accompanied the poet into barracks and was with him
until the end of his days. But he could be kept in his place by
dint of ignoring him; he had been fought back into the unconscious again when Rilke had established spiritual continuity
with his pre-war days in Paris; short-circuiting the years
1914–1919 exactly as he had done with those other dark
years 1885–1890, which had been relegated to the region of
nightmares whence they had thrown shadows terrifying and
grotesque over *Malte Laurids Brigge,* shadows from which
Rilke had fled in panic as far as Africa and Egypt. Sedlakowitz' letter was a challenge to Rilke's method of treating
his intimate, tormenting malady. The convalescent inhabitant
of Castle Berg decided to accept it. The retrospective account
he gave to his former master of his childhood's agony has the
formidable energy of long-delayed utterance; and the sledge-
hammer blows directed against the institution responsible are
deadly, measured out with an unfaltering hand. Behind the
sinister academy looms the grim spectre of war, not invoked
by the writer, but inevitably in his thoughts. Indeed, he could
not think of one without the other, and now combined them in
one long reasoned cathartic condemnation; analysing their
effect upon himself with words which apply with equal force to
the boy and to the man: 'Exhausted, physically and spiritually
maltreated...I stood...enfeebled and ravaged before the
steepest walls of my future.'[1] If the fortress of poetry had to
be scaled in 1890, the rampart of the elegies towered im-
pregnably above him in 1918. Such was the effect of mili-
tarism on this great modern poet.

The letter is more than a mere condemnation; it is a confession, more truly a justification, of his spiritual life. He
could never have led it at all, he maintained, had he not suppressed the memory of the undeserved torments he had

---

[1] *B. 1914–1921,* p. 352; to General Sedlakowitz from Castle Berg, Canton
Zurich, December 9, 1920.

endured. By doing this, he had saved the poet within him from extinction. This vindicated in his own eyes his present determination to blot the war-period out of his life. What had saved him before should save him again, a conscious process of elimination. But that his spirit was alive to make it, and had survived both St Pölten and the war was a miracle which he attributed as far as the first experience was concerned to his complete submission under an inexplicable fate. This faculty of absolute subjection he later came to recognise in Dostoyevski's novels and in Russia as a quality inherent in the Slav soul, a quality by which it can escape from oppression and bondage into a fourth-dimensional freedom of its own. In offering this explanation to Sedlakowitz for the fact that the military academy had not broken his spirit for good and all, Rilke was also rationalising his passive acceptance of the intolerable phenomenon of war. The letter as a whole is, therefore, of crucial importance. It released long-suppressed emotions and memories; and as an *apologia* for his refusal to face them it was entirely satisfactory and convincing. Better far to write *The Book of Hours* and *New Poems* than to rake up a tragic past. It must also have reassured him that he was on the right lines as far as the elegies were concerned. And last of all, since he was human, it must have given him exquisite relief to tell one of his former gaolers exactly what he felt about prison-life. For, however benevolently disposed Sedlakowitz may have felt to Rilke at the academy, he seems to have done nothing at all to soften his lot there, and was probably unaware of his sufferings. Where ignorance is bliss, it is folly to be wise. General Sedlakowitz could have written a cynical gloss on that proverb after reading Rilke's letter.

It is disappointing, after this forthright and penetrating epistle, to come upon one of those regrettable Christmas letters to his mother, which Rilke still felt it incumbent upon him to write. The display of mystical sentimentality he made about Christmas at all times is a disconcerting feature of his life; for he remained bitterly hostile to its founder; and although inconsistency, especially in a poet, is far from being a vice, there is apt to be something a little slippery about Rilke's

Yule-Tide greetings; and this particular letter is saturated with insincerity, and as unreal as the mother to whom it was addressed.

Was it poetic justice, that the flood of inspiration rising at the turn of the year was dammed by a sentimental obstruction? If so, it was a terribly cruel revenge. Rilke was torn away from Berg early in January, just when he was beginning to write. He was away for a fortnight, but the interruption proved fatal, and Castle Berg was not to see the wheel of the elegies come full circle at last. No one, the Princess Thurn and Taxis lamented in her book about Rilke, could ever leave poor 'Serafico' in peace; once again he was needed to 'save' someone, and was urgently summoned to Geneva. Salis, unnecessarily discreet since the princess had mentioned the town, spoke mysteriously of somewhere 'in West Switzerland'; and Katharina Kippenberg seems not to have been in the secret; for she blamed the failure of inspiration on a sawmill erected near the castle which drove Rilke away by its excruciating noise. It was something more personal than that. The poet himself told Countess M. in piteous but vague and general terms that urgent and painful circumstances, whose claims he had to allow, had forced him away. As Geneva was the place, Baladine Klossowska was probably the person. Certainly it was some woman who thus thwarted his inspiration at the eleventh hour. He was too much surrounded by women at all times and far too dependent on them not to have to pay for their homage now and again by sympathetic attention in moments of stress. But in spite of Marie Thurn and Taxis' statement that he was never left in peace, he had actually until now so conditioned his emotional life that women had not seriously interfered with his work. Latterly, however, there had been practically no work to interfere with, so that he may have relaxed his vigilance in a dark hour for himself. For it was a dark hour when he was sundered from Berg; a catastrophe which he compared with the crisis of his mobilisation, since it had a precisely similar effect on his uprising inspiration. This time however the cause was less sinister, being life with a capital 'L'. It underlined the fact that Rilke's relationships with women were rather more normal than they had been in the days when he declared that artists could have and should have no private life, or when he had later bewailed his incapacity to love. He was now at pains to weigh the rival claims of life and art, a rather ponderous subject:

Everyone after all experiences only one conflict in life under various guises and proceeding from different directions. My conflict is to reconcile life and work in the purest sense. Where it is a question of the infinite incommensurable labour of the artist, the two tendencies are in conflict. Many have solved the difficulty by taking life lightly, by snatching stealthily from it what after all they needed, or by turning its values into stimulants, whose turgid inspiration they then hastily threw into their art. Others found the solution in turning away from life, in asceticism, and this is certainly a much cleaner and truer way than the greedy snatching at life for the sake of art. But this too is out of the question for me. As my creative powers derive in the last resort from the most direct admiration of life, from the daily inexhaustible wonder at it (how else could I have come to my art?) I could not but consider it a lie against life if I ever arrested its flow towards me. Any such denial would revenge itself by appearing as hardness in my art, however much the latter might gain potentially by such a denial. For who could be quite open and receptive on such a sensitive plane, if he had a mistrustful, restrictive or timid attitude towards life?[1]

Shorn of its magniloquence this statement claims that Rilke left Berg from a high sense of his duty to life. One may perhaps do him greater justice than he does himself by believing that his heart was involved. Certainly when life had threatened a few weeks before to flow towards him in the shape of a visit from his daughter Ruth, he had had no compunction whatsoever about arresting it. Fundamentally his problem with women was and had always been the difficulty of keeping them at bay. He needed them so much up to a certain point, but they needed him more. Like Emma with Jane Fairfax, he was always doing more than he wished and less

[1] *B. 1914–1921*, pp. 380 f.; to Countess M. from Castle Berg, Canton Zurich, March 10, 1921.

than he ought. He loved to help and to heal them lightly, in passing, or from a distance. He was even now engaged in writing edifying letters to an unknown young woman, a fitting pendant to his earlier uplifting epistles to an unknown young poet. But women are uncompromising realists, and they wanted more than that. When they interfered with his inexorable devotion to his work, he generally refused to tolerate them, as both Katharina Kippenberg and Salis testify. It can have been no ordinary affection on his part that led him to leave Berg in January 1921; and the whole unsettling episode was still uppermost in his mind when he saw the Princess Thurn and Taxis the following June:

I am in perpetual anxiety about Serafico (she wrote in her journal at the time). Will they never leave him in peace? Will he never find the woman who loves him enough to understand what he needs, and to live for him alone without thinking about her own insignificant little life? Poor Serafico, how anxiously he kept on asking if I did not believe that there must be a loving creature somewhere, ready to take a back seat whenever the voice of inspiration called him. The answer was difficult; for he is asking for nothing less than that a woman should give him her whole heart and ask nothing in return. The question would be very naïve and egotistical, if one did not recognise in it the masterful will of his destiny which no power on earth can arrest. And if this woman exists, how is he to find her? Yet he cannot live unless the atmosphere of a woman surrounds him. I have frequently been disconcerted by the extraordinary attraction women exercise over him. He has often told me that he can only converse with them, that they are the only human beings he understands, and the only ones he cares to associate with....But then comes the moment of flight, when he retreats from any and every tie...and then again the old sorrow, the same suffering as before....I see no solution.[1]

It is one of the most painful problems which artists have to face, although Rilke was probably unique in combining such utter dependence on women with so fierce a desire for solitude; and the princess may well be forgiven for despairing of a solution. And yet there does seem to have been one

[1] Thurn und Taxis, *op. cit.* pp. 89 f.

mysterious human being who could have doubled the parts of mistress and maid, the little French girl called Marthe. Too waif-like to make any demands on him, she had strayed into his heart, and if she did not possess it, she remained there still. He wrote to her during the war, and he wrote this of her just before they met in Switzerland at Begnins-sur-Gland:

My heart is wrung in a strange way: Marthe, whom I discovered aged seventeen in the utmost misery, was my *protégée*, a working-class girl, but with that downright genius of heart and mind probably only to be found in French girls. What amazement, what indescribably full, indeed overflowing, happiness she gave me during a certain period by her alert understanding of all that is greatest and best, in which she even outdistanced me. I doubt if any other human being has ever made it so clear to me to what extent a spirit can unfold itself if one provides it with a little space to live in, a little quiet, a scrap of blue sky.[1]

In a life which may truly be said to have been a poetical one, Marthe is perhaps the most poetical of all those charming, graceful, fascinating and sometimes mysterious women who crowded round the hero. There was a tone in his letters about her, the princess said, which he never used about anyone else. Too little is known about the connection to hazard a guess as to why Rilke did not keep her with him in Switzerland. His fear of encumbrances was such, that he would not even possess a dog; nor were his finances assured enough perhaps to undertake the responsibility of her upkeep. But temperamentally she seems to have been made for him, and spiritually she was his creature. He sent for her; he must have paid for her to come and see him in Switzerland, because he needed her so much; but, far from sending for his daughter Ruth, he firmly if kindly restrained her from coming to see him. She made the proposal in the winter of 1920, causing him some uneasiness, until he bethought himself of the expedient of buying her off. She was going to be nineteen in December, and already her birthday wants were in his hands. They included lessons in music, history of art, French con-

[1] *B. 1914–1921*, pp. 274 f.; to Countess M. from Begnins-sur-Gland, Vaud, September 26, 1919.

versation and mathematics; some help with her winter clothes, and a humble request for pocket-money. After anxious consultation with Kippenberg, her father decided to grant everything she asked for and to add the sum of money which would have been spent on the journey to Switzerland, since he had already half promised to give her that. It was an unprecedently handsome birthday present, but it covered Christmas too; and as it ensured his solitude at Berg, he probably considered it cheap at the price. It was certainly ironical that, after all this scheming and contriving to be left to himself, life proved too much for him and forced him into its service after all.

It was a fatal interruption; and Kippenberg's flying visit after his return, although heartening and reassuring in many ways, still further prolonged the divorce between Rilke and his genius. The magic had somehow gone from Berg. When he left it for good on May 10, 1921, no poetical miracle had occurred. Nevertheless, it had witnessed and contributed to his healing, and its place on his private map, which included Moscow, Paris, Toledo, Ronda and Duino, was assured.

During the next few weeks Rilke's headquarters were situated at Etoy, where he lived in a pension called Le Prieuré, and seemed less disposed to mourn the loss of Berg than one might have expected. This was probably because he had abandoned all hope of completing the elegies, and was therefore glad not to be daily reminded of his failure by the castle and the gardens which had witnessed his hopes. So certain was he now that he would never finish the cycle that he decided to publish the four completed poems with the fragments as they stood. They had been in Kippenberg's hands since July 1918, and Rilke read the fragments to the Princess Thurn and Taxis when they met at Etoy and Rolle in June 1921. Then he told her of his intention. She was horrified, and used all her eloquence to dissuade him, much as Eckermann had striven with Goethe not to publish the draft-scheme of *Faust II*. In both cases it would have been tantamount to a confession that no more was to come, and an almost insuperable handicap to further inspiration; especially probably with

Rilke whose discouragement about the elegies was partly pathological. He gazed at the princess in stricken silence as she assured him vehemently that she knew he would finish the cycle; and he told her later that it was her unshaken faith in him which had prevented him from fulfilling his purpose to publish and be damned. He therefore owed her a debt of gratitude which nothing could repay.

Great men are rarely over-much influenced by gratitude; other and much more dynamic forces mould and sway their lives. Rilke's genius had only apparently consented to abandon the elegies; actually it was impelling the poet to the spot where the buried treasure was to be unearthed. Rilke had set his friends in motion to find a substitute for Berg; the number of proposals witness to his magnetic personality, to his widespread fame, and to the desire felt by those in the know to be associated with what he clearly believed was to be the masterpiece of his life. Negotiations were opened in Rome and Carinthia; the Countess Schaumburg suggested her castle in Bohemia; his Venetian friends, the Valmaranas, renewed their entreaties to honour their house in the Euganean Hills; Elizabeth Schmidt-Pauli investigated seven German castles for him; and the Princess Thurn and Taxis would have been overjoyed to see him established safely in the garden-house of Castle Lautschin. But Rilke's genius gave no sign of approval to these various schemes; on the contrary, the poet jibbed like a restive horse when they were mentioned. He had somehow grown to dread the houses of the great. He was by now an expert on the subject, and knew better than anyone else where court-shoes tend to pinch:

The V[almarana]s have no real notion of what I need; and the Princess T. too is incapable of grasping it. She has a sort of idea that on the whole I can manage with a minimum of requirements; but she has neither the understanding, the love nor the patience to realise how absolutely essential the ten requirements are which must be included in the minimum laid down, if my existence is to be protected, serene and fruitful.

He added that the aristocracy had for centuries been accustomed to consider the practical problems of life in the last resort as servant-problems; and this, he concluded bitterly, was the reason that no one was really comfortable in their marvellously run houses. As for himself, he knew too well what, should he go to Lautschin, was *not* to be expected there.[1]

These words of course were not meant to be repeated and should never have been published. The lady who betrayed Rilke's trust in her discretion is one who claims that he was more than mortal and withholds innocent information about dates and numbers of letters. If Rilke showed an 'almost human ingratitude' in this peevish outburst, a very human jealousy of the fairy godmother of the *Duino Elegies* underlies its publication, which is far more damaging to the poet than to the princess. A life led in aristocratic houses may be replete with the drawbacks Rilke complained of, but he had suffered them gladly again and again rather than live in poverty and independence. Nor had he now any churlish desire to bite the hand that fed him. He merely made the mistake of confiding his feelings in an untrustworthy person. Nevertheless, there was a lack of taste and of true delicacy of heart in delivering this kind, generous and trusting old friend of his into the hands of her successor, the same kind of indelicacy which was apparent in some of his dealings with Rodin. But Rilke's taste, exquisite on the whole, was not reliable, as some poems and a great deal of prose bear witness; and his spiritual health had suffered from the discouragement at Castle Berg. It is perhaps more than a coincidence that during the same period as this letter, he was giving way to an old obsession of his: poking about in the rubbish and refuse-heaps near Etoy, unearthing unsavoury and senseless objects, and meticulously describing them in his journal. Perhaps the obtrusive cleanliness of Switzerland was responsible for this relapse into morbid curiosity. And yet it was to be in this over-hygienic and spiritually sterilised country, as his genius subconsciously knew, that he was to complete his life's work. It may have been this inarticulate knowledge which made him speak so impatiently and harshly about the hospitality of the princess, rationalising an urgent instinct to keep away from Lautschin

[1] Salis, *op. cit.* p. 70; to Nanny Wunderly-Volkart from Etoy, May 17, 1921.

at all costs; for during the whole of his life Rilke was never in any doubt as to what was best for his genius.

.   .   .   .

It may have been also the aggravating sanity of the Swiss which accounted for Rilke's relapse into spiritualism, causing him to attend *séances* at Bâle, and to devour the once so heartily despised treatise by Schrenck-Notzing. It is more likely however that, despairing of direct communication, he was once more seeking inspiration from indirect sources. The result was the mystifying episode of the *Poems by Count C. W.* Both to the Kippenbergs and to Marie Thurn and Taxis (always very gullible about ghosts) Rilke declared that these verses were dictated to him by a gentleman dressed in eighteenth-century clothes who haunted Castle Berg. For three nights in succession the great living poet played medium to the dead; but he sent him about his business when the count began to dictate Italian lines. To Nanny Wunderly-Volkart Rilke told a different tale, declaring that the whole story was a poetical game of make-believe. Incapable of any production of his own, he had invented Count C. W. as a pretext for writing poetry on a low plane of concentration, much as a woman might knit. He therefore refused to accept responsibility for these poems or to include them in his published works; for he considered (and Salis agrees with him) that they were not up to standard.

One or two of them have nevertheless seen the light of day; and the poem beginning *In Karnak 'twas* which appeared in the *Inselalmanach* for 1923, if not at the height of Rilke's greatest poems, is nevertheless unmistakably his; and shows, as the preamble to *The Son* had done many years ago, the sudden uprush of inspiration. Clinging to the fiction of Count C. W., Rilke began this poem in a wilfully trivial manner, using the kind of negligent rhymes that a minor poet, who was also a man of the world, might be expected to trifle with. But the theme resisted this treatment; hardly were the ruins of Karnak in sight and that solitary pillar which haunted Rilke to his life's end, before the language and the thoughts rose to meet them; rose, wavered, rose again, and relapsed in the last line into triteness and triviality. C. W. therefore, whatever the rights or the wrongs of the case, had not lived in vain.

Even more important probably in liberating Rilke's mind was his translation of Valéry's *Cimetière marin*, completed in June 1921. He had by then called a halt to his versions of Michelangelo's poems; and though he himself was satisfied with this work, Michelangelo was too great for him, too incomprehensibly great. Rilke diminished his stature, softened his outlines, straightened out his syntax, but could not re-create him. Much the same thing happened with Valéry's great poem; as an effort to communicate the impression made by the original, it failed. The imitation is fairly close, but the greatness is gone. Yet this in no wise detracts from the importance of the undertaking. Brooding over this glorious poem, which describes the rebirth of inspiration, Rilke caught fire from it, quite apart from the magic some of the ideas exerted over his mind. He had long since realised that the tools of his craft which he had vainly sought for in the Rodin period lay very near to his hand, in long, confessional letters, and in translations from other languages into his own. But never before had any mind worked so directly on his; never had any of his translations been so opportune, so prophetic of what was to come.

There were, or there had been, other signs. That odd little essay, *Primal Sound*, written in 1919, and proposing the queer but fascinating experiment of taking phonographic readings from the suture of the human skull, whose indentations, according to Rilke, strongly resemble those which the human voice makes on a wax cylinder, was fantastic possibly, but revealing too. For it was hardly more than a pretext to insinuate rather slyly and shyly some of those overweening ideas about art which Rilke had hitherto kept for his private diary or for his most intimate friends. On the eve of his greatest poetical achievement, they filtered out and challenged the public eye, which was about to be challenged much more violently by the strangest perhaps of all the strange poems our century has produced.

Chapter V

THE CRISIS, 1921–1922

1. *Muzot*
2. *Angels*
3. *Orpheus*

CHAPTER V

THE CRISIS, 1921–1922

1. *Muzot*

Switzerland's 'noble revenge', as Rilke put it, for the insult of the lowered blinds was to give him the castle of Muzot, the historic site where *Duino Elegies* came to completion and which sheltered Rilke during the last years of his life. That he chose this rather formidable habitation from among the number of possible refuges open to him, after many doubts, anxieties and even fears, accompanied by the usual havering and wavering, will not seem strange to those who recognise in his early descriptions that sense of a challenge to his spirit, of danger looming, which had informed his feelings for Paris and Duino. Castle Muzot, discovered by chance from a photograph in a hair-dresser's window in Sierre, was a forbidding little tower, in natural surroundings which reminded Rilke of Provence and Spain, and whose slightly austere magnificence he characterised as biblical, overwhelmingly great and not typically Swiss. The so-called castle dated back to the thirteenth century, and proved far from easy to inhabit. Indeed, as Rilke picturesquely said, it was more like donning an armour than moving into a house. He refused at first to contemplate spending a winter there; and had his kind friend Werner Reinhart of Winterthur (who first rented Muzot for Rilke and then bought it) not allowed him complete freedom in the matter of the tenancy, the poet would probably never have settled there at all. As it was, after weeks spent in making it habitable, with the assistance of Baladine Klossowska, the difficulty of finding a housekeeper threatened to jeopardise the venture; and when at last that problem was solved in the early days of August, months passed by before Rilke could reconcile himself to the idea that Muzot was to be, temporarily at least, his home. 'It isn't Berg', he wistfully told his correspondents; nor was the valuable Frida Baumgarten to be compared to the peerless Leni; nevertheless, that grim little tower pulled him up to it and into it: it was the very acme of solitude, the very essence of the past:

Un très petit château terriblement seul dans un vaste site de montagnes assez tristes; des chambres antiques et pensives, aux meubles sombres, aux jours étroits, cela me serrait le cœur. Mon imagination ne pouvait qu'elle n'ecoutât dans votre intérieur le monologue infini d'une conscience tout isolée, que rien ne distrait de soi-même et du sentiment d'être unique. Je ne concevais pas une existence si separée, des hivers eternels dans un tel abus d'intimité avec le silence, tant de liberté offerte à vos songes, aux esprits essentiels et trop concentrés qui sont dans les livres, aux génies inconstants de l'écriture, aux puissances du souvenir.[1]

Valéry's phrasing and his choice of words recreate the dual aspect of the intense spiritual isolation reigning at Muzot when Rilke was in residence. Its original solitude and remoteness, penetrated by the presence of his abysmally lonely spirit, produced an atmosphere which the sensitive, civilised Frenchman, heir to a social tradition unique in the world, recognised as dangerous and subtly inhumane; for Rilke had in truth come to a pass when his one desire was to be alone, 'if possible for ever'.[2]

The subconscious rhythm of our lives can hardly be perceived, and may even be interrupted, when the conscious rhythm is affected by those of other personalities. Rilke, who did nothing by halves, was an extremist in his personal relationships; superficial social contacts slid almost imperceptibly into spiritual intimacies which made alarming inroads on his time, his attention, his inner self. Unless he was physically cut off from his kind, he was actually severed from the source of his poetry. He now felt it to be an imperative duty, it was certainly a vital necessity, to find his way back to that. The rivalry between personal intercourse and his work had come to a head in the interruption at Berg when life had

---

[1] Paul Valéry, in *Reconnaissance à Rilke*, Les Cahiers du Mois 23/24, Paris, 1926, pp. 9 f.

[2] *B. 1921–1926*, p. 70; to Ilse Blumenthal-Weiss, from Muzot, December 29, 1921.

momentarily won the day, and the reaction to his art was all the stronger now. His fellowship with that he felt to be older than anything else; all his memories, his whole nature was bound up with it; it was insisting on its rights, and telling him the hard and simple facts that his personal communications were filched from his work; that personal intercourse hindered aesthetic expression; that any living thing which made demands on him was a gravely disturbing factor and must be kept at a distance. Rilke obeyed this injunction to the letter; he shut himself up in Muzot for the winter, alone with a taciturn housekeeper, and even refused a watch-dog, so as to be responsible for nothing and nobody but his work. Meanwhile, hundreds of letters reached him from girls, women and young poets asking for help and advice. Rilke was never loth to give counsel from a distance, nor did he neglect any other portion of his vast correspondence, which he dealt with as thoroughly, as whole-heartedly and as fastidiously as he decorated and furnished Muzot; writing letters, few indeed of which were less than four pages in length, many of them being much longer, all of them beautifully written, thoughtfully phrased and carefully composed. They were perhaps less a means of communication with the outside world, than a method of getting into touch with himself, partly by self-expression, partly by clearing away the accumulated external pressure of other minds on his own. They became noticeably rarer as the great event of his life drew near. The solitude he created round him in Muzot played a large part in hastening its approach.

Another contributing factor was his discovery of Paul Valéry's poems. They aroused that kind of enthusiasm which releases the creative instinct; and, by transferring Valéry's rhythms into his own modes, Rilke set his mind vibrating with an energy which developed into sound. But perhaps even more important was the fact that, as in the days when he learnt about Cézanne, the achievements and destiny of another artist seemed to explain and justify his own poetical existence:

Paul Valéry derives from Mallarmé; about twenty-five years ago there appeared a remarkable essay (*L'introduction à la méthode de*

Leonardi da Vinci) which he has now—in 1919—published with an extraordinarily fine preface. But to begin with Mallarmé meant to find oneself, with the next half-step forward, standing in silence, *dans un silence d'art très pur*. And this is what happened. Valéry fell silent and studied mathematics. And only now, during the war, 1915 or 1916, the necessity of aesthetic expression made itself felt again (all the purer for the interruption) in the man of fifty years old. Everything he has produced since then is extremely individual and important.[1]

' *Un silence d'art très pur*'; here was a magic formula for a healing balm. Rilke was still four years short of fifty, and Valéry's impressive silence had lasted for a quarter of a century; his own barren decade lost its formidable aspect and now appeared under an auspicious guise, as if a cooling shadow heralding rain had passed over the face of a fiercely consuming sun.

Into the deep rhythm of a silence which could almost be heard, muffled echoes from the life beyond his tower penetrated fitfully but could not disturb him. Kippenberg could be trusted to cope with the financial side of the engagement and approaching marriage of young Ruth Rilke. Let whatever was suitable be done according to her father's means, and some generous but sensible arrangement made as soon as possible. For his own part, he could even do without pocket-money at Muzot if necessary whilst the rate of exchange was so terribly against him; and it was perhaps just as well to be without the means to leave his tower even for a day. A benign letter or two to his daughter, and a kindly telegram confirming Kippenberg's satisfactory proposals; then the world retreated again. And something, not forgotten but overlaid by plans of escape and journeys of discovery, by emotional crises and urgent house-huntings, began to stir and whisper. Perhaps Ruth's engagement played its subterranean part in *Sonnets to Orpheus* and *Duino Elegies*. Here was a young girl, and his own daughter too, about to embark upon marriage. Rilke took it very much for granted as a grati-

[1] *B. 1921–1926*, p. 75; to Lou Andreas-Salomé from Muzot, December 29, 1921.

fying, but natural event. It was tiresome that the announce-
ment of her engagement had betrayed his whereabouts to the
world at the very moment when he most wanted seclusion;
but it did not upset him as it would have done if he had really
loved Ruth. Is it possible that he had never really loved her,
because he had had a premonition when she was an infant that
she was going to marry young, that she was not destined for a
virgin's death, nor yet for a tragic love-life? If it was true
that he had foreseen her future, it would account for his
benevolent aloofness throughout and the absence of any
antagonism towards her affianced husband now. She was not
one of those mysterious, fascinating young girls whom to wed
is to slay. Two years ago one of these had died just as she was
attaining maturity: Wera Ouckama Knoop, a beautiful child,
a wonderful dancer, a radiant, poetical young creature, a
playmate of his own sturdy matter-of-fact little daughter.
Wera and her sister had once come to tea with him, and he
had told them about the ghosts of Raymondine and Polyxène.[1]
Now she was a ghost herself, and her mother Gertrud had
written to congratulate him about Ruth's engagement. On
November 26, 1921, Rilke answered this letter in a fashion
that probably surprised the recipient, for it was more intimate
than their friendship had hitherto been. Restraint and reticence had always marked Gertrud's dealings with the poet
whom her husband Gerhard had sought out in Paris in 1909.
The two men took to each other, and Rilke made a habit of
calling on the Knoops whenever he was in Munich. He wrote
very movingly to Gertrud when Gerhard died in 1913, and
negotiated with the *Inselverlag* on her behalf in the matter of
her husband's unpublished works. During the war they met
occasionally in Munich, but not very often. She hesitated to
obtrude herself on the time and attention of the poet who was
more surrounded than he liked and with whose desire for
solitude she selflessly sympathised. Whenever they did meet
she felt it to be a rare and beautiful occasion. In her gentle
and unobtrusive fashion she was a friend to the whole family,
for she admired Clara and was devoted to Ruth. It was

[1] These details were communicated to me by Frau Ouckama Knoop.

therefore natural that she should write to Rilke about the engagement, for they corresponded occasionally, although at long intervals. Rilke's answer, however, showed that the relationship had grown closer on his side since her daughter's death. It is one of those important confessional letters which occur at crises in his correspondence, and which were generally addressed to Lou Andreas-Salomé or Marie Thurn and Taxis. Not quite as intimate and outspoken as these, it nevertheless lays bare the state of his inner life when he wrote it; his gentle indifference to Ruth's marriage; his dire need for absolute solitude; the continued spiritual injury of the war; a helpless feeling that he would never be able to justify the colossal expenditure of every sort of assistance that had been made on his behalf; what the landscape of Valais meant to him; the disastrous effect upon his creative powers of human companionship and intercourse; his belief that it was not so much aesthetic expression he was seeking as the spiritual and invisible centre of his own being; the revelation Valéry had been to him; and finally the real reason why he was writing to her so confidentially. It was the nearness of Wera to him which had brought him so near to her mother. Perhaps one day Gertrud would write to him about her dead daughter; he wanted to take part in her death; and he asked that some small thing she had loved might be laid aside for him, if possible something that she had often handled. The account of Wera's illness and death which Gertrud thereupon wrote for him reached him on January 1, 1922, bringing with it a deep sense of obligation to the poet. It was like a challenge and a command.

How unpredictable are the workings of human actions upon the pattern of our lives. Ruth Rilke fell in love and became engaged, thus causing Wera's mother to write and congratulate the slightly bored but benevolent father. All unwittingly she moved the key-log and it shifted; gradually the movement spread to other tightly wedged and stationary blocks of inert inspiration. Imperceptibly they gave way, began to float and yielded to the current; gently at first and then rapidly swept along by the river which had not been able to dislodge them all these weary years.

Rilke was either unconscious or mistrustful of what was happening. Up to the very last moment he repeatedly complained of his continued incapacity to concentrate owing to the effect of the war: on September 25, on November 26, on December 15, on December 29, 1921, on January 12, and twice on January 28, 1922. On February 2 he felt himself in the power of his spirit and began to write, but not the elegies, as he fully expected and intended to do; in their place there came a series of sonnets addressed to Orpheus, penetrated by the invisible presence of Wera and by visions of the metamorphosis she had undergone. On February 5 the first sequence of *Sonnets to Orpheus* was finished. A copy of these twenty-six poems was sent to Professor Strohl in Zurich and another on February 7 to Gertrud Ouckama Knoop with a short covering letter, quietly but tremulously reflecting the emotions he had undergone in writing the sequence. On February 9 he awoke with another sonnet on his lips; this he despatched to Gertrud as a substitute for one of the poems which retrospectively seemed to be 'empty', a mere conduit for the spirit of poetry flowing through and beyond it. At five o'clock that same evening he sent off a telegram to Nanny Wunderly-Volkart: 'Seven elegies now practically complete. Joy and wonder.' On his way back from the post-office the eighth and the ninth formed and completed themselves in his mind round earlier fragments. Late that night he wrote to Kippenberg that the elegies were there; that he was over the mountain, and that nine long elegies and a second part of 'fragmentary poems' belonging to the same stratum were now ready to be published whenever Kippenberg liked. On February 11 by six o'clock in the evening Rilke had completed the tenth elegy, cancelling a longish earlier passage of which he kept only the twelve opening lines of the present poem. On that same day he wrote to Lou and Marie Thurn and Taxis announcing the glorious news that all ten elegies were finished. But they were not finished yet. A last burst of inspiration seized him, which produced between February 12 and 20 yet another elegy, now the fifth in the cycle, and another series of *Sonnets to Orpheus*, embracing twenty-nine poems. Rilke rejected the original fifth elegy in favour of the later one, and it was not published until after his death.

Assuming that both fifth elegies were conceived and composed at Muzot (though part of the original poem seems to belong to 1913–1914), Rilke finished four elegies from longer and shorter fragments and wrote three completely new ones in the space of about a week. That is to say, only the present fifth and seventh elegies of the cycle belong entirely to Muzot. According to Rilke's dating the same holds true of the eighth as well, but this can only be accepted as accurate if by fragments he meant fragments in verse. On February 10, 1922, he wrote to Nanny that the eighth and ninth elegies had completed themselves in his mind as he walked back from the post-office, 'round shorter and longer earlier fragments'.[1] As no verse fragments of the eighth elegy were found, Salis suggested that Rilke was possibly referring to the sixth elegy, a proposal which brings this statement into line with Rilke's subsequent date-scheme of the composition of the cycle. Nevertheless, the fragments were there, in his Spanish diary and in two subsequent letters, one of which at least he did not send off. And even if none of these prose passages was accessible to him in Muzot, the fragments were vividly present in his mind, as can be seen by comparing them with the relevant passages in the eighth elegy.[2] With this modification, here is the scheme as vouched for by Rilke:

First Elegy: Duino, 1912.

Second Elegy: Duino, 1912.

Third Elegy: Duino, 1912; Paris, 1913.

Fourth Elegy: Munich, 1915.

Fifth Elegy: Muzot, 1922.

Sixth Elegy: Toledo, Ronda, 1912; Paris, 1914; Muzot, 1922.

Seventh Elegy: Muzot, 1922.

Eighth Elegy: [Spain, 1912–1913; Paris, 1914; Munich, 1918]; Muzot, 1922.

[1] Cf. Salis, *op. cit.* p. 95, and note on p. 217; also Heinrich Cämmerer, *R. M. Rilkes Duineser Elegien*, Stuttgart, 1937, p. 151.

[2] Cf. *B. 1907–1914*, pp. 347 f. and *B. 1914–1921*, pp. 177 f. with *G.W.* III, pp. 294 f.

Ninth Elegy: Spain, 1912–1913; Muzot, 1922.
Tenth Elegy: Duino, 1912; Paris, 1914; Muzot, 1922.

There is also the teasing little fact to be accounted for that, to judge by a letter to Frau Amann-Volkart from Muzot, not dated, but placed by the editors at the end of December 1921, Rilke was working quietly and laboriously at the tenth elegy before the crisis came.[1] The whole story of the composition of the elegies is obviously even more intricate than it appears on the surface; one cannot attempt to unravel it while so many relevant letters and other documents remain unpublished; and it will probably never be fully known, since so much of the work was unconsciously done. Rilke was so certain himself of a cycle of poems to be realised, that I am inclined to postulate a revelation of the whole in Duino in 1912, which refused to be completely put into words. He laboured unremittingly to recapture it, and was rewarded by many periods of partial illumination. Finally, in February 1922, it was repeated, and he managed to write it down, an undertaking which was certainly lightened by all that he had thought and written during the ten intermediate years. This hypothesis accounts for the ecstatic way in which he broke the news to his friends, which is consonant neither with his usual extremely modest reports of poetical achievements, nor yet with the calm of fulfilment with which a man writes 'finis' to his life-work.

The tone of the various missives he sped across Europe: to Nanny Wunderly-Volkart, to Anton Kippenberg, to Lou Andreas-Salomé and to Marie Thurn and Taxis, all within two days of each other, is indeed rapturous, exultant, awe-stricken and almost vainglorious. The letters were written with a hand still shaking from an event which he felt to be of cosmic rather than personal import. A nameless storm, a spiritual hurricane had threatened, he said, to split the fabric of his whole being asunder. He had groaned aloud for days and nights as long ago in Duino; but that terrific experience had been nothing to the superhuman endurance which had been demanded of him in Muzot. He found himself issuing

[1] Cf. *B. 1921–1926*, pp. 71 f. with *G.W.* III, p. 308. The editors, however, on more than one occasion have placed undated letters inaccurately.

vast commands to the universe, and answering its signals with thundering salutes. He had only survived by a miracle, enduring indescribable things in an 'elemental disorder' during which he could think neither of food nor of rest; undergoing imperious dictation from unknown forces, instrument and agent in one. This is strange language to use, but both Plato and Nietzsche would have accepted it; for the most lucid and beautifully balanced mind that has ever existed and the most overwrought of imaginations coincide in their description of poetical inspiration as divine possession, and justify the incoherent phrases, the staccato style, the overweening pride manifested by Rilke whilst he was finishing *Duino Elegies*.[1] For twenty years he had denied the validity of inspiration and had preached and practised the doctrine of humble, patient work. But he was now in the grip of something different from aesthetic creation. Both he and Nietzsche felt that they were mediums for a spirit more powerful than themselves. Hölderlin underwent the same experience. All three, each in his very different way, aimed at transgressing human boundaries, and the minds of two gave way under the strain. The spirit which possessed the third was less dynamic and dangerous. *Duino Elegies*, finally brought to the surface by a violent spiritual earthquake, did not destroy the author, who was reserved for a less problematical end.

2. *Angels*

The most conspicuous feature of *Duino Elegies* is Rilke's attitude to his own poetry, which underlies the whole cycle, an intensely personal point of view revealing a dangerously isolated mind. Deserted by inspiration during the long period which preceded the inception of *Duino Elegies*, he was to meet the same fate again and again during the following decade. The cycle is the battle-ground of his desperate efforts to win over a fierce and radiant foe; and the scene of a darker conflict, a long, grim struggle with the demon of doubt. Mis-

[1] Cf. Plato in *Ion* and Nietzsche in *Ecce Homo*.

givings as to his own poetical mission, dark suspicions of the validity and power of poetry itself in life and the universe often assailed his mind. The cosmic creativeness of art, the faith in which he had been sustained from the days of the Tuscan journal onwards, seemed to be in question. This spiritual uncertainty has left its mark on *Duino Elegies*. Hardly less harrowing, if on a less exalted plane, was the problem of his human existence, the utter isolation of his genius, the loneliness of his mind, accompanied by sharp stabs of fear that he, and not the world, might be in the wrong. He found some measure of relief in equating his tragic lot in life as a poet with man's position in the universe, which he represented as completely isolated and divorced from nature too. This analogy between his own sufferings and the cosmic desolation of mankind gives to *Duino Elegies* what human significance this strange cycle has. Although Rilke still discriminated sharply between men and artists as between two different species, a belief which dated from the Tuscan journal, nevertheless, as a background to his personal conflict and his personal confessions can be seen a vision of life as a whole. He used the pronoun 'we' in the main as a royal plural for Rilke; but sometimes too for poets in general and occasionally for human beings, as members of the same tragic race.

He saw the world we inhabit as Bunyan saw Vanity Fair, as a city of sorrow situated in the great land of grief. This beautiful, mysterious and glamorous country was inhabited by the noble race of lamentations, once all-powerful throughout the land, but now fallen from their high estate and shunned by the inhabitants of the city who congregate in the garish and strident consolation-market, jostling each other before the gaudy booths, drinking the popular 'deathless' beer and chewing cheap distractions. Just outside the city walls, lovers, children and dogs approach nearer to reality and nature; and it may even happen that some young man from the town meets with a girlish lamentation and follows her through the meadows. But only the youthfully dead realise the full extent of her beauty and charm, and are guided by her

into the heart of the mighty, dreaming land, with its ruined
castles, its tear-trees, its fields of blooming melancholy, its
flocks of affliction, its silent ambiguous sphinx and its unfamiliar, significant constellations. Such wayfarers do not
linger for long, however; bidding their guides farewell, they
depart to go down into the mountains of primeval pain, and
not even the noise of their footsteps will be heard from the
depths of that soundless fate.

The contrast between the blatant vulgarity of the city and
the serene loveliness of the ancient land surrounding it, given
up to the cult of the dead and inhabited by a race of mourners,
is not only a glorification of sorrow and pain as greater and
more beautiful than joy, but also an affirmation of death as
a better and more enlightened state than life, an echo from
many and many a poem in the past. The extreme beauty of the
vision (which even the ingenuity of the allegory cannot hide)
and the literally hypnotic quality of the verse arouse the
species of emotion described by a brother-poet as 'being half
in love with easeful Death', an effect which Rilke's more
proselytising pronouncements do not produce.

The city of sorrow which offers a bird's-eye view of
humanity as a whole shows that almost savage contempt for
ordinary mankind which Rilke often betrayed, but which
gave place in some other poems and passages in the cycle to
greater understanding. Not that his persistent gentleness
to women, including obeisance to protective motherhood,
marked any progress in his earlier views; nor yet his glorification of heroes, since they typify those who die young. But
there is a sensible widening of his sympathies towards lovers,
now given rank as an almost Fourierian 'couple' whose
emotions provide the highest standard of value attained by
ordinary humanity, comparable with, but generally represented as a little lower than, the achievements of poets and
artists. In every one of the ten elegies they are invoked to
measure the ultimate possibilities of the human race, and the
balance sways now this way, now that. But generally love is
represented as weighing less than art. Permanent union,
cosmic reality, immortality and realisation of death; some-

times lovers seem to achieve all this, more frequently it eludes them. On the whole, the emphasis is on the transience of their emotions, as, beautiful but evanescent, wan and a little help-less, they drift forlornly past. Rilke's real enthusiasm was still reserved for the young girls and women who were victims of love. But his sympathies were now more divided. Hitherto, all those forsaken mermaidens had been contrasted with coarse, brutal, or at the best insensitive men who were the merest *dilettanti* in the exacting art of love, scapegoats one and all for Rilke himself and his tragic incapacity to satisfy his own unattainable demands in that difficult relation-ship. His radiantly innocent young girls had been involved in scenes of brutality, horror and death in his immature imagin-ings. Later he kept them apart. Etherealised womanhood and mortal corruption pursued two parallel lines in *Malte Laurids Brigge*, although the cancelled passage of the two young lovers embracing in the Morgue shows that his fantasies had not radically changed. What made all such juxtapositions so distressing emotionally, physically so re-volting and aesthetically so questionable was that they were two forcibly sundered parts of an integral whole which Rilke did not affirm explicitly until *Duino Elegies*. He came near to doing so in *Requiem for a Friend*; but wrath clouded his utterance and masked the true reason for his recoil. The painful, ugly, sinister and grotesque side of life, first isolated from his poetry, and then included in it, but still in an un-assimilated form, mounted steadily in *The Book of Poverty and Death* to the exclusion of almost everything else in *Malte Laurids Brigge*. Now at last it was completely fused into a tragic vision of life. Resolved into its element, the mysterious origins of sexual desire, it was analysed and revealed with unfaltering force and magnificent imagery by Rilke in the third elegy. This was the dark fertile soil from which sprang his fear of love the slayer, his intense desire to save women from their destiny, his gospel of renunciation, his abiding distrust of men as lovers, and his tormenting dreams.

The squeamishness of his youth, the cruel fastidiousness in the requiem for Paula, the emotional suicide of Malte, were all rooted in his tragic realisation of the origins of life. The childhood terrors so graphically described in the novel were now correlated with their subconscious cause, the menace of his blood. It lurked for the child at night and seized upon him in his dreams, dragging him down into primeval, antenatal regions, spiritual ravines and abysses, where blood-sated monsters couched and ravening beasts gave chase. This fierce, fascinating, luxuriant jungle of hereditary instincts lay outside the province of a mother's protectorate. Nor could any young girl quell the storm of ages which first love aroused in the veins of the youth. His dark forbears were desiring her in him; women were hating her, and dead children were clamouring to be born. It was in this aspect that the young male lover as last took his rightful place in Rilke's work—the hero of a conflict whose victims had hitherto entirely monopolised the poet's sympathy. That perhaps was why the early *Maidens' Songs* were balanced by *Angels' Songs*, and why a host of shining angels preceded the third elegy of this cycle. The absolutely pure and radiant guardian angel replaced the vital menacing male in Rilke's youth; one might almost say that he exorcised him. Now they were contrasted, and a space found in Rilke's vision of life for its central manifestation. He had been fully aware of the importance of male sexuality and of its close connection with aesthetic creation, even of its fundamental innocence, as one of his letters to Kappus proves;[1] but intellectual and emotional convictions do not always harmonise; and here for the first time he experienced brotherly sympathy for the young male whose relationship to himself had hitherto inspired nothing but antipathy.

Nevertheless, he still interpreted the antithesis between men and women entirely in favour of the latter, and very much on the lines of Schiller; as witness *Antistrophes*, begun in 1915, completed during the elegy-crisis in February 1922, and originally intended for the fifth poem in the cycle. Here he was still on old ground, as was also the case in his continued reverence for childhood combined with passionate pity,

[1] Cf. *D.B.* pp. 22 ff.; dated from Worpswede, July 16, 1903.

apparent in the third and fourth elegies. This emotion deriving
from self-love and self-pity (as did also his yearning sympathy
for women) had inspired in 1914 a magnificent elegy on
childhood, omitted from the completed cycle probably for the
same reason which may have led him to exclude *Antistrophes*
too, the realisation that their presence would overweight the
balance on the human side. Yet the cancelled and incomplete
poem on childhood is a masterpiece of language and psychology, in close organic connection with the third elegy. Rilke
represented in the unfinished poem not those terrors of childhood which had been described in the other, but the terror of
being a child, isolated in the universe and impossible to
protect; a tragic situation, giving way to a worse one, the
gradual descent from that sublime loneliness to the sense of
being ousted from it, no longer an integral part of what he
feared, but outside it, disunited, betrayed, already gravitating
towards the empty desolation of being a man. The still unbroken integrity of childhood was what Rilke passionately
mourned as Schiller and Wordsworth had done before him.
All three regarded children tremulously and reverently, as
pure, innocent and undefiled, inhabiting a world from which
we are exiled. For Schiller this was a state of nature, a golden
age, from which man emerged as a dualistic being, potentially
greater and nobler, aware of the conflict between his senses
and his soul and striving upward. The child was innocent
because it was ignorant. Man was ethical where the child was
amoral. Rilke started from the same premises to arrive at a
diametrically opposite conclusion. Childhood in his view was
much the more valuable state. Intuitively aware of the nature
of life and the universe, artists in embryo; and like all artists
helpless, apprehensive, unprotected and alone, children died
into manhood before they could utter their thoughts. Their
natural protectors could not safeguard them from the
terrors lurking in their subconscious minds, nor save them
from life, which was waiting to seize them. Do what they
would, in *Malte Laurids Brigge*, in the third elegy and in the
unfinished poem, mothers were ultimately powerless to
protect their sons.

The fundamental difference which Rilke saw between childhood and adult humanity was the child's unconsciousness of death which it shared with the whole brute creation, thus belonging to the great cycle of nature, to that category which Schiller called naïve, in complete integration with universal life. Rilke differentiated man from nature, not by the power of reason or the ethical direction of the will, but by his consciousness of death in which, extremely poetically, he saw man's tragic destiny to lie. His earlier, doctrinaire notion of 'personal death' was not proclaimed in the elegies, and left little trace on his deepened vision of mankind. Increased understanding and greater emotional sincerity beautify the eighth elegy which, with the third, is concerned with humanity in general, even if the tragic awareness is the prerogative of the poet. Rilke's sympathy for mankind as a whole, for ordinary unhappy human beings, whoever or whatsoever they may be, is strongly marked in this poem. It silenced his earlier reproaches to them on the score of their frivolous attitude to death. The lovelessness underlying that criticism was swamped by compassion. He now believed that, far from really ignoring it, they were so cruelly conditioned as never to be able to forget it. This was their tragic fate; this distinguished them from the brute creation, from the serene, untrammelled beasts, calmly proceeding godwards, unaware of death, whole, complete, their gaze directed outwards. Lions roaming the jungle in their glory, he had exclaimed in the fourth elegy, know nothing of impotence until it comes. But man, forever conscious of his mortality, was not free to live fully, unquestioningly and undividedly. Whatever he did, thought or saw, it was always as one about to take leave; the whole life of man was one protracted farewell. It was his cruel destiny always to be playing opposite to death, and nothing but that: opposite always and for ever.

The city of sorrow certainly deserves its name; and the inhabitants are to be pitied rather than blamed, for the hand of fate is heavy on them. They are out of tune with the finite and out of touch with the infinite except during their pathetically brief childhood; the dark inheritance in their blood endangers

their loves; and only those can be called happy who vanish
away early from their death-ridden lives into the soundless
realms of outer darkness and primeval pain. This, in so far as
Rilke considered his fellow human beings sympathetically,
was how he regarded them; whilst even the relatively happy
beasts were represented as obscurely and uneasily longing
for the antenatal womb; and both nature and art were considered to be supremely evanescent. Against this sombre
background the drama of *Duino Elegies* was played out in
the poet's mind, a conflict with a threefold aspect. The first
reflected Rilke's lifelong doubt as to 'whether the highest
kind of activity is creating works of art or being in love';[1] the
second revealed his tormenting search for his poetical destiny
or mission; and the third, closely connected with it, his
homeric struggle to win a foothold for himself as a poet in the
universe and to stake out a claim for the cosmic significance
of poetry. All three aspects helped to inspire the vision of the
angels in *Duino Elegies* and to determine Rilke's relationship
with them.

Like nearly every other symbol in the cycle, the angels had
a long and chequered history behind them. They derived from
visual, and fertilised spiritual experiences. The Italian pictures
he had seen in Florence and elsewhere, notably Giotto and
Botticelli, almost certainly supplied him with the actual
symbol he used in his poetical adolescence to resolve his
sexual conflicts. The guardian-angel in *Early Poems* and the
choirs of angels standing round painted Madonnas performed
no positive functions, but were radiantly pure. A more vital
vision was inspired by Vogeler's sketch of the Annunciation
which Rilke saw in Worpswede. This produced a rhapsody in
prose on the dynamic force of angels on mankind, whom they
approached like a rushing, menacing, terrifying but finally
purifying whirlwind. This is the first hint of something
daimonic about the angels, who were used more convention-
ally in *Tales about God* and in a contemporary *Annunciation*.
In *The Book of Monkish Life*, however, a problematical element made its appearance. They were described as believing

[1] E. C. Mason, *Rilke's Apotheosis*, Oxford, 1930, p. 38.

in the light more than in God's dark power; and Lucifer, prince in the land of light, sought shelter among them. Biblical notions of fallen angels were responsible for this conception. But Rilke's fear of what their very presence denied dictated the description of the 'strange and terrible' choir of angels surrounding the Madonna who, in being delivered of Christ, had not given birth to God, and whom the angels did not comfort. Ruth Mövius identifies this description as a composite version of two of Botticelli's pictures, which she reproduces in her book.[1] She may be right, and it is true that the angels surrounding these two desperately sad Madonnas are making no attempt at comfort. But they are benevolently detached, certainly not strange and terrible. Rilke, having touched on the daimonic, satanic and sinister side of angels, illuminated a mournful aspect in *The Book of Pilgrimage* and in *Angels* in *The Picture-Book*. They had forgotten how to fly in the first poem, and were like heavy birds, ruins of birds, resembling pining penguins. In the second poem they had forgotten how to sing, and drifted languidly about with tired mouths, dreaming of sin, silent in the gardens of paradise, like so many intervals in God's might and melody, though when they spread their wings, they gave birth to a wind which seemed to be stirring the leaves of the book of creation.

These angels, like those in *The Book of Hours*, were not quite at one with God. In Rilke's vision of the Last Day, he imagined them pressing round God with a terrible beating of wings, their hundred thousand eyes full of unspoken accusations, mute and awful protestants against the fatal decree. But the God in this vision was the God of resurrection, the Christian God, whom Rilke was attacking, so that here he was on the side of the angels. The radiant guardian-angel in *The Picture-Book*, fierce, vital, positive and splendid, spoke of miracles as if they were knowledge, of men as if they were melodies, and of roses as if they were flaming events taking place in his eyes. But he never named God, and the poet waited for a command to question him. Except for *Angels*, the

[1] Mövius, *op. cit.* p. 36.

angels in this collection are glorious and terrible, like the apparitions in the Old Testament; whereas those in *Early Poems* are obviously derived from the New. In *The Gazer* the poet wrestled with an angel in the spirit as Jacob had wrestled in the flesh, and was blessed in being conquered by something mightier than himself. An awful austerity and divine power of wrath were attributes of *The Angel* in *New Poems*; and inexorability in *The Temptation*. In *Mission* Rilke interpreted that moment in Mohammed's life when he was keeping vigil on a night of Ramadan and saw the vision of an angel, who seized him with a strong grasp, crying 'Recite!' Rilke's angel commanded his victim to read; but the notion of a mission being forced upon a poet-prophet was the same. Finally, after the inception of *Duino Elegies* with its host of radiant, terrible and unapproachable angels, a revealing poem written in Toledo, *To the Angel*, brought out the magnitude of Rilke's longing for recognition by that divine being, and the reason for it:

> Shine, oh shine, and make the stars look down
> Upon me; for I fade away.[1]

At the outset of Rilke's poetical career angels had offered the passive resistance of radiance to the dark, tumultuous forces of life. The instinctive and primitive symbolism which had shaped them endowed them with dynamic life, so that they became active antagonists to all that is unworthy in man. Glorious and menacing, they challenged him to mortal combat, from which they emerged victorious, whilst he was defeated, but greater than before. The myth of Jacob wrestling with the angel inspired Rilke with gathering intensity as the desire for the 'blessing' grew. Expanded into a cosmic conflict, it moulded the internal structure of *Duino Elegies*, and haunted the poet's mind until the day of his death, as can be seen in his letters.[2] It perfectly symbolised his own most vital experience, the incalculable nature of inspiration, its

[1] *S.G.* pp. 5–6. El Greco's angels clearly affected Rilke's conception in *Duino Elegies*.
[2] Cf. *B. 1907–1914*, pp. 196, 275 and *B. 1921–1926*, p. 356.

dangers, its glories, its inexorability. Rilke's defeats and
victories in the struggle, one of the intensest of human conflicts, were given universal proportions in the cycle; so that
the whole is essentially a mystery play even down to the
allegorical element, so conspicuously present in the tenth
elegy. Rilke's angels were the protagonists in a drama which
had gradually shifted from the human to the superhuman
plane. Behind it was the fierce resolve to force the angels'
blessing, to attract their notice, to enter into their consciousness, to be recognised and accepted as belonging to the same
sphere and contributing something to the absolute beauty
which they represented as well as the forces of spiritual inspiration. For the Duino angels are too truly a poetical creation
to be completely susceptible of rational interpretation, and too
complex to stand for any one idea. Rilke's idolatry of art as
the supreme creative power became incarnate in them; a more
mysterious and less ambiguous piece of symbolism than his
previous use of the word God to represent an emergent
aesthetic creator. These angels had none of the protean
nature of the God of *The Book of Hours*; they were far more
arresting and terrible in their utter aloofness, and self-
sufficiency, as befitted beings who were not in a state of
becoming but of eternal and immortal existence. Their
absolute beauty annihilated human standards; and Rilke
could only avert his personal destruction as a poet by accepting the challenge implicit in their very being. This is the
drama inherent in *Duino Elegies*.

Although the angels have a structural part in the elegies,
this is poetically less important than the fact of their presence,
which drenches the cycle with radiance, giving it greater proportions and a deeper rhythm. They are exciting, dangerous,
forbidding; informed with a vitality which discharges itself
upon the reader like an electric shock. Whenever the sound of
their wings is heard, life becomes intensified, sometimes
almost to the limits of endurance. For these dazzling beings
are terrible and unnerving. They seem to deny, if not the
existence, then the validity of human life, love, suffering and
endeavour. They are utterly remote and completely self-

absorbed. Far from mediating between God and man, or
interceding for humanity, they stand like a liquid barrier of
fire between man and his maker; they encompass the whole
horizon with their glory, with a blinding radiance too
beautiful to be borne. They would not hear us if we called;
and if they did, if they lifted us up, or even approached one
step nearer, we should perish. Who are they?

> Earliest triumphs, and high creation's favourites,
> Mountain-ranges and dawn-red ridges
> Since all beginning, pollen of blossoming godhead,
> Articulate light, avenues, stairways, thrones,
> Spaces of being, shields of delight, tumults
> Of stormily-rapturous feeling, and suddenly, singly,
> Mirrors, drawing back within themselves
> The beauty radiant from their countenance.[1]

Spiritually male and overpoweringly virile, these angels
were sexless beings, divine antitheses to the natural man. The
dark mystery of the origins of sex was unfolded in a region
empty of angels in the third elegy; and the gallant young
heroes of the sixth stood in no discernible relation to them.
Nor were they mentioned in the eighth elegy, where the
knowledge of death prevailed. They did not distinguish
between the two provinces, Rilke declared in the first elegy,
and were often unaware whether they were among the living
or the dead. The human drama of birth, heroic life and death
did not affect them. It remained to be seen if they could be
compelled to acknowledge the spiritual aspirations of man, to
which they also appeared completely indifferent.

The first elegy forms as it were the exposition of the action
about to be engaged between Rilke and the angels, whose
passive manifestation was absolute art, but whose active
aspect, if they could be prevailed upon to show it, would be a
mighty whirlwind of inspiration. This highly personal, indeed
autobiographical, poem reflects Rilke's state of mind at
Castle Duino in 1912, and is elegiac in tone and content.

---

[1] *G.W.* III, pp. 264–265; based on Leishman and Spender's version in
Duino Elegies, London, 1939, p. 33.

Rilke confessed to the Princess Thurn and Taxis, after the poem was written, that the inspiration which had produced it was such a terrible experience that he feared its recurrence.[1] This is strongly brought out in the opening lines, where the poet partly despairs of attracting the angels to him and partly fears his immediate annihilation if they should approach him; coming to the conclusion that he could not use them poetically any more than he could use human beings. For his utter isolation in the world of men was the second subject of the poem, concentrated in the central fact that he was incapable of love. His yearning for it was so great however that it distracted him from his poetry. There was nothing for it but to sublimate all this frustrated longing into the symbolism of the early prose *Fragment*, and confess once more in his own idiom that he did not love the living but virgins who were dead.

Rilke's painfully tenacious spirit was still labouring with that early experience which had produced the original *White Princess*, some violent emotional shock which had been buried in his subconscious mind where it found incredibly fertile soil. It struck deep, and tangled roots grew, spread and branched up and out, driving the branches down again into the earth, whence they threw up fresh shoots to go through the same process as before, so that the inextricable but monotonous luxuriance of a banyan forest was the result. The wearisome prevalence of pathetic young girls and tragic women in Rilke's work, and their persistence in his translations needs no further pointing out at this stage of the present study. It is with a sinking heart that one hears them eddying back into the elegies, a ghostly choir of voices striking upon Rilke's ear, and confirming him in his mission to immortalise their love. What is more, it almost seems as if Gaspara Stampa were to be added to the list of Rilke's vocal heroines, which already included the Virgin Mary and Mary Magdalene, Alcestis and Eurydice, Elizabeth Barrett Browning and the Countess of Noailles, Marianna Alcoforado and Louïze Labé, to name only a few of the more important names. The mission to glorify this ill-starred lover-poet seems indeed like a work of

[1] Cf. above, p. 225.

supererogation. Nor can one feel much more enthusiasm for
the other cognate task, to magnify all the youthfully dead of
either sex, thus weaning them gently and consolingly from
life to death. Three requiems and countless other poems and
prose passages had already, one would think, exhausted this
theme. In spite of the beauty of the language it betrays no
fresh inspiration and no stirring of the poetical waters. Rilke
felt this himself, since he came to the conclusion that the
youthfully dead did not need him, or at least not for long, and
that therefore he had no real mission to them; but they were
his only source of inspiration, since their departure and the
sense of loss they left behind them set the world swinging to
the rhythm of musical laments, as Linus had done of old. This
first elegy is in fact a bitter confession of poetical and emotional bankruptcy, the inexhaustible theme of his contemporary letters. Were it not for the presence of the angels at
the beginning of the poem, one would almost be ready to give
him up.

But the vital, magnetic power radiating from them came
from Rilke himself and was more clearly manifest in the second
poem. Human love shrank almost to nothingness when he
surveyed that dazzling host; for love was tragically ephemeral, and they were beyond all time. Heroically he set himself to establish the one possible connection with them; that of
contrast between their absolute beauty, glory, intensity and
might and the feeble, evanescent nature of mortal emotions
and aspirations. Perpetually evaporating into the universe
and vanishing, might not all this nevertheless have some
almost imperceptible effect upon it? Those shining angelic
mirrors, eternally reflecting their own glory might, without
meaning to and certainly without noticing it, catch something
emanating from us on the way; so that we might be present in
their features just as much or as little as the vagueness on the
countenance of a pregnant woman. This was barely conceiv-
able; but the angels in the whirlwind of their return to themselves would be totally unaware of it.

If Rilke did not actually reject love in favour of art in this
poem, he showed more clearly than in the first elegy his dis-

satisfaction with it as a poetical subject, and his willingness to relinquish it. Gaspara Stampa faded from his mind altogether when he turned to his interpretation of sex in the third elegy, representing it as an elemental, dangerous, subversive force which had nothing to do with art, at the very antipodes from the radiant angels of his desire; yet paradoxically enough it was a force which inspired him here with some of the finest poetry he ever wrote, and heralded his later phallus-worship rooted in the creative power of sex. This however was still to come. Rilke's main preoccupation in *Duino Elegies* was with his supra-terrestrial opponent.

The crisis in his conflict with the angel occurred in the fourth elegy, in which poem he braced himself to coerce by sheer will-power the austere and reluctant daimon of poetical inspiration. It is a hard poem in more senses than one; hard to like, even when the intellectual difficulties it presents have been partially overcome, on account of its hard tone of contempt for all human values and its convulsive efforts to transcend them. It came from an atrophied heart and an arrogant mind, rigidly determined to divorce life from art at any cost, and there is something grotesque about the endeavour. Yet, for all its grimness, it has tragic proportions; since the violent effort to constrain inspiration met with no apparent success, and the poet reached the nadir of despair. After a bleak and wintry survey of the false position of man in the world and of the pitiful inadequacy and hostility of his human relationships, Rilke hissed him off the stage, irritably and impatiently rejecting himself as an actor in the theatre of life, and as a poet of such dramas. Far better to replace man by a puppet which, however lifeless, was at least solid and full, whereas the human actor was flabby. The puppet had enjoyed almost as long and quite as varied a symbolical career in Rilke's works as the angels.[1] In fact it had been through even more vicissitudes, for the very word, *Puppe*, was ambiguous and could be used either for dolls or for marion-

---

[1] Cf. E. C. Mason, *Lebenshaltung und Symbolik bei Rainer Maria Rilke*, pp. 82 ff. for an exhaustive and fascinating analysis of the puppet-symbol in Rilke's work.

ettes, including the thought-associations inherent in its third meaning of chrysalis, often present when Rilke was speaking of dolls. The word was chameleon-coloured, and Rilke used it with the most bewildering, shifting, kaleidoscopic effects. For the pure doll, the doll *an sich*, he had the most devastating contempt, apparent in his essay on the subject and in the final lines of the unfinished childhood elegy. It stood for the inertia of dead matter aping human form, and therefore treacherous and deceitful in its supine insensibility. Amongst other things it symbolised that puppet-god man has made in his own image, for ever unaware of adoration and stone-deaf to prayers. The marionette, on the other hand, represented art quickened by life and roused the kind of reverence Rilke felt for all spiritually animate things. But since a motionless marionette is almost identical with a lifeless doll, Rilke, past-master in ambiguity, used *Puppe* at times, and notably in this poem, to convey his dual attitude towards art, a deep-seated discord, never quite resolved and particularly strident in this poem. For although art, or the puppet, seemed preferable by far to life, nevertheless its disillusioning nature, its apparent impotence to act on life, was also represented. The puppet created by man stood, not for absolute art, but for human approximations to it, and in particular for Rilke's own poetry, whose inadequacy in face of the war was the saddest lesson he ever learnt. Hence his insistence that the puppet was filled with sawdust, that its face was completely inexpressive, and the wires all too visible. Having dismissed his fellow human beings from his life, this was what he was faced with, and he had to face it out in utter isolation from his own kind. In June 1914 he had come to believe that he had reached the limits of what the most fervent and devouring contemplation of objects could achieve, a belief expressed in *Turning-Point* and *Woodland Pool*. More, he suspected that he might have done violence to the things he had thus transmuted into art because he had been deficient in love. The hard lesson of love was his next and most urgent task. This criticism of *New Poems* and of Rodin's method was carried a step further in the fourth elegy, where, however, love was replaced by external inspiration.

There was no love, either human or aesthetic, but desperate anxiety in the gaze Rilke directed at the inanimate puppet whilst he waited tensely in the empty theatre before the grey, deserted, draughty stage. There was not a soul beside him; he had banished his friends and lovers, and even those of his blood and in his blood had left him to practise his magic alone. Self-dedicated, he watched and waited for the miracle which was to reward his utmost effort. He would and must compel the angel to descend at last and manipulate the strings of the seemingly lifeless marionette. 'Far above our heads the angel then will play.' The disturbing human element having been eliminated, art and inspiration would perform a real drama, a cosmic event, leaving mortals to their botch-work. This ultimate triumph took place in an uncanny silence and in his mind's eye. There was no motion on the stage, no sound of whirring wings, and nothing whatever happened. Then an anguished voice was heard, Rilke's voice crying out to the hours of his childhood, the magic interlude fit for pure creation. But how is a child to know, and who is there to tell him? Ask rather who the murderers are that take his young life from him. The puppet was probably responsible for this emotional collapse, and those wrathful mutterings. Tenacious as Rilke's mind was, he must have remembered the part assigned to the puppet-theatre in *Frau Blaha's Maid* as vividly as his own childish experiences with dolls. These memories of early disillusion and later horror of child-birth were fused in the grim closing lines of the poem. In vain had he sublimated the latter emotion in Christ-Child and Virgin Mary fantasies (immaculate conception and virgin birth), the strangled infant of the prose story was still present in his mind and haunted the end of the fourth elegy, where an ugly, painful, choking death was prefigured for the defenceless victim. Whether this interpretation is correct or not, the desperate appeal to childhood would seem to prove conclusively that the angel of inspiration had not accepted the burnt offering of human love Rilke had made in the poem.

The fifth elegy still leaves the matter in doubt, although it illuminates it vividly. For here the marionettes came to violent, indeed to galvanic life and performed an amazing *danse macabre*, in dramatic contrast with the inert and motionless puppet of the preceding poem. Although actually the last poem to be written, this acrobat elegy probably germinated in Rilke's mind contemporaneously with the fourth, since the theme was suggested to him by Picasso's *Saltimbanques*, over which he brooded for months on end in the summer and early autumn of 1915 before he wrote the puppet-play elegy. In 1922, when so much that had been stagnant in his mind began to stir, the stock-still group in the picture broke up too, performing fantastic gyrations, and leapt on to the stage whence the marionette had vanished. But the stage had disappeared as well; the acrobats were performing in the open air and in the street for everyone to see. There was some strange compulsion behind their actions, some eternally unsatisfied will, but certainly not the angel who had tarried in the fourth elegy. Nevertheless, he seemed to be watching them, or at least to be aware of them out of the corner of his eye; for these bewildering and tragic figures were artists of a sort, achieving the utmost it is possible to achieve without real inspiration and true love. Rilke, having rejected love for art's sake in the fourth elegy, now represented art without love in the fifth as the most tragically evanescent and unstable manifestation of life. It is therefore a pendant and an answer to the puppet-play poem, and as truly in its right place as the original fifth elegy (*Antistrophes*) would have been incongruous and irrelevant. If the puppet had represented the utter dependence of art on inspiration, the acrobats stood for the votaries of art for the sake of art. Metrically as well as imaginatively the poem is a *tour de force*, being a representation of virtuosity and skill gone almost mad, taking one's breath away as such performances are meant to do. The rush, the strain, the fever and the fret of these hectic and agile performers is so verily a dance of death, that the final merging and re-composition of the group into a tableau of love fulfilled after death is almost demanded by the dynamics of the poem. It also serves to illuminate the ambiguity of the symbolism prevalent throughout. The acrobats are artists in a wide as well as in a narrow

sense, and *dilettanti* in love as well as in art. If Rilke wished to
show the brittle brilliance of art as an end in itself (a doctrine
he had once subscribed to, but always with metaphysical
reservations), he also aimed at exhibiting the failure of even
the most highly skilled experts and untiring exponents of the
art of love. His personal belief that men are mere virtuosos in
this matter and women the only true artists, and that therefore
love will never be perfect in this world, glimmers through the
poem. All the active acrobats are male. The little girl is
merely hoisted into various positions, carried about, over-
leapt and triumphantly displayed as proof of their dazzling
skill. A personal confession obtruded itself here. There can be
no question, to anyone who knows Rilke, but that the child-
acrobat stands for himself. He was the little boy who would
sometimes smile tremulously through his tears towards his
'rarely tender' mother whilst making frantic and incessant
efforts to win applause. Something of the physical strain of
life at the military academy and René's hopeless efforts to
shine at drill and on horseback is present in these lines; and
memories still remoter; pathetic attempts to earn approval
when he was dressed up in his best clothes and proudly
paraded for show.

The shattering of the eerie silence and solitude of the
fourth elegy which takes place in the fifth, the glorification of
love above artistry and possibly even above art, are accompanied by references to an angel which certainly diminish the
significance of the radiant beings in the opening poems of the
cycle. This angel appears in a more familiar (and therefore a
more contemptible) guise as a being of compassion and love.
Addressing him as one who would certainly hear and probably
obey, Rilke charged him to pluck the tremulous smile from the
face of the child-acrobat and to preserve it in an urn. Moreover the angel seemed to be watching the troupe and to have
fore-knowledge of its future transmogrification. The cloudy
residuum of self-pity in Rilke's feeling for the little acrobat
accounts for the sentimental injunction to the angel; the fact
that the latter seems to know the place where after death the
lovers will perform truly inspired and beautiful feats shows

his characteristic wavering between love and art. Here, as if in reaction to the fourth elegy, he gave the palm to love. His tormenting doubts as to his own personal rightness in choosing a poet's life and as to the greatness of poetry altogether also account for his hymn to heroes in the sixth elegy, where they are exalted above the rest of mankind, because they live dangerously, pressing onwards towards fruition in death, whereas we linger merely to bloom. This poem, like his early *Cornet*, was written under the compulsion of that life-long love for those who died young which must have been intensified by the war, thus adding perhaps greater enthusiasm to the lines when he completed or recast this elegy in 1922. His conviction of the greater glory of death was founded upon a rock. Yet this was embedded in dark, submerged hatred and abhorrence, loathing and fear of dying. Nakedly expressed in *Malte Laurids Brigge*, it dictated during the war a terrible poem called *Death*. It had racked his mind ever since the days of *The White Princess* and probably before. It was too elemental to be conquered; but let those who had conquered it be extolled.

The fifth and sixth elegies mark that pause in the conflict between Rilke and his great antagonist which often comes after a crisis has been reached; a pause in which waverings and doubts beset his mind for having made his great refusal in the fourth elegy in the name of art. Art seemed less attainable and less desirable than it had done before the sacrifice, and heroes of a different kind from himself more greatly admirable. Human values reasserted themselves and the heroism of human endeavour. But in the seventh elegy Rilke turned away from them finally. More, he explicitly abandoned the poetical mission he had accepted in the first elegy to glorify the tragic women-lovers of the past. At the beginning and end of a most magnificent courting-song he abjured love and the beloved too; since if he called to her she would bring in her train all those dead and gone young maidens who wanted to live again, and come back to this world. They had not yet learnt the lesson of the seventh elegy, that the only real world is within us, and that life is one long transformation. Rilke had at last found the formula for his cosmic mission and a

connecting link between himself and the angel. He still
dreaded that awful being unutterably, he still called 'Come'
and 'Avaunt' in the same breath; he still wished to keep him
at a great distance; but during the course of the poem Rilke
brought into the consciousness of the angel the mighty
achievements of human art. That world of towering cathedrals
and soaring columns was vanishing away from sight. The
rushing spirit of the age which cared more for power than
form was destroying the monuments and temples of the past.
And where they still stood, they were already partly invisible,
altogether overlooked by many who neither saw them with
their bodily eyes nor transformed them with the eyes of the
mind. Rilke displayed them to the angel, whose eyes received
them; and there, upright and saved in his gaze, they remained.
More, the angel was challenged to confess his astonishment, to
glorify those works, and to proclaim the miracle that man,
encompassed by an incomprehensible fate, had peopled space
with such magnificent monuments, which were great, even
when measured against his own stature. So too was music, and
lonely, unrequited love. But they, belonging to the invisible
kingdom, needed no transformation to immortalise them.
Architecture and sculpture, vanishing from the apparent
world, were eternalised in the angel's eyes.

In the fluctuating rise and fall which marks the movement of
the cycle, the eighth elegy goes subsiding into the depths
after the triumph in the preceding poem. This hymn to the
brute creation is tragic in the extreme, a bitter contrast
between the beautiful unconsciousness of death which marks
out the beasts that perish, and man's incessant and despairing
awareness of it. One is therefore prepared in the ninth elegy
for Rilke's flat denial of the eternal value and significance of
human emotions, pain and even love, which had still counted
in the seventh elegy. But all our spiritual experiences shrink
to nothingness beneath the eternal stars and are not worth
uttering either there or here. What then remained for the
poet to do? The same task he had undertaken in the seventh
elegy, but now contemplated under a more universal aspect.
His mission, the only valid poetical mission, was to the world

of things, animate and inanimate, which belong to the here and now and not elsewhere. It was they who needed the poet in order to become immortal, and it could only be done here. Let him transform bridges, wells, gateways, pitchers, fruit-trees, windows, houses, at the most towers and columns, in his inmost heart; nay, let him thus transform the whole earth which was demanding to rise again invisibly within him, and thus to be translated into the angelic sphere. Then the angels, who can only apprehend what is invisible, will marvel at this hymn of praise to humble, simple things. They will receive them and rescue them from oblivion. We, whoever we may be, are here simply and solely for this.

Nietzsche said in *The Birth of Tragedy* that the world was justified, but only as an aesthetic phenomenon. Rilke came to the more extremist conclusion that existence was justified only in so far as it was aesthetically active; and he narrowed the sphere of art to include only visible phenomena, expressly stating that emotions such as sorrow and love should be left to the angels to utter, since their power of feeling immeasurably transcends ours.

It was more truly a personal confession than an aesthetic which he gave voice to in the seventh and ninth elegies. He was repudiating not only his early emotional poetry but also his later attempts to express things as they were in *New Poems*; they were now to be represented as they never really imagined themselves to be, they were to be transformed. This was his procedure in *Sonnets to Orpheus*, which is the practical pendant to the theoretical aim; and there was therefore the best of reasons for the triumph and affirmation of existence present in both these elegies. Rilke, an isolated, individual poet, had achieved recognition from the angels; he had dis-covered a channel of communication. If beauty was absolute, eternal and unattainable, all that was imperfect and temporal could be translated into that angelic sphere by the magic of poetry; and the poet who could do this might well uplift his voice in a paean of praise and exultation to the assenting choir of angels; he had at last attained the farther end of his grim insight into life.

The tenth elegy opened with this statement; the last in a cycle in which humanity as a whole, and especially lovers, heroes, children, beasts and things, had all been seen in their tragic aspect. For even the beasts who know not death obscurely long to return to the darkness of the womb; even the greatest works of art fade away and vanish from mortal ken. Whilst man himself, cruelly compassed round about by death, at the mercy of sinister antenatal forces, helpless to arrest the descending course of his existence, wanes ineffectively away. In spite of the poet's triumph, this world is one of sorrow; and for this reason, if for no other, it is outside the angels' ken. In a cancelled passage in the tenth elegy, Rilke drove this point home. Should a grief-stricken man lure an angel to his side, banking on his curiosity, the latter would come with a darkened countenance, and, powerless to comprehend sorrow or pain, would imitate the man's laments, as one copies the call of a bird.[1] So that the angels who tarried to hear the hymn of praise at the beginning of the poem vanished and were seen no more when the last sad dirge was raised.

There is a strange picture, once seen and never forgotten, of a man drowning in a lonely, ominous sea. Emerging for the last time from the still and deadly waters, he is past hope and beyond help. An almost intolerable awe distends the pupils of his eyes; but the frantic fear, the stark panic of the preceding struggle is already stiffening into the awful serenity of death. The horizon is completely surrounded by a host of glorious and terrible angels, waiting in utter impassibility for the end. One shudders to think that into these inexorable hands the soul of the dying man may be delivered. Yet one has an irrational hope that they are a subjective vision riding his panic-stricken mind.

This appalling picture is a visual equivalent of *Duino Elegies*. The last seconds in the life of a drowning man are filled with memories of the whole of his past existence, it is said. In the same way, all the poetical thoughts Rilke had

---

[1] This cancelled passage has been printed and rather inadequately commented on by Hermann Pongs in *Dichtung und Volkstum*, 1936, XXXVII, pp. 97–99.

experienced rose to the surface in this ultimate struggle; the whole of his spiritual life was lived through again, shot through by a vision of such beauty and terror as could be vouchsafed only, one would think, to a poet in mortal peril of spiritual annihilation. All this first happened in a blinding flash in Duino in 1912, for the first elegy contains the whole cycle in embryo. The final complete repetition of the initial experience brought the formulation (if not the revelation) of the poetical mission elaborated in the seventh and ninth elegies. It also acted on the grouping of the various poems in a species of composition which revealed Rilke's battle with and for inspiration, his conflict with doubts and with his own protesting heart. So that, if the angels represent a vision of light, the cycle as a whole reproduces the tragic struggles of a drowning man who would seem to have gone under irrevocably at the end of the tenth elegy.

But the cycle is not nearly so simple and unambiguous as this reading of it claims. On the contrary, it is one of those baffling and controversial works, so often written by poets who have passed their creative prime, in which poetry is subordinated to the philosophical content and to the didactic aim; in which beauty is not enough unless vouched for by truth. Obscurely aware of treachery to their art, such writers wrap up their meaning in veils of obscurity and offer intellectual puzzles instead of mystery itself. In spite of its intricate symphonic structure, its creative language, the pure magic of some of the poetry, and the simple beauty of some of the thoughts, the strongest impression produced by *Duino Elegies* is an unquiet feeling of treacherous depth, a sensation so vivid and so unremitting that one is justified in concluding that Rilke had experienced it too, and had realised that the attempt to sublimate his emotional and aesthetic experiences on to an astral plane was a desperate and dangerous venture. If the cycle as a whole seems to represent the vision of a drowning man whose breaking eyes behold austere shapes of glory, the abstract depths from which he had risen are part of that vision too. The poem, in fact, is not only susceptible of philosophical interpretation, but actually seems to demand it.

It has not demanded in vain. Deep has unhappily called audibly unto deep. Donning their diving-suits (latterly all of the regulation Existence-Philosophy pattern), German critics have boldly gone down where Rilke went under, emerging spluttering to the surface, a great roaring in their ears and full of submarine knowledge. The fault lies in the poem itself, which will not let its readers merely look and listen. Its obscurities are too challenging, its intellectual appeal too direct, its philosophical bent too obvious. For it was not the mythological sea from which Rilke rose to chant his paeans and his dirges. It was the ocean of abstract speculation which had engulfed the poet. Herein lay a tragedy; a tragedy which is enacted again whenever the poem is interpreted; and which is none the less tragic when, as sometimes happens, it develops into farce.

3. *Orpheus*

Although the first sequence of *Sonnets to Orpheus* preceded and heralded the final elegy-crisis, whilst the second followed and concluded it, both sequences belong chronologically and by their inspiration to a later period. They are like molten lava issuing from the depths of Rilke's mind and ejecting in the process petrified blocks formed during a previous eruption. The fundamental experience behind them, the biographical genesis of which stretched back through Wera and Paula to the days of the Tuscan journal, was Rilke's sudden recognition of himself in the legendary singer Orpheus. All great poets have moments at least when they become aware that they are but manifestations in time of the eternal spirit of poetry, a consciousness often deepened by the sensation that life itself is seeking utterance through them. Until Rilke wrote his *Sonnets to Orpheus* such moments had been overlaid by the much more persistent and vivid experience of spiritual isolation. This had only once been completely dissipated when, in the summer of 1914, his personality had seemed to merge with the spirit of mankind prostrate before the god of war. The miracle was not repeated, however, and Rilke's herculean

efforts to achieve direct contact with the transcendental spirit
of poetry formed the theme of *Duino Elegies*. The goal was
not attained, and the poet was forced to magnify his own
highly individual genius and unique point of view into something of cosmic value, because he could not surrender himself
to an infinite and impersonal power. The distance between
himself and the angels was not diminished; it remained as
great as before. There is nothing of inexorability or otherness
in Rilke's relation with his master Orpheus with whom he felt
himself to be one, whilst appearing far less arrogant in his
natural acceptance of a metaphysical affinity than he had been
in his apparently abject adoration of the angels. Towards
mankind, too, the sonnets are considerably more humane than
the elegies; human beings were no longer inflexibly excluded
from the sphere of poetry; they were tacitly allowed to be fit
objects and even subjects of song, although Rilke's ineradic-
able distaste for life as we know it and live it remained.
Mysterious often and sometimes disdainful as the sonnets are,
they nevertheless give the impression of universality while
the elegies astound by their unapproachable intensity. It is
as if Rilke's eyes, once opened to his affinity with Orpheus,
saw affinities everywhere.

His kinship with the magical singer of Greece was in the
nature of a revelation, as well it might be. The outstanding
fact about Orpheus, according to Western Europe, was his
descent into the underworld to bring back Eurydice, and the
tragic failure of the venture. All his life Rilke had been doing
just this; following young girls and women down into the
shades and trying to rescue them from oblivion. The first and
seventh elegies strongly suggest that he was aware of the
hopeless nature of this mission for all the magic of his verse.
Here was a startling mystical similarity, great enough
certainly to make a small engraving of Orpheus with his lyre
seen through a shop window impel the nascent sonnets to
group themselves round this name. Actually, the resemblance
between Rilke and Orpheus went far deeper than this and was
even more mysterious; for the legend about Eurydice,
although it was known to the Greek classical writers, was not

much emphasised by them. Euripides touched on it in *Alcestis*, as if Orpheus' undertaking had been successful;[1] Plato referred to it in the *Symposium* in terms which strike oddly on modern ears:

> . . . Orpheus, the son of Oeagrus, the harper, they [the gods of the underworld] sent empty away, and showed him an apparition only of her whom he sought, but herself they would not give up; because he appeared to them to be enervated by his art, and not daring like Alcestis to die for love, to have been contriving how he might enter Hades alive; moreover, they afterwards caused him to suffer death at the hands of women, as the punishment of his cowardliness.[2]

The version as we know it to-day comes from Virgil and Ovid, and has inspired many poets since then, amongst them Rilke in *Orpheus, Eurydice, Hermes*. But it was not this episode in Orpheus' legendary life which caused his name to be famous among the Greeks from the sixth century downwards. Although his descent into Hades was of great importance, his aspect as a passionate lover was almost certainly a later development. 'Anyone who realizes Orpheus at all' (said Jane Harrison) 'would feel that the intrusion of desperate emotion puts him out of key.'[3] In the eyes of the Greeks he was the magic musician, and more than that, the founder of a great religious reform, the holy high priest and prophet of the god Dionysus, whose savage rites he purified and civilised, and from whose mythical history he deduced a doctrine, enjoining a way of life on his disciples, so that they might become one with the god they worshipped, divine, and thence immortal. The orphic religion was based on the belief in successive reincarnations of souls, until that pitch of purity was attained which meant escape from the wheel of life and death. This was to be achieved by rites and by asceticism, particularly by abstention from animal food, logically forbidden to the orphics, since they held that souls might inhabit beasts. They further believed in the mixed heavenly and

---

[1] Euripides, *Alcestis*, ll. 359–362.
[2] Plato, *Dialogues*, tr. Jowett, 2nd ed. Oxford, 1875, II, p. 31.
[3] J. E. Harrison, *Prolegomena to the Study of Greek Religion*, 2nd ed. Cambridge, 1908, p. 603.

earthly nature of human beings, in the tragic dualism between soul and body, the divine origin of the former, the inglorious nature of the latter, a tomb, a prison from which the soul desires desperately to escape.

Modern thought inclines to-day to the belief that Orpheus had a real existence in remote antiquity, a belief clearly held by the Greeks who did not worship him as a god. This possibility is strongly suggested by the very individual personality which permeates the descriptions of him, his putative sayings and the doctrines attributed to him. This personality is so far from being shadowy, that its effect upon two modern scholars has been sharp and clear:

> Orpheus is first and foremost the musician with magic in his notes. . . . The influence of Orpheus was always on the side of civilisation and the arts of peace. In personal character he is never a hero in the modern sense. His outstanding quality is a gentleness amounting at times to softness. . . distinguished. . . from most of his fellow-men, by a type of quiet mysticism rare in any age.[1]

> . . . there is always about him a touch of the reformer's priggishness. . . this aloof air, this remoteness, not only of the self-sufficing artist, who is and must be always alone, but of the scrupulous moralist and reformer. . . who. . . draws men and repels them, not by persuading their reason, still less by enflaming their passions, but by [the] sheer magic of his personality. It is this mesmeric charm that makes it hard even now-a-days to think soberly of Orpheus. . . . Orpheus is utterly sober. . . . The notion of kinship with the brute creation harmonized well with the somewhat elaborate and self-conscious humility of the Orphic. . . .[2]

The remarkable resemblance between the impression made by Orpheus and that made by Rilke will justify and explain these quotations. It accounts for the affinity that the twentieth-century German poet felt for the musical magician of Greece, which the latter's personality, still persistent and still strong, could make him realise through the countless ages which separated them. The sensitiveness of the modern poet divined

[1] W. K. C. Guthrie, *Orpheus and Greek Religion*, London, 1935, pp. 39, 40, 56.
[2] Harrison, *op. cit.* pp. 461, 471, 473, 589 f.

the similarity without the aid of scholarship, for he was no
Hellenist, and probably knew nothing about Orpheus that
every schoolboy does not know. But this includes the legend
of the creative and transforming power of his music, a legend
which haunts English ears to the lines:

> Orpheus with his lute made trees
> And the mountain tops that freeze
>   Bow themselves when he did sing:
> To his music plants and flowers
> Ever sprung; as sun and showers
>   There had made a lasting spring.
>
> Everything that heard him play,
> Even the billows of the sea,
>   Hung their heads and then lay by.
> In sweet music is such art,
> Killing care and grief of heart
>   Fall asleep, or hearing, die.

Paul Valéry had newly paid his tribute to this magical power
in *Orphée*:

> ...Je compose en esprit, sous les myrtes, Orphée
> L'admirable!...Le feu, des cirques purs descend;
> Il change le mont chauve en auguste trophée
> D'où s'exhale d'un dieu l'acte retentissant.
>
> Si le dieu chante, il rompt le site tout-puissant;
> Le soleil voit l'horreur du mouvement des pierres;
> Une plainte inouïe appelle éblouissants
> Les hauts murs d'or harmonieux d'un sanctuaire.
>
> Il chante, assis au bord du ciel splendide, Orphée!
> Le roc marche, et trébuche; et chaque pierre fée
> Se sent un poids nouveau qui vers l'azur délire;
>
> D'un Temple à demi-nu le soir baigne l'essor,
> Et soi-même il s'assemble et s'ordonne dans l'or
> A l'âme immense du grand hymne sur la lyre![1]

Here, in the transparent radiance of Greek symbolism, was to
be found the apotheosis of art as a cosmic, creative, trans-

---

[1] P. Valéry, *Poésies*, Paris, 1930, pp. 13 f.

forming force, which Rilke had tried to achieve in the God of
The Book of Hours and the angels of *Duino Elegies*. The simple,
inevitable discovery, so long retarded, was made at last. The
functions and the destiny of Orpheus were clearly a mythical
counterpart of Rilke's, and therefore of all poets and of poetry
itself. The symbol had that magical simplicity and depth, that
universal validity and acceptability which only the Greeks
have ever been able to achieve. Almost at the end of his
poetical career Rilke ceased to strive after esoteric symbolism
and surrendered to the power of the greatest poetical
mythology the world has known. Orthodox Russia, the
Bible, the Apocrypha and the Koran had hitherto supplied
Rilke with his mythical framework at the expense of violent
ambiguities. His aesthetic religion accorded better with
Orpheus, a god moreover strongly impregnated with traits of
the Egyptian death-cult with which Rilke felt strong poetical
affinities, as the tenth elegy shows. He saw shining through
the figure of Orpheus the features of an ancient vegetation-
deity, the ancestor of all those mysterious gods who have
descended into the underworld; and the notion of a spirit of
vegetation in which 'the phenomena of birth, death and rebirth take place before our eyes in the flowering and withering
of plants in their seasons'[1] fused in his mind with the myth of
the magical singer.

Although the presence of *Orphée* in Valéry's poems (which
Rilke discovered in 1921) may well have been partly responsible for the flash of revelation, Valéry's real contribution
to *Sonnets to Orpheus* is to be found in *Le cimetière marin*, the
first of his poems to be translated by Rilke. It contains a
magnificent passage on biological metamorphosis, the
cardinal doctrine of the sonnets, and it fired Rilke's imagination. In much the same way as his conception of 'personal
death' flowered from a chance remark in *Marie Grubbe*, so too
Valéry's poetical statement of a biological fact seems to have
set Rilke's mind alight with metamorphic visions; to which the
divine little dancer in the French poet's dialogue *L'âme et la*

---

[1] Guthrie, *op. cit.* p. 55. Guthrie inclines to believe that Orpheus was not a
faded vegetation-deity; and he was certainly not so regarded by the Greeks.

danse almost certainly contributed, notably with regard to Wera. Valéry's influence on Rilke was as fundamental as Jacobsen's and Rodin's. All three affected him so deeply as to be definite and dynamic inspirations which altered his vision of life.

But inspiration is in reality collaboration. Orpheus, in his dual aspect as a poet of the under and the upper world with magical powers in both regions, accorded so exactly with Rilke's own deepest feelings about poetry and poetical destiny that he would appear almost fated to use this myth as a personal symbol. He had seen no such close connection when he told the tale of Orpheus and Eurydice in *New Poems*, although his sympathy with the poet who went down into the underworld betrays kinship. Nevertheless, Eurydice, who had attained that further and better state of being and was unconscious of the human drama in which she was involved, was the focus of interest, the meaning of the poem. Rilke would never have identified himself with a willing agent of physical resurrection. The unwilling and wrathful Christ in *The Raising of Lazarus* is far more truly a symbol for himself than Orpheus in *New Poems*. But in the sonnet sequences, the mortal, tragically mistaken poet-lover was merged in a God presiding over mysteries of life and death; whilst Eurydice was replaced by Wera, whom Rilke had no desire to raise from the dead.

This lovely child, who first began to dance, and caused a sensation among those who saw her by the art of motion and metamorphosis innate in her soul and mind, suddenly told her mother that she could and would dance no more . . . (this was just when she ceased to be a child). Her body underwent a strange transformation, becoming curiously heavy and massive without losing its lovely eastern form . . . (and this was the beginning of the mysterious glandular trouble which was so soon to cause her death) . . . . In the time that remained to her, Wera went in for music, and finally abandoned that for drawing, as if the dancing which had been denied were manifesting itself more and more discreetly.[1]

[1] *Inselalmanach*, Leipzig, 1937, pp. 113 f.; to Countess Margot Sizzo from Muzot, April 12, 1923.

A month before these details reached Rilke he had almost certainly read Valéry's prose dialogue *L'âme et la danse* which he was later to translate into German, and which contained, among many other deep and beautiful things about dancing, Socrates' definition of it as a pure act of metamorphosis.[1] One can well imagine the effect such a description would have on Rilke, always vitally interested in the transforming power of art. It must have quickened his imagination, an effect traceable in at least one of the sonnets; and, filled as his mind was just then with the image of Wera, the whole dialogue must have brought her still closer, almost uncannily close:

> If one were to read about this, it would touch one closely enough, even though it concerned some young girl whom one had not known. But it concerns Wera, whose mysterious, strangely concentrated charm is so unutterably unforgettable to me and so uncannily easy to evoke....[2]

In joining the serried ranks of dead young girls living in Rilke's heart, Wera transformed them all into music, a rhythm vibrating through the spheres of life and death, so that the whole of existence became a song, and mourning was transformed into rapture. She fitted without violence into the ancient mythical framework, from which Rilke borrowed the story of the magical singer who went down into Hades and possessed himself of its secrets; who thereafter was torn to pieces by the Maenads, but whose head and lyre could not be silenced. His connection in the underworld with a young dancing-girl represented the fusion of the legend of Eurydice with the personality of Wera.

Strange resemblances with the orphic religion itself (of which Rilke probably had only the vaguest notions) are dis-

---

[1] The dates are as follows: on November 26, 1921, Rilke wrote to Wera's mother asking for details about her death. These reached him on January 1, 1922. Valéry's dialogue was published on December 1, 1921 in *La revue musicale*. Rilke had a copy in his possession in March 1922; it is therefore reasonable to suppose that he procured it on its appearance, as he was reading Valéry with such enthusiasm at the time.

[2] *B. 1921–1926*, p. 83; to Gertrud Ouckama Knoop; no date or address; speaks of receiving her account of Wera's death on 'the first evening of the new year' (1922).

cernible in the themes treated in the sonnets, where the dualism between soul and body, the doctrine of reincarnation, the belief in the possibility of magical transformations, and of union with the god shimmer mistily through the lines, while the emphasis on life in the underworld pervades the whole. All this must be attributed rather to a temperamental affinity between Rilke and the Greek orphics than 'influence' in the usual sense; and if one is tempted to see an echo of their expressed desire to escape from the wheel of life in his burning wish for metamorphosis, his perfervid glorification of the whole of existence distinguished him sharply from that mysterious religion whose aim was to be done altogether with the cycle of birth, life and death.

Transformation under many aspects is the main theme of the first sequence. Orpheus' song became a tree of sound in the first sonnet, and the wild beasts came from their lairs to assemble round it, whilst he built temples in their ears. The singing god then magically transformed Wera into music, creating her by means of a marvellous song which quivered into the likeness of a young girl who slept in the poet's ear and dreamed life and the world, but had no desire to awaken. Real song is existence, and none but the god can sing it; mortals are rendered impotent by the warring dualism of their nature. Yet Orpheus is always with us, since all poets, and all singing, are incarnations of the god:

> For Orpheus 'tis. His metamorphosis
> In this poet and the next. No need to seek
> For other names. But hearken once for all:
> 'Tis Orpheus when there's song. He comes and goes.[1]

He rules over the double kingdom of life and death; lifting up his lyre in the underworld, eating of poppy-seeds with the dead, and able therefore to magnify the whole of existence. He comes and goes perpetually, as the poets come and go, roses blossoming, falling and dying, only to bloom again. But wherever and whenever their voices are uplifted, it is in praise. In that realm the voices of our lamentations are

[1] *G.W.* III, p. 317; Sonnet I, 5.

transformed into a serene constellation by the naiad of the weeping stream, who lifts the sparkling precipitate of our tears high into the placid heavens. The transmutation of sorrow into a shining glory (of mourning into music) is one of the doctrines of the sonnets. In the double kingdom all voices become eternal and mild.

Life comes from death, and archaeological discoveries are bringing back into life much that seemed to have been lost for ever. The ancient Roman sarcophagi, now used as water-troughs or basins for running water and springs; or those lying open in the cemetery near Arles, filled with flowers and humming life are like mouths once closed in death and now speaking again. We have probably been through a similar silence; our brooding countenances seem to answer both yes and no to strange intimations. But we are baffling creatures. There should be a constellation called *Horseman* to stand for the close relationship and the immeasurable distance between the god and the brute in us; yet even such a constellation would be a misleading figure. But our real life is in such symbols, belonging as we do to a wider kingdom than this world and being in spiritual connection with it, antennae feeling out for antennae through space. The peasant who tills the soil never reaches down to where the seed is transformed into summer; but the earth is bountiful, and the relationship is there. For the fruits of the earth belong both to death and to life.

> With vine-leaves, flowers and fruit how much we dare.
> They speak not only of the seasons' wending,
> Clear, dappled things from darkness upward tending
> The bloom of jealousy perhaps may bear
>
> Felt by the dead the while the earth they harrow.
> What do we know of their part in the game?
> It has been long their custom all the same
> To mingle with earth's clay their liberal marrow.
>
> But is it of their own free will or no?
> And does this fruit, work of dull slaves, come creeping
> Clenched like a fist, to us their lordly foe?

Are *those* the lords who by the roots are sleeping,
Not grudging us from their abounding riches
This thing cross-bred from dumb brute force and kisses?[1]

Les morts cachés sont bien dans cette terre
Qui les réchauffe et sèche leur mystère.

. . . . .

Mais dans leur nuit toute lourde de marbres,
Un peuple vague aux racines des arbres
A pris déjà ton parti lentement.

Ils ont fondu dans une absence épaisse,
L'argile rouge a bu la blanche espèce,
Le don de vivre a passé dans les fleurs!
Où sont des morts les phrases familières,
L'art personnel, les âmes singulières?
La larve file ou se formaient des pleurs.

Les cris aigus des filles chatouillées,
Les yeux, les dents, les paupières mouillées,
Le sein charmant qui joue avec le feu,
Le sang qui brille aux lèvres qui se rendent,
Les derniers dons, les doigts qui les défendent,
Tout va sous terre et rentre dans le jeu![2]

Rilke's sonnet and the lines from *Le cimetière marin* show the power of a biological fact on one poet, and his statement of it on another. They also show the difference between the powerful realistic imagination of someone trained to face facts, and the fanciful play of a less disciplined mind, sensationalising and dramatising them. For Rilke could not allow the natural process to finish where Valéry so magnificently left it. He must suggest a more esoteric development, and demonstrate further in what subtle ways human beings contribute to the perpetual metamorphosis going on all round them. The act of eating an orange dissolves it back into the stream of life, makes it part of ourselves;[3] and we can still

---

[1] *G.W.* III, p. 326; Sonnet I, 14.

[2] Paul Valéry, *Poésies*, pp. 189 f.

[3] This is an elaboration of what Socrates said in *L'âme et la danse*; Paris, 1931, p. 13: *Chaque bouchée qu'il sent se fondre et se disperser en lui-même, va porter des forces nouvelles à ses vertus, comme elle fait indistinctement à ses vices.* Cf. *G.W.* III, pp. 325, 327; Sonnets I, 13 and I, 15.

further advance the metamorphic activity by dancing the
orange, scattering its fragrance into the air, which is thus
transformed into a warm, scented southern climate.

Behind the ceaseless process of natural transformation
there goes on, according to Rilke, the mysterious phenomenon
of the reincarnation of souls, changing our disinherited
brothers into mute, anxious, appealing dogs, who in some
former life have sold their human birthright for a mess of
pottage; and now, bewildered and betrayed, gaze on their
usurpers like shaggy Esaus. The same strange force operates
through the laws of heredity; the ancestor, the root and the
spring of the genealogical tree, repeats himself and his
dormant possibilities again and again in succeeding generations, until at last he achieves himself in the poet, and the
race is at an end. Nor was Rilke unaware of evolutionary
changes. He concentrated upon the latest and the most
striking, the manner in which civilisation and man himself are
being altered, and man is being weakened, by the passionless
power of machines. Nevertheless, behind all the clangour and
uproar of these driving and serving forces Orpheus' song
persists.

> Though the world change as fast
> As clouds dislimning,
> Home to the age-old past
> What's done is winging.
>
> Over the thrust and throng,
> Freer and higher,
> Still lasts your prelude-song,
> God with the lyre.
>
> Sorrows we misunderstand,
> Love is still learning,
> Death, whence there's no returning,
>
> No-one unveils.
> Song alone over the land
> Hallows and hails.[1]

[1] *G.W.* III, p. 331; Sonnet I, 19; based on Leishman's more pleasing but
slightly less accurate version in *Sonnets to Orpheus*, London, 1936, p. 73.

Although Rilke still lamented human ineffectiveness in the face of sorrow, love and death, it was in a new, gentle and compassionate manner, almost as an accomplice in guilt, but for the grace of Orpheus, whose creature he was no more and probably less than the gallant little Russian horse, scampering with hobbled fetlocks and tossing mane out on to the wide spaces of the steppe to the sound of his master's voice. The orphic rhythm coming full circle in the steppe-pony also throbs in the seasonal metamorphoses of the year. Spring turns the earth into a little child, who has escaped from her taskmaster with the hoary beard; and having learnt the hard lessons lurking in roots and stems can now play and sing with the children outside. How different this kind of motion is from the mad hurtling through space, against which Rilke, another and an equally impotent Faust, warned this Euphorion-like generation; imploring them at least to turn their thoughts away from the beauty and complexity of aeroplanes, to the spaces they are traversing, that they may become those far-distant bourns. Determined though he was to glorify all existing things and to worship metamorphosis, Rilke could not affirm with any conviction the changes accomplished by the march of history and the industrial revolution. Our modern methods of haste and luxury, our mechanised lives have separated us from the gods of old; our sacred fires now burn in boilers; our strength has entered automatic hammers, and we are swooning like exhausted swimmers. Forcing his thoughts back again into mythical regions, he concluded with a description of Wera's translation from life into death, and of Orpheus' fate at the hands of the Maenads; declaring that his voice was still singing on in birds and beasts, in rocks and trees; and that we should never have heard and answered it, had he not, all those dim ages ago, been cruelly torn to pieces.

The first sequence of sonnets is like an illustration of the various ways in which metamorphoses may be accomplished. First and foremost are the magical transformations, then the musical or aesthetic, which are another form of the magical; emotional or spiritual changes come next; then the biological, the transmigratory, the evolutional, the seasonal and the historical; the whole introduced, interspersed and finally resolved by the mythological figure of Orpheus, the immortal singing god.

The second sequence is much less closely knit, and is in a much less obvious connection with the legendary hero. Something esoteric and inexplicable takes his place; whilst greater sadness alternating with fiercer determination to glorify all things makes the atmosphere of the whole far less serene. Nevertheless, two of the poems at least and many of the lines can hardly be equalled for sheer wizardry in the whole of Rilke's work. The transformations undertaken or described are subtler, stranger, more delicate than those in the first sequence. Tenuous and enigmatic, the world we know seems to be shifting and subsiding beneath our feet and perpetually changing before our eyes. The act of breathing, an invisible poem, a wave from a waxing sea, and now part of the winds and the air—the first sonnet as it evaporates in this way is symptomatic of the others, in which smiles vanish into mirrors, and looks are lost for ever among the glowing coals; roses emerge from wild eglantines, and cut flowers exhale into the air the very moods of the girls who plucked them. Loving it and believing in its existence, the saints of old created a pure white unicorn from nothingness; children pass away and are lost beneath falling balls; temples of quivering stone are erected in waste space by the magic of music, surrounded by menacing destructive machines. Murmuring away to itself the marble fountain changes into a mouth of mother earth whispering secrets into her own ear; and the swirling and whirling young dancer transforms her motion into a magical tree whose branches bear beautiful pitchers and vases shaped by no earthly potter's wheel.[1] This is an isolated instance of the way our superfluities tend to overflow foaming into art, under the pressure of whatever fate. Parks, statues, buildings, obelisks were lavished in the past. Now they are replaced by frantic speed describing curves of flight. Gold is the master now; and the jaundiced eye of a copper coin transforms the

---

[1] This is the poem in which the influence of *L'âme et la danse* seems indubitable.

holy, humble beggar into a dusty corner underneath a ward-robe, where money would inevitably be lost. Relativity, inter-relations, transitoriness, vanishings and change occur and recur in all the poems. The wide-open anemone, unable to close its petals at night, is in relation with countless worlds, receptive of their power and will in a manner which we, violent and longer-lived, will never achieve. We are shut to so many things, not even aware of the solidarity of our souls; flattering ourselves that we are merciful, because some instruments of torture have become antiquated. We would be differently merciful if the great god of mercy seized upon our souls and made them aware. As it is, the distance between human beings is greater far than that between the stars; perhaps this is because we are measured with the rod of real life, and cannot complete the cycle in our partial existence here, where fishes appear to be dumb; yet surely somewhere, elsewhere, their language is spoken plain to hear? Whence come those glorious fruits of consolation, if not from that double kingdom where angels congregate in the trees and a far longer summer lasts than our brief seasons know? We are the heavy-weights of the world; we oppress and depress flowers and things; we bawl and we caterwaul stridently amidst nature's harmonious cries; oh, that Orpheus would accord our voices into a rushing stream bearing on its flood his head and his lyre. But though Orpheus is always trying to heal within us, we are always tearing the wound open again, and crucifying him afresh. It is small wonder that, holding such views of humanity, Rilke should have issued such categorical commands to desire and attempt metamorphosis, entry into the double kingdom, parting and death; which he did in two strongly doctrinal sonnets, the one preaching a sermon on the text of the will-to-metamorphosis; the other (he called it the most valid of them all) elaborating the injunction: 'Always be dead in Eurydice.'[1]

Savagely critical as Rilke was about man in relation to nature in this sequence, his glorification of existence as a whole, far from being diminished, was reaffirmed with an intensity, an exaggeration, that makes it slightly suspect.

[1] Cf. *G.W.* III, pp. 354 f., 356; Sonnets II, 12 and II, 13.

Allowing for the hackneyed point of view that every prospect pleases in the universe and only man is vile, the rigid commandment (sometimes it sounds like the crack of a whip) '*dennoch preisen*' (magnify and glorify nevertheless) is the language of an overseer to slaves. Even the slaughter of innocent birds by a particularly shady trick must be no matter for rebellious mourning. Killing is one of the aspects of the sorrow we wander in, and everything that happens to us is right. The loom of life is like a Persian carpet, wonderful and beautiful, even if the thread of one's own existence is part of a pattern of torment. We are only just when we praise in the teeth of disillusion and despair. However unendurable the agony of existence, it must be accepted and affirmed, if necessary by transforming oneself into the agent of torture, the better to understand that too. It is all very austere and unattainable, this gospel of submission and acceptance. Yet it was not held quite so dogmatically as this account indicates; for it was based on the belief in the indestructibility of the soul, if not of the personality; and once at least Rilke paused to weigh this doctrine against the theory of annihilation, without coming to a definite decision.[1]

Altogether the second sequence with its bitter criticisms of man, its heart-searchings, its final mournful farewell to Wera, and its tragic consolation to her friend, is more in tune with Rilke's previous poetry than the first. Man's isolated position in nature; the tragic rift between childhood and maturity; the glorification of poverty; the lament for sculpture and architecture as bygone arts were among his perennial themes; whereas both sequences magically transform objects dear to him in the past. For the mere description and glorification of change tending always towards invisibility and death does not limit Rilke's orphic activities in the sonnets. His aim was to say things in a manner which should transform them, to give them magical names.[2] In *New Poems* he had bent his eyes and

---

[1] *G.W.* III, p. 372; Sonnet II, 27.

[2] Cf. Hans-Egon Holthusen, *Rilkes Sonette an Orpheus*, Munich, 1937; a most interesting and exhaustive investigation along these lines, to which I am much indebted in the following pages.

his mind to the task of seeing and saying things as they really are, inwardly as well as outwardly; to describe them as they would describe themselves if they were able to speak. In *Duino Elegies* he expressly stated that his mission now was to say them differently, so that they themselves would be surprised, to transform their inner and outer reality into invisibility. One after another of the subjects he had treated in *New Poems* and elsewhere were here submitted to the new process: childhood, maidenhood, death, dancing, roses, fruit, mirrors, sarcophagi, parks, fountains, the unicorn, beggars, art and things; they were now transformed into inhabitants, not of this world, nor of the next, but of the double kingdom in which we really have our being; they became more mythical than had been the case before, charged with deeper significance. *The Coat of Arms* in *New Poems* for instance was a faithful description of a coat of arms including the inner meaning of the heraldic symbols. In Sonnet I, 17 Rilke reproduced a genealogical tree, its roots in the underworld, its branches and stems in the upper, through which the rising sap of poetry invisibly flowed. It was both a poetical and a mythical way of saying *Stammbaum*, almost like an inaudible pun. Mirrors, whose mystery had haunted his poetry and his prose, were placed in relation with a greater mystery by imagining them to be animated by Narcissus, released and fulfilled at last. This name transforms the mirror into a magical object, eternally reflecting and comprising itself, unfathomable and impenetrable. Whilst, by christening the dog 'Esau in his hairy skin', he brought that humanised victim of the supremacy of man into the stream of the great myth of the transmigration of souls. All these various poems, by transforming familiar objects, may be said to recreate them; but the strongest effect of such magical making is to be found in the poem about the unicorn which Rilke had described so exquisitely in *New Poems* and with fascinated sympathy in *Malte Laurids Brigge*. In *Sonnets to Orpheus* he set himself to produce the unicorn almost as a conjurer produces a rabbit from his sleeve. At a given moment the fabulous animal which had been fed upon the possibility of its

existence raised its head in the space left empty for it and grew
One Horn (*Einhorn*). Such was the magical compulsion in the
name that the beast was there too. These are only a few,
although they are perhaps the most outstanding, examples of
what Rilke was doing in the sonnets: translating things he had
loved and studied in the past from the world of art into the world
of myths, where they lead a double life, have a dual personality
and inhabit two different spheres, each of which is an aspect of
the other and both of them subject to Orpheus, the poet-god.

But nothing that one can say about these poems can render
the precise effect Rilke achieved in some of them; nor can this
be done by translation. The sonnet addressed to the marble
fountain for instance is pure imitative magic from beginning to
end; and there is such power in some of his incantations that it
needs very little imagination to believe that the object invoked (the Karnak obelisk is an obvious example) is actually
there in the poem. Nevertheless, like other magicians all the
world over, Rilke sometimes failed to delude. The rhythmic
summons to the fettered horse is clumsy; the puns about the
'roots and stems' learnt by the infant earth are too slick, and
the whole simile is forced. In attempting to be abysmally
simple and unutterably mysterious at one and the same time,
he occasionally lapsed into pure inanity:

> Only those who dwell
> beyond can drink that spring we
> only hear,
> when the god has beckoned to them, hushing.
> We are offered nothing but its rushing.
> And the lamb's far stiller instinct's clear
> When it begs us for a bell.[1]

This may be nonsense, but it is orphic nonsense, comparable
to the affirmation of the orphic mystic: 'A kid, I have fallen
into milk'; of which Jane Harrison pertinently said:

The quaint little formulary is simple to fatuity. Mysticism, in its
attempt to utter the ineffable, often verges on imbecility.[2]

---

[1] *G.W.* III, p. 359; Sonnet II, 16, tr. Leishman and communicated privately to
the author.

[2] Harrison, *op. cit.* p. 594.

Rilke seems undoubtedly to have been temperamentally and
spiritually akin to the orphic mystics. But he did not share
with the Greek genius that power of creating myths which
irradiate life with poetry and mystery. Although the Orpheus
he hymned in these sonnets is partly his own creation, all that
is most quickening, fascinating and revealing in the figure of
the poet-god is a legacy from Greece. *Sonnets to Orpheus*, like
Duino Elegies, are a one-man vision; they do not interpret
existence in the grand mythological manner. They are orphic
by their partly esoteric, partly doctrinal character; but above
all they share with the legendary founder of that religion a
magical, musical, spell-binding power. Some of the sonnets
radiate those baffling rays which the genuine crystal gives out.
One gazes and gazes into the heart of the stone, but one
cannot penetrate to the focus of light emitting the dazzling
fountain. If one looks long enough, the crystal becomes
cloudy, then deceptively clear, and finally will show nothing
more revealing than one's own insignificant thoughts. For
the purpose of magic lies in the process. This is what makes it
so potent and also so disillusioning. Spells, abracadabra,
mystical numbers, incantations—their value lies in themselves.

Bemused and enchanted, one realises only after Rilke's
charms have ceased to work that the will-to-metamorphosis,
the doctrine of the sonnets, is as of little avail to mortal men
as the earlier injunction to die one's own death, which indeed
it strongly resembles. No human power can stay or hasten
the course of nature's cyclic rhythm. The strongest magic
ever brewed, the most dynamic spiritual energy, the divinest
poetry are so much waste energy here. Positively the will-to-
metamorphosis can achieve nothing; negatively it approximates to Schopenhauer's will-to-death, but without that great
mythical monster, the will-to-life, to give it heroic significance. To enjoy the sonnets without a qualm it is best to read
them as poetry and to ignore as far as possible the rather intrusive doctrine. Rilke was and remained a far greater poet
than prophet. As the priest of an esoteric life-and-death cult
he may be ignored; but as one of the great magical musicians
he will never fail to enthral; and it was the timely revelation of
his kinship with Orpheus that brought music back into his art.

Chapter VI

THE END, 1922–1926

1. *Personal Death*
2. *Last Words*
3. *Transformation*

CHAPTER VI

THE END, 1922–1926

1. *Personal Death*

When the hurricane of inspiration which had produced the elegies and sonnets died down, Rilke, far from collapsing, did not even seem particularly exhausted. He stayed quietly on in Muzot where Marie Thurn and Taxis, Baladine Klossowska and the Kippenbergs visited him in the spring of 1922. It need hardly be said that readings of *Duino Elegies* and *Sonnets to Orpheus* by the tremulous author to his transported friends were the main feature of these visits, an unforgettable experience for everyone concerned. Rilke then allowed himself a little summer holiday with the Klossowskas at Beatenberg above the Thunersee, after which he returned contentedly to Muzot where he spent the winter translating Valéry's *Charmes*. The spring of 1923 brought more guests to his door, among them the princess again, this time with her youngest granddaughter. Then a natural desire for movement and sociability overcame him, and for a more worldly kind of life than he had led in the past. Swallow-like flittings hither and thither across Switzerland now became the order of the day; motor-trips in Nanny Wunderly-Volkart's car and visits to different friends marked the summer of 1923, which included a cure at Schöneck on the Vierwaldstättersee. Rilke returned to Muzot early in November, intending to go into winter quarters after this rather restless summer and devote himself to his work. But towards the end of December he was in a sanatorium in Valmont near Montreux, under the care of a Dr Hämmerli, who remained his physician to the last. Although complaints about his health had begun in January 1923, and had continued steadily throughout the year, it was not until now that a fatal march was stolen upon him by the enemy in his blood.

His doctor was not alarmed, but Rilke was. Something fundamental had happened to him; something so terrible and terrifying, that it had altered him, he maintained, as radically as the catastrophe of 1915. His patient's livery had precisely the same effect upon him as the soldier's uniform, cutting him off from nature, from the sky, from trees and flowers. He felt that they and he were in different worlds. The shock of his first intimate acquaintance with real illness since the fevers of his childhood was of the kind that opens the door to panic, which from now onwards lurked in his mind. It was the shadow thrown by his personal death, the destiny so fearfully described in the eighth elegy. The fear of the impending change, rarely acknowledged and wonderfully controlled, was the great central fact of Rilke's emotional history from now onwards until his death. His sabbatical period of rest from mental torments and freedom from tyrannical visions had been brief indeed; and he was in a dreadful predicament now between his nervous temperament which forced him to fear death and his arduous belief that it was the greater and better part of life. He clung to that faith more desperately than ever, almost frantically indeed in his famous commentary on the elegies; and he tried to rationalise the dread in which he lived by attributing it to dismay at the wedge driven by illness between his body and soul. His repeated fervid declarations that they had always lived in the completest concord until then are not convincing; but his dislike of an outsider mediating as a doctor between himself and his body is painfully credible.

In accordance with the sensational psychological trend of her monograph, Lou Andreas-Salomé doubtless stressed too much Rilke's sense of an irreconcilable dualism between his spirit and his flesh. But it was there. He spoke in 1912 of the frightful misuse the body made of the soul, referring in another letter to his own physical nature as a trap or a snare. His undeviating dislike of male lovers and his personal conflicts in the erotic relationship strengthen the assumption that he was often torn between the spiritual and the natural man; whilst his fascinated analysis of the horror and grandeur, the

cruelty and elemental beauty of sex in the third elegy was
made by no serene and sunny pagan mind. His continued
allegiance to Marianna Alcoforado as the perfect lover and his
unconquerable contempt for men in this capacity ('botchers,
dilettanti, usurers of emotion') is vouched for by a letter
dated December 29, 1921;[1] and two months before he died he
was still hoping to undertake those translations from Gaspara
Stampa which were half promised in the first elegy in 1912.[2]

But during and after the spiritual upheaval which completed
the elegiac cycle in the spring of 1922, a revolution occurred in
Rilke's attitude towards sex in men; although whether or not
his unconscious mind was really liberated from its ancient
fear cannot be determined. His relationship with Baladine
certainly seems to have been a more normal and pleasurable
liaison than usual, one of the symptoms or one of the causes of
that change of heart which is visible in some of his writings.
It is a tragically ironical change, considering how near he was
to death, and may have been an involuntary recoil from it; nor
must it be forgotten that Rilke was drained of spiritual energy
after the blood-letting of the elegies and sonnets, and that
nature was reasserting her rights.

Yet the inevitable reaction after the storm of inspiration in
1922 was nothing like so severe nor so close to a mental
collapse as it had been after *Malte Laurids Brigge*. Rilke
suffered certainly, although he was less voluble on the subject
than he had been before and during the war. He had after all
performed his mission and completed his master-work;
gratitude for this achievement upheld him, and the sense of
freedom too. Unhappily, however, his mind was now released to contemplate anew the tragic prospect presented by
the world.

What it must have been like to leave the sphere of the
elegies into which he had been gradually absorbed since his
escape from Germany in 1919, and to find himself still inhabiting post-war Europe can be vividly imagined by all those

[1] Cf. *B. 1921–1926*, pp. 69 f.; to Ilse Blumenthal-Weiss from Muzot.
[2] *V.B.* pp. 452 f.; to Anton Kippenberg from Hôtel Bellevue, Sierre, October 27, 1926.

whose endeavours to lead a spiritual life are at the mercy of even more drastic disturbances now. Having created the elegies and sonnets Rilke could no longer live in them. They were projected outside himself, and his eyes were turned outwards too. What he saw and heard disturbed, alarmed and finally appalled him. The misery, hatred and brutality seething in Europe had nothing to do with him; and yet, even in his remote little fortress-refuge, he was involved in them. He could not ignore them, yet they were beyond the sphere of his influence. The world was being transformed by forces which had nothing in common with poetical inspiration; and the facile doctrine of the sonnets, to affirm and glorify everything that is, proved its impotence here, very much to Rilke's honour. His lamentations and accusations were such, that Salis still dared not publish the more vehement ten years after the poet's death. His liberty of movement and his financial position were both adversely affected by currency and other regulations, but he bore this philosophically. What distressed him beyond bounds was the failure of Germany to achieve spiritual regeneration after the war. He blamed her present state of misery on her slavish worship of the false gods of material prosperity and political aggrandisement. Bewildered, hopeless and helpless, one of the few great poets then alive saw where all this was tending and recoiled from it in anguish, only to find within himself the tormenting dread of illness and death.

Rilke fought this fear as best he might by mental occupation. He went on with his translations of Valéry's poetry and prose at intervals until he died. By April 1924 he had also a small volume of original French verse to his credit; and German poems came to him as well from time to time. But no great theme had as yet emerged from the vision of life of the elegies and sonnets, so that his mind was frequently forced to contemplate its approaching dissolution. He returned from Valmont to Muzot on January 21, 1924, mentally and physically shattered; yet he remained there alone for almost three months, an experience he never repeated again except for brief periods. No wonder that when Valéry came to see him at Easter, he was disturbed by the extreme isolation of spirit emanating from Muzot and its host. Numerous other guests followed the French poet. The Kippenbergs came for the second time and Clara was with her husband in Muzot for ten days. She did not belong to that small inner circle to whom the glad tidings of the elegies had been immediately announced; indeed, she did not hear of the great event until the following May in a letter which kindly equated its importance in his life with the approaching wedding of their daughter. Her husband also thought it necessary to tell her, or to remind her, that his great poetical achievement was the elegy-cycle. This alone would show how far apart they were in 1922; but they drew nearer together now. Each succeeding letter of the twelve published in the last volume is more intimate than the last. Schuler's death, which she reported to him, stirred up emotions common to both husband and wife, for they had attended his lectures in Munich and were united in their admiration for him. Clara's enthusiastic reception of the elegies also warmed Rilke's heart and melted his cool friendliness. The delightful humour which she of all his correspondents most readily evoked accompanied the thawing-process, and something that was almost family feeling began to stir. His mother, his wife, his daughter and her child were often in his thoughts; Christmas and birthday presents and wishes flew hither and thither between them all. He was as generous in money matters to them as his resources allowed; and he felt kindly and pitifully about his mother when her own mother came near to death in May 1924;[1] whilst the last Christmas letter he wrote her in December 1925 is more loving and less mystically exalted than these annual epistles usually were.[2] Filial piety, marital and paternal affection remained however platonic. Rilke refused Clara's warm invitation to visit his family, so that he died without seeing his granddaughter. He also felt unequal to receiving Ruth at

---

[1] Cf. *V.B.* p. 385, where Rilke says that Phia Rilke had been obliged to interrupt her cure in Karlsbad to see her own aged mother die. Both Salis and André Germain however say that Rilke's grandmother survived him.

[2] Published in the *Inselschiff* for Christmas 1936.

Ragaz in the autumn of 1925, and indeed his state of health bears him blameless for that. But he eagerly welcomed Clara's visit to Muzot in May 1924, after a complete separation of five years, which Rilke believed to have been longer still.[1] Husband and wife made the most of this meeting, discussing among other things the difficult art of being grandparents from the financial point of view. Clara then went on alone to Meilen, where she met Nanny Wunderly-Volkart, who took a great liking to her, and reported very favourably on her to Rilke. He passed the good news on to his wife, as unaware as she that the situation was ironical; but he sighed over her persistent impulsiveness in a letter to Kippenberg. The visit, however, had strengthened the slender bond between them at a time when Rilke needed all the sympathy and support he could procure. After she left, he very soon began his restless flittings again. From the end of June until October he was here, there and everywhere, and nowhere alone for long. With Nanny in her car, with Marie at Ragaz; with other friends in Ouchy, with Edmond Jaloux in Lausanne; darting rapidly from one place to the next, like a gull before a storm; fluttering off to Muzot again in the autumn, and finally driven back to Valmont early in November.

The late summer and autumn of 1924 were characterised by Rilke himself as one of the worst times in his life; for he little knew, when he made that statement, what was to follow. Valmont did him very little good and was ruinously expensive. After staying there much against the grain for two months, he left abruptly for Paris on January 6, 1925, determined to ignore his symptoms and to forget all about his illness. He probably hoped to cure himself by going back to the centre of his life; for when had Paris ever failed him before, however stricken he had been? He was also irresistibly drawn there by his longing for intellectual society, and by his intense interest in the contemporary Parisian intelligentsia. He did not expect to find himself regarded as one of them; but the partial

---

[1] Cf. *B. 1921–1926*, p. 269, where Rilke says that he had not seen Clara for six or seven years, with Andreas-Salomé, *op. cit.* p. 87. If Clara really saw Rilke off from Munich to Switzerland in 1919, the period was only five years.

translation into French of *Malte Laurids Brigge* which had
appeared in 1923 had taken Paris by storm, and he was overwhelmed with invitations.

An almost Proustian atmosphere surrounded him *du côté de
chez la princesse*, as the wits of the time called the exclusive
circle into which Rilke was now admitted; and if Valéry was
too busy to see much of the German poet owing to his candi-
dature for membership of the *Académie française*; and if Gide,
after undergoing an operation, made off for the equatorial
regions, still there were enough poets, artists and men of
letters left to make for intellectual exhilaration. He enjoyed
all this greatly at first; but the real Rilke, whom he always
distinguished sharply from the 'other' Rilke, was not lulled
into forgetfulness by flattery and fame. He was soon exhausted by the exacting life of a literary lion, and longed
for the Paris he had known as an obscure, poverty-stricken
young poet in the years before the war. At first he believed
that it had greatly changed; but after a while he found his
way back and realised that it was the same as before, gigantic
and unalterable. But it did not grant him relief from his
mental and physical anguish:

But neither victory nor relief came to me. Imagine that the
obsession...was stronger and mightier than Paris. It became the
suffering of one long defeat; and if I greatly out-stayed my time in
Paris, right into August, this was only because I was ashamed to
return to my tower in the same fetters as before.[1]

An attack of influenza towards the end of April, which
brought him very low, contributed its quota to his hidden
misery in Paris. He must have felt himself to be going under
in the same maelstrom of terror which had sucked Malte
down; and yet he could dissociate himself from what was
actually happening to him, and talk for hours on end to
Maurice Betz about his former literary scapegoat in connection with the complete translation of *Malte Laurids Brigge*
which Betz was preparing under the author's eye. Recapitulating those excruciating torments in his present state of

[1] Andreas-Salomé, *op. cit.* p. 99, not dated; the omission marks are not mine.

mind must have been an eerie occupation. Small wonder that
he wrote so few letters and made so few entries in his note-
book during the eight months he was in Paris; and perhaps it
was because he could not trust himself to see more of her that
he postponed his meeting with Marthe until the eve of his
departure.

When at last he returned to Muzot after visiting Milan and
Lake Maggiore, he felt so unutterably wretched that he
decided to try a cure at Ragaz towards the end of September.
All to no avail. A peculiarly distressing affection of the
mucuous membrane inside his mouth now attacked him,
swellings which hindered him in speaking and set up a phobia
inhibiting speech after the external symptoms had yielded to
treatment. From this moment onwards his terrors became
more definite and therefore more acute. Fear of cancer
tormented him, of internal poisonings, of a stealthy physical
conspiracy against him housed in his own flesh. Such thoughts
were with him perpetually, so that he was often almost beside
himself with apprehension.

In the throes of this emotion he composed his last will and
testament in Muzot on October 27, 1925, and sent it sealed to
Nanny Wunderly-Volkart. In his covering letter to her written
in French, and in the German directions on the envelope,
he stated that the document contained a few personal wishes
to be carried out in the event of some illness which would
'more or less remove me from my own jurisdiction'.[1] And
he began the will in much the same way: 'Should I fall into
a severe illness which might finally disorder my reason....'
He clearly found it very difficult to use the verb 'to die' and
the substantive 'death'. When he was obliged to do so in the
next paragraph, it was in a deliberately casual manner;
'Should I chance to die in Muzot, or anywhere else in
Switzerland....' Yet the will is not misleading; it was not
written in the event of insanity, which he did not fear, but to
give instructions about his death, which he dreaded profoundly. He wished for no priest by his bedside; he gave
directions about where he was to be buried, about what form

[1] Salis, *op. cit.* pp. 176–178 gives the text of the will.

the gravestone should have and what inscription it should bear. He was facing death resolutely and preparing for it; but the poet who had apostrophised it so often did not now utter its name.

One of the clauses in this singular will directed that he should be buried neither in Sierre nor yet in Miège, as this was perhaps what the unknown old woman had meant by what must *not* be done if the restless night-wanderings of poor Isabella were to be avoided. This is an allusion to the ghost of Isabella de Montheys, *née* Chevron, who was said to haunt Muzot and the churchyard of Miège where her two lovers, bitter rivals, lay buried. Rilke felt her presence in the little castle; and the Hôtel Château-Bellevue in Sierre, where he often stayed and where he accommodated his guests, also seemed to him to be peopled with apparitions and to echo with ghostly noises. To hear him talk about it, said Betz, was like watching him weave a strange web of memories and phantoms in which he was enmeshed himself.[1] The old woman mentioned in his will may have been one of the Muzot peasants with whom Rilke often discussed the local ghost; or she may have been either the medium or the control in one of those *séances* he occasionally attended. But he had progressed much farther in his views on spiritualism since the crisis of 1922. In 1912 at Duino and again in 1921 at Berg, table-rapping, automatic writing and spooks had been in the nature of a substitute for the angels he had lost from view; or perhaps it would be truer to say an attempt to force them to manifest themselves by the use of magic. But he had now had his revelation, and it was one which transcended occult manifestations of a more material kind. So that when, in June 1924, Nora Purtscher-Wydenbruck, a niece of Marie Thurn and Taxis, wrote to him about her psychic experiments and asked for his views, he was in a position to make an authoritative statement.[2]

[1] Betz, *op. cit.* p. 196.
[2] Cf. *B. 1921–1926*, pp. 277–284; from Muzot, August 11, 1924. Nora's two letters and Rilke's last answer are to be found in *Maandblad voor geestelijke Stroomingen*, Amsterdam, November, 1937. The whole number deals with Rilke and the occult. I am indebted to Dr Pickering of Manchester University for help in reading it. The letters themselves are given in German.

Curiously enough her letter, hinting at sensational dealings with the spirit-world, reached him in Ragaz where he and Marie Thurn and Taxis were collating the results of former and recent experiments, at some of which he had been present. He told Nora that he had attended hardly any other *séances* except those held in the Taxis circle ten years ago, where he had been only a spectator; and that unfortunately he had never been able to find a trustworthy medium, otherwise he would have eagerly sought to add to such experiences, which he believed to concern humanity vitally and to be extremely valuable as long as they were not used as an escape from life, but were related to the whole of our existence. Mysterious though the occult element in life might be, it was only one mystery amongst countless others, and not in his opinion so great as the one discernible in his own poetical achievement and in certain manifestations of nature. It helped to complete his vision of life, but in a perfectly natural way. Nor did he now incline to ascribe psychical influences to external causes, as he had in the past. They came, he was convinced, from our unconscious minds, whose depth reached down into infinity where space and time are not, into universal as against individual 'being', where the dead, the living and the unborn are indistinguishable. These notions which recall Rilke's thoughts about the unconscious in the third elegy, and about the state of death in the tenth, and which permeate the sonnets, deprive spiritualism of its sensational and shady elements. He was resolute enough in his affirmation of the whole of life not to weight the scales in favour of the 'undiscovered country'. This letter is in fact a stronger proof of the validity of his vision than the epistle to Hulewicz sixteen months later in which he tried to push it too far. Nora responded on August 29, 1924 with accounts of hair-raising *poltergeist* phenomena, prophecies, trances, messages from the 'other side', written and spoken in that familiar psychic jargon which is so singularly unimpressive.

In his reply Rilke maintained that he had been deeply affected by her account of the behaviour and messages of her spirits and controls; and that the very sheets of paper on which all this was written subtly affected the atmosphere of his room as with an urgent presence. He begged to be allowed to keep the letter for a time before sending it on to her aunt; but he finished the short and tremulous effusion with the following words:

And do not change. Do not divert your love from visible things. But go on loving what is good, simple and ordinary: animals and things and flowers, and keep the balance true.[1]

This rather touching appeal represents the 'small beginning of love' (to quote from the fourth elegy) which Rilke was beginning to experience during the last months of his real life for his fellow human-beings as such. Real humanity, real distress for the sufferings of another as against exquisite poetical sympathy and counsels of perfection are manifest in a letter to an unfortunate author who had been unjustly accused of plagiarising passages from his early monograph on Worpswede. The unfounded charge stung Rilke and disturbed him quite as much as if it had been made against himself.[2] And warmth of heart rather than subtle psychological understanding informs his letters to Lisa Heise, whose sufferings made him really unhappy although he did not know her, because she was so clearly a victim of the cruelty of the times.[3] As for his own old friends, his feelings for them certainly did not decrease. His regard for Kippenberg, founded on the rock of gratitude, had developed with the years into an almost beautiful emotion, irradiating their literary and financial affairs as well as their human intercourse.

The *Inselverlag* must have recouped itself again and again for the sums paid out to Rilke during his lifetime; but Kippenberg was rewarded before the poet died by the devoted affection of a man who was far more often beloved than loving. The last tragic note Kassner received also shows an unsuspected depth in Rilke's feelings. Whilst, though Marie Thurn and Taxis noticed some witchery lacking in his later

---

[1] *Maandblad voor geestelijke Stroomingen*, p. 92, September 5, 1924.
[2] Cf. *B. 1921–1926*, pp. 274–277.
[3] Cf. *F.B.* pp. 41–47, 48–55.

letters, this was certainly not emotional warmth. Their friendship was closer than ever, to judge by their numerous meetings, and by a remark Rilke made to Kippenberg. She had always understood his poetry, he said; but this comprehension deepened and became completer every year. As for Lou Andreas-Salomé, not only did he make her privy to his panic fears, but she was the one friend to whom accounts of his illness were sent. He believed that she could help him; and although the three letters she wrote in this connection proved vain, he clung to the fixed idea, that at least she would understand. She, the Kippenbergs and the princess remained to the end of his life proof of his capacity for steady and enduring friendship. He could also truthfully conclude his last published letter to his wife by saying that his thoughts and his wishes came to her from his heart.[1] To which statement one cannot but add the rider that it was only an atrophied organ as far as she was concerned. The riches of his temperament were showered during these last years most abundantly perhaps on Nanny Wunderly-Volkart, to whom he wrote even more informally, intimately and racily than he had done to Clara in the past. And although the letters to Baladine Klossowska have not been published, one divines, from the very fact that she settled him into Muzot and helped him to furnish it, something more natural and less tense than in his previous emotional adventures. But Monique Saint-Hélier's descriptions of him, frightened, fascinating, sorrowful,[2] and the tone of some mysterious *billets-doux* in the last volume of the correspondence illuminate a highly poetical approach to women; and this is also manifest in his passion for a little Belgian girl of thirteen whom he met at Ragaz and for that 'beautiful Egyptian' who was innocently to precipitate his death. Well might older friends like Katharina Kippenberg and Marie Thurn and Taxis miss something of his peculiar enchantment in his conversations and his letters. There was only enough of that now for the very young. The last volume of the correspondence hints as much. It was not for nothing

[1] *B. 1921–1924*, p. 340, from Muzot, November 17, 1925.
[2] Cf. M. Saint-Hélier, *A Rilke pour Noël*.

that Rilke reached his fiftieth year before he died. Life, which had been unable to change him radically even with the aid of war, found, as it generally does, an effective ally in time. The sententiousness of age began to cast long shadows over his irridescent personality which had hardly even seemed adult until now. Time was gradually transforming him from a poet into a commentator and from a shrinking hermit into a lionised literary man. He asked Kippenberg for interleaved copies of the elegies and sonnets so that he could annotate them for his own use and for his friends; and he almost collaborated in *Reconnaissance pour Rilke*, so anxious was he that this European tribute to his fame should not be lacking in substance;[1] he who had earlier believed that fame was synonymous with disaster.

They were both hot at his heels when his fiftieth birthday overtook him on December 4, 1925, bringing with it shoals of letters and telegrams from all over Europe which had to be answered if possible. But his herculean labours with his correspondence were interrupted by another forced sojourn in Valmont which lasted until the end of May 1926. A slight improvement in his condition allowed him to escape from the clinic to a hotel near by from which he visited Lausanne, where he met Jaloux again, and Vevey. Then he went back to Muzot, firmly determined to be done with sanatoriums for good. He was obliged to put up at the Bellevue Hôtel in Sierre, for repairs were in hand at Muzot, and he left it for Ragaz in July in order to meet the Princess Thurn and Taxis. They were both in wretched health and low spirits, but full of plans for a next and merrier meeting, by no means foreseeing the imminent end of their long friendship. Then Rilke returned to Sierre early in October. Before October 24, 1926, a strange and fatal accident occurred which precipitated his death. It seemed quite unimportant at the time, a mere scratch on his hand made whilst gathering roses. But it was the opportunity for which the mysterious malady in his blood was waiting. Rilke had been right in diagnosing the presence of a lurking enemy. He was actually far gone in leuchaemia before the

[1] Cf. *V.B.* pp. 440 f. and 424 with Betz, *op. cit.* pp. 228 f.

symptoms became apparent in the infection set up by the
scratch on his hand, a rare and torturing disease due to an
excess of white corpuscles in the blood. When at last
Hämmerli was able to recognise it, Rilke was as good as dead.
The roses which the poet was gathering are said to have been
presented to the last of the girls he loved. This was a beautiful
young Egyptian, a recent acquaintance who was driving over
to Muzot to visit Rilke on that ominous day in October and
arrived two hours late. She found her lover waiting for her in
the middle of the road, declaring that he had followed all the
adventures of her drive from afar, and had known just when to
expect her.[1] Girlhood, roses and death, three of Rilke's recurrent poetical subjects, were combined here for the last
time, echoing back through the *Requiem for a Friend* to that
eerie *Fragment*. But this time it was not the virgin, it was
Rilke who was to die; and from this point of view, it could
certainly be said of him that he died his own personal death.

Not that Rilke made any such claims. He asked for nothing
now but his own individual illness. Once more back at
Valmont, he is reported to have exclaimed to Nanny
Wunderly-Volkart when she entered the sick-room: 'Help me
to my own death';[2] but otherwise he avoided the word, whilst
insisting that he was suffering from a disease unique to himself, which he attributed not to bacteriological but to metaphysical causes. He suffered agonies of pain; but almost until
the end he seemed unaware that he was dying, and was full of
plans for a journey to the South of France. When in his long
conversations with Hämmerli about his sickness and sufferings
the word 'death' seemed imminent, he always broke off and
began to speak of other things. The poet who had glorified
death throughout his life was silent about it at the last. Not
from any lack of courage. He refused those opiates which
would deaden his consciousness, and finally died, his eyes
very wide and blue. It was in a room with a southern aspect,
and an incomparable view over the lake, for everything

---

[1] Cf. André Germain, 'Rainer Maria Rilke et la France', *Revue française de
Prague*, XVI, no. 75, 1937.

[2] Salis, *op. cit.* p. 202.

possible was done for him, including specialists and consulta-
tions. Towards the end he refused to see even Nanny
Wunderly-Volkart. Except for the presence of the doctor and
the nurse he died, as he had lived, alone; surrounded by every
care and comfort, and suffering the tortures of the damned.

2. Last Words

When Kippenberg visited Rilke in April 1924, the poet told
him to go ahead with the collected edition of his works. He
might possibly write another poem or two, and undertake
this or that piece of translation; but his real work was accomplished with *Duino Elegies*; he had said what it had been laid
upon him to say. Hardly had he uttered this poetical *Nunc
dimittis* before the idea of a new work in prose which should
be to the elegies and sonnets what *Malte Laurids Brigge* had
been to *New Poems* began to take shape in his mind, reminiscences of his childhood and of Russia, urgently willing him
to write.[1] Wise after the event, one sees now that this was
inevitable. *The Book of Monkish Life* had formed the prose
precipitate, *Tales about God*, in which the deistic elements
separated out from the poem, found expression. *Malte
Laurids Brigge* was the reverse side of the medal struck to
honour art in *New Poems*; it depicted the anguish of the
creator and the horror of life. Some kind of answer to the
elegies, some modification or denial was almost bound to
come from this poet of progressive reactions. The story of his
spiritual existence was not finished in 1922; his ideas about
God had gained in depth and interest since he no longer
equated the divinity with art. They were in a state of pregnancy, heralding some new birth. The emergence of deity,
whom Rilke now defined as a direction of love but not an
object of love, was probably but no longer obviously still a
tenet of his creed; the 'indescribable discretion' which he
claimed for the relationship between them, his insistence that

[1] Cf. *V.B.* p. 472; Salis, *op. cit.* pp. 185, 199; Betz, *op. cit.* pp. 56, 58, 148,
281.

faith was not the right attitude towards God, his explicit
preference for the fierce hebraic and islamic deities combined
with a continued adherence to the 'Russian' God; all this
suggests some organic modification of his former conception.
Between February 12 and 15, 1922, Rilke began a prose *In
Memoriam* to Verhaeren sandwiched in between the tenth and
the fifth elegies, which developed into that fictitious letter
from a young workman about God which has caused so much
interest and comment.[1] As a statement of his own religious
views whilst he was writing the elegies, fervent, unorthodox,
impassioned views, it is certainly of great importance, containing as it does Rilke's most slashing attack against the
Christian religion. The young workman gives many reasons
for rejecting Christianity as entirely unsuited to the spiritual
needs of modern men and women; but his strongest reproaches were levelled against the Christian denial, tacit or
otherwise, of the divine nature of sex. Rilke's antagonism to
Christianity and hostility to Christ had hitherto been based on
his dislike of resurrection and mediation. The more familiar,
indeed time-worn, objection to its asceticism was now raised
with all the emotional ardour of the newly converted. The
same slightly callow and far from original notion of the
sanctity and purity of the flesh informed a genuine letter in
March 1922 and was combined with a diatribe against modern
religions for their ethical and therefore superficial treatment
of 'our greatest and most intimate secret'.[2] Rilke saw no
other hope for humanity but to live their sexual life in the
protective zone of some phallic divinity, who would perhaps
be the first to bring back to mankind the host of gods absent
for so long. Could the sexual act, he continued, but be replaced in its rightful position in the very centre of the world,
the immediate result would be that gods would stream and
pulse through it once more as of old. This invocation to
phallic deities is at least as startling coming from Rilke as his

[1] Cf. *A.W.* II, p. 392 for this information; the *In Memoriam* is still unpublished; the letter is printed in *A.W.* II, pp. 294 ff.; and also in Rainer Maria
Rilke, *Über Gott*, Leipzig, 1934, pp. 27 ff.

[2] *B. 1921–1926*, pp. 126 ff.; to Rudolf Bodländer from Muzot, March 23,
1922.

salute to the god of war in 1914. Had his rash prayer been answered, and that primitive cult been re-established, he would have proved of all men the least fitted to survive under its empire. But one cannot affirm the greatness and glory of existence as a whole, unless one gives a central and splendid position to sex. Rilke had hitherto given this place of honour to death. Rightly or wrongly he believed that in the elegies he had gone beyond this and had glorified life as a whole. He repeatedly reaffirmed this *Credo*, and wished it to be taken seriously. But his fantastic lip-service to phallic gods, contrasted with the sombre splendour of the third elegy, may well make one doubt whether he had in truth conquered his abhorrence of sex any more satisfactorily than his terror of death;[1] whether in fact (and this is the crucial point) his own interpretation of the elegies is valid.

Another new element which crept into Rilke's letters after the spring of 1922 further complicates this vital question. It is a rational as opposed to a poetical approach to life, a position almost thrust upon him by his increasing fame and the consequent spate of letters asking for advice and for critical opinions on the work and the promise of would-be young poets. Like Goethe's, when he deflated young Eckermann's literary aspirations, Rilke's counsels were extremely sound and often most unpalatable. Kind, sympathetic, acutely critical and devastatingly honest, his letters of advice were nearly always negative pills with a coating of positive sweetness. He warned his young correspondents against everything most dear to the heart of youth: against inspiration, against formlessness, against rebellion, against exclusive devotion to their art, against publication, and sometimes even against writing at all. He had attained the bleak years of discretion and was particularly vigilant about the follies he had perpetrated himself, such as rushing into print too early and neglecting to provide oneself with a profession as a subsidiary occupation. Rilke was sensitive on both these counts,

---

[1] The German poem *Eros*, *S.G.* p. 124, written early in 1924, and the longer French poem of the same title, *Poèmes français*, pp. 19 ff., reproduce roughly the attitude of the third elegy.

for which he excused himself by an appeal to the unfavourable social conditions prevailing in his youth; echoing the eternal refrain of age, that things were much easier for the young people of to-day. This particular piece of ripe wisdom was peculiarly inappropriate to the situation of the post-war youth of Germany, but such is the language of sages.

Besides being besieged on all sides for professional and personal advice, Rilke was also badgered for autographs and was continually being approached for permission to translate and illustrate his works and to set his poems to music. Invariably courteous, he was adamant about the last two proposals and sometimes reluctant to yield to the first. But those who wrote to him for information about himself were not sent empty away. A retrospective, autobiographical vein runs through many of the personal letters as well; but the most outstanding feature of the late correspondence is Rilke's strange eagerness to analyse his poetical development and expound his works for the benefit of total strangers. Some of these were engaged upon studies of his writings, and must have been extremely gratified when their tentative and diffident enquiries met with such a voluble response from a poet whose aloofness and remoteness were legendary by now.

This self-exegesis has its painful side. The unhappy necessity which modern poets are under to explain and even annotate their works for the uninitiated was upon him; for he now clearly wished to reach a public which could not understand him. He was no longer a self-sufficient artist, he was a prophet-poet, with all which that office entails. He would beg such critics as approached him to write again, to keep in touch with him and to ask him more questions. He even recommended the use of *questionnaires*, and took endless trouble filling in forms and supplementing them by pages of explanatory matter. How much more nonchalantly he had dealt in the past with similar missives from the outer darkness! And this zealous collaboration with his critics was all the more disconcerting because he still clung to the notion that he never read anything that was written about him.

Such Olympian indifference had actually always been an idea rather than a reality. Ever since 1907, when the threat of a German reprint in book-form of Ellen Key's well-meant essay about him had hung over his head, Rilke had formed the habit of warning his various interpreters that it was his fixed and unalterable custom not to read criticisms of his works in order to protect his unconsciousness and preserve his poetical integrity. What he really wished to guard against was the shadow of personal responsibility which had fallen over Ellen Key's monograph. No one can blame him for sheltering behind this convenient fiction which saved him endless trouble and the appearance of discourtesy when zealous critics and admirers presented him with copies of reviews, lectures, theses and books dealing with his own works. In reality he seems to have scrutinised such offerings fairly closely before tossing them aside. He certainly characterised two of them briefly and brilliantly in a letter to Clara, even quoting a passage from one which 'had happened' to catch his eye; whilst maintaining both to his wife and the authors that he could not and would not read them.[1] The discovery made in 1907 that Cézanne, his *nonpareille* amongst artists, had resolutely ignored the critiques of his paintings certainly hardened him in the belief that his own abstention was equally unswerving. In 1921 this delusion had become a fixed idea which forced Rilke and his critics into truly Gilbertian situations. Some would send him their books and articles, and receive charmingly worded acknowledgments, regretfully acquainting them with his unalterable rule and giving very solemn reasons for it. What must have been their surprise as they read on, to find their methods criticised, their errors identified, their knowledge supplemented, their sympathy appreciated, or their championship hailed? Others, having asked for and received valuable inside information of a psychological nature about influences and the genesis of works, would be told in all seriousness that the part-author of the prospective treatise would be unable to read it, because it was his high duty to shield himself from the very enlightenment he had dispensed,

[1] Cf. *B. 1906–1907*, pp. 156, 238 f., 250, 286, 317 f., 353.

lest it should reveal to him his unconscious processes and thereby injure them.[1] Yet so suggestible, not to say gullible, are human beings, that these very critics have blazed abroad (as he meant them to) the curious legend of Rilke's complete and utter ignorance of the critical works he inspired. It still flourishes hardily (although the correspondence disproves it) in the teeth of Carlyle's optimistic *dictum* that a lie cannot be believed. Rilke's disingenuousness in this matter is one instance among others of his powers of self-deception, causing misgivings to arise about his general reliability. But no one who takes himself as seriously as Rilke did can be completely trustworthy.

Of the seven correspondents to whom he unburdened himself about various aspects of his life-work, the two most important are Witold Hulewicz, his Polish translator, and Hermann Pongs, the well-known writer, whose contributions to Rilke-criticism are amongst the most valuable that have been made. But extremely interesting information can be gleaned from his other exegetical letters; and all of them, fourteen in number, have been drawn upon in the following attempt to define Rilke's attitude towards himself and his poetry at the end of his life.[2]

About his own early works he was acutely critical and far more cruel than he allowed himself to be with the young writers, whom he discouraged so much (one suspects) because they reminded him of his *bête noire*, René Rilke. He had nothing but cold contempt now for that dim and insincere little poet. And the worst of it was that the farther he went with his utter condemnation, the farther his publisher went in reviving his *juvenilia*. Rilke had not been averse from publishing *Early Poems* in 1909, and had allowed *First Poems* to come out in 1913 without uttering a protest. But when Hünich wished to bring out *Life and Songs* in 1919 he met with violent opposition. The lack of integrity and truth

---

[1] Cf. *B. 1921–1926*, pp. 59 ff., 62, 154, 172 f., 249 f., 374.

[2] Cf. *Dichtung und Volkstum*, 1936, xxxvii, no. 1, pp. 100–115 for Rilke's three letters to Pongs; and *B. 1921–1926*, no. 13 to Heygrodt; nos. 48, 78, 85, 105, 106 to Hulewicz; nos. 80, 81 to Schaer; no. 111 to Fischer-Colbrie; no. 119 to an unknown young friend; and no. 121 to Korrodi.

manifest in his youthful work now seemed to Rilke to dis-figure *Early Poems* too, and caused him retrospective shame. He told Heygrodt, who was writing a monograph on Rilke's lyric poems, that he had made a fundamental error in his book by taking the early verse into account, not to mention those 'wretched little tales' in prose. To Pongs' suggestion that it might be worth while to collect and publish these stories, he opposed a strenuous negative. They were utterly devoid of value, partly because of his mangled and martyred adolescence, and partly because (verse being his native idiom) he had been unable to write an even tolerable prose in his youth. But his early verse was little better, and should never have been published; it was execrable stuff, written to con-vince his sceptical family that he was a poet. His sensitiveness on the subject was heightened by the fact that Kippenberg had finally wrung permission from him to publish *From Rainer Maria Rilke's Adolescence* in 1921, containing early verse, prose sketches and dramas. The edition was limited to ninety-nine copies and Rilke sent one to Nanny Wunderly-Volkart, saying bitterly that he considered these documents of the 'young Rilke' *inavouable*.[1] He addressed the prime instigator, Hünich, with a sad little poem to the effect that he felt he must be 'slightly dead' already not to have been able to hinder the publication.[2] Which sheds a rather sinister light on the posthumous publication of *Adolescent Tales and Sketches* in 1930, bringing those 'wretched little tales' before a much wider public, and making them accessible to critics who can neither ignore nor admire them.

Rilke's root-and-branch condemnation of his early manner just stopped short of *The Lay of the Love and Death of Cornet Christopher Rilke*. He considered it fundamentally unimport-ant, it is true, and written in an intolerable mixture of verse and prose; yet its youthfulness moved him now that he was really getting old; and he regarded with a deprecating tenderness this gallant little thorn in his aesthetic flesh. He was less indulgent to *The Life of Mary*, written in 1912, but

[1] Salis, *op. cit.* p. 157.
[2] F. A. Hünich, *Rilke Bibliographie*, Leipzig, 1935, I, p. 85.

deriving from a considerably older stratum. He dismissed it summarily as 'unimportant'; and indeed its Catholic setting must have been peculiarly repugnant to him now. Nor need one wonder at the rather cold glance he cast in passing on his *Auguste Rodin*. Cézanne had taught him in 1907 how little he knew about art, and the exuberant enthusiasm of the monograph had been rather cruelly curbed by his subsequent knowledge of Rodin. Neither the man nor his work seemed to Rilke now to be purely admirable, and there was no mention of Rodin in the seventh elegy which sang the dirge of sculpture and architecture on earth. Possibly Rilke would have hesitated towards the end of his life to include Rodin's masterpieces among the eternal 'things'. But if this were so, he was as emphatic and as grateful as he had ever been about the incalculable influence and inspiration the 'mighty master' represented in his life. His longest and most reasoned statement on this subject was made to Pongs; and, though he slightly altered some of the facts in his own favour,[1] he gave the essential truth of the relationship and stressed the magnitude of his debt to Rodin, a theme to which he constantly recurred in his self-explanatory letters.

His analysis of Tolstoy's temperament in the letter to Pongs of October 21, 1924 showed understanding and breadth of vision, flavoured with a pinch of retrospective rancour which made him deny his early adoration of this strange genius. He owed Tolstoy no debt of any kind, and was right to exclude him from the list of great Russian writers who had influenced him. But it is decidedly odd, and indeed inexplicable, that Dostoyevski's name should also have been omitted.[2] I am inclined to account for it by Rilke's markedly anti-Christian bias. This had already precipitated him into the posture of a phallus-worshipper and was to lead to some remarkable mental antics later. It might well have inhibited him from acknowledging a debt to the greatest Christian

---

[1] He said that he at first refused the invitation to Meudon, and only yielded to telegraphic pressure. The letters do not bear this out. He also rather naturally made it appear that he left Rodin of his own accord.

[2] *B. 1921–1926*, p. 246; to Schaer from Muzot, February 26, 1924.

writer of modern times. It was almost certainly a strong
desire to differentiate between his poetical love for the poor
and Tolstoy's practical Christianity which led him to be so
exceedingly garrulous to Pongs about his own unsocialistic
tendencies. These were clearly manifest as early as *Tales
about God*, where he deprecated any attempt to ameliorate the
lot of the poor; but the love he expressed for them there and in
The Book of Poverty and Death was too close to Dostoyevski's
'protoplasmic humanity' not to approximate to Christianity.
Hence perhaps both the silence on the one count and the
volubility on the other.

The silence about Dostoyevski is all the more noticeable
because the journeys to Russia and all that they had meant to
him were now in the forefront of Rilke's mind for the first
time since he had come under the sway of Rodin and had been
ensnared by Paris. The enchantress had let him go during that
brief but pregnant visit in the autumn of 1920. She was still
there when he returned in 1925, but she had resigned her
empire over him in favour of that glamorous land he had never
quite forgotten during all his subsequent journeys. Now the
memories came rushing back as unaccountably and as ex-
citingly as the little horse he had seen long ago by the Volga,
which galloped with tossing mane into the *Sonnets to Orpheus*.
Rilke's meetings with various Russian friends, old and new, in
Paris strengthened, though they did not initiate, his surrender to
the past. The letter he wrote to the artist Leonid Pasternak in
the year of his death is so full of longing and of living love for
Russia and all things Russian as to be profoundly moving. He
had earlier dwelt very emphatically on the importance of
Russia in his life to several correspondents, but this is
different. What he said of post-war Russia, that she had withdrawn into her secret roots and was invisibly there in the
dark preparing for a rebirth, may or may not prove to be
prophetic; but it exactly describes what had happened to
Russia in Rilke's own mind. The vision had penetrated to the
very roots of his being, sending up *The Book of Hours* as it
struck downwards, and thereafter discernible only by slight
upheavals on the surface. The puerile local colour of *Tales*

about God, the affectations Russia produced during Rilke's
unreal period; the strangeness of *The Tsars*; occasional
striking descriptions and penetrating remarks, written and
oral, showed that it was working underground and sending up
filaments into his consciousness. These increased during the
years 1924 to 1926 in his letters and in his conversations.
Russia was preparing for her rebirth in Rilke's mind; he
was beginning to relive the 'Russian miracle' and was
waiting to put it into words. His openly expressed intention
to write a book about it was accompanied by illustrative tales,
a preliminary oral stage through which he had also passed
when *Malte Laurids Brigge* was taking shape. But another
force was working against it. His childhood hung like an evil
star over the Russian horoscope. Stories of his early youth
were also being retailed at the same time; for his lifelong
conviction that he ought to achieve an aesthetic crystallisation
of those sorrows had not left him. Perhaps he intended to
combine both subjects in an autobiographical work. If so, I
for one do not mourn the loss of his childhood's recollections.
Even in his last years, when he was able to see the humorous
side of some episodes, he was still too prone to self-pity on the
subject as a whole for aesthetic detachment.[1] But his untimely
death probably deprived posterity of a greater work than
Malte Laurids Brigge. The Russian secretary whose services
Rilke engaged in the early autumn of 1926 was almost
certainly chosen with a view to this book, whose outline one
can vaguely imagine, but the tone and texture of which are the
really interesting problems. It seems at least possible that
Rilke's sense of humour, which was vivid and vital, might at
last have been allowed to collaborate with the other powers of
his mind in a work of imagination. This would have given it
that breadth of perspective and that human validity hitherto
lacking, because he had deliberately suppressed an essential
part of his vision of life from aesthetic expression. Wit of the
first order, flashing out in his letters and his conversations,
had made its mark on his poetry. The fifth and tenth elegies
are impregnated with it, even containing some fascinating

[1] Cf. for instance M. Saint-Hélier, *op. cit.* pp. 14 ff.

poetical puns and elaborate conceits. But humour had been banished after the very unsuccessful effort to make use of it in *Tales about God*. Irony at the most had occasionally been allowed to intrude. But no one would guess from Rilke's published works that one of his outstanding gifts was the faculty of seeing human beings, situations and life itself in divinely comic aspects. His works suffer from this suppression; not because they lack humour where it would have been out of place, but because they assume that it is non-existent for the purpose of poetry. It was an element of reality he refused to acknowledge, a part of life which he did not transform into art; hence the rarefied atmosphere of his poetry, the feeling of dimensional constriction, of something inhumane.

Meanwhile the humour was there, a vital part of Rilke's make-up, transporting his friends by its spontaneous and irresistible appearances, fascinating posterity when it appears in his letters. It was gaining the upper hand towards the end of his life, or so I believe; for it began to encroach upon hitherto sacred subjects, such as the ill-starred visit to Yasnaya Polyana. It might have overflowed into art at the last and given a radiance to his book about Russia, which would certainly also have included Rilke's deepened conception of God. And this is all the more likely because, during and after the elegy-crisis at Muzot, a vision of life emerged subtly but essentially different from the tragic conception of the destiny of man which had moulded *Malte Laurids Brigge* and the earlier elegies. Unfortunately Rilke's *Ultima Thule* (the title I would have given to his Russian book) is not there to compensate us for the less inspiring side of his altered focus on life; this, on the other hand, is all too clearly discernible in his late interpretations of *Malte Laurids Brigge* and *Duino Elegies*.

It was partly reaction, partly the probable effect of *Malte Laurids Brigge* upon sensitive young minds, which first made Rilke lower his ground. He was not willing to accept the responsibility for what he had written, any more than Goethe had been for *Werther*. Goethe turned whole-heartedly, one might almost say venomously, on his unfortunate scapegoat and held him up to ridicule. Rilke had a more divided mind. He tried to justify the novel and at the same time to prove that it did not mean what it seemed to convey—a despairing rejection of life. The elements which had destroyed Malte were not in themselves destructive, he protested, but the reverse side of great positive forces. The book should be read against the current, as it were, otherwise it would do more harm than good.[1] In an undated letter assigned by the editors to the year 1921, he went a step farther, and declared that the bitter reproaches in the book were not directed against life, but against our lack of strength to enjoy the countless earthly riches intended for us.[2] This is quibbling. For our lack of strength is part of life and part of tragic destiny. The ethical judgment contained in the word 'intended' presupposes a loving and benevolent father whose generosity is ill-requited by a band of weak and whining children. Such an interpretation of *Malte Laurids Brigge* deprives it of all claim to greatness; and the advice to read it backwards is (like all other cautionary tales) aesthetically preposterous.

Rilke's famous explanation of *Duino Elegies* made for the benefit of Hulewicz and posterity is more important and far more complicated.[3] It gives no adequate idea of the cycle, which is interpreted entirely from the standpoint of the sonnets and the seventh and ninth elegies. This has a dire effect on the mystery and subtlety of the whole, its tragic beauty and its host of angels.

Their creator was, alas! a true modern poet in this, that he analysed these symbols theoretically. As early as 1909 he defined angels as beings who assert and will existence, as life itself magically transmuted by art, so that everything ugly and depraved becomes a positive and radiant angel.[4] Toledo, which gave a great impetus to the development of the cycle, also clarified Rilke's intellectual attitude to the mysterious beings who dominate it. He described Toledo as the speech

[1] Cf. *B. 1907–1914*, pp. 195 ff., 207 f.

[2] Cf. *B. 1921–1926*, p. 19. This letter was written in September 1920 to Baladine Klossowska; not to 'a young girl' therefore.

[3] *B. 1921–1926*, pp. 330–338; postmarked Sierre, November 13, 1925.

[4] *B. 1907–1914*, p. 74.

used by angels when they tried to communicate with men;[1] and as a city equally visible to the living, the dead and the angels, a focal point for these three different angles of vision.[2] In 1915, when he was writing the fourth elegy, he spoke of Toledo as the vision of a blinded angel gazing inwards, and added the revealing statement that it was perhaps his mission to represent the world from this angle and not from the human point of view.[3] The aesthetic result would be true art, completely objective and dispassionate, radiating its own intense emotional life, but unapproachable and withdrawn:

...it would be presumptuous to expect assistance from a work of art. The human tension it contains is not directed outwards. But its inner intensity, without becoming extensive, can by its presence create the illusion that it is an aspiration, a challenge, an act of courtship, of overwhelming love, an incitement to rebel, a mission; all this is due to its own rightfulness and is not its function. And this deception practised between art and forsaken mankind is like all those priestly deceptions by means of which, since the beginning of time, what is divine has been promoted.[4]

The priestly deception, the illusion of a challenge thrown down to man by the angels, is the great leading idea of the elegies, whose author achieved his supreme ambition in 1922 when the world of art, and therefore of human aspiration, was made visible to the angels in the seventh elegy and invisible to man in the ninth; whereas in the first and second elegies Rilke had gazed at the angels and then back to earth, dazzled, bewildered and defeated. The gospel of transformation was the new element in the cycle; it seemed to Rilke now to dominate it completely, so that in the letter to Hulewicz he passed over in silence the life-and-death conflict with his daimonic opponent, and implicitly denied the profoundly tragic views on childhood, on sex, on the doom of death encircling humanity and on the isolation of man in the universe which the poem contains. Restricting himself to the sonnets, to the seventh, and particularly to the ninth elegy, Rilke

[1] B. 1907–1914, p. 246.　　　　[2] B. 1907–1914, p. 249.
[3] B. 1914–1921, p. 80.
[4] F.B. pp. 7 f.; dated from Soglio, August 2, 1919.

propounded a metaphysical doctrine which can only be accepted as one-sided, and which is more fantastic than mysterious, more eccentric than poetical. Shorn of their radiance, ambiguity and menace, the angels have dwindled to an abstract idea: they are those creatures in whom the transformation of the visible into invisibility, which humanity is performing, is already completed; they stand for the higher degree of reality of what is invisible; and are 'terrible' because we still cling to what we can see, loving it whilst we transform it. One need only look back to the inspired description of the host of angels in the second elegy to realise what they lose by this doctrinaire interpretation.

There are three main leading ideas in Rilke's commentary on *Duino Elegies*. The first is an emphatic declaration that the cycle is a definitive affirmation of life here and now. In the seventh elegy there was undoubtedly a triumphant declaration of the glory of being here. But otherwise such rapture about life as occurred was inspired by the world of plastic art, of nature and of things, because these were susceptible of transformation, and therefore of recognition by the angels, the ultimate test of value. By extension, the life, or the moments, of such human beings as take part in the great task of transformation could also be strongly affirmed. But in the ninth elegy Rilke seemed to postulate this for himself alone. And life as we know and live it, organic, functional, dynamic life, had no real place in his scheme. Whilst art as we know it which uplifts and transports must disappear, if it is to find its centre of gravity in his universe, the world of platonic ideas. It is a tenable position, and has been held by all idealistic philosophers; but the very desire to translate the whole of life into another sphere is a criticism of its present surroundings.

The weakness of Rilke's position as the universal lover of life is also apparent in his second leading idea, the contention that in *Duino Elegies* life and death were shown to be two equal parts of a greater whole; so that to affirm life was to affirm death too. His affirmation of death had always been an essential doctrine in his metaphysical creed; but, until the

sonnets, this had been at the expense of life, whenever they
were contrasted. The orphic sequences explicitly glorified
both aspects of the state of being. The elegies as a cyclic
whole did not. In the first poem the angels were certainly
represented as being unable to distinguish between the two
spheres; but their utter disregard of everything pertaining to
humanity would account for that. The poet himself was on the
side of death in the first elegy, and again in the sixth, where
the heroes are glorious because they choose to die young. In
the eighth the knowledge of death was tragically conceived,
from which exceptional concession to human sorrow Rilke
swerved away in the tenth elegy where the farther land was
contrasted in its mystery and beauty with the garish, shallow
life we live and know. Rilke's retrospective attempt to force
the unity of conception behind the sonnets on to the elegies as
well will not stand the test of a close examination. But his
present feverish insistence that he worshipped this life was
probably not due to aesthetic preoccupations. Why should he
have denied his belief in spiritual as against earthly values?
Why should he have been at such pains to assert that his
gospel of transformation was not a criticism of life as we know
it? A man capable of dreaming such dreams as Rilke could not
and did not accept the world he lived in. He offered instead
the solution of an out-and-out extremist, to spiritualise it out
of existence, to make it actually what it already practically
was for him, invisible and unearthly. This is not only a
perfectly comprehensible point of view, but one with which
all idealists will sympathise. It will not square, however,
with the declaration made to Hulewicz that his notions about
life and death were rooted in a purely earthly, deeply earthly,
blessedly earthly consciousness. The truth was (and he confessed as much) that he was above all things anxious to avoid
the appearance of Christian asceticism. He dreaded lest
Catholic conceptions of the next world and of eternity should
be applied to *Duino Elegies*, or lest his angels should seem to
have anything in common with those of Christian mythology.
His antagonism to Christianity is the clue to the puzzle of his
unsatisfactory interpretation of the elegies. He was almost

forced to represent himself as a pagan in order to underline the difference between his notions of life and death and the Christian conception of their relative value. For Rilke's instinctive hostility was the real bar between his views and Christian metaphysics. His spurious enthusiasm for sexual intercourse, his incongruous cult of phallic divinities, his rather pallid paganism, and the glorification of life which he now stridently claimed for *Duino Elegies* were all pieces of anti-Christian propaganda. Far from illuminating the mystery of the cycle itself, his letter to Hulewicz tends to darken counsel, the more so as the orphic doctrines of the will-to-metamorphosis and of the unity of the kingdom of life and death, taken over from the sonnets, the first inherent in the seventh and ninth, the second in the tenth elegy, were only a fraction of the vision of life which inspired the cycle as a whole.

The third leading idea, the actual theme of transformation, is a commentary on the ninth elegy, a prose paraphrase in parts, leading to a further and more fantastic development. For Rilke suggested that the transformation of visible objects into invisible vibrations would not only introduce new wave-lengths into the universe; but, since matter is merely differ-entiated oscillations, it would create new bodies, metals, constellations and milky ways, hardly a consummation devoutly to be wished from his point of view, but rather a vicious circle, if not a *reductio ad absurdum*. We are the bees of the invisible, he said, frantically collecting the honey of this world to store it in the great golden invisible hive. Evidently the parallel holds more closely than he thought. This honey is to be used for purposes other than those intended. By our unremitting labour to render the visible world invisible and therefore immortal we shall be adding on a colossal scale to existing visible matter. Sisyphus' stone and the Danaides' sieve are as nothing to this. If all the worlds of the universe are rushing (according to Rilke) towards invisibility as their next nearest reality, ought we not to beware of introducing the principle of *perpetuum mobile* by creating new worlds to rush? Should these belong to the category of stars which (again according to Rilke) vanish immediately into the eternal consciousness of angels, no harm if but little good will come of our interference. But what if they prove to be worlds which depend for their progress on beings who slowly and laboriously transform them again and so on *ad infinitum*? This was the pitfall which beset his feet when he attempted to make out a megalomaniacal case for the conception behind the elegies. It was great enough in all conscience, tragically great. But its cosmic significance, the conflict between man and the supernal powers, had little to do with the apocalyptic fantasia Rilke now embroidered on the theme. This itself was an eruption from the past, another outbreak of that high-flown idealism about art which had inspired the final paragraph in the Tuscan journal in his youth and moulded another exalted passage in Rome.

If the letter to Hulewicz was even more extremist and extravagant, this was so perhaps because Rilke was already in the throes of one of those prosaic reactions which were apt to set in after his sustained flights of imagination, and was therefore overstating his case. Taking the letter as it stands, however, one can only marvel at the heights of frantic self-assertion to which his belief in the cosmic creativeness of art finally led him. And at the depths of bathos too. Rilke's declaration in the seventh elegy that the things of art were passing away from this world may not seem excessive to lovers of the past in this age of steel. But, since architecture was the main theme of this passionate if triumphant dirge, one cannot but remember that, even whilst he was writing it, the sky-line was being sculptured in New York, the greatest architectural event since the Moghul Empire, and that Rilke knew nothing of either. Invincible ignorance about America went farther still in the letter, which reproduced a very natural and very common dislike for shoddy ready-made goods. But the conclusion he drew was preposterous. An American house, vine or apple had nothing in common, he categorically stated, with the building, the fruit or the grapes into which the hopes and thoughts of our forefathers had entered; they were in fact only bogus 'things'. This denial of spiritual life to a whole continent, this almost insane assumption that the rhythm of nature, the deep organic connection between life and death (the central theme of the sonnets) did not hold good in the New World reveals Rilke as having attained the very nadir of bombastic nonsense. It recalls two sinister prophecies he had made at the inception of *Duino Elegies*. He had foreseen that a course of psycho-analysis would cast out the devils which tormented him, but probably the angels as well;[1] and he had quoted the Old Testament adage, that no man can behold an angel face to face and live.[2] Rilke's work on the elegies from 1912 to 1922 had been a long, perilous and revealing piece of self-analysis. It had laid bare two ancient wounds, his subconscious horror of sex, and his mortal terror of death. It is doubtful if it healed the first, almost certainly it did nothing to soothe the latter. But it cast out the demon of sexual inhibition from his conscious mind, and the radiant, menacing angel departed with it. Taboo and fetish were now outgrown. Meanwhile Rilke had seen his God's proxy face to face; the letter to Hulewicz would seem to suggest that the poet of *Duino Elegies* had not survived that vision.

The question as to whether the cycle as a whole is more triumphant than tragic will be answered in every case according to the bias of the individual reader. Both elements are there: and one can lay the emphasis at will on either. But the triumph is dated 1922 and the despair reached its nadir in 1915. Concentrating on the victory in the letter to Hulewicz, Rilke ignored the bitter defeat and the rejection of life in the fourth elegy, which remained for many years his final word. He rarely acknowledged that this was the case. On the contrary, though dating the other elegies, and acknowledging the fragments written in Toledo and Paris in 1913, he continually asserted that the work on the cycle had been completely interrupted by the war,[3] a statement emphatically repeated in the letter to Hulewicz. Intimate friends undoubtedly knew the truth; for Rilke had read them the poem at the time, and they later received copies of the cycle accurately dated by the poet

---

[1] *B. 1907–1914*, pp. 180 f.   [2] *B. 1907–1914*, p. 196.
[3] Cf. *B. 1921–1924*, pp. 212, 219, 224, 238, 264, 333, 347, 371.

himself. But the general impression he aimed at creating was that the miracle of 1912, consummated in 1922, was to all intents and purposes the same revelation, interrupted but not otherwise affected by the war. This was at most the dramatic truth of the situation; since the fourth elegy, written in utter despair and hatred of life, represented man as waiting tensely for a revelation which was withheld. The bitterness of this defeat threw a dark shadow over the tragic themes of the three first poems, but lost much of its sting when it subsided finally into the cycle as a whole. So that Rilke was both right and wrong in tacitly denying its crucial importance. Right from his present standpoint which half obliterated it; disingenuous in making it appear that his vision of life had never been tragic and had not been affected by the war. This was perhaps a form of that metaphysical vanity which so clearly underlay his present attitude to the elegies.

Rilke was now firmly convinced that he was a vehicle for inspiration in the literal sense. The poems by Count C. W., the elegies and sonnets had all in their different ways been 'dictated' to him, an explanation which did him good service in the matter of his French verse. After he had temporarily called a halt to his translations of Valéry's *Charmes* early in 1923, Rilke began to amuse himself by writing original poems in French, an occupation which he continued throughout the years 1924 and 1925. The French language, in which many of his intimate letters to Nanny Wunderly-Volkart were written, was now almost a second mother-tongue to him: and he sometimes switched over from German to French when writing to her in a manner which (whilst it would cause a purist to swoon) shows that he was equally at home in either.[1] The atmosphere and associations of Valais made it natural for him to express himself poetically in the tongue spoken all round him, and the refreshment of using something like a 'little language' instead of his own formidable and exacting idiom, of playing where he was wont to travail so sorely, lured him on and on to shake one fascinating little poem after another from his magician's sleeve. Valéry published a few of them in

[1] Cf. Salis, *op. cit.* pp. 65 f.

Commerce in 1924, whereupon the fat was in the fire and hissings and splutterings arose from the more benighted German journalists about 'Frenchification' and 'double-dealing'.[1] Although the papers which attacked him on this score were only scurrilous little rags, whereas the reputable dailies defended him, Rilke took the accusation very much to heart. He went to see a journalistic friend of his, Walter Mehring, almost daily when they were both in Paris in 1925, with bundles of press-cuttings which Mehring was to use for his defence; and when he could not come in person he wrote.[2] Nor did he stop there, in spite of his feint of complete ignorance of what was written about him and of utter indifference to public opinion. Two of his self-explanatory letters dealt rather piteously with the subject.[3] He 'had happened to glance' at an article about him by an old friend, Fischer-Colbrie, which referred to the vexed question, and wrote to the author giving an abbreviated psychological life-story to account for his French poems; protesting very earnestly against the explanation some of his defendants had offered, that he had deserted his mother-tongue because his country and particularly Stefan George's circle had failed to recognise his genius. In another letter to yet another champion, Eduard Korrodi, written three months later, he was at great pains to prepare a soft place for his French poems to fall on. They were about to appear in book-form and Rilke, anticipating further criticisms of a patriotic nature, frankly enlisted Korrodi's sympathy and support in the press. He blamed himself for his 'weakness' in permitting publication; and to both correspondents he sheltered himself behind the fiction of a 'peremptory dictation'. Nothing had been farther from his thoughts, he declared, than to write, let alone to publish, French verse; but he had been forced to yield to spiritual pressure from within and to Valéry from without.

---

[1] *Verwelschung* is a much bitterer term of reproach than the English equivalent; *doppelzüngig* means both bilingual and double-faced, which throws an interesting light on German mentality.

[2] Cf. *Die literarische Welt*, January 14, 1927, for these and other details on the subject.

[3] *B. 1921–1926*, no. 111, December 18, 1925 and no. 121, March 20, 1926.

Rodin's doctrine of daily labour had been totally vanquished now by Rilke's inspirational experiences, which did indeed resemble spiritual dictation far more closely than unremitting work. Once converted to the view of inspiration in the literal sense, he held it as strongly as he had earlier advocated the gospel of toil; and there is a malicious description by Raymond Schwab of Rilke boring a reunion of literary men in Paris by a long-winded account of his 'automatic' writing:

Dans ce salon, où l'on avait commencé par faire cercle autour de lui, peu à peu les gens s'échappaient discrètement, tôt fatigués par la loquacité de Rilke parlant droit devant lui, expliquant, sans nul regard à l'effet produit, par quel automatisme son rêve se traduisait en mots incontrôlés quand il passait de la prose aux vers, activité selon lui essentiellement différente—je n'ai vu personne souligner à ce point la différence, ni, ma foi, écarter de soi avec tant de rapidité, et, aussi, d'insouciance, les auditeurs, en déduisant trop généreusement des choses trop importantes.[1]

Spite apart, that last phrase ('deducing too generously all too important things') sums up Rilke's attitude to his poetry as reflected in his later letters, but his attitude towards life and fate was less portentous and much less tragic than before. His sufferings at the military academy and during the war could still draw from him accents of profound sorrow; but the wound dealt him by the latter was partially healed by the miracle of the elegies. Otherwise his retrospect was unclouded. The terms in which he referred to Jacobsen, Rodin, Verhaeren, Cézanne and Valéry, to the places he had loved and the countries he had visited give the impression of a rich, varied and essentially happy life. This serenity of outlook is all the more remarkable because from his intimate letters it is clear that the shadow of sickness threw a dreadful darkness over his mind; that his mortal illness and the mortal terror it inspired were the real events of his emotional life after 1923. But above and beyond the emotions he could not control, his intellect affirmed the beauty of existence in general, and in particular of his own. In doing this, he may have been sailing under

[1] Betz, *op. cit.* p. 143.

false colours, in which case it was all the more gallant on his part to nail them to the mast.

The foregoing attempt to reconstruct Rilke's spiritual history during the last four years of his life from the material available has led me to believe that the completion of the elegies had been a climax and a crisis, but not the end. Had there been no sign of change in Rilke himself after 1922, one would have been almost forced to accept his own verdict of April 1924, that he had said his last word; for it is difficult to see how the poet of *Duino Elegies* could have surpassed those flights of imagination, or how the orphic lyrist could have added anything essential to his vision. The crucial letter to Hulewicz, however, makes it clear that Rilke was attempting just this; and the late poem called *Music*[1] is a pointer in the same direction. For the change was there. The struggle to complete the elegies, which had been partly pathological, was over at last. Less concentrated on himself, Rilke was more sympathetic and more aware of others than he had been in the past. His poetical temperament was achieving something like normality; but it would be unwise to deduce from this that Rilke's future works would be less interesting and unique. On the contrary, the letter to Hulewicz hints that they might be markedly eccentric; but Rilke's prose was never at any time a safe guide to his poetry. As a thinker he was approximating ever more closely towards the end of his life to that other extreme idealist, Friedrich Schiller. They had been separated in the past by the latter's robust and rational optimism, which the author of *Malte Laurids Brigge* and the early elegies certainly did not share. But they held many views in common nevertheless: the nobility and purity of women; the wholeness and integrity of childhood; the essential innocence (Schiller called it *naïveté*) of nature. The similarity of these notions now became more recognisable. *Antistrophes*, the original fifth elegy, written in 1922,[2] for all its far greater imaginative beauty, is uncannily like *The Dignity of Women*, and is impregnated with the same antithetical and dramatic technique.

[1] *A.W.* I, pp. 363 f.; December 1925.
[2] *G.W.* III, pp. 457 ff.

Can Nature remember the jerk...,[1] describing man's unique position in the universe, and no longer attributing this to his consciousness of death as in the eighth elegy, approximates very closely to the differentiation made by Schiller. Nor is this all. *When winged rapture...*[2] and '*Nor spirit nor yet fervour will we lack'*...,[3] instinct with lofty idealism didactically expressed, are so startlingly like *Ideal and Life*, especially the latter, even to the swing of the rhythm, not to mention the gospel of ceaseless spiritual endeavour, as to make one blink and rub one's eyes. The subtle suggestiveness, the vague allusiveness, the intricate rhythms of a Rilke to be giving way to the abstract lucidity, the pounding metres and the dramatic emphasis of a Schiller? Can it be true? It would seem as if Rilke's latter-day rational optimism had in sober fact brought him to the cross-roads where Germany's greatest didactic poet can be found, resting between two tragic periods and declaiming inspiriting verse. How long the poet of *Duino Elegies* would have tarried in this spot, one cannot say; but it seems unlikely that he would have made more than a brief halt before passing onwards. For his development into the seer-sage was already an accomplished fact. More of a visionary than a thinker, his future prophetic utterances, however didactically framed, would surely still be surrounded by an element of mystery and poetry. As for his prose, were it not for the letter to Hulewicz (and this ought not to be taken as a clear indication of what was to follow, since it is largely anti-Christian propaganda), one would postulate for the contemplated book on Russia mellow serenity and sweet reasonableness moulding fantasies neither grim nor unearthly. Humour might have added breadth to the perilous depths and glorious heights of earlier visions; so that this book might have gained in perspective and humanity what it lost in strangeness. The dream he only dreamed in 1899 and 1900 might have come true. But it is all conjectural. Nor are we on much surer ground when, leaving unsolved the problem of what was never written, we turn to contemplate the handful of

[1] *S.G.* p. 89; December 22, 1923.   [2] *A.W.* i, pp. 364 f.; February, 1924.
[3] *A.W.* i, pp. 365 f.; August 10, 1926.

German poems, the translations from Valéry and the volume of French verse which the poet left behind him when the man gave up the ghost.

3. Transformation

It is certainly not possible to hazard any prophecies from the heterogeneous collection of German poems which now calls for attention, and which the author characterised in the following fashion in 1922:

The only thing that might hold me for a time is the rather difficult arrangement of that second part, which, as you already know, I intend to entitle 'Fragmentary'. Actually the ten great completed poems [the elegies] could easily be published alone, although the volume would in that case be rather slender. But it is not in order to give it a bulkier appearance that I should like to put in a word for that second part; it is because those poems, akin to the elegies and contemporary with them throughout, would otherwise never be published at all. This is the more likely, because I can hardly imagine myself issuing any mere collection of poems in the future that have accumulated gradually without originating in a common impulse.

To come back to the 'Fragmentary' poems. In this section I should include in the first place everything that was already broken, so to speak, before it came to light by those uncontrollable convulsions of my whole existence—shattered, and only capable of being produced in pieces. In the second place there would be poems which, though they were brought forth whole, remained incomplete. In both cases only such work would pass my judgment as is, even at the surface of fracture, still expressive, shapely, a 'thing'.[1]

Rilke did not publish this 'Fragmentary' section as a second part to the elegies. It appeared posthumously in the collected edition of his works, and since then three other arrangements and collections have been printed.[2] None of

---

[1] *V.B.* pp. 358 f.; to Anton Kippenberg from Muzot, February 23, 1922.

[2] *Gesammelte Werke*, III, 1930, pp. 379–473; 57 poems. *Gesammelte Gedichte*, IV, 1933; 81 poems. *Späte Gedichte*, 1934; 110 poems. *Ausgewählte Werke*, I, 1938, pp. 307–369; 61 poems; all dated. I refer to *Späte Gedichte* (*S.G.*) wherever possible, since it contains the majority of the poems; otherwise to *Ausgewählte Werke* (*A.W.*).

them is a complete compilation of Rilke's last poems and unpublished verse; all of them overlap considerably; most of
them are confusingly arranged; but even when grouped together according to their subjects, as Mr Leishman has done
in his translation,[1] they do not belie their fragmentary nature.
The rough chronological order followed by Dr Zinn,[2] which
more or less underlies *Late Poems* too, brings the accuracy
of Rilke's judgment into strong relief. Hardly one of these
poems predates the elegies of 1912 and most of them are so
clearly broken bits of poetical lava ejected during and after the
prolonged volcanic disturbance of the years 1912 to 1922 that
they are apt to arouse greater intellectual than aesthetic
interest. Nevertheless, some of them are peculiarly beautiful,
whether complete in themselves or not. The early *Sketch for a
Saint George*, the *Raising of Lazarus*, the *Harrowing of Hell*,
the war-hymns, the poem to Hölderlin, the ode to a flag, the
requiem on the death of a young boy, all these (and there are
others) make a direct poetical appeal. But the bewildering
and fascinating fragments are in the majority. *Antistrophes*
and the incomplete elegy on childhood, just not included in
the masterpiece, have that curious attraction, part pity part
nostalgic dreams, which the caryatid from the Erechtheion
arouses in Hellenists when they visit the British Museum.
I for one regret the exclusion of the childhood elegy from
Rilke's cycle almost as much as I deplore the absence of the
marble maiden from the temple she used to grace. And one
finds oneself scrutinising the other elegiac and orphic *débris*
and splinters in a cognate frame of mind. Incomplete, partially
destroyed or torn away from their surroundings, they have
the extra-aesthetic glamour of ruins and relics. Appealing,
expressive 'things', they bear the mark of a great period
upon them, a period that is past. To spend a day over them
is not unlike pottering about some excavated archaeological

[1] Rainer Maria Rilke, *Later Poems*, tr. by J. B. Leishman, London,
1938.
[2] In *A.W.* I; Dr Zinn's review of *Späte Gedichte* in *Dichtung und Volkstum*,
1936, is invaluable. He also helped Mr Leishman in the latter's important
commentary on Rilke's *Later Poems*; and he has been most generous in answering my questions.

site, reconstructing the demolished temples in one's mind, and
identifying sherds, coins, and some miraculously unshattered
jar with different layers of civilisations. Amidst these fragments, most of them recognisable as belonging to a well-
defined Rilkean stratum, one sometimes stumbles on a poem
that seems radiant and new, as if rising by spontaneous
generation from the backwash of the tidal wave which had
submerged Rilke for so long and had wrought such devasta-
tion in his poetry. There is a strange mythological poem of
the dawn of mankind and the birth of a smile which is unlike
his other visions; promethean and fierce, with a mysteriously
beautiful apolline ending.[1] But the poem which seems to me to
be crucial is the late *Music*[2] to which I have already referred,
prophetic of things to come and pregnant with promise. Rilke
had early realised the danger (if danger it can be called) which
music threatened to his poetry. When he turned from Russia
to Rodin, he was fleeing away from music into the refuge of
the temple of art; and his distrust of inspiration was an aspect
of his distrust of music, which imperilled his aesthetic integrity. It was the emotional, intoxicating, dionysiac element
which he feared, its lawlessness and overwhelming power.
A very interesting passage in a letter to Marie Thurn and
Taxis written in Toledo in 1913 shows that he had absorbed
Schopenhauer's and Nietzsche's views and recoiled from their
conclusions. But the mathematical, the intellectual, what he
called the true side of music, 'the law itself', the sacred
number appealed strongly to him; he would have liked to
make it impossible for music to be manifest in any other
way.[3] The poem *Overwhelm me, oh music*[4] of the same
period expresses a despairing conviction that such creative,
rhythmical music did not, and never would, exist. In 1915,
however, he already saw its power to transform feelings, as
he put it, into audible landscapes;[5] and in 1925, in the poem in

---

[1] *S.G.* pp. 79 f.; cf. E. Zinn in *Dichtung und Volkstum*, XL, p. 129 for the
genesis of this poem written during the winter of 1920 to 1921.

[2] *A.W.* I, pp. 363 f.; December 1925.

[3] Thurn und Taxis, *op. cit.* pp. 66 f.

[4] *S.G.* p. 77.

[5] *A.W.* I, p. 363.

question, he appealed to it as the great transforming universal force:

> Beat on the earth: earthen it sounds and muffled,
> Dull and beshrouded with our purposes;
> Beat on the stars, they will themselves discover.
>
> Beat on the stars: numbers unseen, untold
> Fulfil themselves, whilst atoms radiate
> Increasing power through space. Look and behold:
> For what on earth is ear when notes vibrate
> Is somewhere also eyesight. Domes of state
> Arch themselves upward into realms of gold.
>
> For somewhere music *stands*, and somewhere far
> This light falls into ears, like distant chiming;
> Tis only for our senses that they are,
> Or seem, divided. Twixt their different timing
> Nameless superfluity ever swings....
>
> Music, thou water of our earthly wells,
> Thou ray that falls, thou tone that mirrors, thou
> Blessedly wake beneath our wakening spells...
> Thou more than we...from every why and how
> Set free....[1]

This is more than a versified repetition; it is a poetical metamorphosis of a portion of the Hulewicz letter of a month before. The fantastic notion of new worlds arising from the process of making this world invisible is here transfigured into a dream of music recreating by its vibrations this visible world; so that somewhere else, in that other sphere where our sense-differentiations do not obtain, it will be completely manifest. This poem is another proof, if proof is needed, that Rilke's poetry and prose were two such different languages that they could not express the same thoughts, however great the effort to make one repeat the other. It is also clearly impregnated with Schopenhauer's belief that music is the metaphysical expression of the physical universe. This belief ranged Rilke consciously on the side of a power to which he

[1] *A.W.* 1, pp. 363 f.

had always been subject.[1] Openly so in *The Book of Hours* and *The Picture-Book*; unwillingly so perhaps in *New Poems*, where music is nevertheless magically present like the 'breathing of statues' as he was to call it in 1915. Those apparently plastic poems owe the greater part of their witchery to the almost unearthly music in which they breathe. *Duino Elegies*, on the other hand, only transcended reflective poetry when music mastered the poet who was trying to break it in. Happily in vain; for it came flooding back irresistibly into the sonnets.

His present belief that music alone could transform the world seemed to demand that Rilke, like Socrates before he came to die, should devote himself to music in a special sense and must discover a new instrument, if those symbols which had appeared and reappeared in so many different guises since he first began to write were to be sung to sleep in this world that they might enter the next. There was such an instrument ready to hand: the language of Villon, Racine and Valéry, which can produce the purest and most intellectual music ever formed. Valéry's responsibility in the last metamorphosis Rilke's poetry underwent needs no pointing out. It began with simple translation, the transposition of Valéry's poems from French into German. Rilke was almost intoxicated by his success; but that was probably because the beauty of the original dazzled him. He was apt to be well pleased altogether with his achievements as a translator, which were in strict fact rather mediocre. In dealing with Valéry he failed on the whole to render the beauty of expression, and frequently of thought. I am far from blaming him for this. There is such strong magic in Valéry's music that not only would it not yield to Rilke; but like a powerful magnet it caused his poetical needle to waver violently and erratically. But he was not finally thwarted. He began to write in the language which he could not translate into his own, an experiment he had already made in his early days with Russian, and which came even more naturally to him now. The temptation

---

[1] I use music in a wide sense. Rilke had very little feeling for real music; and, like Goethe, only began to appreciate it towards the end of his life.

to remodel Valéry's themes in Valéry's idiom must have been almost irresistible; but Rilke did not push this venture very far, contenting himself with three arresting sketches.[1] He was extremely diffident of these products of his 'idle hours'. German critics do not take the *Poèmes français* seriously, and are inclined to regret them; the French have been politely appreciative; but they know and love their own language too well to be deaf to the obvious weakness of Rilke's touch on his new instrument. His French poems will probably never rank very high; for they are *juvenilia* in a sense. Rilke himself acknowledged that he felt young again, very young, when he wrote them. They represent only tentative, almost embarrassed beginnings; but the volume is nevertheless from start to finish an exercise in poetical transformation, in which his formidable intellectual qualities have yielded the field to something more innocently spiritual.

In the *Quatrains Valaisans* he repeated an experiment he had made in those far-away days in Prague when he had tried to express in verse the atmosphere of his surroundings. He now felt a strong desire to do the same for the Valais. But the facile rhythms and the lilting rhymes of *Offering to the Lares* were no longer in his power. On the contrary, so rigorous was he in his search for the exact poetical equivalent of the country surrounding Muzot, that its own native idiom appeared to him to be the only appropriate medium. This, I imagine, is why he started to write in French, only to discover that he was becoming a new, younger and different poet in the process.

Now the themes which interested him far more vitally than natural descriptions were not bound to any particular surroundings in time or space, and could be expressed (with a difference) in any language. His work on Valéry's poems showed him that translation is transformation. What was even more startling was to find that in original composition, not only the poems but the themes themselves underwent a metamorphosis when transposed from one language to another. This discovery revolutionised his ideas about trans-

---

[1] *La Dormeuse, Cimetière* and *Narcisse* in *P.fr.*

lation, which now appeared to him unnatural.[1] But the idea of transposition must have appealed irresistibly to the poet of *Sonnets to Orpheus*. What had undergone the compulsion of magic in the sonnets was exposed to music in *Poèmes français*, a new kind of music which he had never used before, and which he did not manipulate faultlessly, but which is nevertheless the potent factor in the last evolution he was to give to his dreams.

Turning over the leaves of *Poèmes français* one seems to hear, fluttering melodiously towards invisibility, the disembodied spirits of persons and things, of symbols and themes which had been Rilke's life-long companions. They make the German equivalents (delicate, subtle, shadowy even as they had appeared before) seem by contrast almost full-blooded and robust; for they have suffered a further remove from reality. But the process would not have ended there. The French Rilke would have reacted on the German poet; was, I believe, already reacting on him. The vigour, the dramatic tenseness, the vividness and the plastic power of the German *Eros* and *Magician* are almost like a protest against their French equivalents;[2] and *Corne d'abondance* and *Paume* seem to be of set purpose less ponderable and more spiritualised than *Cornucopia* and *Palm*.[3] Taking *Eros* and *The Magician* in conjunction with Rilke's semi-promethean myth[4] and the poems in Schiller's vein, one is tempted to prophesy that the more tenuous, the more subtilised, the more remote and the more elusive the French poet became, the more virile, the more dynamic, the more vivid and nervous his German double would have appeared.

The poems which I have instanced are concrete and relatively glaring examples of the intangible difference which the change of language made in Rilke's visions. It is a change which does not assault the reader's mind, but filters slowly down into it, and for which transubstantiation is perhaps a

---

[1] *B. 1921–1926*, p. 267.

[2] Cf. *S.G.* pp. 124, 125 with *P.fr.* pp. 19 ff., 178.

[3] Cf. *S.G.* pp. 133f., 149 with *P. fr.* pp. 14 f., 12. All these eight poems belong to the year 1924.

[4] *S.G.* p. 79. This was relatively early (1920–1921); but it shows the latent drama released in *Eros* and *Der Magier*.

better word than metamorphosis. This does not apply however to the case of *Le Drapeau*, the post-war answer to the
German poem of 1914.[1] This is a piece of conscious international propaganda in lofty didactic language, a tongue too
truly cosmopolitan to have any special flavour of its own.
Otherwise to absorb *Poèmes français* at the end of Rilke's
life-work is to take part in a process of evaporation, a rather
heart-breaking experience, as one after another of his great
themes dwindles and begins to drift towards invisibility,
rather haltingly accompanied by the music of *douce France*:

> Faut-il vraiment tant de danger
> à nos objets obscurs?
> Le monde serait-il dérangé
> étant un peu plus sur?
>
> Petit flacon renversé
> qui t'a donné cette mince base?
> De ton flottant malheur bercé
> l'air est en extase.[2]

It has come at last. Chartres, the columns, the pylons and
the sphinx, whose disappearance was foretold in the seventh
elegy, have really vanished away; and nothing is left of that
magnificent world of 'things' but a small overturned scent-
bottle whose fragrance is perfuming the air. Even the pillar
of Karnak which had survived almost eternal temples in the
sonnets is no more. Rilke's last requiem remained to be
sung; and it was, fittingly enough, a *requiescat in pace* for the
things he had loved all his life. Not for the things of art, but
for the *lares et penates* which he visualised as lost. For his
household gods were to be lost; he was about to lose them,
since he was about to die. Not that he made this statement
openly; the poem would have been far less poignant if he had:

Vous souvient-il de ces choses que l'on a perdues le lendemain,
Une dernière fois elles vous implorent
en vain
de rester auprès de vous encore.[3]

---

[1] Cf. *S.G.* p. 36 with *P.fr.* p. 48.
[2] *P.fr.* p. 51. [3] *P.fr.* p. 151.

Irresistibly the memory recurs of Rilke frantically packing and hunting high and low for those exasperating yet beloved objects which were playing at hide and seek with him.[1] This time he would not be able to take them with him. What would their life be like, he wondered, when it was no longer the life of the man who had loved them? Would they have long regrets in the morose dust which would surround them; or would the vague happiness of being just matter steal upon them again? In this poem, the animated, characteristic household things are reverting to matter and losing their individuality. But, if not so explicitly as in this poem, it is much the same story in the French verses about children, young girls (nothing now but two little breasts), animals and the ancestors in our blood. His attitude towards them was unchanged; but they seem to be dwindling away, whilst indeterminate angels drift hither and thither among the windows and mirrors, the fountains and water-nymphs, the playthings and dolls, orphans and prisoners, all of whom we have met before. It is eerie indeed to hear in French the ghostly echo of the magnificent reverberations of the elegies and to watch the magic mirror of the sonnets melt into liquid music. But most fascinating of all it is to observe what happened to Rilke's roses.

It was certainly not Rilke who invented the simple and rather sentimental symbolism, by which roses stand for love, and also for evanescence and death. The romantic poets, and in particular Heine, had played perpetually on the kind of theme which inspired Matthew Arnold's famous poem: 'Strew on her roses, roses....' It was probably Heine who fathered Rilke's yellow rose presented by the lad to his lover, and laid by her next day on his grave, the dewdrops now replaced by tears.[2] And it was only a step or two farther towards the macabre to visualise the rose-wreath wound by the lover in his mistress' hair as a crown of thorns, the symbol of dead love-nights, the tired blossoms expiring on her brow and shedding livid petals into her lap.[3] It was a natural transition for Rilke to represent

---

[1] Cf. *ante*, p. 214.   [2] *G.W.* i, p. 113: *Traumgekrönt*, 1897.
[3] *G.W.* i, p. 238: *Advent*, 1898.

them a little later as maidens walking in twos and twos behind
the garden wall, arms round each other's hips, the red roses
singing, the white ones gently drooping and falling.[1] Sickliness, decadence and grotesquerie were early elements in his
feelings about these flowers.

The first time he really experienced the nature of a rose
made its mark on his poetry until the end of his life. This was
on the expedition to Hamburg, when he invented the caress of
laying a red rose gently on his closed eyes and keeping it
there until its freshness was barely perceptible and its softness
was like 'sleep before sunrise'.[2] This discovery, merging in
his mind with the 'tired' roses on Paula's hat and with his
feeling that her girlhood was in danger, produced that remarkable *Fragment* in which a youth and a dead girl, love and
death, virginity and red roses opening on closed eyes were
brought into such unholy proximity,[3] riveted together and
exhibited once more in *Requiem for a Friend* where Paula's
violated ghost and the ravished rose on the poet's writing-
table were confronted, the one as a guilty, the other as an
innocent victim of an unnatural fate.[4]

But the simple idea of restfulness and sleep which underlay
the baroque distortion of the *Fragment* was capable of real
poetical development. I believe that it mingled in Rilke's
mind with Jacobsen's famous description of Marie Grubbe
among the roses and his musings on a yellow rose to Mary
Gneisenau in 1906 to produce the bewilderingly beautiful
Rose-Bowl in *New Poems*.[5] The two epistles to Mary about the
rose she sent to him when she returned Marianna Alcoforado's letters are laboured, portentous and far too ponderous
for the object described which he was identifying with forsaken womanhood, trying meanwhile to keep Mary herself at
a distance. The poem is exquisite, so absolutely exquisite as to
stand in no need of the introductory verse in which various

[1] *G.W.* I, p. 285: *Mir zur Feier*, 1899.
[2] *B.u.T.* p. 336.
[3] *B.u.T.* pp. 336 ff.
[4] *G.W.* II, p. 327.
[5] Cf. *G.W.* III, pp. 110 ff. with *B. 1906–1907*, pp. 73 ff., 128 ff.; and J. P.
Jacobsen, *Sämtliche Werke*, Leipzig, n.d., pp. 6 f.

examples of brutality and cruelty are cited for the sake of an irrelevant contrast. But the flowers in the poem are all-sufficient and self-sufficing. They are pure beauty, inner reality unfolding itself before our eyes, offered for our contemplation, incapable of giving more than that. As the petals open one by one like eyelids, they reveal countless sleeping lids closed over inner sight. For all these flowers, each one different from the next, each peerlessly lovely, contain nothing but themselves. They have transformed all the external influences of life into a handful of inwardness. They are like beautiful women, but still more in this poem like a symbol for the process and function of art. They stand for the inner reality of beauty even more clearly in *The Heart of a Rose* in the second part of *New Poems*.[1] Here the essence of the roses overflows until the whole summer becomes a room, a room in a dream.

The metamorphosis of the single into the double rose, of the chalice with a simple edge into a body of light surrounded by robe after robe, was the theme of a poem in the sonnets, and its mysterious, unnameable scent another aspect of its alluring charm.[2] There is no doubt that roses cast a spell upon Rilke. Monique Saint-Hélier recounts how he once sent her some fading flowers to die with her, because he was going away. His description of a vase of falling roses in *Late Poems* represents him as keeping them in his room until they were really dead, when he embalmed their petals in books and used them for *pot-pourri*.[3] And indeed it is noticeable that, from the *Fragment* onwards (with the single exception of the poem in the sonnets) Rilke's roses were always explicitly in enclosed spaces: in death-bed chambers, in his study at night, in rose-bowls, bringing summer into a room, bestrewing the chimney-piece as they shed their petals. And even in his garden at Muzot, they seemed to be clad in pink silk boudoir-gowns and red summer dresses,[4] like carefully tended and cherished, fragrant and fragile hothouse blooms.

It would be inaccurate to say that the atmosphere of these

[1] *G.W.* III, p. 225.   [2] *G.W.* III, p. 346.
[3] *S.G.* p. 163.   [4] *V.B.* p. 448.

poems is oppressive. But it is true that the air in *Les roses*
breathes upon us more sweetly; and that, whether represented
as indoors or out of doors, the roses in the French poems have
a more natural charm, which even shines through the tender
conceits the poet invented to describe them. They are almost
spirit-roses, repeating in a more ethereal sphere the gestures
and the postures of their German predecessors; symbolising
the same things, but more simply and more delicately:

> Abandon entouré d'abandon,
> tendresse touchant aux tendresses...
> C'est ton intérieur qui sans cesse
> se caresse, dirait-on;
>
> se caresse en soi-même,
> par son propre reflet éclairé.
> Ainsi tu inventes le thème
> du Narcisse exaucé.[1]
>
> T'appuyant, fraîche claire
> rose, contre mon œil fermé,—
> on dirait mille paupières
> superposées
>
> contre la mienne chaude.
> Mille sommeils contre ma feinte
> sous laquelle je rôde
> dans l'odorant labyrinthe.[2]

For Rilke, although he was still addressing, picking and playing with the roses in French, was doing it more gently; more
intimately and yet more cautiously, as if he really knew now
how fragile they were. And an even fuller enlightenment came
over him at the end of the cycle:

> Rose, eût-il fallu te laisser dehors,
> chère, exquise?
> Que fait une rose là où le sort
> sur nous s'épuise?

---

[1] *P.fr.* p. 85; cf. *G.W.* III, pp. 110 f.
[2] *P.fr.* p. 86; cf. *G.W.* III, p. 111 and *B.u.T.* p. 336.

Point de retour. Te voici
qui partages
avec nous, éperdue, cette vie, cette vie
qui n'est pas de ton âge.[1]

It was almost like a death-bed repentance for his lifelong treatment of roses which he had plucked so often and caressed so much, as children maul the animals they love; and he had deflowered them too by using them as symbols for death. It was a genuine repentance. Light, fresh and cool as the poems in *Les Roses* are, unobtrusively caressing, Rilke took a further step, and renounced them completely in the prose poem *Cimetière*. The final line in the requiem on 'things' showed that he had begun to deprecate the violation inanimate objects suffer by being exposed to human thoughts. How much more must flowers and roses suffer under the domination of mankind?

Y-a-t-il un arrière-goût de la vie dans ces tombes? Et les abeilles trouvent-elles dans la bouche des fleurs un presque-mot qui se tait? O fleurs, prisonnières de nos instincts de bonheur, revenez-vous vers nous avec nos morts dans les veines? Comment échapper à notre emprise, fleurs? Comment ne pas être nos fleurs? Est-ce de toutes ses pétales que la rose s'éloigne de nous? Veut-elle être rose-seule, rien-que-rose? Sommeil de personne sous tant de paupières?[2]

This is the matrix of the pearl of poetry which he wrote for his grave-stone:

Rose, oh pure contradiction, joy
To be no-one's sleep beneath
So many eyelids.[3]

The sensation of 'sleep before dawn' which he had courted a quarter of a century earlier at the expense of a rose, he now renounced, preferring to worship from a distance the flower he baptised '*rose-seule, rien-que-rose*', a lovelier phrase by far than all the exquisite compliments lavished on her in the past. Something rather ruthless and intrusive in his passion for the flower vanished in these magical words, whose sensitive

[1] *P.fr.* p. 95.   [2] *P.fr.* p. 112.
[3] *A.W.* I, p. 369; October 27, 1925.

restraint, simplicity, chivalry and poignancy are essentially
French. Rilke relinquished the rose, and his other themes too
began to slide away from his grasp when transposed from
German into that courtly language which does not exaggerate
and never insists.

Perhaps it was the 'dying fall' of dissolution which informs
the rhythm of these ethereal lyrics. But the puzzle of two
different poets writing two different languages at the end of
Rilke's life remains. The one was a wistful dreamer of
exquisite dreams; the other a vigorous writer with extraordinary spiritual power. It is possible at least that the
Russian 'novel' would have shown yet a third aspect of Rilke,
in which, unlike the far-away *Tales about God*, humour and
godhead might at last have emerged together in triumphant
accord.

Conclusion

CONCLUSION

The course of Rilke's life will probably remain bewildering
even when the factual basis of his existence comes to be
solidly established. To follow his travels, peregrinations and
emigrations is rather like watching the restless flickerings of
some shimmering fish darting hither and thither in a trans-
lucent element which is not one's own, even if one has seen all
the places he visited, read all the books, and knows all the
languages and works of art which chiefly allured him. For
these constituted the fluid element in which he lived and
moved freely, and on which too he roamed and roved like a
pirate on the seas of poetry. That organic growth into and
with the surrounding world which shapes most life-lines for
all to see was absent from his. In its stead such a number of
haphazard encounters, of almost random relationships, of
strange and indeterminate friendships, of ephemeral love-
affairs, of literary connections, of poetical associations and
aristocratic acquaintances that one is almost driven to deny
fundamental human value to any of them. For Rilke expended
himself poetically on nearly all his friends and correspondents,
whose number mounts into the hundreds;[1] this constituted his
real emotional adventures; there was neither time nor energy
for deeper and more exclusive feelings.

In a note-book kept for Lou Andreas-Salomé there occurs
a passage in which Rilke revealed the hidden reason for his
etherealised human affections. Harking back to that strange,
trance-like moment under the olive-tree at Duino, when the
present vanished from his consciousness and his body became a
mere ghost from the past, he remembered how often ever since
the days of his childhood he had experienced similar states, and
acknowledged that since he had surrendered himself finally to
such influences, he had been cut off from his own kind:

Something gently separative kept a clear, almost shining interspace between himself and human beings, across which it was

---

[1] There are well over two hundred recipients in the published correspondence
alone, not counting the letters disseminated in journals and books.

certainly possible to exchange isolated communications, but which absorbed every relationship into itself and, becoming saturated in the process, condensed into a smoky mist, so that the participants were deluded. He was still unaware of how far his remoteness was recognised by those others. As far as he was concerned himself, it gave him a certain freedom he had not known before with human beings. The small beginning of poverty by which he was the lighter gave him a unique mobility amongst those whose hopes and cares were in and for each other, who were bound to each other in life and death. He was still not immune from the temptation to confront their state of encumbrance with his lightness, although he realised by now how deeply he deceived them by so doing; since they could not know that he (unlike the hero) had not attained to his kind of victory by experiencing personally their fettering ties and the heavy air of their hearts; but outside, in a spaciousness so little adapted to humanity, that they would certainly call it emptiness. The only quality with which he might appeal to them was his simplicity. It was reserved for him to speak to them of joy when he found them too much entangled in the counter-parts of happiness; and perhaps also to communicate to them some aspects of his intercourse with nature, things which they neglected or only attended to incidentally.[1]

This passage was written towards the end of Rilke's life, and the separation was expressly represented as having post-dated the experience in Duino in 1912. Whilst never so complete and final as he here rather complacently declared it to be, this divorce from his fellows, which he realised far more clearly than they did, was the outstanding feature of his personal relationships. He profoundly influenced all those who knew him well, but was not much affected by them; the only clear exception to both statements being his early connection with Rodin, in which art was the determining factor. Rilke was phenomenally susceptible to aesthetic influences, to atmosphere, to latitude, to landscapes, to the past, to spiritual forces subtle, sublime or terrible; but not to human beings as such. He had skipped the chapter of mankind, as he phrased it to Heydt in 1913, and gone straight on from things and

[1] B. 1921–1926, pp. 312 f. Not dated, but placed by the editors among the 1925 letters.

animals to angels.[1] From Paris onwards certainly, if not before, his greatest friends were chosen vessels into which he poured his dreams, aspirations, problems, rapture and despair, greatly deepening and widening their hearts in the process, sometimes probably breaking them, but hardly ever relieving his own. For their similar outpourings he kept a well of sympathy and wisdom situated outside the dwelling-place of that aloof and lonely self. Many were those who stole up to it and heard its gentle rhythmic murmur, beautiful, impersonal; ever-recurrent in those letters of advice, sympathy and condolence which flowed so smoothly from his pen. It was another matter if anyone tried to force an entrance into the place beyond. Then a different note was raised behind the fast-closed door—pleading, protesting, fluent but embarrassed, volubly adamant all in one. This is the story one reads in the letters. In actual social intercourse it is probable that Rilke's exquisite and daunting courtesy was his chief weapon against his fellows and particularly against women.

There were, of course, degrees in that confidingness which was the main feature of his closest friendships; there were also exceptions to his immunity from love and passion; but on the whole the artist maintained the upper hand in the conflict with the natural man, who was no very formidable adversary, although an extremely eloquent victim. The word formidable, on the other hand, exactly describes Rilke's genius, which no one, not even Rodin, could enslave for long; which the war could not deflect from its course; and against which matrimonial, paternal, economic and social claims were powerless. Gently but inexorably he drifted or floated away from all ties into that region where they do not obtain, into the spaciousness outside where he could mingle with nature, things, the dead and the past and communicate with his fellow human-beings across a shining interspace. It was his paradoxical destiny to be free, a fate with a double aspect, the most glorious reward and the most bitter of punishments.

Superficially regarded Rilke's life might well be entitled a poet's dream. Extreme poverty, romantic solitude and sublime

[1] Cf. *B. 1907–1914*, p. 275.

aspirations flourishing in strange and beautiful places and attracting towards them as time went on all the most glamorous elements society disposes of: men and women of genius and taste with the power to gratify poetical wishes. Beauty and greatness were brought to his door when he was not wafted away towards greatness and beauty. The strength of his dream was such, so dazzling the star that beckoned him onwards, so potent the spell of his personality, that everything life has to offer to a poet was showered upon him, including the tenderest love. Even his death, brought about by the loveliest flower picked for a beautiful girl, has a fairy-tale element in it which seems to remove Rilke completely from the ugly and sordid side of existence under which we all suffer so much.

But the cruel, disfiguring and agonising manner of his taking off would be enough to spoil this picture, even if one did not know from his letters how dark the background was, how acutely Rilke suffered under the military academy, poetical sterility and the war; and most of all perhaps under his tragic lovelessness. Certainly the background was sufficiently dark in itself, and moreover stained with self-pity. And the fascinating figure in the foreground wears an ambiguous expression, disguising its ruthless purposes under a saintly exterior. Rilke never acknowledged, even to himself, that in choosing the arduous artist's course he was pleasuring his own will and obeying an irresistible inclination. The highest and hardest of duties, the divinest and austerest of missions, these were the sanctimonious phrases he used as a weapon to keep life at bay. They fall like a shadow across the poet who needed no such self-justification, and who should have loved his art truly enough not to deny in this implicit fashion that it was a worthy end in itself. This crack on the surface of Rilke's character was due to a flaw in the lambent crystal itself and profoundly affected his art. Perhaps the hard struggle he had with his father in his youth to become a poet at all was responsible for the fracture, which produced not only much private hypocritical patter but also his distorted and magnified ideas about the cosmic functions of art.

Yet the word hypocritical is probably inaccurate; for Rilke in all sincerity took himself far too seriously; this made him pharisaical about humanity as a whole, whom he gently pitied and despised, thanking the god of art that he was not as they. At other times, the tragic side of his difference and consequent isolation would overwhelm him; so that he oscillated violently between self-esteem and self-pity under the influence of self-love. These emotions, expressed by a beguiling, subtle and imaginative mind with infinite variations and modulations, inform the rhythm of his letters and of *Malte Laurids Brigge* as well as the tone and tenour of *Duino Elegies*.

But much of Rilke's poetry was altogether free of them, inspired as it was by the external world beyond us which he knew and understood far more intimately than the life of men and women on this mysterious earth. From *Early Poems* down to *Poèmes français* he gave proof of having penetrated much farther into the nature of things than is possible to most of us, and of entering by this means into spheres not generally accessible. His poems often read like keepsakes or relics of voyages of discovery, aesthetic symbols of spiritual experiences which are yet by some incomprehensible magic the things or the persons themselves. Everywhere represented except in his very early verse, this poetry is most densely concentrated in *New Poems*, where explorations into legends, works of art, animals, flowers, things, people and periods of the past resulted in an almost inexhaustible variety of themes, handled strangely but surely by one who knew and loved their inner essence, their unique individuality. The few men and women he created in this way will live on and live ever as monuments to his art on exactly the same plane as his statues and cathedrals.

How dim in comparison and wan, how wearisome in their monotony are those pervading presences in which Rilke embodied his judgments on human values:

Is it possible, that one should know nothing of those young girls who after all are living? Is it possible that people say 'women', 'children', 'boys', and have no glimmering of a notion in spite of all their education, that these words have had no plural for centuries, but only countless singulars?[1]

Out of Malte's own mouth one must condemn Rilke. This passage, so often quoted in his favour, defines his own constant practice. 'Women', 'young girls', 'children', 'lovers' and 'heroes' people his poetry and prose, plural personifications of his ideas about womanhood, girlhood, childhood, love and early death. His obsession with certain subjects was too strong to allow him to let well alone. In *Alcestis* and in *Orpheus, Eurydice, Hermes*, for instance, he achieved the utmost beauty, suggestiveness and economy of expression for his ideas about girls, marriage, women and death. Would that he had stopped there, realising that the theme which had already inspired *The White Princess*, the *Maidens' Songs* and many other poems was now exhausted. But no. He went on labouring it until his death, always from the same point of view, the pathos of girlhood, the piteousness of womanhood, and oh, the pity of love. Deprived of all individuality, seen only as potential or actual martyrs to men, this depressing plurality of the female persuasion becomes finally so wearisome that the reader's patience snaps. In the same way, although less insistently, Rilke dehumanised the poor, projecting into his abstract conception of them that beauty, simplicity and integrity of soul which made of them a vague and indistinguishable mass. Wherever in fact he was concerned with human values he created types, recognisable anywhere as his, to wit his poems about childhood, subtle though they are. In many such renderings however the poet by his language prevailed over the thinker, who actually had nothing very original or interesting to say about humanity itself and only a few although strong convictions about it.

Originality of expression is also far more remarkable than creativeness of thought in Rilke's attitude to death. Few great writers have described it so often and yet revealed so little of its mystery. The two monstrously long letters he wrote to Countess Margot Sizzo from Muzot in 1923 can be whittled down as regards subject-matter to the truism that the

[1] *G.W.* v, p. 30.

dead go on living in our hearts; and to the meaningless statement (repeated with italics in the letter to Hulewicz) that death is that side of life which is turned away from us, and which we do not illuminate.[1] Rilke's doctrine about death, his repeated affirmations of its greatness and glory show less inspiration and vision than poets like Plato, Shakespeare, Goethe and Tolstoy, who were content to reflect upon its unfathomable mystery or to dream of the immortality of the soul. Rilke wished to claim a greater knowledge of the subject than is given to mortal man, and at the same time to evade the question of immortality, about which he was extremely doubtful. Spiritual arrogance, intellectual confusion and a tormenting obsession inform his dogmatic utterances on this theme. But when poetry purified his thoughts, or when the emotion of fear got hold of him, then some unforgettable lines would flash out, revealing the nature of the mind which moulded them and of the quivering imagination at work.

The spirit of poetry came very near to achieving in the works of Rilke something approximating to pure art in *New Poems*, in some of the *Sonnets to Orpheus* and elsewhere. But it was clearly pressing forward to something else. One can see it at work in the Tuscan journal and creatively active on a grand scale in *The Book of Monkish Life*, which invoked a future God, a coming God and the human heart awaiting him. This is a mythological conception whose inspirational value for Rilke was manifest in the poem itself, and which seems to be fraught with universal possibilities:

Deity is thus the next higher empirical quality to mind, which the universe is engaged in bringing to birth. That the universe is pregnant with such a quality we are speculatively assured. What the quality is we cannot know.... Our human altars still are raised to the unknown God.... As an actual existent, God is the infinite world with its nisus towards deity, or, to adopt a phrase of Leibniz, as big or in travail with deity.... Deity is a nisus and not an accomplishment.... Even the blind fear of natural forces... attests the religious conviction of some overpowering thing in the world.[2]

---

[1] Cf. *Inselalmanach* for 1937, pp. 104 ff.

[2] S. Alexander, *Space, Time and Deity*, London, 1920, II, pp. 347, 353, 364, 382.

To read Alexander's chapters on deity is like listening to 'the soul of the wide world dreaming of things to come'; but the poetical imagination behind this vision had been fed on a steady, devoted contemplation of life as it actually is. Rilke's far more poetical rhapsody was inspired by a lesser dream and was arbitrarily exclusive, where Alexander's was all-embracing. Rilke's emergent aesthetic creator was a highly specialised deity, a poetical symbol based on a profound misconception of the real relationship between religion and art. Both manifestations of one spirit, they are mutually interdependent to a large extent, but neither creates the other, and it is a violent falsification of the mythological process to represent art as its beginning or end. Rilke believed, or forced himself to believe, that the part was greater than the whole; and this was only possible because he had no conception of the whole, because he had gone down an aesthetic backwater and was cut off from the main stream of humanity. The God whom he himself later abandoned emerges from *The Book of Hours* like an unfinished work of art, mutilated by changes of conception within the cycle, and out of all proportion to its damaged greatness. No altars, one may safely prophesy, will ever be erected to Rilke's unknown God whose solitary worshipper, having poured out a spate of glorious poetry to his own creation, fell silent and then stole away. This poetry only flags, and the reader with it, when the meaning of the cycle either forces itself upon the attention or becomes intellectually obscure. It can be enjoyed as pure religious poetry, and is enjoyed in this way by many Christians who take the word God at its face-value; it can also be interpreted to fit in with various philosophical systems on account of its ambiguity; but as creative mythology it has little inspirational power.

Rilke tried again. The direct way through mystery in *The Book of Hours* was abandoned in favour of the indirect method through art in *New Poems*. The attempt to create his God was followed by the experiment of creating as if he were that God, which brought him by a different route to the confines of his powers, to the periphery of his individual circle, to the limits where the deity of art holds sway. But he was not beaten yet.

On the contrary, his ambition soared higher still. In *Duino Elegies* he set himself to represent humanity, life, death, the world and the universe in terms of the divinity of art. His poetry, now charged with intellectual meaning, became more philosophical, and therefore less poetical. Was it nevertheless a greater vision than the more spontaneous *Book of Hours?* On a larger canvas, it was an even more striking instance of that illusory idealism, of that anarchical egotism in German philosophy which Santayana has characterised with such extraordinary penetration:

It is a wager or demand made beyond all evidence, and in contempt of all evidence, in obedience to an innate impulse....To take what view we will of things, if things will barely suffer us to take it, and then to declare that the things are mere terms in the vision we take of them—that is transcendentalism. Thus it is from Kant, directly or indirectly, that the German egotists draw the conviction which is their most tragic error. Their self-assertion and ambition are ancient follies of the human race; but they think these ...passions the creative spirit of the universe.[1]

Every word of this description is applicable to Rilke's vision of the universe as finally stated in *Duino Elegies*. As the expression of his own spiritual desires, of his highly individual, tragically isolated and nobly vain-glorious mind, it has a great and lasting value. As an interpretation of life and poetry it has less, though still some, significance. As a mirror held up to the universe, it has no general validity, being mere private symbolism. Human beings live abjectly perhaps but hopefully under the fetish gods of primitive tribes; they live fearfully and yet happily under Vishnu and Siva; they are serene and contemplative under Brahma and Buddha. Jehovah exalts them by turns and casts them down; they live gloriously and dangerously beneath the slopes of Olympus, rapturously and fiercely under the sway of Dionysus. They try to be good, loving and merciful beneath the shadow of the cross; they are virile and fatalistic where the crescent

[1] G. Santayana, *Egotism in German Philosophy*, 2nd ed. London, 1939, pp. 16, 31, 51. I have omitted the word 'vulgar' from the last sentence as not applicable to Rilke.

rules. But they have no real existence in the minds of Rilke's angels, who belong to a sphere from which human beings are for ever outcast. As a profoundly tragic record of the isolation of genius, *Duino Elegies* is unparalleled in the history of poetry. It is like the vision of a martyr at the stake, born of excruciating torments as a compensation for them, utterly personal and subjective, and unique rather than universal. This is not the stuff from which mythologies are made.

Sonnets to Orpheus have a different aura, since Rilke here made use of a living mythological conception which he developed poetically along its original lines. In doing this he entered the stream of German Hellenistic tradition, and became part of an important whole, with recognisable affinities to his predecessors. Looking back over the history of the gods of Greece in Germany since the days of Winckelmann one is struck by a certain parallelism between their dynastic vicissitudes in ancient and modern times. The German classicists worshipped Apollo whose high priest was Goethe. A later generation surrendered to Dionysus, ecstatically hymned by Nietzsche. And now Rilke civilised and moderated that wild worship by the magic music of Orpheus. But these several victories were only partial and precarious advantages over a common foe, the might of Christianity. Goethe wavered in his famous *Prologue in Heaven*, began to give ground in *Elective Affinities*, and paid lip-service at least to Catholicism at the end of *Faust II*. Hölderlin attempted a reconciliation between Dionysus and Christ in *Bread and Wine* and in the tragic figure of Empedocles. He did not achieve it. Heine vacillated between the Hebrew and the Hellene all his life, but finally chose the passion-flower in preference to the vine. Nietzsche called himself Dionysus or the Anti-Christ; but it was something more ambiguous than blasphemy (ambiguous though blasphemy always is) which caused him to entitle the story of his life *Ecce Homo*. None of these poets, not even Goethe, ever really threw off the shackles of Christianity; and Rilke's open hostility to Christ showed him chafing at his bonds. But he attacked religion in a manner very similar to Euripides' use of mythological legends. He either illustrated their intolerable nature, as in *The Last Judgment*, or he interpreted them sceptically, as in his poems on Christ, or deduced from them the direct opposite of their original meaning, as in his version of the Prodigal Son. But he confused the issue by drawing on orthodox Russia, on the Bible, the Apocrypha and the Koran as well as on Greek art and legends for his own mythological background. He became at once clearer and more convincing when at the last he proclaimed his religion in the name of Orpheus and identified himself with the magical singer. In doing so he certainly gave a mythological flavour to those strange poems. The most marvellous among them are documents of that external world where Rilke was more at home than among his fellows. These authentic revelations, characteristic of his greatest poetry, are taken as all such knowledge is taken, on trust. One can only experience these things through him; but to see and hear through his eyes and ears is to believe. The dogmatic and doctrinal element in the sonnets, on the other hand, the consciously mythological element, is weak. In so far as it is biologically true, it is self-evident; in so far as it is an incitement to transformation, it is of no avail. But the orphic tradition is so strong even to-day, it is so highly charged with mythical and poetical associations, that it will be thanks to this password, if at all, that Rilke may perhaps in the future be seen to possess mythological significance.

The real bent of his genius, though he forced it into religious channels, was aesthetic. So much so indeed that he magnified art into a religion at the dictates of that passionate self-assertion he was at such pains to disguise. The works chiefly impregnated with this quality are dazzling but deluding. They are 'like a sort of shooting star, with no guarantees for the future'.[1]

[1] Santayana, *op. cit.* p. 138.

BIBLIOGRAPHICAL NOTE

The formidable body of Rilke-literature is so unequal in value, that I have thought it best to indicate in the footnotes those biographical and critical works to which the present study is indebted. The most conveniently arranged and comprehensive bibliography is to be found in J.-F. Angelloz, *Rainer Maria Rilke, l' Évolution Spirituelle du poète*, Paris, 1936. Several important works have appeared since then, most of which have been analysed by E. C. Mason in *Rilke's Apotheosis*, Oxford, 1938, a survey of Rilke-criticism. The first volume of *Rilke Bibliographie*, Leipzig, 1935, covers the period up to the poet's death, and is extremely useful. The second volume has not yet appeared. A good deal of information can be gleaned from the lists of books and journals containing contributions and letters by Rilke in *Philobiblon*, Vienna, Leipzig, Zürich, 8. Jahrgang, Heft 10, 1935.

Rilke's published works are in a chaotic state. Leaving out of account the many and various separate issues of individual works and poems, the main collected edition in six volumes presents many notable gaps. It omits all those *juvenilia* which were published in a limited edition during the poet's lifetime, containing verse, prose and plays. This is now extremely rare. Nearly all the prose sketches were later included in a volume of early prose, uniform with the main edition. Rilke's critical and other contributions to journals from 1896 to 1905 were collected and printed privately after his death in a volume which is now unprocurable. The French poems have been published in France, and there is a collected edition, now out of print but still obtainable. Several separate editions of the late German poems repeat and supplement each other and the main edition. Finally a recent selected edition of Rilke's works in two volumes prints poems from all these sources as well as from hitherto unpublished material. There remain several original works and translations which are not represented in any of these numerous collections and selections. They are out of print and often very hard to come by. I give them first in the following list.

The state of the letters is one of inextricable confusion. There is a good deal of overlapping between the chronological series and the collections according to correspondents. Worse still, the very con-

siderable number of letters printed earlier in books and journals
have been almost entirely omitted from the general edition. The
three volumes of letters published in 1939 covering the period
1892–1914 and replacing four earlier volumes running from 1899 to
1914 (now out of print) contain 160 pages less than the edition they
have supplanted. About 80 new letters have been added to the
previous material at the expense of an early diary and about 180
letters and extracts from letters. Both editions are needed to complete each other, and neither can be considered as the standard
collection. I quote from the earlier and fuller edition as a general
rule and from the later only when referring to the new material it
contains. The abbreviations used in the footnotes are indicated in the
following lists.

A. Works

Leben und Lieder. Bilder und Tagebuchblätter, Strassburg and
    Leipzig, 1894.
Das tägliche Leben, Drama in zwei Akten, Munich, 1902.
Worpswede, Bielefeld and Leipzig, 1903.
*Paul Valéry, Eupalinos oder über die Architektur. Eingeleitet durch
    Die Seele und der Tanz*, Leipzig, 1927. [Translation.]
Ewald Tragy, Munich, 1927–1928, privately printed.
Aus der Frühzeit Rainer Maria Rilkes. Verse. Prosa. Drama (1894–
    1899), Leipzig, 1921.
Gesammelte Werke, Leipzig, 1927, 6 vols. = *G.W.*
Erzählungen und Skizzen aus der Frühzeit, Leipzig, 1928 = *E.u.S.*
Verse und Prosa aus dem Nachlass, Leipzig, 1929 = *V.u.P.*
Gedichte. Liebhaberausgabe, Leipzig, 1930, 4 vols.
Späte Gedichte, Leipzig, 1934 = *S.G.*
Bücher, Theater, Kunst, 1935, privately printed.
Poèmes français, Paris, 1935 = *P.fr.*
Ausgewählte Werke, Leipzig, 1938, 2 vols. = *A.W.*

B. Letters

Briefe und Tagebücher aus der Frühzeit, 1899–1902, Leipzig,
    1933 = *B.u.T.*
Briefe aus den Jahren 1902–1906, Leipzig, 1930 = *B. 1902–1906.*
Briefe aus den Jahren 1906–1907, Leipzig, 1930 = *B. 1906–1907.*
Briefe aus den Jahren 1907–1914, Leipzig, 1933 = *B. 1907–1914.*
Briefe aus den Jahren 1914–1921, Leipzig, 1937 = *B. 1914–1921.*

Briefe aus Muzot aus den Jahren 1921–1926, Leipzig, 1935 = B. 1921–1926.

Briefe aus den Jahren 1892–1904, Leipzig, 1939 = B. 1892–1904.

Briefe aus den Jahren 1904–1907, Leipzig, 1939 = B. 1904–1907.

Briefe aus den Jahren 1907–1914, Leipzig, 1939 = B. 1907–1914, 2.

Briefe an seinen Verleger, Leipzig, 1934 = V.B.

Lettres à Rodin, Paris, 1931 = L.R.

Dreizehn Briefe an Oskar Zwintscher, Chemnitz, 1931 = Z.B.

Briefe an einen jungen Dichter, Leipzig, n.d. = D.B.

Briefe an eine junge Frau, Leipzig, n.d. = F.B.

INDEX OF NAMES

Afanasev, A. N., 74 n., 75 n., 78, 82 n., 84
Aïssé, 208
Albert-Lazard, L., 271
Alberti, R., 272
Alcoforado, M., 183, 208, 242 f., 273, 328, 363, 407
Alexander, S., 421 n., 422
Alfieri, V., 200
Amann-Volkart, Frau, 315
Amélie, 227
Amenophis IV, 253
Andreas-Salomé, L., 21 ff., 29, 46, 49 ff., 66 n., 67 n., 118, 131 n., 139, 141 n., 145 n., 150, 151 n., 153 n., 154, 155 n., 156 n., 157, 171, 179, 181, 214 n., 215 n., 222 f., 229, 233, 238 n., 239, 255, 263, 268, 269 n., 270 f., 310 n., 312 f., 315, 362, 366 n., 367 n., 372, 415
Anduze, C. d', 208
Angelloz, J.-F., 38 n., 121 n., 426
Arnim, B. v., 193, 208
Arnold, M., 406
Arvers, F., 208

Balzac, H. de, 142, 186
Bang, H., 205
Baudelaire, C., 194, 209, 230
Baumgarten, F., 307
Becker, K., 110 f.
Becker, M., 92, 95
Becker, P., see Modersohn-Becker, P.
Beerbohm, M., 78 n., 172
Beethoven, L. v., 107
Bell, Clive, 253
Bellman, C. M., 265
Betz, M., 54 f., 57, 367, 369, 373 n., 375 n., 395 n.
Beuret, R., 142, 144
Blake, W., 4
Blumenthal-Weiss, I., 308 n., 363 n.
Bodländer, R., 376 n.
Bodman, E. v., 122 n.
Boecklin, A., 107
Bonin, E. v., 159
Bonz, A., 30
Bossuet, J. B., 243

Botticelli, S., 68, 323 f.
Bourges, C. de, 208
Brandes, G., 158
Browning, E. B., 177, 183, 328
Browning, R., 200
Bruckmann, E., 271
Brutzer, S., 52 n., 53 n., 61 n., 64, 66 n.
Buchheit, G., 92 n.
Büchner, G., 274
Bülow, F. v., 49 n., 50
Bunyan, J., 317
Burckhardt-Schatzmann, H., 287

Cämmerer, H., 314 n.
Carossa, H., 254, 270, 274
Cervantes, M. de, 230
Cézanne, P., 109 f., 185 ff., 189, 309, 379, 382, 395
Chadwick, N. K., 80 n., 82 n., 83 n.
Charles VI, 208
Charles the Bold, 208
Chehov, A., 51, 62, 64 ff.
Choiseul, Duchesse de, 193
Christian IV, 208
Cladel, J., 162
Clermont, M. A. de, 208
Cocteau, J., 190
Commynes, P. de, 205

Dante Alighieri, 230, 243
Darwin, Charles, 3
Däubler, T., 274
Dauthendey, M., 230
David-Rhonfeld, V., 15 n., 16 ff., 31, 38, 46, 118, 128
Dehmel, R., 33, 95
Delp, E., 258 n., 272
Desbordes-Valmore, M., 208
Die, Comtesse de, 208
Dietrichstein, A. v., 268, 272
Dobržensky, M., 286
Dostoyevski, F., 16, 61, 64 f., 210, 230, 295, 382 f.
Dreyfus Case, the, 142
Drojin, S. D., 51 ff., 65
Du Bos, C., 32 n., 52, 54 n., 57, 61 n., 66
Duncan, I., 190

Duse, E., 209, 235ff., 289

Eckermann, J. P., 300, 377
Einstein, A., 3
Euripides, 200, 342, 424

Faehndrich, A., 159, 176, 187, 190, 234, 242, 244
Fedor Ivanovich, 80, 171
Fiedler, H. G., 125n.
Fischer-Colbrie, A., 380n., 394
Flaischlen, C., 45n.
Flaubert, G., 274
Fofanov, K. M., 65
Forman, Buxton, 95n.
Freud, S., 3
Fried, 16f.
Froissart, J., 205
Fürstenberg, E. v., 288
Fyet, A. A., 65

Ganghofer, L., 15n.
Garshin, V., 65
Gebser, H., 228
George, S., 23, 30, 230, 255, 394
Germain, A., 365n., 374n.
Gezelle, G., 274
Gibson family, 157
Gide, A., 205, 208f., 230, 237, 243f., 273, 367
Giotto de Bondone, 323
Gneisenau, M., 159, 174, 183, 234, 264, 407
Goethe, J. W. v., 49f., 88, 152, 193, 200, 204f., 208, 230, 242, 274, 300, 377, 385, 402n., 421, 424
Gogh, V. van, 108
Gogol, N. V., 64
Goncharov, I. A., 65
Goncourt, E. and J., 156
Gorki, M., 59, 64
Greco, El, 228, 245, 253, 265n., 325
Griboyedov, A. C., 65
Grimm's Dictionary, 155
Guérin, M. de, 243f.
Guthrie, W. K. C., 343n., 345n.

Hämmerli-Schindler, T., 361, 374
Harrison, J. E., 71n., 342, 343n., 357
Harrison, M. C., 85n.
Hauptmann, C., 92ff., 103
Hauptmann, G., 38, 40, 92, 100, 131
Heine, H., 13, 31ff., 40, 406, 424
Heise, L., 371

Hellingrath, N., 254, 263, 270f.
Hetsch, R., 93n., 114n.
Heydt, E. von der, 159, 214n., 256n., 270
Heydt, K. von der, 159, 162f., 176, 214n., 217f., 221, 228, 235, 256n., 270, 416
Heygrodt, R. H., 380n., 381
Heymel, A. W. v., 254, 270
Hilbert, I., 272
Hirschfeld, C., 20
Hofmannsthal, H. v., 33, 200, 205, 230, 237, 261, 270
Hölderlin, F., 4, 230, 240f., 251, 274, 316, 424
Holitscher, A., 122n., 142n.
Holm, K., 66n.
Holthusen, H.-E., 355n.
Huch, F., 130n.
Hulewicz, W. v., 66, 370, 380, 386, 389ff., 396f., 401, 421
Hünich, F. A., 380f.

Ibsen, H., 38, 202, 209, 230
Ivan the Terrible, 75, 80, 171
Ivanov, A. A., 64

Jacobsen, J. P., 33, 39ff., 42n., 75, 112, 117, 146, 148, 155, 158, 167f., 205, 210, 230, 274, 346, 395, 407
Jaloux, E., 210, 366, 373
James, Henry, 195
Jammes, F., 155, 209
Jarintzov, N., 78
Jean de Dieu, 208
Jerusalem, K. W., 204
Jowett, B., 342n.

Kafka, F., 245
Kalckreuth, W. v., 112, 190, 203
Kanitz-Menar, L., 159
Kant, I., 423
Kappus, F. X., 148, 177, 237, 320
Kassner, R., 221, 237ff., 371
Keats, J., 95
Kessler, H. v., 221
Key, Ellen, 27n., 30n., 50, 56, 147ff., 155ff., 172ff., 176, 182ff., 186, 213n., 379
Keyserlingk, P. v., 254, 267
Kierkegaard, S., 6, 129
Kippenberg, A., 111n., 174, 188f., 191f., 215n., 216n., 217f., 221,

223, 229 ff., 234 f., 237, 241, 245, 262 n., 270, 274, 278, 287 n., 288, 300, 303, 310, 313, 315, 361, 363 n., 365 f., 371 ff., 375, 381, 398 n.
Kippenberg, K., 111, 217 f., 223, 234, 241, 256, 260, 270, 272, 284, 288, 292, 296, 298, 303, 361, 365, 372
Kleist, H. v., 97, 230
Klossowska, B., 290, 296, 307, 361, 363, 372, 386 n.
Knoop, Gerhard Ouckama, 190, 234, 311
Knoop, Gertrud Ouckama, 270 f., 284 n., 311 ff., 347 n.
Knoop, J. and M. v., 182, 218, 223
Knoop, W. Ouckama, 311 f., 340, 346 ff., 352, 355
Koenig, H., 111 n., 272
Koenigswald, H. v., 265 n., 266 n.
Korrodi, E., 380 n., 394
Kottmeyer, G., 134 f.
Kramskoy, I. K., 64, 93
Krylov, I. A., 65

L. H., 278
Labé, L., 208, 243 f., 328
Lamb, Charles, 60 f.
Lawrence, T. E., 49
Leibniz, G. W. v., 421
Leishman, J. B., 203 n., 265 n., 281 n., 327 n., 351 n., 357 n., 399
Leni, 290, 293, 308
Lenin, V. I., 79
Leopardi, G., 95
Leppin, P., 15 n.
Lepsius, R., 100
Lermontov, M. U., 51, 65
Lespinasse, J. de, 208
Levitan, I. L., 64
Liliencron, D. v., 33, 44
Lomonosov, M. V., 65

M., Gräfin, 288, 291, 296, 297 n., 299 n.
M., Mme., 235
Mackensen, F., 94
Maeterlinck, M., 41, 42 n., 74, 123, 169
Magnus, L. A., 85 n.
Mallarmé, S., 309 f.
Marlowe, C., 230
Marthe, 63 n., 235, 239, 290, 299, 368
Marwitz, B. v. d., 265 ff., 276, 279

Mason, E. C., 4 n., 20 n., 323 n., 330 n., 426
Max, de (actor), 190
Mehring, W., 394
Mercoeur, E., 208
Michelangelo Buonarotti, 69, 72 f., 98, 100, 262, 274, 283, 304
Michelet, J., 156
Modersohn, O., 89, 92 n., 93, 97, 100, 103, 105, 107 ff., 113 f.
Modersohn-Becker, P., née Becker, 89 ff., 93 ff., 96 ff., 100 ff., 117, 121 n., 131, 187 f., 190, 231, 275, 340, 407
Moissi (impressario), 236
Mönckeberg, C., 123 n.
Mont, P. de, 123 n.
Montaigne, M. de, 274
Montheys, I. de, 369
Mövius, R., 69, 122 n., 131 n., 324
Mühll-Burckhardt, D. v. d., 286 n., 287
Münchhausen, A. v., 260 n., 270, 272
Münchhausen, T. v., 254, 270
Muther, R., 143

N. N., 234
Nádherný, S. v., 187, 218
Nekrasov, N. A., 65
Nietzsche, F. W., 4, 21 ff., 26, 29, 252, 316, 337, 400, 424
Nietzsche, L., 22
Noailles, Comtesse de, 238, 242, 328
Nordeck zur Rabenau, J. v., 159, 184 n.
Nordeck zur Rabenau, M. v., 264, 272
Norlind, E., 157 f.
Nostitz, H., 272

Obstfelder, S., 204
Oltersdorf, Frau, 218
Oscar, see Fried
Otrepyov, Grischa = false Demetrius, 208 f.
Overbeck, F., 96
Ovid, 342

Pasternak, L., 383
Pauli, G., 123 n.
Picasso, P., 272, 333
Pickering, F. P., 369 n.
Pissarro, C., 185 f.
Pitoev, G., 290
Plato, 316, 342, 421

Poletti, Signora, 236
Pongs, H., 27n., 57, 111f., 338n., 380ff.
Proust, M., 4, 230
Purtscher-Wydenbruck, N., 369f.
Pushkin, A. C., 65

Racine, J., 200, 402
Ralston, W. R. S., 74n.
Rambaud, A., 74n., 75n., 76
Reinhart, H., 287
Reinhart, W., 307
Reventlow, F. v., 26, 46, 122n.
Reynolds, J. and M., 95n.
Rilke, Clara, née Westhoff, 83n., 90, 93f., 95, 97, 99ff., 105n., 106ff., 110n., 111, 114n., 116ff., 121ff., 125f., 128f., 134f., 139, 141n., 143, 144n., 145, 147, 149f., 152, 154, 157ff., 163n., 164f., 171f., 175ff., 190ff., 213n., 214n., 217f., 222, 231ff., 239f., 270, 273, 275, 311, 365f., 372, 379
Rilke, Jaroslav, 19
Rilke, Joseph, 13f., 16
Rilke, Ruth, 123, 125, 129, 147, 156, 158, 161, 179, 181f., 186f., 217f., 231, 270, 273, 275, 297, 299, 310ff., 365
Rilke, Sophia (Phia), née Entz, 13f., 129, 172n., 365n.
Rilke, Sophia, 13
Rodin, A., 59, 100f., 125ff., 130f., 140, 142ff., 157ff., 172, 174f., 179, 181, 184ff., 190ff., 209, 231ff., 237, 239, 241f., 264, 270, 285, 302, 304, 321, 346, 382f., 395, 400, 416f.
Romanelli, Signorina, 187
Rybnikov, R. N., 74n., 75n., 79, 82n., 83n.

Sachs, Hans, 132
St Francis, 169
Saint-Hélier, M., 18n., 372, 384n., 408
Salis, J. R. v., 9, 289n., 290, 296, 298, 302n., 303, 314, 364, 365n., 368n., 374n., 375n., 381n., 393n.
Santayana, G., 3, 423, 425n.
Sappho, 208
Sauer, A., 221
Savonarola, 68
Schaer, A., 380n., 382n.

Schaumburg, Gräfin, 301
Scheibel, G., 110n.
Schenk zu Schweinsberg, E. v., 193, 272
Schill, S. N., 52ff.
Schiller, F., 85, 320ff., 396f., 404
Schlözer, L. v., 182, 269n.
Schmidt-Pauli, E. v., 18n., 272, 301
Schobloch, R., 190
Scholz, W. v., 20
Schönaich-Carolath, E. v., 128, 159, 190
Schönburg, Prinz, 286n.
Schopenhauer, A., 4, 358, 400f.
Schrenck-Notzing, A., 241, 303
Schubert, F., 95n.
Schuler, G., 272, 365
Schwab, R., 395
Schwerin, L. v., 159, 171, 176, 228, 234
Seckendorff, G. v., 265f.
Sedlakowitz, General, 16, 18, 57, 86n., 112, 293ff.
Shakespeare, W., 230, 421
Shaw, G. B., 164
Sieber, C., 17n., 122n.
Sievers, M., 25n.
Sizzo-Crouy, M. v., 346n., 420
Socrates, 347, 402
Sokolov, the brothers, 79
Solms-Laubach, M. zu, 159, 184n.
Spender, S., 327n.
Spinoza, B. de, 274
Stalin, J., 79
Stampa, G., 208, 328, 330, 363
Stanhope, Hester, 49
Stauffenberg, Dr v., 268
Steindorff, Professor, 223
Strindberg, A., 230, 274
Strohl, Professor, 313

Taubmann, E., 272
Teweles, H., 125n.
Thurn und Taxis-Hohenlohe, A. v., 255n., 260, 270
Thurn und Taxis-Hohenlohe, M. v., 61n., 63n., 215n., 216n., 218, 222, 223n., 225n., 227, 230, 234, 236, 239f., 243, 258, 259n., 260, 270, 272, 275, 287, 291, 296, 298ff., 303, 312f., 315, 328, 361, 366, 369ff., 400
Thurn und Taxis-Hohenlohe, P. v., 227

Tolstoy, A. K., 65
Tolstoy, L. N., 49ff., 54ff., 60, 63, 65, 97, 112, 120, 144, 146, 172, 230, 237, 274, 382f., 421
Tolstoy, N., 51, 53, 61
Tolstoy, S. A., 164
Trakl, G., 254, 274
Turgenev, I. C., 64
Tyutchev, F. I., 65

Uexküll, D. v., 183
Uexküll, G. v., 159, 183
Uexküll, J. v., 159
Ullmann, R., 234, 271

Valéry, P., 304, 308ff., 312, 344ff., 350, 361, 364, 367, 393ff., 398, 402f.
Valmarana, P. di, 239
Valmaranas, the, 287f., 301
Vasilyev (painter), 64
Veltzé, Colonel, 260f.
Verhaeren, E., 237, 264, 270, 274, 376, 395
Verrall, A. W., 200
Villon, F., 402
Virgil, 342
Vladimir I, 74
Vogeler, F., 99

Vogeler, H., 86, 92, 94ff., 103, 106, 234, 243, 323
Vogeler, M., 92n., 94
Vogué, E. M. de, 127
Vyeryesai, Ostap, 76

Wassermann, J., 20n., 21
Wedekind, F., 38
Weinmann, J., 118n., 127, 149
Werfel, F., 230, 274
Westhoff, C., see Rilke, Clara
Wichert, Dr, 232
Winckelmann, J. J., 424
Woolf, V., 66
Wordsworth, W., 321
Woronin, H., 46, 49
Wunderly-Volkart, N., 9, 287, 289f., 292, 302n., 303, 313ff., 361, 366, 368, 372, 374f., 381, 393

Yeats, W. B., 274

Ziegler, Colonel and Lily, 290
Zinn, E., 91n., 399
Zola, E., 186
Zuloaga, I., 155
Zweig, S., 261n., 269, 274
Zwintscher, O., 141n., 150, 162n.

INDEX OF WORKS

A. Original Works in German

About Girls (*Von den Mädchen*), 96, 102

About God (*Über Gott*), 376 n.

Adolescent Tales and Sketches (*Erzählungen und Skizzen aus der Frühzeit*), 381

Advent (*Advent*), 31, 33, 35, 97, 406 n.

Alcestis (*Alkestis*), 115, 183, 200 f., 420

All in One (*Alle in Einer*), 39, 99 n.

An Apparition has been granted us (*Wir haben eine Erscheinung*), 252 f.

An Experience (*Erlebnis*), 227

Angel (*Der Engel*), 325

Angels (*Die Engel*), 132, 324

Angels' Songs (*Engellieder*), 36, 320

Anniversary (*Das Familienfest*), 39

Annunciation (*Verkündigung*), 323

Antistrophes (*Gegen-Strophen*), 320 f., 333, 396, 399

Apostle (*Der Apostel*), 23, 25 f., 38

Archaic Torso of Apollo (*Archaïscher Torso Apollos*), 196

Aschanti (*Die Aschanti*), 170

Auguste Rodin (*Auguste Rodin*), 166, 184 f., 196, 220, 232, 273, 382

Aunt Babette's Death (*Der Sterbetag*), 39

Birth of Venus (*Geburt der Venus*), 157

Book of Hours (*Das Stunden-Buch*), 67 n., 72, 131, 148, 150, 152, 155, 167, 169, 188, 220, 225, 246, 253, 257, 273, 295, 324, 326, 345, 383, 402, 422 f.

(1) Book of Monkish Life (*Das Buch vom mönchischen Leben*), 67 ff., 76, 87, 100, 104, 167, 194, 323, 375, 421

(2) Book of Pilgrimage (*Das Buch von der Pilgerschaft*), 131 f., 134, 167, 324

(3) Book of Poverty and Death (*Das Buch von der Armut und vom Tode*), 148, 150, 166 ff., 170, 277, 319, 383

Books of a Lover (*Die Bücher einer Liebenden*), 243

Can Nature remember the jerk... (*Weiss die Natur noch den Ruck...*) 397

Catechumens (*Die Konfirmanden*), 170

Childhood Elegy (*Lass dir, dass Kindheit war...*), 245 f., 321, 331, 399

Christ Child (*Das Christkind*), 38

Christ Visions (*Christus-Visionen*), 25

Coat of Arms (*Das Wappen*), 356

Cornucopia (*Das Füllhorn*), 404

Crowned with Dreams (*Traumgekrönt*), 32 f., 406 n.

Daily Life (*Das tägliche Leben*), 130 f.

Death (*Der Tod*), 335

Dolls (*Puppen*), 13, 240, 243, 245, 331

Dragon-Slayer (*Der Drachentöter*), 78, 83 f., 130, 170

Drill-Class (*Die Turnstunde*), 18, 88

Duino Elegies (*Duineser Elegien*), 29, 111, 223, 258, 285, 288, 294 f., 296, 300 f., 302, 310, 313 ff., 316 ff., 341, 345, 356, 358, 361, 363, 373, 375, 377, 385 ff., 395 ff., 398 f., 402, 406, 419, 423 f.

First Elegy, 224, 229, 243 f., 314, 327 ff., 335, 339, 341, 363, 387, 389, 393

Second Elegy, 224, 229, 244, 314, 329 f., 387 f., 393

Third Elegy, 229, 244 f., 314, 319 ff., 327, 330, 363, 370, 377, 393

Fourth Elegy, 272, 282, 314, 321 f., 330 ff., 371, 387, 392 f.

Fifth Elegy, 272, 313 f., 332 ff., 376, 384, 396

Sixth Elegy, 228f., 244f., 314, 327, 335, 389
Seventh Elegy, 314, 335f., 339, 341, 382, 386ff., 390f., 405
Eighth Elegy, 313f., 322, 327, 336, 362, 389, 397
Ninth Elegy, 313ff., 336f., 339, 386ff., 390f.
Tenth Elegy, 313, 315, 317f., 326, 338f., 345, 370, 376, 384, 389f.

Early Poems (*Frühe Gedichte*), 34, 220, 273, 323, 325, 380f., 419
Equal and Free (*Gleich und Frei*), 38
Eros (*Eros*), 377n., 404
Evening in Skåne (*Abend in Skåne*), 157
Ewald Tragy (*Ewald Tragy*), 19ff., 23n., 26
Experience of Death (*Todeserfahrung*), 200

Falconry (*Falkenbeize*), 198
Fiddler (*Ich war ein Kind...*), 93
First Poems (*Erste Gedichte*), 221, 380
Five Hymns (*Fünf Gesänge*), 249ff., 261, 276, 280, 399
Flight (*Die Flucht*), 38
Fragment (*Fragment*), 89, 102, 105, 113, 115, 117, 328, 374, 407f.
Fragments from Lost Days (*Fragmente aus verlorenen Tagen*), 119
Frau Blaha's Maid (*Frau Blahas Magd*), 88, 90, 115, 332

Gazer (*Der Schauende*), 325
Grave-Digger (*Der Totengräber*), 43, 105n.
Grave-Gardener (*Der Grabgärtner*), 43, 89
Guardian Angel (*Der Schutzengel*), 132

Harlots' Graves (*Hetärengräber*), 157, 197
Harrowing of Hell (*Christi Höllenfahrt*), 265f., 399
Heart of a Rose (*Das Roseninnere*), 408
Hoar Frost (*Im Frühfrost*), 38
House (*Das Haus*), 39

I will praise thee oh Flag...(*Dich will ich rühmen, Fahne...*), 261, 399, 405

In Karnak 'twas (*In Karnak wars*), 303
In Memoriam to Verhaeren (*Erinnerung in Verhaeren*), 376
In my Honour (*Mir zur Feier*), 31, 34f., 132, 407n.
Island, North Sea (*Insel, Nordsee*), 203

Lace (*Die Spitze*), 196
Last Judgment (*Das Jüngste Gericht*), 88, 100, 103, 132, 169, 199, 425
Last of their Line (*Die Letzten*), 130
Late Poems (*Späte Gedichte*), 399, 408
Laughter of Pán Mráz (*Das Lachen des Pán Mráz*), 39
Lay of the Love and Death of Cornet Christopher Rilke (*Die Weise von Liebe und Tod des Cornets Christoph Rilke*), 44, 172, 220, 257, 273f., 381
Life and Songs (*Leben und Lieder*), 31, 380
Life of Mary (*Das Marienleben*), 234, 243f., 273, 381
Little Mother (*Mütterchen*), 38
Loneliness (*Einsamkeit*), 170
Lonely (*Der Einsame*), 170
Lover (*Die Liebende*), 170

Madness (*Der Wahnsinn*), 170
Magician (*Der Magier*), 404
Maidens' Songs (Maidens, Songs of the Maidens, Prayers of the Maidens to Mary) (*Mädchengestalten, Lieder der Mädchen, Gebete der Mädchen zur Maria*), 36, 46, 91, 115, 148, 198, 320, 420
Malte Laurids Brigge (*Die Aufzeichnungen des Malte Laurids Brigge*), 29, 40, 65, 139, 150, 152, 155, 175, 185, 190f., 204ff., 220ff., 226, 229, 235, 243, 262, 273, 276f., 294, 319, 321, 335, 356, 363, 367, 375, 384ff., 396, 419f.
Memory (*Erinnerung*), 170
Mission (*Die Berufung*), 200, 325
Mountain Air (*Höhenluft*), 38
Music (*Musik*), 396, 400

Neighbour (*Der Nachbar*), 170
New Poems (*Neue Gedichte*), 157, 175, 194ff., 206, 208, 221, 225f.,

New Poems (*cont.*)
227, 273, 295, 325, 331, 337, 346, 355f., 375, 402, 407, 419, 421f.
New Poems I, 184, 188, 220
New Poems II, 190f., 192, 220, 235, 408
'Nor spirit nor yet fervour will we lack'... ('*Nicht Geist, nicht Inbrunst wollen wir entbehren*'...), 397
Now and at the Hour of Death (*Jetzt und in der Stunde unseres Absterbens*), 38

Offering to the Lares (*Larenopfer*), 31f., 124n., 403
Old People (*Greise*), 39
Orpheus, Eurydice, Hermes (*Orpheus, Eurydike, Hermes*), 115, 157, 201ff., 342, 420
Overwhelm me, oh Music... (*Bestürz mich, Musik...*), 400f.

Palm (*Handinneres*), 404
Picture-Book (*Das Buch der Bilder*), 79, 87, 121, 132ff., 152, 170f., 172, 175, 220, 273, 324, 402
Pierre Dumont (*Pierre Dumont*), 18
Poems by Count C. W. (*Gedichte des Grafen C. W.*), 303f.
Pont du Carrousel (*Pont du Carrousel*), 170
Portrait (*Bildnis*), 235
Prayer (*Gebet*), 121
Presentiment (*Vorgefühl*), 170
Primal Sound (*Ur-Geräusch*), 304

Raising of Lazarus (*Auferweckung des Lazarus*), 265f., 278, 346, 399
Reflexes (*Reflexe*), 130
Requiem for a Boy (*Requiem für einen Knaben*), 282, 399
Requiem for a Friend (*Requiem für eine Freundin*), 110, 112ff., 118, 190f., 203, 220, 319, 374, 407
Requiem for Gretel (*Requiem*), 134f.
Requiem for Kalckreuth (*Requiem für Wolf Graf von Kalckreuth*), 112, 190f., 203, 220
Rolling Pearls (*Perlen entrollen*), 91n.
Rose-Bowl (*Die Rosenschale*), 183, 407

Sacred Spring (*Heiliger Frühling*), 39

Saint (*Die Heilige*), 170
Samskola (*Samskola*), 158
Secret (*Das Geheimnis*), 39
Sketch for a Saint George (*Skizze zu einem Sankt Georg*), 281, 399
Son (*Der Sohn*), 132ff., 167, 171, 303
Songs of Mary (*Marienlieder*), 234, 243
Sonnets to Orpheus (*Die Sonette an Orpheus*), 29, 111, 116, 223, 258, 310, 313f., 337, 340ff., 361, 363f., 370, 373, 375, 383, 387, 389f., 392f., 402, 404f., 406, 408, 421, 424f.
Spanish Trilogy (*Spanische Trilogie*), 265n., 266
Storm-Night (*Sturmnacht*), 170
Straining so hard against strong Night...(*So angestrengt wider die starke Nacht...*), 281 and n.
Stranger (*Der Fremde*), 196f.
Strophes (*Strophen*), 104, 106
Swan (*Der Schwan*), 200 and n., 278

Tales about God (*Geschichten vom lieben Gott*), 67, 71ff., 87f., 98f., 100, 132, 147, 156, 158, 169, 173, 188, 220, 253, 273, 323, 375, 383f., 385, 411
How it befel that the Thimble became God (*Wie der Fingerhut dazu kam, der liebe Gott zu sein*), 75
How old Timofei sang on his Death-Bed (*Wie der alte Timofei singend starb*), 77
How Treachery came to Russia (*Wie der Verrat nach Russland kam*), 75f.
Song of Justice (*Das Lied von der Gerechtigkeit*), 76
Temptation (*Die Versuchung*), 325
Thunderstorm (*Gewitter*), 240
To Hölderlin (*An Hölderlin*), 261, 399
To the Angel (*An den Engel*), 325
Tsars (*Die Zaren*), 79ff., 170f., 198, 384
Turning-Point (*Wendung*), 240, 331
Two Prague Tales (*Zwei Prager Geschichten*), 38, 55

United (*Einig*), 38

Vigils (*Vigilien*), 38
Voice (*Die Stimme*), 39
Voices (*Die Stimmen*), 170 f., 198

When winged rapture... (*Da dich das geflügelte Entzücken...*), 397
White Princess (*Die Weisse Fürstin*), 27 ff., 38, 41 ff., 45 f., 91, 94 f.,
115, 130, 148, 156 f., 169 f., 198, 235 f., 328, 335, 420
Wild Chicory (*Wegwarten*), 31
Without being Present (*Ohne Gegenwart*), 38
Woodland Pool (*Waldteich, weicher, in sich gekehrter...*), 331

B. French Poems

Poèmes français, 377 n., 393 f., 402 ff., 419, 426
   Cimetière, 403 n., 410
   Corne d'abondance, 404
   Dormeuse, 403 n.
   Drapeau, 405
   Eros, 377 n., 404
   Magicien, 404
   Narcisse, 403 n.
   Paume, 404
   Quatrains Valaisans, 403
   Roses, 406 ff.

C. Translations

L'Ame et la Danse (Valéry), 347
Centaure (de Guérin), 243
Charmes (Valéry), 361, 393, 402
Cimetière marin (Valéry), 304, 345
De l'Amour de Madeleine (ed. Bonnet), 243
Lay of the Band of Igor (Russian epic), 51, 65, 153
Lettres portuguaises (Alcoforado), 243, 273
Poesias (Michelangelo), 262, 274, 283, 304
Retour de l'Enfant Prodigue (Gide), 243, 273
Sonnets from the Portuguese (E. B. Browning), 177, 183, 188, 242, 243 f.
Quatre-vingt Sonnets (Labé), 243 f.

CAMBRIDGE: PRINTED BY W. LEWIS, M.A., AT THE UNIVERSITY PRESS